BALKAN PREHISTORY

The period from 6500 to 2500 BC was one of the most dynamic eras of the prehistory of south-eastern Europe, for it saw many fundamental changes in the ways in which people lived their lives. This up-to-date and authoritative synthesis both describes the best excavated relevant Balkan sites and interprets long-term trends in the central themes of settlement, burial, material culture and economy.

Prominence is given to the ways people organized themselves, the houses and landscapes in which they lived and the objects, plants and animals they kept. The key developments are seen as the creation of new social environments through the construction of houses and villages, and a new materiality of life which filled the built environment with a wide variety of objects. Against the prevailing trends in European prehistory, the author argues for a prehistoric past riven with tension and conflict, where hoarding and the exclusion of people was just as frequent as sharing and helping.

Balkan Prehistory provides a much-needed guide to a period which has previously been inaccessible to western scholars. It will be an invaluable resource for undergraduates, advanced students and scholars.

Douglass W. Bailey is Lecturer in European Prehistory at the School of History and Archaeology, Cardiff University. He has carried out extensive fieldwork in Bulgaria and Romania.

BALKAN PREHISTORY

Exclusion, incorporation and identity

Douglass W. Bailey

London and New York

First published 2000
by Routledge
11 New Fetter Lane, London EC4P 4EE

Simultaneously published in the USA and Canada
by Routledge
29 West 35th Street, New York, NY 10001

Routledge is an imprint of the Taylor & Francis Group

© 2000 Douglass W. Bailey

Typeset in Goudy by
Florence Production Ltd
Printed and bound in Great Britain by
TJ International Ltd, Padstow, Cornwall

British Library Cataloguing in Publication Data
A catalogue record for this book is available
from the British Library

Library of Congress Cataloging in Publication Data
Bailey, Douglass W. (Douglass Whitfield), 1963–
Balkan prehistory : exclusion, incorporation and identity /
Douglass W. Bailey.   p. cm.
Includes bibliographical references and index.
1. Antiquities, Prehistoric–Balkan Peninsula.
2. Prehistoric peoples–Balkan Peninsula.
3. Balkan Peninsula–Antiquities. I. Title.

GN845.B28 B35 2000   99–057122
939′.8–dc21

ISBN 0–415–21597–8 (hbk)
ISBN 0–415–21598–6 (pbk)

For my father,
L. SCOTT BAILEY

CONTENTS

CONTENTS

ILLUSTRATIONS

FIGURES

TABLES

PREFACE

This book developed over the past ten years or so as, first as a student and then as young lecturer and excavator, I have tried to grapple with the prehistory of south-eastern Europe. As my ignorance of the region and its archaeology has receded I have remained concerned over the absence of a linguistically accessible synthesis and interpretation of what must be one of the world's most extraordinary periods of prehistory. The classic text, still on course syllabi but long out of print, is Tringham's *Hunters, Fishers and Farmers of Eastern Europe 6000–3000* BC, which will be 30 years old when the present volume appears. Since Tringham carried out her early research and wrote her seminal text, the practice of archaeology, the amount of information available and, perhaps not least importantly, the modern geopolitics of eastern Europe have changed fundamentally.

Where once a desire to study east European prehistory required preliminary campaigns of survey merely to find the relevant language courses or textbooks, today a visit to almost any bookstore or website provides a choice of self-taught language courses in every language necessary. Visa requirements are, marginally, less rigorous and travel and accommodation are no longer the romantic expeditions they once were. Politically, for most east European countries membership in western economic, political and military organizations is following the first ten years of financial and socio-economic networking.

The position of archaeology and archaeologists within the Balkans has also changed. However, it is unfortunate (some would say tragic) that, if anything, archaeology and archaeologists in most Balkan countries are worse off than, perhaps, they have been ever before. The assured financial support and ideological primacy available during the decades of marxist socialism collapsed with the Berlin wall in 1989. Current budgets are thin, if provided at all; if the situation is drastic for national institutes and academies, then it is worse for archaeologists and museums in the provinces. The opening of eastern Europe which has followed the political changes of 1989 has not been accompanied by equally significant increases in support to disciplines such as archaeology (Bailey 1998).

The present volume is offered as one step in the path towards a more comprehensive and theoretically informed understanding of the Balkans from the beginning of the Neolithic through the beginning of the early Bronze Age. As such it attempts to take Tringham's project forward; in many ways it is dwarfed by the scope and achievements of the earlier work. In other ways, I hope the reader will agree, it moves in new directions. Regardless, I hope that it will provide a platform upon which future progress will be made.

D.W. Bailey
Stanton, September 1999

ACKNOWLEDGEMENTS

To work in a foreign environment requires the accommodation, generosity and understanding of a great many people. The process of researching and writing this book has been no exception. My deepest links are with colleagues in Bulgaria and to them I offer very sincere thanks for their patience. Many thanks to Stefan Alexandrov, Ivan Gatsov, Vasil Nikolov, Nilolai Sirakov, Henrietta Todorova and many others, for taking the time to discuss their important projects and research. I will never be able to repay Ivan Panayotov and Ilke Angelova for their support and help.

In Romania Siliva Marinescu-Bîlcu and Dragomir Popovici helped to introduce me to Romanian prehistory. Radian Andreescu, Mihai Tomescu, Christi Mirea and Marian Neagu were generous with their time and patient with my early ignorances. I owe a further debt to Paul Halstead and Kostas Kotsakis who directed me through difficulties with the Greek scene. A major obstacle to carrying out research on Balkan topics is access to many very short-run periodicals or obscure and out of print publications. The staff at the library of the Ashmolean Museum in Oxford helped to remove most of this obstacle.

Thanks are due to Bill MacKeith, who improved the text immeasurably at the copy-editing stage and saved me from many potential embarrassments. Except for Figure 5.8, which was drawn by Mike Hamilton, all of the line-drawings were prepared by Howard Mason. Howard's many suggestions and critical queries about the book's illustrations have had obvious consequences for the appearance of the volume. I am in his debt. Thanks as well to Don Shewan, who prepared the maps, and for doing so from a frustratingly wide range of detailed originals.

While on the subject of maps, it would be impolite of me not to offer a special note of gratitude to the officials and ministers of the Bulgarian Ministry of the Interior, Border Police and State Militia, who freed me from the time-consuming commitments of a field-project I was involved in several years ago. They have been a constant inspiration to me, especially during those times when I have felt my powers of concentration failing. To you bastards, I hope that the fact that this book has appeared and that I survived your unpleasantness causes you untold displeasure.

ACKNOWLEDGEMENTS

In Cardiff, I must apologize to students who sat through what must have seemed like endless lectures in which new ideas were given their first airings. I hope that they realize how important their critical comments have been. To Amanda Banham, Jo Seely and Steve Trick many thanks for arguing through the central tenets of the book with me. Steve Mills provided cutting comment where required: much appreciated. Rick Shulting suffered through early drafts of the main chapters. I am fortunate to work in a department which is both understanding and generous in making time for research to be completed; many thanks to my colleagues.

Two people have seen this project through from its beginnings. The first is Vicky Peters at Routledge who, very early on, placed her faith in both the idea of the book and in my position to produce it. The second is Alasdair Whittle, who ploughed through prospectuses, chapter drafts and the final version with, perhaps sado-machochistic, enthusiasm. If the finished product has value it is due, in the main, to his many suggestions and criticisms.

None of the research or writing which went into this volume would have been possible without the support of my family, especially the understanding of my wife Emma and our son Alexander and daughter Hannah. Apologies for the many lost weekends. Most fundamentally, however, it is my father who has been the constant inspiration for all of my academic work and it is to him with much love and great humility that I dedicate the pages which follow.

INTRODUCTION: BALKAN PREHISTORY (6500–2000 BC)
Fundamental changes in human behaviour

Sometime in the second half of the fifth millennium BC, several people were talking and working together inside a house in a small village in what is now north-eastern Bulgaria. The village was now well established, having grown up over a long period of time, through many generations of people's births and deaths and many episodes of abandonment of old crumbling houses and replacement with new ones. The village sat next to a thin stream which, having risen in the mountain foothills to the south, wound its way northwards, past the village, eventually joined by other streams before emptying into a larger river which, in turn, swung 100 km or so to the east before it emptied into the Black Sea.

The men and women chatting together in the house were casually sorting out and repairing digging tools; some were made of antler, others had short wooden handles lashed to a thin heavy piece of stone which had been ground into the shape of an adze. The tallest of the men was adding the final red lines to the simple patterns of rhomboids and angles which ran along the freshly replastered walls and the curved roof of the oven. Outside the house a child was playing with a little clay statue left over from an initiation ceremony. Next to her, three older members of the group were arguing about which of the younger cattle should be slaughtered.

Regardless of their decision, any slaughtering would have to wait until they knew when the meat would be required. This of course depended on what the Old Man decided. When did he want the most people in the village? When did he want them to start digging over the soil and sowing the seed corn? In a small, dark room, deep within the house, the Old Man and a younger woman were arguing about just this question of the appropriate timing of the planting. She thought that the ground was already dry enough. He decided. They would wait another week. He told the others to cut the calf's throat now and hang it so it would be ready in six or seven days' time.

1

Up in the hills south of the village, a small group of people sat on the edge of a wooded terrace and talked; they looked out over the plain, watching thin lines of smoke rise through the thatch of three of the buildings in the village. The buildings and the village itself rose out of the flat plain like a small hill. If they had looked out over the plain earlier that morning, they would have seen that the low spring sun had raised a blanket of fog across the cool earth of the valley floor; the fog had been thickest along the stream. They would have seen that the fog hid everything but a few roofs which poked up and marked the presence of the village. Two weeks ago the people had stopped on the hill and had looked out and seen smoke from only one of the buildings. When the time was right, they would come down into the plain and set up camp nearer to the village; they would smell the meat, hear the songs and see the cattle led out along the stream.

While the group on the hill watched, down in the village, in a second house, another group of people were busy cleaning off and inspecting the biggest and finest of their most brightly decorated bowls, pans and dishes; most of the pots had survived the winter, a few were cracked and would be repaired, only one was in a hopeless state. While some sorted out the fancier pots, others were unwrapping parcels they had brought with them from downriver. A girl was making a necklace, threading bright white shell beads onto a leather cord and tying other beads of bone and fired clay onto a large piece of fabric.

In a third house, people were busy mixing a sticky paste of coarse wheat-flour with water and, in a domed oven, cooking little flat loaves which they piled up on a low bench against the wall of the largest room. This house had a weary and lived-in look; under the smell of wood-smoke and the sweet aroma of baking bread ran a dank, remnant stench of stale sweat and sour urine which had strengthened during the winter just ending. When the first frosts had come at the end of the autumn, the rest of the villagers had moved off downstream with a few cows and sheep; in this dank house Bogdan, an elderly man, and two of his young grandsons had stayed behind to overwinter. They had lived in this house and looked after the rest of the animals in the village.

Through the colder months, the pigs had snorted and routed around and through the empty houses, had borne their litters and, basically, annoyed everyone. The cattle and sheep bedded down each night in various buildings and rooms. In the coldest part of the winter, the animals were given fodder, mostly straw kept from last summer's harvest; some, especially the cows which were with calf, were given barley. By the beginning of spring, two calves and half a dozen lambs had been born and survived; one calf had been stillborn.

It was in the house where the bread was being baked that Bogdan had spent the winter along with the two boys; while the children saw to the animals and kept the fire burning, Bogdan had grown weaker and weaker. First he couldn't manage to get to the door to take a leak and had had to pee in the corner of one of the smaller rooms. One day he couldn't get up from bed and, finally, one morning his body was stiff and cold to the boys' touch. They had wrapped the body in an old blanket and dragged it into the cold, little, outer room where it had lain; it had only started to stink as the warmth had returned to the early spring sun.

Together, the whole village community would bury Bogdan. His age gave him some status but in fact he wasn't really anyone special, although the boys would have said otherwise. The body needed burying and the village needed a burial both to re-anchor their community for the agricultural year and to refocus young and old minds on whom they relied to make the important decisions. They would bury him just before they started working the soil. The calf would have been slaughtered and hung; the shell necklace would be finished, the copper axe fitted with a wooden shaft and Bogdan's body wrapped up, properly this time, ready to be carried from the house to the burial area across the stream.

By the time they had started roasting the heavy shank of the calf, the stragglers from the hills had started to come down. The village would soon be full. When the Old Man started singing by the side of the grave, the villagers and travellers came out from the buildings and carried the body to the open hillside where the Old Man sang. Together they would look back at the village and bury Bogdan; his body was tightly wrapped in a new cloth which had a few shiny metal discs tied onto it next to the rows of white and red beads. In the pit, with the body, they would place the new copper axe, a few marvellously long flint blades and a couple of freshly made but poorly fired pots. Later that night they would all eat too much. The meat would be shared out, some to everyone, though the Old Man would make sure that the right pieces made it to the right people. The next day the whole group would break up again into separate households; some would carry antler picks into the plain over the ridge and start to turn the soil and plant the seed; the two boys would start packing Bogdan's house with branches, twigs and all of the chaff and straw left over from the winter's fodder. When the house was lit it would burn well, maybe even throughout the night. After the fire the boys would go to live in another household and begin new lives.

So began another spring in the village of Ovcharovo.[1]

By the end of the fifth millennium BC, the Balkans was a vibrant place to be; perhaps the most dynamic part of Europe at this time. Monumental

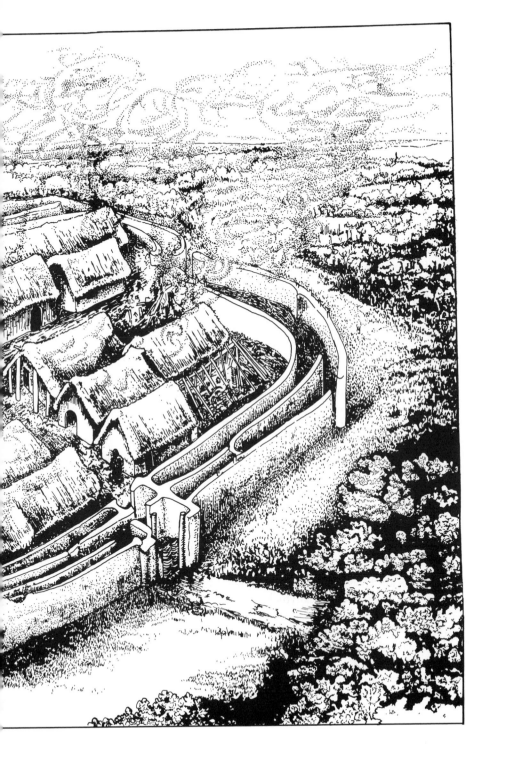

villages like the one at Ovcharovo were increasingly filling many land-scapes, marking out and anchoring communities to particular places. Houses and households were increasingly important centres of activities and social interaction. In several regions extramural cemeteries were attached to these villages. The majority of burials in these cemeteries were simple single inhumations of men, women or children; most had very few, if any, grave-goods. Some burials, however, were extraordinarily equipped with jewellery made of exotic shells, copper or gold, or with large, heavy cutting tools, such as axe-adzes, axe-hammers and chisels made of extravagant amounts of copper. Gold was hammered flat and cut into discs or zoomorphic shapes and sewn on to the deceased's clothing or hair. In the most sensational grave assemblages, found on the Black Sea coast at Varna and Durankulak, gold objects found in individual graves reached more than 1000 in number and weighed many kilograms.

Visually exciting materials and objects were not limited to funerary contexts; in addition to flint, bone, stone and antler tools and ceramic vessels used and stored in houses, small clay figures, fashioned to resemble people or animals, were widespread. By the end of the fifth millennium BC, therefore, the landscapes of the Balkans were extraordinary places full of a wide range of economic activities, social ceremonies and the routines of a daily existence which was centred on long-extant villages.

Three thousand years earlier, the same landscapes would have been unrecognizable. There were no villages, nor any houses, temporary or permanent, and there was no formal disposal of the dead. People went about their lives with a comparatively impoverished inventory of tools or other items. Most objects were made of flaked stone; many were made of bone, wood, antler and other perishable materials. There was no pottery, let alone any objects made of copper or gold. The people of these earlier Balkans lived very mobile existences, relying on their knowledge of the climate, the environment and the patterns of availability of animal and plant communities.

FUNDAMENTAL CHANGES IN LIVING

This book is an investigation of the changes in the ways people lived their lives. It is about the changes which separate the earlier Balkans from the material, settlement and burial activity that developed into the dynamism of the late fifth millennium BC. As such it focuses on the period from 6500 BC, when these changes began, through the sixth and fifth millennia BC, when they reached their fullest expression, and into the fourth millennium BC when another sequence of fundamental changes began. Thus, in traditional terms this book is about the Neolithic and Copper ages of south-eastern Europe. While there are chapters on what came before and what

6

came after, the core of the book investigates a series of principal changes in how people lived their lives within these periods.

In terms of geography I have taken the Balkans to include northern Greece, Bulgaria, southern Romania, Serbia, the eastern Hungarian Plain and north-west Anatolia (Figure I.2).[2] In this region, during the period concerned, there were significant changes in three critical areas of human behaviour: material culture; mobility and the spatial organization of communities; and the expression of individual and group identities. Within each of these areas there are important issues which the following chapters examine.

Material culture

Perhaps the most obvious element of the difference in the post-6500 BC Balkans rests in the variety, quantity and material of the things which people made, used and discarded. Critical to a better understanding of the Balkans at this time is a group of the significance of this increase in quantity and the introduction of novel materials and processes of creation. Thus, for example, we need to know what is the significance of the appearance of ceramic pyrotechnology across the Balkans in the middle of the seventh millennium BC. What did the earliest potting consist of, who did it and for what purposes? What was the inspiration and what were the consequences of the adoption of this new technology? Similar questions must be asked about the appearance, usage and patterns of deposition of other materials such as copper and gold or exotic marine molluscs such as *Spondylus*.

Also, important questions revolve around the social significance of geographically broad patterns of similarities in the form and decoration of these new objects. Why did long-term trends in decorating ceramic vessel surfaces reveal moves towards an increase in complexity of pattern and technique? Why did highly decorated pottery disappear from Balkan inventories after the middle of the fourth millennium BC? Why were there broad similarities in forms of early metal objects?

Much of the new material of the post-6500 BC Balkans was well suited to use in the creation of explicitly and intentionally expressive objects. Some, such as anthropomorphic and zoomorphic figurines, were clearly representational; others, such as the geometric designs of decoration applied to the surfaces of pottery and tools and onto the walls of buildings, are more enigmatic symbols. How do these visually evocative objects fit into the contemporary developments in Balkan communities? Questions about the role of material culture, both the expressly symbolic and representational and the more routine, but no less significant, mundane materials and objects lead to an examination of the degrees of sedentism and the spatial contexts in which these objects were made, used and deposited.

7

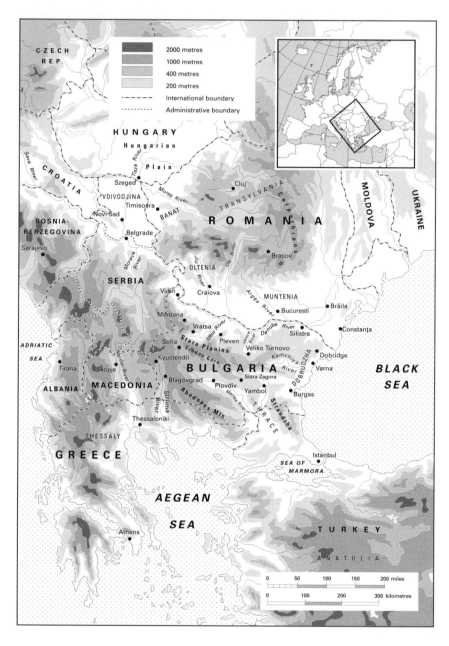

Figure I.2 Map of key geographic features of the Balkans

Mobility and spatial organization

Changes in the scales of mobility and the patterns of the spatial organization of communities make up the second major element that distinguishes
the post-6500 BC Balkans from what came before. Some of the most significant issues that need to be examined concern people's occupations of
special places in the region's varied landscapes. Why did people start to
mark out and occupy, with varying degrees of permanence, specific sections
of particular landscapes? What was the significance of the different architectural forms, methods and materials used? Why did some people build
small huts out of saplings, branches and twigs which they placed over
shallow pits? Why did others construct large, multi-roomed buildings out
of sun-dried blocks of mud which they stacked on top of stone foundations? How are we to understand the architectural and social significance
of these differences?

Equally importantly, what is the significance of loosely defined collections of the short-lived pit-huts and the more ordered and longer-living
aggregations of substantial surface-level structures? Can we call one a camp
and the other a village? Can we refer to the long-lived large buildings as
houses and the flimsier structures as huts? If so, what are the social and,
perhaps, political inferences which can be drawn from such distinctions?
What do these patterns in the records of architecture and mobility reveal
about the people who built these structures and settled down in these places?
What can we learn about their interrelationships on both the individual
and group levels? These questions about the spatial relationships within
and between communities lead on to the investigation of identity.

The expression of identity

Together, the developments in architecture and in material culture suggest
that new importances were being placed on people's desires to create, declare
and, undoubtedly, dispute the identities of individuals and of groups of
individuals. How did people make statements of identity? What physical
equipment and, now invisible, ceremonies were required? Were particular
materials, such as gold and copper, better suited for use in ceremonies
devoted to the declaration of identities? Why did people declare particular
elements of their character which they wished to express in a public manner?
Equally, how did they downplay or hide other components of their personae?
Similar issues need to be investigated for groups of people, whether they
were settled village communities or more mobile hunting and foraging or
herding groups.

Issues of identity lead on to issues of social structure, organization and
intra- and inter-group politics. What do all of these patterns in building,
burial, economy and material culture tell us about the structure of social

relationships? Can we come to any more interesting conclusions than traditional dichotomous claims for egalitarianism or hierarchy, matriarchy or patriarchy?

In this discussion of this book's key issues, there is no mention of shifts in economic strategies, of the change from food-gathering to food-production, which have been the hallmarks of European prehistory since Gordon Childe's monumentally influential work on the Neolithic revolution (Childe 1936). In the present volume, economy is considered but not as a primary determinate of social behaviour. If there are important changes in the patterns of plant and animal exploitation then they are addressed in other ways. The critical economic enquiry asks whether or not the significance of new plants and animals is to be found in terms of nutrition. Are the post-6500 BC changes in the sources of nutrition important in themselves or do they have greater significance in the light of the new ways in which people chose places in which to establish villages and in the social and political consequences of planting new crops and grazing new species of animal? Linked to these issues are questions of how we are to understand apparent changes in the scale of economic activity. For example, what were the different dimensions of cereal-growing which developed after 6500 BC? Can we speak of a shift from small-scale garden horticulture to larger, field-based agriculture? What about similar issues of scale and intensity of the tending, herding and breeding of animals? What would have been the social consequences and the requirements of the different methods, strategies and scales employed?

EXPLANATION

The other main issue addressed, though indirectly, in this book is a consideration of how we, as twentieth-century archaeologists, are to think and write about the days and lives of people who lived and died over 6000 years ago. The introductory narrative at the start of this chapter is an attempt at one possibility. It tried to get down to the level of the individuals who lived in the Balkans and to get a whiff of their daily experiences. Another level of approach will be found in the description and ordering of scientific data which forms the backbone of the chapters which follow. This is a regional approach to the millennia under consideration in which the individual is subsumed, appearing only occasionally. A third level of explanation is full of bigger concepts which try to draw together grander patterns of behaviour over periods of time well beyond the limits of human life, even as extended through ancestral lineages. This last level is met in the book's final chapter where priority is given to proposing higher-level schemes of human behaviour which run through the many millennia at the core of this book. The intention is to work each different level of explanation to equal advantage to extend and refine our understanding of Balkan prehistory.

THE ORGANIZATION AND STRUCTURE OF THE BOOK

The major task of this book is to investigate the archaeological issues outlined above in light of the evidence available. It does this by examining the better excavated, recorded and published sites which date from between the Balkan late Pleistocene and the early Bronze Age, a span of 40,000 years. In this sense, there is difficulty even before we begin; the number of detailed, well excavated sites where appropriate attention has been given to the spatial relationship of finds and to the study of the reality of strati-graphic relationships, and not to loose conceptions of phases based solely on changes in ceramic typology, is limited. Smaller still is the number of sites where environmental factors have been satisfactorily addressed, if considered at all.

Some regions of the Balkans are better sources of quality information than others. In some cases the task is made easier by recent country-based syntheses such as Andreou, Fotiadis and Kotsakis' review of the Greek scene (Andreou et al. 1996) or the less recent, but still informative, booklet by Dumitrescu, Bolomey and Mogoşanu for the Romanian situation (Dumitrescu et al. 1983). For other regions, such as eastern Hungary, synthetic studies in English and other western languages have a longer history (Kalicz 1970; Bognár-Kutzián 1972; Kosse 1979; Kalicz and Raczky 1980–1; Sherratt 1983a and b, 1984; Raczky 1987). In Serbia, major collab-orative excavation projects such as Selevac (Tringham and Krstić 1990), Opovo (Tringham et al. 1985, 1992) and Divostin (McPherron and Srejović 1988) provide important benchmarks of research and initial points of access to the region's archaeological record; detailed synthetic works are available in local language (e.g., Brukner et al. 1974). Other recent studies, such as Radovanović's synthesis of the Danube Gorges site help to refine our understanding of particularly complex parts of larger regions (Radovanović 1996a).

In almost every case, however, I have attempted to use the original source publications; in some cases this has been linguistically less difficult (as for the Bulgarian publications) than in others (as for the Greek records). For Bulgarian prehistory for example, the classic works are Todorova's masterful synthesis, *Kammeno-mednata Epokha v Bulgariya* (1986) and Todorova and Vajsov's *Novo-kammennata Epokha v Bulgariya* (1993). The most detailed site reports come from the Bulgarian Academy of Sciences *Razkopki i Prouchvaniya* series (Todorova et al. 1975, 1983; Raduncheva

11

1976; Panayotov and Dergachov 1984; Panayotov 1989; Nikolov 1992a); other detailed reports come from international collaborations (Georgiev *et al.* 1979; Demoule and Lichardus-Itten 1994; Hiller and Nikolov 1997). For each region, however, I have attempted to provide the reader with as complete as possible a bibliography to sources in local publications for the key sites and local period or regional syntheses.

Thus, while I hope to have avoided one potential obstacle to synthesis, the linguistic one, other problems are more difficult to sidestep. The long-engrained protocol of severing archaeological geographies with the modern borders of political nation-states makes pan-Balkan synthesis difficult. Equally disruptive are inter-national differences in research agendas where varying interpretive and explanatory goals and political constraints have contributed to the difficulty of aligning the modern study of what, in many cases, were homogeneous archaeological entities. Further differences between regions is evident in the quality and quantity of publication and in the depths of detail available. It is not surprising, therefore, that it has not been possible to treat each separate region with the same level of precision.

In attempting to synthesize without descending into unnecessary confusion, the chapters which follow make little reference to the traditional names of culture complexes (but see Figure I.3). The trend across Balkan prehistoric archaeology has been to ascribe differences in material culture, burial or settlement to differences in cultural groups, named after one key site which is deemed to represent a distinct group of people; thus one reads of the Krivodol-Salcuţa-Bubanj Hum culture group or the Spanţov phase of the Boian culture or the Körös culture. While it is impossible to acquire any familiarity with the region without first understanding the geographic or chronological relationships of these cultural constructs, once they are learned it is perhaps best to recognize that much variation exists within any generalized 'culture'. There is also the fact that many of the existing cultural schemes have little interpretive value beyond bare description.[3] Thus, for the purposes of this book, I have kept references to different culture groups and subgroups to a minimum, preferring to write in terms of modern geography and absolute chronology. Furthermore I have kept to a minimum references to the long-established local sequences of phases such as upper Palaeolithic, Mesolithic, Neolithic, early Bronze Age; I have done this for the simple reason that each of the different countries of the Balkans uses slight variations on the sequence, especially with respect to end of the fifth and the beginning of the fourth millennium BC when late Neolithic, final Neolithic, Eneolithic, Copper Age, and even early Bronze Age may refer to the same period of calendar years. The goal in all of these simplifications is just that – simplification – so that the reader, whether student or more advanced scholar, can move through the text without the distraction of the need for a cultural glossary.

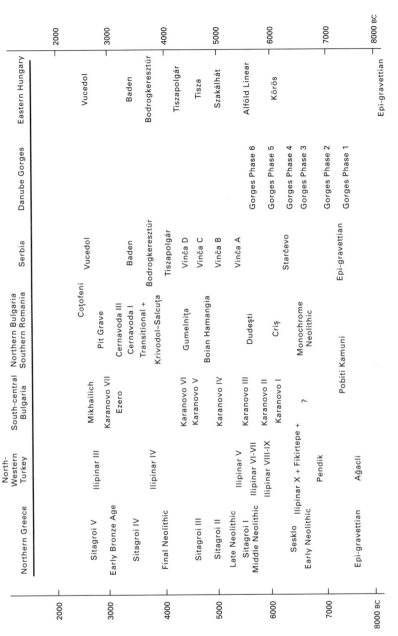

Figure 1.3 Key cultural complexes relevant to the following chapters

Chapter topics

The key developments of human behaviour in the Balkans on which this book is focused occurred between 6500 and 2500 BC. These four millennia occupy the attention of Chapters 2–7. Some readers may wish to start straight in with Chapter 2 and skip Chapter 1, which looks, briefly, at the Balkans during the long, local upper Palaeolithic and sets the scene for the major changes which occur after 6500 BC.

Chapter 2 is the first of three chapters which examine the thousand-year period between 6500 and 5500 BC. It considers the different ways in which people marked out particular places in the landscape and established small camps and larger villages. The chapter provides the cornerstone to the book as it distinguishes among three key regions: one to the south, encompassing northern Greece; a second to the north and west consisting of the lower Danube, Serbia and the east Hungarian Plain; and a third, positioned between the first two, in south-central Bulgaria. Additional, brief comment draws parallels with contemporary events in north-west Anatolia.

In Chapter 3 attention is directed to important new elements of material culture which appeared during the thousand years after 6500 BC. Discussion focuses on the early use and subsequent development of ceramics for making vessels and various other objects. The discussion considers the making and use of numerous material novelties such as representational objects like anthropomorphic figurines, sealing stamps and more enigmatic decoration of tools and other objects. Chapter 4 completes the discussion of the 6500–5500 BC period by examining the evidence for continuity or change in the working of flaked stone, the treatment of the deceased and the managed exploitation of plants and animals.

Chapters 5 and 6 examine the Balkans from 5500 to 3600 BC. In Chapter 5 attention focuses on the continuities and expansions of building activities (as seen in, among other things, the spread of tell villages) and the acceleration of economic activities. Chapter 6 investigates the developments in mortuary behaviour and the expanding range and character of new elements of material culture which include the early uses of copper and gold.

In Chapter 7 a brief look is taken at the end of the long period which occupies the preceding five chapters. Discussion includes a look at the most dramatic changes in settlement, burial and material culture which distinguish post-4000 BC Balkans from the 2500 years which preceded. In Chapter 8 the reader is invited to step back and consider the long-term changes (and continuities) which run through Balkan prehistory from the seventh to the fourth millennium BC. Suggestions are made as to why developments occurred when and where they did and what might have been their stimuli and consequences.

1

SETTING THE SCENE
The Balkans before 6500 BC

The main issues of this book begin in the next chapter with the discussion of the fundamental changes evident in the Balkans from 6500 BC. To fully appreciate their significance, however, it is important first to set the scene by examining the region before this date. In the present chapter, discussion focuses on the late Pleistocene and early Holocene and includes a brief introduction to the upper Palaeolithic which, as suggested below, runs from c. 50,000 BP. A complete discussion of the Balkans during this period requires a book of its own.[1] Here, attention is restricted to a few key sites, the most important trends in climate, lithic acquisition networks and developments in human behaviour such as the spatial organization of activities within sites and early forms of expressive material culture. We turn first to the beginnings of the upper Palaeolithic and note differences between it and the core areas of the European Palaeolithic; then we examine the evidence for early symbolic expressions of individual and group identities.

THE EARLY BALKANS

There is good evidence for a human presence in the Balkans from the middle Palaeolithic onwards, although the number of sites is limited (Darlas 1995).[2] As in other regions, the transition from activities and sites of Archaic *Homo sapiens* and Neanderthals marks a significant break, with important changes not only in human subspecies (the appearance of Anatomically Modern Humans) who possessed new cognitive abilities but also in the types of artefacts made and used, the range of activities carried out and the places in which activities were focused.[3]

Transition to the upper Palaeolithic

In the Balkans, the changes which mark the earliest appearance of modern humans, as documented at Bacho Kiro at 46,000 BP, were not as drastic as elsewhere in Europe. Sites with early upper Palaeolithic material suggest that the transition was gradual. At two key Bulgarian caves, Bacho Kiro and Temnata Dupka, the evidence for a measured transition includes types and frequencies of diagnostic material culture and patterns of environmental, climatic and faunal continuity which, significantly, were dissimilar from contemporary events in the core areas of Europe in the late Pleistocene.

Containing a long sequence of both middle and upper Palaeolithic activity, the cave at Bacho Kiro is an important site for understanding the Palaeolithic of Bulgaria and the Balkans. The site is located in the Strazha ridge on the northern border of the Stara Planina and thus sits between the moderately continental climate of the Danubian lowlands to the north and the sub-Balkan mountains and the Thracian plains of Mediterranean climate to the south.[4] The sequence at the cave runs through fourteen layers which range from Atypical Charentian (layer 14) through non-Levallois Mousterian (13), Levallois-Mousterian (13/12), Mousterian (12), Bachokirian (11), Aurignacian (6a/7), Tardi-gravettian (5 and 4) and Neolithic (2–1).

One of the most significant results from Bacho Kiro was the identification of a local industrial complex, the Bachokirian, which has been identified as transitional from middle to upper Palaeolithic (Kozłowski 1979; Kozłowski et al. 1982). Found in the earliest upper Palaeolithic layers at the cave (layers 11/I–IV, 9, 8, 6b/7 and 7), the Bachokirian is defined by a predominance in the proportion of retouched blades over other forms such as retouched flakes, end-scrapers and splintered pieces. Particular, diagnostically important tools, such as burins, and truncated and notched pieces, occur rarely in these early assemblages. Indeed, burins and carinated end-scrapers only appear in the later layers of the site's upper Palaeolithic sequence (layers 6a, 6b and 7). An absolute date from the beginning of layer 11 places the sequence at 43,000 BP (Mook 1982). Kozłowski and Allsworth-Jones have noted similarities between the content and structure of the Bachokirian assemblage at the eponymous site and of that from the lower layer at Istàllösko in Hungary (Ginter and Kozłowski 1982; Allsworth-Jones 1986). Dates from the latter site of 44,000 BP confirm the contemporaneity. Svoboda and Simán (1989: 288) have argued that the Bachokirian is best understood as a transitional phenomenon similar in significance, if not necessarily in material culture, to other transitional phenomena in other parts of Europe, such as the Szeletian and Bohunician.

Aurignacian assemblages, the definitive material of the early upper Palaeolithic, appear at Bacho Kiro in the phases after the Bachokirian, at Temnata Dupka and at several other early sites, such as Istállosko; the assemblages are similar to early Aurignacian material from the Near East such as that found at Boker Tachit area A (Allsworth-Jones 1986: 197–8). The content of the early Aurignacian assemblages at Bacho Kiro reveals a gradual development of this phase; this is especially clear in the appearance

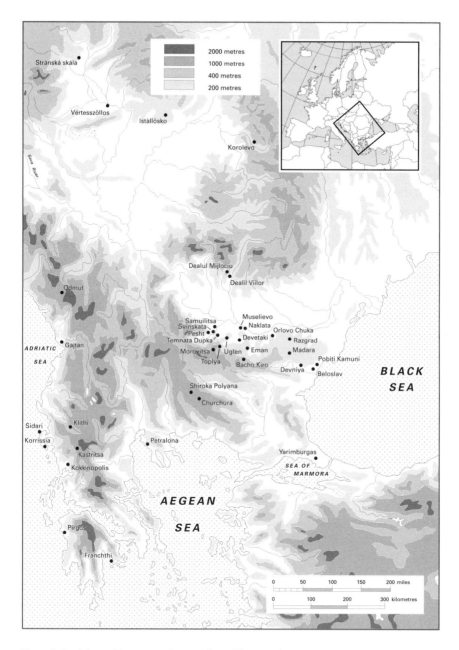

Figure 1.1 Map of key sites discussed in Chapter 1

of the small numbers of bone points and an increase in end-scrapers and retouched tools in layers 9, 8, 7/6b and 7. Typical Aurignacian elements, such as high end-scrapers, are not present. It is only in layers 6a and 7 that a typical Aurignacian assemblage appears at the site; the frequency of end-scrapers equals that of retouched blades, and bone points (with round cross-sections) appear more frequently as, for the first time, do carinated end-scrapers and burins.

Climatic, floral and fauna components of the transition

In terms of at least some of the earliest upper Palaeolithic material, therefore, the transition to the upper Palaeolithic appears as a gradual shift and not a sharp replacement of entire sets of tools and technologies. Fundamental to the background of the transition were the contemporary climate, flora and fauna. This environmental background reinforces the suggestion that the late Pleistocene Balkans was distinct from regions to the north and west.

Three types of plant communities existed over central and eastern Europe in the run-up to the late glacial maximum at 18,000 BP: periglacial-tundra, periglacial-steppe and boreal forest. The first two of these existed in environments where permafrost was present. The third, boreal forests, was confined to enclaves in southern Europe, in the east Carpathians and in the Ukrainian upland (Starkell 1977: 360). What is significant in a comparison of the Balkans with central, western and northern Europe is that during the pleniglacial, from 75,000 to 20000 BP, the southern extent of permafrost reached no farther than 48° latitude and even at 18,000 BP no further than 45°; thus even during the late glacial maximum the most southern extent of permafrost did not reach beyond the Danube.

During the last interglacial and full glacial, between 128,000 and 13,000 BP, therefore, the Balkans was not affected by the inland ice, permafrost, tundra or arctic desert or forest tundra that developed in areas to the north and west (Starkell 1977: 363, figure 7). During the late interglacial and the first part of the early glacial (128–75,000 BP) the Balkan landscapes alternated through cycles of deciduous forest and forest-steppe. During the rest of the early glacial and most of the full glacial (from 75,000 to 13,000 BP), cycles of forest-steppe varied with those of steppe conditions (Starkell 1977: figure 7). The presence of forest-steppe and steppe also suggests that the Balkans was less dramatically affected by glaciation than were regions to the north and west.

The Balkans did not, however, avoid completely the effects of the climate changes which were having more monumental effects in other regions. Van Andel and Shackleton (1982) have argued that the sea-levels of the late glacial Aegean and Adriatic were 100 m below their modern levels. At 18,000 BP the northern Aegean and northern Adriatic seas were large coastal plains, rich enough in plants and animals to support mobile or semi-permanent groups of hunters, foragers, gatherers and fishers throughout the year (van Andel and Shackleton 1982: 451). The post-glacial loss of these rich coastal plains and their resource abundances may have stimulated the shift in exploitation patterns noted by Geoff Bailey in the Epirus region (G. Bailey 1992; G. Bailey et al. 1983a, 1983b). Here new upland areas came into use at this time, as seen at the Klithi rock shelter and the Kastritsa cave. Klithi was only used between 16,000 and 10,000 BP: before and after these periods human activity was confined to the Kónitsa plain.

The now submerged coastal shelf of the western Black Sea would have been a similarly productive resource zone. From 16,000 BP the European ice-sheets began their retreat in the face of warming conditions. Sea-levels in the Adriatic and Aegean rose to within 25–40 m of their current levels and covered much of the rich coastal plains (van Andel and Shackleton 1982). The same process occurred in the Black Sea, especially along the western and north-western coasts, where the modern shoreline lies 100–150 km from its position during late Pleistocene (Ryan et al. 1997a, 1997b).

Animals and refugia

While much of Europe was suffering the rapid expansion of ice-sheets as they reached their maximum southern extent and thickness at 18,000 BP, there were less drastic changes in the plant and animal populations of the Balkans and the Mediterranean. In its position as a palaeoecological transition between the Mediterranean and European biotopes, south-eastern Europe, during the coldest periods, was home to refuge populations of thermophilous taxa of plants and species of animals (G. Bailey 1992: 8; 1995a: 519). In northern and western Europe, at this time, unglaciated areas were periglacial steppe and supported woolly mammoth, reindeer and horse. In the south-east a lowering of temperature and the related increase in aridity facilitated the spread of open steppe, a reduction of tree cover and the development of landscapes which supported grazing by herds of deer, cattle and steppe ass (G. Bailey 1992). Similar conditions undoubtedly dominated southern and eastern Bulgaria and perhaps northern Bulgaria and southern Romania.

Clive Gamble has identified red deer, horse, bos/bison and reindeer as the four principal species upon which Palaeolithic subsistence was based (Gamble 1986: 101). These species were distinct. They appeared in large numbers and high densities, had body sizes large enough to return the investment of energy expended in their hunting and had reproductive rates rapid enough to support population survival despite losses to hunting. A second group of Pleistocene animals consisted of musk ox, elk, roe deer, ibex and chamois. These animals are distinct from the principal species

19

either in their higher reproductive rates or by lower degrees of migration. Since many of these latter species could be precisely and predictably located in the landscape, they provided reliable alternatives and thus could have been exploited, when necessary, to make up for any failures in hunting the four riskier species of the principal group. The distinction is important as it can help to refine our understanding of hunting activities and site selection.

In their early phases, sites like Bacho Kiro probably served as temporary foci for hunting activities. They were points in flexible, impermanent networks of sites and micro-regions which stretched over large areas. People moved through these networks in search of resources ranging from high-quality materials for tool production, such as good quality flint, to predictably located animals, such as residential species like the ibex and chamois. In the middle Palaeolithic therefore, people came to the Bacho Kiro cave in order to exploit these predictable and residential species which occupied the mountainous micro-regions near the site. During some visits to the cave people capitalized on the less predictable appearances of the more mobile, more productive species such as red deer, aurochs, bison and horse that were at home in the forest and grasslands which also developed from time to time near the site.

Following Gamble's summary of species behaviour during the Pleistocene (Gamble 1986: 103–12), the middle Palaeolithic faunal evidence from Bacho Kiro suggests that use of the cave was conditioned by its position in an area in which migratory forest and grassland species such as red deer and horse could have been taken in combination with mountain species. Availability of the residentially predictable and stable ibex and chamois communities would have provided a degree of security against the possibility of failure in the riskier hunting of the less predictable, more mobile, forest and grassland species of deer and horse. For the upper Palaeolithic at Bacho Kiro the site existed in a colder and drier climate than during the middle Palaeolithic (Madeyska 1982). The area around the cave became increasingly, though not completely, deforested and contained a more open landscape with steppe vegetation.

Through his analysis of the upper Palaeolithic fauna from Bacho Kiro, Kowalski has highlighted the differences between these Balkan conditions and those documented in the late glacial assemblages of western and central Europe (Kowalski 1982). The Bacho Kiro material lacks some species, such as lemmings, which are normally associated with tundra regimes. Bacho Kiro also has a higher proportion of steppe species, contains several steppe species which never reached the more northern regions and includes forest species which had disappeared in central Europe during the coldest phases (Kowalski 1982: 67). Indeed, throughout almost the entire upper Palaeolithic sequence at Bacho Kiro, forest species were present. If analogies in terms of fauna are sought, they are best found in the material from contemporary caves to the east in Dobrudzha such as La Adam and Bursucilor and not to the west and north.

The micro-region around the Temnata Dupka cave, the other key Bulgarian site, was a refuge for animal species during the most drastic parts of the upper pleniglacial (Ginter *et al.* 1992: 329). The presence of elk through the entire upper pleniglacial and the absence of species such as reindeer, which are characteristic for the European periglacial, supports this proposal. The studies of the Temnata rodents and small mammals (V.V. Popov 1986, 1994) and pollen (Marambet 1992) confirm the differences which set the Balkans apart from central and western Europe. Thus, at Temnata, there is no evidence for any of the small mammal species which are characteristic of cold, periglacial conditions in other parts of Europe. Similar distinctions are noted with respect to larger mammals (Delpeche and Guadelli 1992) and birds (Z. Boev 1994). Popov suggests that the Balkans at this time was cooler, but not necessarily colder, than it is today and certainly experienced less extreme conditions than those faced in other regions during the later upper Palaeolithic. The most significant difference between present conditions at Temnata and those of the later upper Palaeolithic has more to do with humidity than temperature. Lower precipitation and lower temperatures would have favoured a domination of landscapes by open vegetation favouring species at home in forest-steppe, bush and dry meadow conditions.

Based on the detailed work undertaken at Temnata Dupka and Bacho Kiro, fundamental differences in environment are evident between east and west-central Europe during the upper Palaeolithic. If additional evidence is needed, a comparison of north Bulgarian conditions with those of Acquitaine in France illustrates the key differences between two otherwise topographically similar regions at the late glacial maximum. In comparison with the west, the annual mean temperature in Bulgaria would have been higher (12°C rather than ±7°C), as would have been the average January temperature (–2 to 0°C rather than –8 to 0°C) and the average July temperature (20–22°C rather than 12–16°C). The annual mean precipitation would also have been greater in Bulgaria (550–600 mm rather than 450–500 mm) (Laville *et al.* 1994: 324). Furthermore, although both regions are located on the southern extremes of large boreal plains, the one in northern Bulgaria did not support large arctic mammals such as reindeer or saiga antelope which are well known from the French context after 19,000 BP. Furthermore, the presence of elk at Temnata highlights its absence at contemporary sites in south-west and eastern France (Delpeche and Guadelli 1992: 208).

To the detailed analyses of Bacho Kiro and Temnata can be added the evidence from Balkan pollen records. Kathy Willis has shown that the late-glacial climatic oscillations documented in north-western Europe pollen records are not present in the Balkans (Willis 1994: 784). Willis studied the pollen records from ten palaeoecological sites in the Balkans containing deposits extending back to the last glacial period between 75,000 and 14,000 BP (Willis 1994). As one might expect, and as occurs in much of unglaciated northern Europe, her diagrams contained indicators for *Artemesia*-Chenopodiacae steppe, thus suggesting drier conditions for the full glacial. Unexpectedly however, the Balkan diagrams also document a continuous presence of coniferous and deciduous tree taxa which would not have been present in the northern regions (Willis 1994: 772). Willis suggested that the evidence for low, but persistent, levels of pollen from temperate tree taxa originated from local refugial populations. Indeed, many temperate taxa appear to have survived in the Balkans throughout the last glacial (Willis 1994: 769). A combination of altitudinal diversity (that is to say, large variations in precipitation and temperature due to changes in topography), little or no ice cover during the last glacial, and July temperatures only 5°C lower than at present suggest that the Balkans provided suitable micro-environments for the survival of temperate tree taxa during the last glacial period (Willis 1994: 769). The vegetational history of the Balkans has not been subject to the immigration of additional taxa at any time from the last glacial to the present. Indeed, the fact that the diversity of present-day plant-life in the Balkans is richer than that of any comparable area in Europe may be due to survival from the Quaternary ice ages of a flora which contains many ancient forms (Willis 1994: 770).

Thus, the Balkans of the Pleistocene glacial maximum was very different from other parts of Europe. The extremes of low temperature and high aridity found to the north and west did not play a major part in shaping the contemporary Balkan environment. Local refugia populations of plant and animal species were present in the Balkans at a time when they did not survive the more dramatic glacial conditions to the west and north.

Consequences of the character of the Balkan late Pleistocene

In light of the detailed evidence for the distinct character of the Balkans during the Pleistocene, the classic reconstructions of middle and upper Palaeolithic human behaviour which have been developed for the core west and north European regions, and which rely on environmentally induced adaptive stress, are not applicable to the Balkans. For example, the explanations for upper Palaeolithic symbolic activities and material culture, such as cave art and Venus figurines in western, central and northern Europe (Gamble 1982, 1991; Mithen 1991), which have been explained as adaptations to periods of worsening climate conditions, find no correlate in the Balkans. It is not surprising, therefore, that the classic upper Palaeolithic cave and figurine art did not appear in south-eastern Europe; there was no

22

adaptive need for them. Although the absence of these more obvious elements of a European upper Palaeolithic suggests that material expression and communication were absent from Balkan communities, good evidence exists in other parts of the archaeological record for the development of social interaction of increasing complexity in the region. Four topics are addressed here: the organization of intra-site space, the acquisition of lithic raw materials, the production and use of high-investment stone tools, and the decoration of the human body.

SPATIAL ORGANIZATION IN THE MIDDLE AND UPPER PALAEOLITHIC

Associations of stone tools and animal bones represent the majority of patterning in the spatial record of the early Balkan sites. There is no record from middle Palaeolithic sites which can be interpreted as an architectural feature and the arrangement of activities within sites was limited. More apparent is the emergence in the upper Palaeolithic of regular fixtures and associated concentrations of material within sites.

The early upper Palaeolithic uses of cave sites such as Bacho Kiro were small-scale, one-off exploitations of sheltered places where tools could be made or repaired and animal carcasses butchered and consumed. Thus in the two earliest Bachokirian phases at the eponymous site (levels 11/IV and 11/III), small hearths (no larger than 0.75 m in diameter) were the foci for concentrations of burnt bone of bovid, horse and bear, flint tools such as end-scrapers, retouched blades and accumulations of ash and charcoal. Similar isolated concentrations appear in the following phase of the site (level 11/II); more material and more hearths were present, although all were not necessarily in use at the same time. One of the hearths in level 11/II was faced with large sandstone blocks and was the centre of the largest concentration of butchered and burnt bone and stone tools; perhaps this is evidence for a limited degree of continuity of use over time, or at least an increase in the investment in the construction of the hearth. The early Bacho Kiro patterns continue with little, if any, variation through the Aurignacian phases of the site (levels 9–10, 6a/7 and 4b).

The evidence for the spatial organization of activities during the Gravettian phases (from c. 30,000 BP) at Temnata Dupka continues the patterns evident at Bacho Kiro from the Aurignacian levels. In the earliest Gravettian phases (levels IXb, IXa and VIII) distinct areas of tool-working are evident as are flat hearths. The following Gravettian II use of the cave (level VIIb) documents a change; a wider range of activities were carried out, including bone-, hide- and wood-working as well as meat butchering. Perhaps most significant is the evidence for the grinding of coloured materials and the discard (or perhaps loss) of a fired-clay bead.

The next major development in activities and their spatial arrangement within the site occurred at the beginning of the Epi-gravettian phase (level III), from c. 17,000 BP, when numerous separate structures with associated concentrations of artefacts were in use. Each structure had a hearth and contained limestone blocks, many of which were used to grind mineral dye. The range of activities included butchering meat and stone-tool repair and production as well as harvesting and crushing plants. The use of mineral dyes is again evident as is the use of mollusc shells from the Black Sea and the Aegean. Perhaps most importantly the hearth in one of the structures (no. 3) had two sequential phases of construction; another structure (no. 6) contains vertically consecutive concentrations of finds. Both structures suggest that the site was now being used repeatedly if not, necessarily, continually. The following phase of cave use (level II) was similar although smaller in size and material inventory.

The evidence from Bacho Kiro and Temnata Dupka therefore documents the development from the early to the later upper Palaeolithic. During the transitional Bachokirian and early Aurignacian, sites were used for short-term, one-off episodes of animal butchery and tool-working or repair. In the later periods, more complex arrangements of structures and activities are apparent, as is the expansion of the range of activities carried out during individual episodes of occupation, if we can consider these uses of caves in terms of occupation and residence. The repetition of architectural features such as hearths and the spatially anchored vertical sequences of material in the Epi-gravettian phases suggest an important shift in how people perceived particular places in landscapes at the end of the upper Palaeolithic. Some places, like Temnata Dupka, were repeatedly chosen as appropriate bases for activities and for longer periods of residence.

Flint acquisition networks

While activities at an intra-site level document small groups of people working and, perhaps, living together in particular caves in the upper Palaeolithic, there is also good evidence for the development of activities which stretched people across the landscapes and regions of the Balkans. As it is clear that networks of sites in different micro-regions were visited by people seeking particular animal species, so also is it clear that lithic material was moving long distances from source to places of use and deposition.

During the middle Palaeolithic, at sites such as Bacho Kiro, material for making stone tools came from considerable distances. There are no flint sources within 100 km of the site and the high proportions of flint tools in several middle Palaeolithic phases document the movement of material or people over at least this distance. Throughout the early upper Palaeolithic uses of Bacho Kiro, flint came from a range of different sources some of which document significantly greater distances of acquisition; flint from extra-local sources came primarily from north-eastern and eastern Bulgaria, especially from the Luda Kamchiya region, with less numerous material from the Iskur river basin in north-western Bulgaria. There is one instance of material – black menilitic slate – coming from the west Balkans or the Carpathians and one instance of obsidian from the Aegean. Diachronically, there is little variation in the frequencies of the differently sourced materials. The material from the north-east and east always predominated although among these two materials, the Luda Kamchiya material was more frequent towards the end of the Bacho Kiro levels (Kozłowki's late Aurignacian phase). The Aegean contact, if one artefact can justify the term, occurs in level 7, Kozłowski's second Aurignacian phase. The absence of absolute dates for these layers makes any more refined comment imprudent.

A more detailed reconstruction of the range and direction of flint mobility is available for the upper Palaeolithic assemblages from Temnata Dupka. While information of the Aurignacian assemblages is yet to be published, the analyses of Gravettian and Epi-gravettian material are available and informative (Kozłowski *et al.* 1992; Kozłowski *et al.* 1994). Detailed mineralogical studies of lithic material from the cave and from outcrops within and beyond the immediate vicinity of the cave, in addition to analysis of the Gravettian and Epi-gravettian assemblages, make it possible to reconstruct trends in the scale and geographic direction of flint acquisition networks (Pawlikowski 1992; Ginter *et al.* 1992; Sirakov *et al.* 1994).

Pawlikowski identified three geographic ranges of lithic sources for the artefacts found at Temnata; he distinguished between materials of local, meso-local and or extra-local origins. The extra-local flint came from six different regions: eastern Bulgaria; north-eastern Bulgaria; the west, including the middle Sava basin and its tributaries in Bosnia; the northwest, including the southern part of mid-Danube basin in northern Voivodjina, the southern Banat and the northern Danube basin; Greece; and southern Bulgaria, including the Rhodope mountains. The material from all of these sources was not found in every assemblage, nor did the popularity of each source remain constant through the uses of the cave.

There are three important phases of the flint source exploitation as seen in the Temnata Dupka material. In the first phase, before the onset of the late glacial maximum, flint from extra-local sources was a significant component of assemblages and included material from the Rhodope mountains in southern Bulgaria and from southern Greece as well as flint from eastern Bulgaria. In the second phase, during the final Gravettian use of the cave at c. 20,000 BP and during the late glacial maximum, extra-local flint decreased and local and meso-local sources were predominant; especially frequent was material from eastern and north-eastern Bulgaria. At this time, flint from the Sava basin and the middle Danube decreased to their lowest proportions and there was little, if any, material from the distant southern sources. In the third phase, during the Epi-gravettian (from c. 17,000 BP), extra-local sources become popular again although materials from the west and north-west now predominated; the Greek and southern Bulgarian material did not reappear. Indeed, in the late phase, the Rhodope region of southern Bulgaria appears to have been part of a different lithic tradition; this can be seen in the material from high mountain sites such as the camp at Orpheus I (Ivanova and Gatsov 1985: 76).

Thus through the upper Palaeolithic, for Temnata Dupka at least, people were engaged in networks of mobility or, at least, networks of acquisition which shifted in geographic scale and direction: from wide-ranging and including both northern and southern Balkan sources; to less wide-ranging and meso-local sources; and, again, to sources that were wide-ranging but focused only to the north and west. While these patterns of direction at the end of the upper Palaeolithic may have implications for later developments after 6500 BC, when the southern Balkans developed in different ways and degrees from did the north, the significance for the upper Palaeolithic is that people had established and maintained contacts over considerable distances. Along these networks of contacts not only did flint move extensively but, perhaps more importantly, people met and communicated with unfamiliar contacts or at least with individuals and groups who spent most of their lives in regions which were distant from their own.

EXPRESSIONS OF IDENTITY IN THE BALKAN LATE PLEISTOCENE

The absence of cave and mobiliary art in the Balkan upper Palaeolithic gives the impression of a period in which explicitly visual human expression was non-existent. This was not the case. Two main examples are presented here; both suggest the production and use of material culture as a component in the expression of individual and group identities. One of the examples, the production and use of bifacially flaked leaf-points, crosses the divide from the middle to the upper Palaeolithic. The other, the decoration of the body with ornaments and mineral-based paints, is more closely associated with later developments in the upper Palaeolithic, specifically the Gravettian and Epi-gravettian.[5] Both have important consequences for our understanding of the interaction of upper Palaeolithic communities.

Bifacial leaf-points

At the end of the middle Palaeolithic and the beginning of the upper Palaeolithic, many sites in the Balkans and in east-central Europe were the foci for the production and use of a particular form of elaborately created cutting tool, the bifacial leaf-point (Figure 1.2). Traditionally leaf-points are assigned to the middle Palaeolithic, are associated with Neanderthal

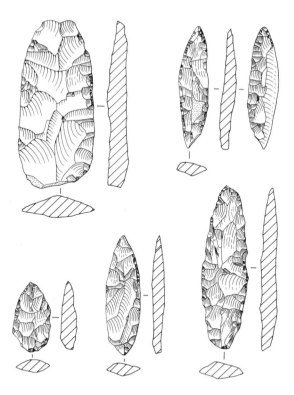

Figue 1.2 Leaf-points from Muselievo (no scale) (after Allsworth-Jones 1986)

remains and Levallois Mousterian materials and thus are usually considered separate from the upper Palaeolithic. In this sense, Kozłowski refers to them as distinctive for the East Balkan Mousterian with leaf-points or the Muselievo-Samuilitsa culture (Kozłowski and Kozłowski 1979). Recently, however, their position has been reassessed and they are now, more correctly, identified as part of a transitional phenomenon which overlapped the later middle and the early upper Palaeolithic (Allsworth-Jones 1986, 1990).

Philip Allsworth-Jones (1986) has made a strong case for the contemporaneity of the early Aurignacian and the leaf-point assemblages of central Europe (e.g., the Szeletian phenomenon). In his comparative study of the material from the sites of Szeleta and Érd, Allsworth-Jones argued that these leaf-point sites and others, such as Istàllösko, were places which people used sporadically for specialized hunting, which included killing bears (Allsworth-Jones 1986). Leaf-point sites may represent, therefore, the locations for special hunting and butchery activities and, as such, record sets of tasks different from those taking place at other contemporary early upper Palaeolithic sites such as Temnata Dupka and Bacho Kiro.

27

The distinction in activities may be one of the factors in the differential distribution of Aurignacian and leaf-point sites in central Europe, as in Moravia, where the former are arranged in a ring in the limestone uplands around a core area along the Váh and Nitra rivers and in which the leaf-point sites are located. Outside of Moravia and eastern Slovakia, the geographic distinction between leaf-point sites and Aurignacian ones is less straightforward. Elsewhere in eastern Slovakia, the Aurignacian appears without relatable Szeletian sites (Gamble 1986: 186). In other cases, as in the north-east and north-central regions of Palaeolithic Europe, Aurignacian sites themselves contain leaf forms, although in limited numbers. In the Balkans proper, assemblages of leaf-points appear at a significant number of sites and are especially well documented in Bulgaria at Samuilitsa, Muselievo, Shiroka Polyana and Temnata Dupka, with isolated and unstratified finds coming from the Rhodope mountains (Ivanova and Sirakova 1995). Further to the south, leaf-points appear at Kokkinopolis and Amalias; to the north they have been found at Ripiceni-Izvor in north-eastern Romania (Păunescu 1981).

Leaf-points are important not only because they suggest that different types of activities were probably taking place at the same time at different sites in central and eastern Europe. They are also important because of the levels of experience, knapping-skill and time required for their production. Anthony Sinclair made a detailed study of the processes and requirements of leaf-point production and their uses for the later, but arguably similar, leaf-point assemblages of the late upper Palaeolithic of Cantabria (Sinclair 1995, 1998). Sinclair suggested that leaf-point forms are significant because of the particulars of their production and use.

On the one hand, leaf-points are the products of elaborate knapping activities. The technical benefit of bifacially flaked tools rests in the efficiency of the cutting edge produced. However, during bifacial thinning, greater and greater degrees of precision would have been required if the project was not to have ended in failure. The final blows required both precision and strength. Success in production required the application of accumulated experience in sequential chains of action and continuous assessments of progress and decision-making. Successful leaf-point production would have depended upon considerable knowledge accumulated through experience.

The creation of a leaf-point also represents a significant investment of time, the amount of which increases with the size of the tool produced. Sinclair suggested that the time required to produce a Solutrean leaf-point ranged from 20 to 30 minutes for a small example (4–5 cm long) to three to four hours for one 10–12 cm long and to as much as eleven hours for the longest pieces (up to 30 cm) (Sinclair 1995: 55). In terms of production, therefore, leaf-points represent significant personal skills in knapping and substantial investments of time. Whether it was intentional or not, a person who produced or used a leaf-point would have been expressing the skills and efforts which they possessed and had invested; undoubtedly these expressions would have formed one component in the way others perceived and identified the leaf-point producers and users.

By studying fracture patterns of the Solutrean leaf-points, Sinclair also suggested that the leaf forms were used for cutting and not, as has been commonly assumed, as projectile points. As elaborately produced cutting tools, leaf-points may have been perceived as special artefacts used in the butchery of carcasses during events of meat redistribution following a kill or hunt (Sinclair 1995). Thus, in addition to making reference to skilled and time-consuming production, the use of leaf-points may have symbolized individual or group control over hunting success and over the distribution of meat among and between hunting groups.

Bifacially flaked leaf-points therefore represent the combined expression of skill and investment in production and in control over the distribution of meat. Both the sharing out of meat and the possession and use, if not also the production, of high-investment leaf-points were powerful parts of the displays of individual or group authority and prestige. Although the material of Sinclair's study is distant in time and in geography from the Balkan leaf-points, similar conclusions can be applied to the latter phenomenon.

Body ornamentation

While the dramatic cave and figurine art of the central, western and northern regions of Europe did not appear in the Balkans, other, expressive but non-representational objects were in use. At both Bacho Kiro and Temnata Dupka, shell, bone, teeth and fired-clay beads are present as are numerous lumps of hematite and traces of hematite and ochre on pebbles and limestone blocks. At other Epi-palaeolithic sites dating to the tenth and ninth millennia BC, such as Cuina Turcului, Climente II and Ostrovul Banului I–II in the Danube Gorges, blocks of graphite as well as animal teeth and shell pendants and bone tools decorated with ochre or engraved ornamentation have been found. Contemporary contexts at Franchthi cave contained 'hand-stones' which bore traces of ochre; a few *Dentalium* shells from the cave also stained with the same material (Cullen 1995: 282). If there is a trend through time in the appearance of beads and hematite, then it is one in which beads are more frequent than hematite in the earlier periods (as in the Bachokirian and Aurignacian levels), with beads and hematite appearing equally in the following period (the Gravettian), and with hematite more frequent in the later period (the Epi-gravettian) (Table 1.1).

Table 1.1 Summary of expressive material culture from the upper Palaeolithic levels of Bacho Kiro and Temnata Dupka (after Kozłowski 1982; Kozłowski et al. 1992; Kozłowski et al. 1994)

Period (site and phase)	Ornament	Use of hematite or ochre
Bachokirian		
Bachokirian (Bacho Kiro 11)	bone pendant	
Bachokirian (Bacho Kiro 11)	perforated teeth (2)	
Aurignacian		
Aurignacian II (Bacho Kiro 9)	perforated rib	
Aurignacian III (Bacho Kiro 6a/7)	perforated bead	
Aurignacian IV (Bicho Kiro IVb)		sandstone slab with hematite
Gravettian		
Gravettian II (Temnata Dupka I/VIIb)	perforated shell (*Galeodea echinophora*)	
Gravettian II (Temnata Dupka V/VI–VII)		stone grinders (2) with ochre
Gravettian II (Temnata Dupka V/VI–VII)		pebble chopper with ochre
Gravettian II (Temnata Dupka V/VI–VII)	fired clay bead	
Gravettian II (Temnata Dupka V/VI–VII)	bone bead	

Table 1.1 continued

Period (site and phase)	Ornament	Use of hematite or ochre
Gravettian II (Temnata Dupka V/VI–VII)		fragment of weathered hematite
Gravettian II (Temnata Dupka I/VI)	shell beads (2) (*Dentalium ergasticum* Fischer)	
Epi-gravettian Epi-gravettian I (Temnata Dupka V/IIIa–VI)		lumps (4) of red ochre
Epi-gravettian I (Temnata Dupka V/IIIa)	perforated shell (*Dentalium ergasticum* Fischer)	
Epi-gravettian I (Temnata Dupka V/IIIa)		small lump and many fragments ochre
Epi-gravettian I (Temnata Dupka V/IIIa)		retouched pebble fragment with red dye
Epi-gravettian I (Temnata Dupka V/IIIa)		pebble with traces of hematite
Epi-gravettian II (Temnata Dupka V/III)		limestone block with traces of hematite
Epi-gravettian II (Temnata Dupka V/III)		many small pieces of hematite
Epi-gravettian II (Temnata Dupka V/III)	perforated shell (*Nassa reticula* L)	
Epi-gravettian III (Temnata Dupka V/I)		cobbles with traces of ochre

Different contexts of identity expression

In the middle Palaeolithic, the materials and practices that contributed to the creation and maintenance of individuals' identities were found in time-consuming and skill-expressive activities such as knapping elaborate tools and foraging and hunting for and distributing butchered meat. In the upper Palaeolithic, new components of material culture and materials can be read as expressions of differences between individuals or similarities among people within particular, probably co-residential, groups. Compared to middle Palaeolithic components of identity expression, the beads, pendants and body-painting were more flexible, less permanent markers of identities.

In both the middle and upper Palaeolithic the acquisition of flint ranged over considerable distances, although the distances were less during the late glacial maximum. Is the emergence of the more frequent and flexible identity markers in the upper Palaeolithic a correlate or symptom of the longer-distance networks of contacts in which people were now participating? Perhaps the movement of people and lithic materials required displays of recognizable symbols made of appropriate materials. One function of the beads, pendants and body-painting may have been to provide such symbols. The other intriguing correspondence is the apparent shift from beads and pendants to body-painting after the late glacial maximum and the contemporary predominance of western and north-western material appearing at Temnata Dupka. Were different types and materials of identity expression linked to particular regions? It is difficult to answer any of these questions with any certainty. Perhaps the best response is to note that such expressions were taking place during these periods in the ways and with the material and activities suggested here. As will be discussed in chapters 2 to 6, the expression of identities changed dramatically after 6500 BC.

WHERE IS THE MESOLITHIC?

If the sequence from the latest middle Palaeolithic through the Bachokirian, Aurignacian, Gravettian and Epi-gravettian is relatively clear and takes us to *c.* 11,000 BC, the following four millennia are less straightforward and in some micro-regions are marked by an absence of sites.

Bulgaria

In Bulgaria, the single site that can be proposed for this period is at Pobiti Kamuni west of the modern city of Varna. Here, in an area of fine-grained sands and dunes between Varna Lakes to the south and the Varna Plateau to the north are unstratified surface scatters of flint tools and debris (Dzhambazov and Margos 1960; Margos 1961; Gatsov 1984a, 1984b; 1995: 73–4); the total area of all of the individual surface scatters covers 50 sq km.

Gatsov's typological and technological analyses of thousands of cores, tools, flakes, blades and bladelets from Pobiti Kamuni suggest that these sites were places of lithic working but not of lithic use. Thus, most cores were in their final stages of use and complete blades or flakes are rare. Among the flakes and blades which are present, over a third have cortex on their dorsal side and thus suggest that initial processing was taking place here. It appears, therefore, that the blades and tools that were produced at Pobiti Kamuni were taken away for use elsewhere.

There are no absolute dates from Pobiti Kamuni and its chronological position is held only by typological and technological similarities with Epi-gravettian sequences in the Danube Gorges (Kozłowski 1982b). Gatsov suggests that one of several periods of activity at Pobiti Kamuni was between the ninth and the seventh millennia BC (Gatsov 1995: 74). This ties in well with the dates for the early phases of the Gorges sites (discussed in Chapters 2 and 3). Pobiti Kamuni was also a focus for activities during the middle and upper Paleolithic as well as the late Neolithic (the beginning of the fifth millennium BC).

Thus, with the exception of the Pobiti Kamuni material, in Bulgaria there is a 4000-year gap between the latest date for upper Palaeolithic material (13,600 BP at Temnata Dupka) and the earliest Neolithic as seen at Gulubnik at the beginning of the seventh millennium BC. Gatsov has blamed the absence of an archaeological record on a lack of research, especially of surface survey, in the areas, such as river valleys, which are most likely to contain early Holocene activities and which may contain the keys to the early Holocene Balkans. Other absences of research into river valley sedimentation processes, the palaeoclimate and the prehistory of the Black Sea coast have contributed to the gap between the Epi-gravettian and the Neolithic in this part of the Balkans (Gatsov 1995: 73).

Serbia and south-western Romania

Further to the north-east, in Serbia and south-western Romania, at the Cuina Turcului rock shelter in the Danube Gorges, several hearths and assemblages of end-scrapers and debitage mark areas of early Holocene flint working and activities (Păunescu 1978; Radovanović 1981, 1996a: 319). In the nearby cave of Climente II people made a simple hearth and marked off part of the cave's interior with stone at some time during the tenth millennium BC (Radovanović 1981; 1996a: 317). At the same site, the body of a deceased individual was placed in a shallow pit along with a bone spear and several lithic tools; part of a child's skull and some teeth were found close by. At Ostrovul Banului a simple hearth was made and used in the tenth or ninth millennium BC and perhaps was set in a shallow dug-out structure (Boroneanţ 1973; Radovanović 1996a: 335). Traces of burnt bones and charcoal, lithics such as end-scrapers, bladelets and flakes and bone tools were also found.

At Odmut in Montenegro phases of activity date between 10,000 and 7,000 BP (Srejović 1989: 490). The Odmut assemblages contain lithic forms which Srejović has used to draw parallels with assemblages at other undated caves: layers VII–V at Crvena Stijena (Basler 1975) and in layer D at Sidari on the island of Corfu (Sordinas 1969, 1970: 10–11). In Serbia and Montenegro, therefore, there is evidence for human activity in the gap between the end of the Epi-gravettian and the beginning of the Neolithic. Based on lithic evidence at least, these activities have links with previous millennia of local late upper Palaeolithic activities, as is seen in layers VIII–V at Medena Stijena (Srejović 1989: 485–90) and layers IX–VIII at Crvena Stijena (Srejović 1989: 490).

Greece

In regions to the south there are two main sites of relevance. The first is the well known cave at Franchthi in the Peloponnesus, where there is a long sequence from 20,000 BP (Jacobsen 1969, 1973, 1981; Payne 1975; Jacobsen and Cullen 1981; Perlès 1987, 1990; Jacobsen and Farrand 1988; Hansen 1991). The early use of the cave was similar to contemporary patterns further north; wild cattle and ass were hunted on the coastal plain and cave use limited to sporadic episodes. The cave probably was part of a larger flexible network of sites which included small camps located up in the hills near the cave (Whittle 1996: 22). At 12,000 BP, after a long period of abandonment, the use of the cave began again. Large game continued to be an important resource but was supplemented, increasingly, by a wide range of fish, shellfish and small game. The presence of obsidian from the Cycladic island of Melos suggests that networks of material acquisition stretched hundreds of kilometres from the site. Cattle, pig, red deer and a range of wild animals and sea-creatures continued to be exploited after 9000 BC with an increase in marine resources, such as tunny fish, after 8000 BC. There are burials in the cave at this time as well; six inhumations and two cremations were found near the cave's entrance (Cullen 1995). One fragmentary burial dates to the following millennium and there are scattered human bones from both of these phases. All but two of the full body burials are of mature and young adults; of the younger individuals one was a nine-month-old infant (Cullen 1995: 274–8). The potential evidence for grave-goods is limited to flint blades, pierced *Cyclope neritea* shells and *Dentalium* beads; the placement of stones over and around one burial may have been intended to mark the place of burial, although they may equally have served no more dramatic purpose than to cover and thus secure the body from unwanted attentions of scavenging animals.

The amount of information available for Franchthi alone makes the site extra-ordinary. Less is known about other sites from these periods in southern

34

and coastal Greece such as Zaïmis near Megara, at Ulbrich, at Sidari on Corfu and Maroula on Kynthos (Markovits 1928, 1932–3; Sordinas 1969, 1970; Honea 1975; Jamet 1982). An important site is the recently discovered cave at Theopetra in Thessaly in northern Greece which contained middle and upper Palaeolithic as well as early Neolithic material; there is evidence for human burial here as well. A full report will help to clarify our understanding of this region in this period (Kyparissi-Apostolika 1995).

North-western Anatolia

Recent surface surveys in north-western Anatolia have identified two distinct types of lithic assemblages which have been dated, based on typological and technological similarities, to the end of the Pleistocene and the beginning of the Holocene (Gatsov and Özdoğan 1994). One type appears along the Black Sea coast west of Istanbul either as sporadic finds or, as at Ağaçli, as larger concentrations of lithics. The most prolific of these sites are on the Black Sea coast at Gümüşdere and Domali, on the coastal dunes along the Dardanelles at Tepecik, by the Manyas Lake at Musluçeşme, and overlooking the Sea of Marmara at Harmidere (Gatsov and Özdoğan 1994).

Lithic assemblages at Ağaçli-type sites include end-scrapers, blades and bladelets, microliths and cores. The majority of cores were in their final stages of exploitation when discarded and, thus, these sites seem to have been places used, temporarily, for the production or repair of tools which were then taken and used elsewhere. At some of the larger sites, such as Ağaçli which covered 1 sq km, there is evidence for upper and middle Palaeolithic activities. Thus as was the case at Pobiti Kamuni in eastern Bulgaria, in the early Holocene, for lithics at least, people continued to exploit sites that had been in use for many millennia.

Despite the increase in our understanding of the late upper Palaeolithic as a result of the results of the north-west Anatolian surveys, there still are very few sites dated to the period between 11,000 and 6500 BC in this region or elsewhere around the northern Aegean. Özdoğan and Gatsov have stressed the fact that the sites that are known have been found close to current shorelines; this is the case both in southern Greece and in north-western Turkey (Özdoğan and Gatsov 1998: 211). Undoubtedly, major factors in the absence of sites from this period in this region, and further north along the Black Sea coastlines of Bulgaria and Romania, were sequential rise in post-glacial levels of both the Black Sea and the Aegean (Özdoğan and Gatsov 1998: 211). Relatively late rises in the level of the Black Sea (at 5500 BC) suggest that a large part of the evidence of human activity which took place during and after the glacial maximum, especially including the early Holocene, is currently hidden under water of the western coasts of the Black Sea.[6]

Was there a Balkan Mesolithic?

Thus, at a time when a distinctive pattern of human activities was marking a Mesolithic phase in many other parts of Europe, there appears nothing significantly similar in the Balkans. While part of this is down to the position of early Holocene research on local scientific agendas and the loss of sites due to sea-level changes, it is equally important to recognize that the Balkan upper Palaeolithic was a long period containing little significant internal change. The 'Mesolithic' may not have existed in the Balkans for the same reasons that cave and mobiliary art never appeared: the changes in climate and flora and fauna were gradual and not dramatic. Voytek and Tringham have made this point for the changes in post-Pleistocene environment in the Danube Gorges (Voytek and Tringham 1989). Furthermore, one of the reasons that we do not distinguish separate industries in the Balkans as Mesolithic is because the lithic industries of the early Holocene were very firmly part of a gradually developing late Palaeolithic tradition (Whittle 1996: 374, n. 25).

CHAPTER CONCLUSIONS

In the light of the research available, it is best to include the record of human activity in the early Holocene, up to 13,000 BP at least, but also perhaps through to the ninth or eighth millennium BC, as the tail-end of an extended upper Palaeolithic. This upper Palaeolithic was a long period characterized by the mobility of human communities within and across regional landscapes, stretching in some periods considerable distances, and increasingly, repeatedly, concentrating activities in particular sheltered places such as caves and rock-shelters (Chapman 1989b: 506; Whittle 1996).

If there are any emerging trends towards the end of this period then they are an increasing focus of activity on the high-biomass river valleys and coasts and a widening of the types of resources which were being used, especially fish and other marine and aquatic foodstuffs. The distinction is striking between these valleys, coasts and marshes on the one hand and, on the other, the wooded lowlands that contained lower ranges of resource availability and where people focused their attention in the millennia after 6500 BC (as discussed in the following chapters). The distinction is important both in terms of the types of daily lives which people were living and in terms of the parts of the landscape on which much modern fieldwork within Balkan prehistoric archaeology has focused, that is, the wooded lowlands, and the consequent continuing absence of early Holocene sites.

Even if the current under-represented settlement of the early Holocene landscapes of the Balkans is fleshed out with a better sample of sites, it is highly likely that the density of communities in any one landscape was low. Furthermore, these communities were more mobile groups and their marking of particular places in the landscape was temporary more than it was permanent. Whittle has followed Binford (1980) and Lieberman (1993) to suggest that such post-glacial foraging communities circulated through the landscapes moving from one place to another in accord with the availability, abundance and variety of resources (Whittle 1996: 34–5). In this sense, the re-use of a particular site represents an episodic re-exploitation of a spatial resource, for shelter or as a short-term base for butchering or tool-working, in a sense very similar to episodes of re-exploiting seasonally available migratory species of animal or ripe fruit or nuts.

The connection of people to places during the long upper Palaeolithic thus was a flexible one with little locking of people to place through time. If the identity of individuals and groups was expressed it was phrased in a simple vocabulary written on the mobile human body. The anchoring of people to place was yet to appear in the Balkans.

SUMMARY

In this chapter I have described in brief the Balkans in the period leading up to the seventh millennium BC. I have argued that from 50,000 BP the region is best defined in terms of continuity and gradual change. In this sense, during the late Pleistocene and the early Holocene, the Balkans were different from other parts of Europe. Less dramatic changes to climate, flora and fauna resulted in less dramatic adaptive, or reactive, developments in material culture. Hence the Balkan absence of classic upper Palaeolithic cave or mobiliary art.

Significant changes did take place during the long gradual upper Palaeolithic. People started to use repeatedly particular places in the landscape. The traces of activity began to resemble something more substantial than just one-off uses of caves for shelter or places for tool-repair and carcass butchery. Increasingly, activities were concentrated around individual hearths and structures within individual sites. People also started to declare personal and group identities by wearing ornaments and by painting their bodies with hematite or ochre. Earlier expressions of identity through knapping skills, effort and time invested in producing elaborate flint-cutting tools as well as using them in events of meat distribution were superceded by the new, more flexible combinations of materials that increased in frequency in the later stages of the upper Palaeolithic. New needs to express identities may have been part of wide-ranging networks of contacts and movements linked to acquiring raw flint. The reconstruction of a long, gradual upper Palaeolithic in which change occurred slowly and mobility was the over-riding theme to the organization of groups of people provides a stark contrast to what was to follow. The Balkans after 6500 BC was dramatically different; these differences are the foci of the rest of this book and in the next chapter we begin by examining one of the most important developments, the marking out of particular places in the landscapes with permanent structures and buildings.

2

BUILDING SOCIAL
ENVIRONMENTS
(6500–5500 BC)

From the middle of the seventh millennium BC, people across the Balkans started to live in new ways.[1] They began to build permanent and semi-permanent structures and they adopted clay firing as the standard technology for making containers. Over the long term, the adoption of permanent architecture and pottery vessels was to have significant consequences in altering people's lives. Other, similarly significant developments are evident. Most obvious is a general increase in the number and range of objects that people made, used and kept within the new built environments. These objects range from bone, stone and antler tools that were all previously widespread technologies, to non-vessel ceramics such as discs and models of houses and furniture, to new plants and animals and, even, to people themselves, as seen in burials and figurine portraiture. Taken together, these elements and technologies were symptoms of profound material changes in the ways people organized their lives and the relationships within and between their communities.

These changes did not appear at one time across the regions of south-eastern Europe; nor, when they did appear in the different regions, did they do so in exactly the same combinations. What is common across the regions, however, is that the changes mark off the post-6500 BC period from the preceding millennia. This chapter examines one of these developments: the creation, delimitation and division of built social environments. Other important developments, such as the firing of clay, the formal treatment of the dead, the managed growth of plants and the raising of animals are examined in Chapter 3.

BUILDING THE SOCIAL ENVIRONMENT

In the seventh millennium BC people began to alter, physically, their natural environments in active new ways. In doing so they refashioned the previously unmarked landscapes of the Balkans. They did this by building

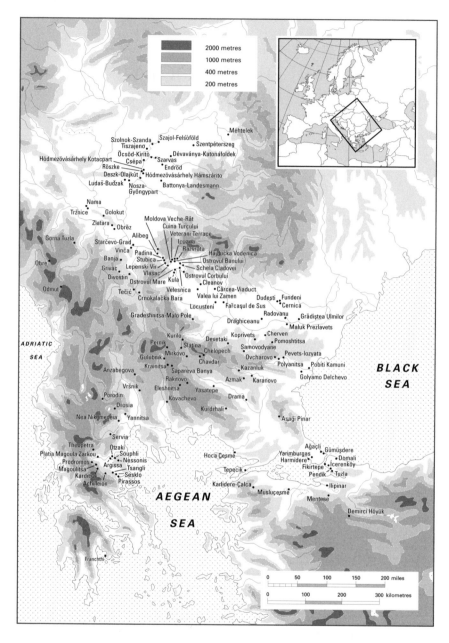

Figure 2.1 Map of key sites discussed in Chapters 2–4

structures of wood, clay, mud and, sometimes, stone and by grouping these structures together into small camps or villages. People marked out and created places to which they assigned particular identities across terrain which for tens of millennia had been open, traversed by mobile foragers, gatherers and hunters. While earlier, more mobile groups had well developed senses of place and had identified particular locations within regions, through valleys and forests, upland and downlands, the means of the new marking of place was significantly different. After 6500 BC people marked out particular parts of landscapes by constructing into and on them semi-permanent and permanent buildings. The form of building varied in different regions and at different times, although by the end of the period considered in this chapter, c. 5500 BC, all regions were physically structuring their environments in broadly similar ways.

At the most general level, one can recognize three regions of formal variation in architecture. To the south, in northern Greece (and especially in Thessaly) people built rectangular structures with stone foundations and substantial timber frames which they covered with clay and mud daub. In some cases, they built walls with sun-dried blocks made by mixing together clay, plants and mud; in a few cases they dug shallow hollows into the ground and erected walls or roofs made of branches and small tree-trunks among which they wove smaller branches and twigs which, in turn, they covered with applications of clay and mud.

In a much wider area to the north and west (the lower Danube, Serbia, the eastern Hungarian Plain) the substantial timber-framed buildings were fewer in number, if found at all. Here, there were almost no buildings with stone foundations or sun-dried mud blocks. In these northern and western regions, two types of structures were common: a roofed, semi-subterranean pit-hut, elliptical in plan; and a surface-level building with rectilinear floorplan and wattle-and-daub, post-framed walls. In between these two regions lay a third area, south-central Bulgaria. Here there were none of the pit-huts which were common to the north or west and although timber and post-framed buildings were built they did not employ the stone-foundations common to the south. More briefly, two other geographically distinct areas are considered below as well: the Danube Gorges and north-western Anatolia.

There are other differences which are less easily restricted to regional classification. In some places people repeatedly repaired and reconstructed buildings in the same place over many human generations; in other areas people abandoned structures after a single period of occupation or use. Regardless of these varieties in technique, materials or degree of continuity, a common theme unites all of the efforts people expended to create their physical environments after the middle of the seventh millennium BC. Each effort succeeded in marking out and enclosing parcels of the landscape from a previously open terrain. In doing this, people created places of particular personal or group importance. Let us consider each region in detail.

41

NORTHERN GREECE

Some time in the second half of the seventh millennium BC,[2] a small group of people stood on the rise of a hillside overlooking a rain-fed river. They dug several simple pits into the ground and, using thick branches and saplings, erected huts over the pits. Around this hillside, on the sparsely forested plain, lived aurochs, fallow and roe-deer. The people who constructed the pit-huts hunted these animals as well as the red deer, ibex, wild cat and wild pig which lived nearby and in the more distant mountainous forests. They also cultivated cereals such as wheat and barley and raised domesticated varieties of cattle, sheep, goat and pig. This was the beginning of the early Neolithic village of Achilleion (Gimbutas *et al.* 1989).

The people who constructed the first simple camp of pit-huts (phase Ia) appear to have used them for not more than, perhaps, fifty years, although there is nothing to suggest that such use was continuous. When excavated, the pits contained thin layers of material, mostly very simple and often crude pottery and some stone vessel fragments (Winn and Shimabuku 1989a: 32–3). Most probably people used these huts as temporary bases or stopping-places at different times in the year when they were busy with various activities such as hunting or tending herds and flocks of domesticated animals.

In the subsequent generation of the camp (early phase Ib), white plaster floors were added to pit-huts. The range of tools and pottery from this phase suggests a longer, more continuous, occupation of the buildings. In the next phase (late Ib), people built more substantial structures. They did not dig pits but constructed the buildings with plastered floors at ground level. For walls, they packed mud onto timber, branch and twig frames which they set on stone foundations dug into supporting trenches. The range and quantity of tools and other artefacts suggest a more permanent use of the buildings and a wider range of activities taking place in and around them. The more stable and durable building methods and materials of construction also suggest that people were creating a place which they intended to use for more substantial lengths of time. Perhaps it is correct to recognize this phase with its sense of longevity of use as the emergence of Achilleion as a village. People rebuilt these more durable buildings in the subsequent phase of occupation (IIa) and added new structures. Activity areas and hearths were set up immediately outside of the buildings; rubbish was thrown into nearby pits. One building contained a domed oven and a clay bench. Similar architecture and divisions of space are evident in the next phase (IIb); the use of open areas between buildings increased and new structures, such as a large circular hearth, and activity areas were in use in the spaces left free of buildings. A phase of apparent inactivity follows (IIIa), although buildings and task areas may merely have shifted to other parts of the village beyond the limited area of the excavation. Buildings and activity return in the subsequent phase (IIIb) with new, well built extramural hearths constructed in the open areas; a stone wall separates one of the cooking areas from new structures. In the village's final phase (IV), buildings were larger, had stone foundations and reveal no reference (in terms of the orientation of floorplan layouts) to buildings of the earlier phases. One of the final-phase buildings contained two separate rooms. Perhaps this suggests further divisions of settlement space: the separation of areas inside a building from the open spaces between buildings was extended by the segmentation of intra-mural space into separate, but linked, units.

The village at Achilleion was built and rebuilt over an 800-year period. By the final phase the village covered an area 200×600 m. There is no reason to assume that the occupation of the village was continuous, nor that every part of the village was used at any one time. Indeed the absence of architectural features and activity areas in phase IIIa suggests that the focus of life in the village shifted with time. Nevertheless the length of time over which people chose to build, work and live in this particular place is striking: they repeatedly recognized an explicitly fixed location as appropriate and desirable for living and doing.

Achilleion is but one, early, example of the way in which people started to mark out particular places in the landscape with small collections of structures and then larger aggregations of buildings. Across Thessaly after 6500 BC people were building rectangular timber-and-clay structures of various sizes (up to 10×7 m) in village aggregations covering as much as 5 ha of the landscape (Demoule and Perlès 1993: 370; Halstead 1995: 13). Some buildings were of sun-dried mud blocks (as at Sesklo, Otzaki and Magoulitsa); others were of timber, branches, clay and mud. In several villages, such as Sesklo, people used both construction materials. Within many villages (as at Achilleion), hearths and cooking equipment were located in open, perhaps shared, areas between buildings. Some villages developed upwards into tell settlements reaching many metres in height and covering several hectares; others developed outwards into very large horizontal spreads of occupation covering larger areas. People built their villages in a diversity of locations: in low foothills as well as in fertile lowlands and floodplains (Gallis 1994). Most were near water sources and some (e.g., Platia Magoula Zarkou) were positioned along streams in actively flooding river plains (van Andel et al. 1995).

Achilleion provides a good early example of people carving their own social environment out of the open landscape, and of their use of timber-framed buildings to create a focus for a wide range of activities. The Achilleion village also offers some initial insights into ways in which people divided up internal space within a village: the eventual use of rooms to divide intra-building space and the separation of activities within buildings from those taking place outside. Equally, the collection of separate, individual buildings in one place may have served to define the interior of the village from activities, people and animals that remained outside its limits.

At a general level, one gains a sense that people were actively and purposefully dividing one building or group of buildings from another. This sense of the demarcation of physical space is heightened when one looks to other villages for evidence of the erection of tangible boundaries. In a number of Thessalian villages (e.g., Souphli, Achilleion), especially during the early years of their existence, people built boundary walls and dug ditches around their communities to mark the spatial limits of the community (Demoule and Perlès 1993: 370). Perhaps they were responding to the increasing density of settlements within the region: some villages were less than 5 km from their nearest neighbour. More likely, perhaps, by erecting village boundaries people were trying physically to differentiate their areas of living and activity from those of others.

Sesklo

The case for boundary definition is especially clear at the village of Sesklo in Thessaly. The village sits on the edge of low hills above a small stream valley; the site itself is flanked by two shallow ravines. The village is spread over three areas (Figure 2.2): Sesklo A, which is the tell itself; Sesklo B, a horizontal spread of occupation on a natural flat surface sloping to the southwest; and Sesklo C, an area of very early occupation marked by pit-dwellings and stone structures. The total area of the site may have been as much as 100 ha although, as at many sites, it is unlikely that all of the areas were in use at the same time; thus during the middle of the sixth millennium BC perhaps only 10 ha were densely occupied (Kotsakis 1995: 125).

In the second quarter of the sixth millennium BC, people made buildings of sun-dried mud and straw blocks on the acropolis of Sesklo A. These buildings were free-standing and several had open areas between them which were kept free of structures; some buildings had courtyards. Buildings were substantial in size (e.g., 'House' 39 was 8.5 × 5.5 m) and contained distinct activity areas with stone platforms, hearths, storage vessels and grinding-stones. Floorplans were precisely delimited and maintained over successive architectural phases (Kotsakis 1995: 126).

Sesklo B was very different. Here cultural deposits are thinner and vary greatly across the area; indeed some parts contain no evidence for activity or building (Kotsakis 1995: 125–30). Space for building in Sesklo B appears not to have been as rigidly regulated as in Sesklo A. Building construction expanded horizontally without constraint and buildings formed tight clusters with shared walls and, perhaps, communal areas for food-processing and storage (Kotsakis 1981). There are also significant differences in the ways in which people constructed buildings: techniques employed at Sesklo

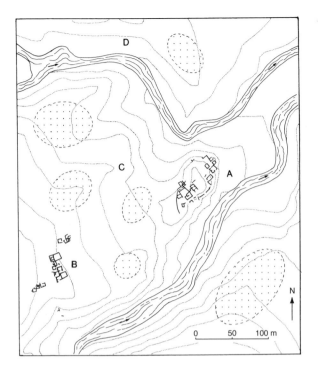

Figure 2.2 Plan of differential land-use at Sesklo in Thessaly (after Kotsakis 1995)

A were more refined than those used at B. Most striking is the demarcation of one area from the other by the creation of a boundary wall which
separates the two, perhaps as much symbolically as physically. There are
also significant differences in the quality of pottery found in A and in B;
these are discussed in Chapter 3.

The composition of villages with several distinct internal areas was not
unique to Sesklo. In certain generations of Achilleion parts of the village
were deemed suitable for rubbish; others for particular activities and building.
At Prodromos there is evidence for shifting settlement between three
contemporary foci of activity and occupation (Kotsakis 1995: 128). At
Argissa there are separate series of ditches and pits (Theocharis 1958, 1973;
Milojčić *et al.* 1962).

At all of these sites the evidence that people physically separated areas
one from the other suggests that they perceived different parts of community space in particular, perhaps exclusive ways. The ways in which space
was divided was not identical in all villages. At Otzaki there appears to
have been little of the need or desire to retain open space which was so
obvious at Sesklo A or Achilleion: structures on the Otzaki tell were erected

45

and successively rebuilt close to each other; indeed many buildings shared walls. It appears that people held building space within this village at a premium. Most buildings at Otzaki had a single room; in some, people constructed buttresses against the interiors of the rooms' walls to support upper storeys. Two-storied buildings were also constructed at Tsangli. Overall, the distribution of buildings within villages may have been based as much on perceptions of where it was appropriate or desirable to build as on any, more functional, factor.

Macedonia

Further north, in Greek Macedonia, people were marking out parts of the landscape in similar ways. During the second half of the seventh millennium BC people erected rectangular post-framed houses on a low rise north of the River Haliakmon and adjacent to an oak forest, a marsh and meadow. This was the village of Nea Nikomedia (Rodden 1962, 1964, 1965; Rodden 1962; Pyke and Yiouni 1996). A ditch surrounded the early aggregation of buildings and suggests that, as in Thessaly, people thought it necessary physically to demarcate the particular area which they deemed suitable or desirable for building and living. In the succeeding building generations of Nea Nikomedeia, people repaired and renewed existing buildings by resurfacing floors and by completely replacing individual structures.

Different parts of buildings and different areas of the village appear to have been perceived in different ways. As was the case at the late phase of Achilleion and at Otzaki, some of the Nea Nikomedeia house interiors were segmented by the construction of partitions. In the earliest phases of life at the village, one, particularly large (10×10 m), building was constructed with parallel rows of heavy timber posts which divided the interior into three sections. The building's contents were also unusual: a collection of five figurines, two large greenstone axes and, most exceptionally, two caches of hundreds of unused flint blades made of exotic raw materials. Several hundred clay discs were also found (Rodden 1964: 114; Halstead 1995: 13).

In Macedonia other early attempts physically to create a built environment out of the open landscape were made close to springs or streams in lowlands (Andreou *et al.* 1996: 575). Field survey in the Grevena region has located more than a dozen open and unconstrained concentrations of material and structures on terraces as well as on low-lying areas near streams. Most sites are less than 1 ha in size and at many mud-block was used as a building material (Wilkie 1993). Further early building programmes have been found in western Macedonia, at Yannitsa B, where a metre-thick layer of early Neolithic material marks relatively long-term use (Chrysostomou 1989, 1991, 1993; Chrysostomou and Chrysostomou 1990). The long, though not necessarily continuous, use of the village reveals, again, people's choices over long periods of time to build and rebuild and to anchor their lives in particular places which they defined in permanent, physical fashion. Similar attachments to particular places were made at Servia (Rhomiopoulou and Ridley 1973; Ridley and Wardle 1979) and at Drosia (Kotsos 1992).

Northern Greece: conclusions

In northern Greece after 6500 BC, therefore, people selected particular places in their natural environments and marked them by using buildings (and rebuildings) to create series of durable, anchored, social environments. In building and aggregating structures into villages (and less permanent camps) and by marking community boundaries with walls and ditches, people parcelled particular areas in the landscape from others. In some cases, by digging semi-subterranean pit-huts, they literally carved out a part of the landscape. In other instances, by enclosing some spaces and activities within walls (and by focusing some activities in open spaces), people segmented the internal space, if not in the small pit-huts, then certainly in the larger village structures. At a general level, in the parcelling and segmenting of space, it appears that people were viewing their immediate and wider surroundings from a new social perspective; at the core of this were ideas about what should and could take place where and, no doubt, who should, and should not, be part of separate activities carried out in different parts of buildings, villages and the larger landscape.

The significance of the intention to mark out particular places and segment their interiors would have been amplified by the durability of the materials and techniques employed. In most cases, parcelling out and segmenting was achieved by creating physical boundaries of varying efficiency. Some boundaries may have been marked in largely symbolic ways. The walls and ditches which delimited village boundaries may have done nothing more than express the sense of the outer limits of community space. Other boundaries were more tangible and restrictive. Thus walls of mud, clay, timber and stone prevented physical access to building interiors or entry from one room to another. Furthermore, the materials used to construct walls made it difficult, if not impossible, for outsiders to see, hear or, even, smell what was occurring inside a building. In this sense these building walls served as barriers to the acquisition of any knowledge of activities and occupants within a structure as much as they prevented, or at least restricted, physical entry or exit.

The permanence of materials and techniques and the long-term patterns of repair and reconstruction lend further importance to the processes of marking, parcelling, segmenting and bounding space after 6500 BC. If the intention was to identify and promote one particular place as a focus for community and small-group activities, perhaps an unintended consequence of the many successive generations of building, demarcating and segmenting space and of living within that space was a continually reaffirming routine of spatially restricted living. Such a routine may have infused these communities with values of bounding and excluding.

Not all building solutions invoked permanence of place; elements of bounding and exclusion may have been but one of several themes in the lives of people in some communities. In many cases structures were erected with less durable materials and techniques. Pit-huts were seldom vertically repeated; where they were, the number of repetitions is low. Furthermore, some walls were built with less durable materials such as smaller saplings instead of heavier timber, stone or sun-dried mud-blocks. In many cases, successive generations of surface-level structures were built horizontally displaced from their predecessors.

Therefore, in some parts of the landscape, people established less permanent, if not ephemeral, links to particular places. These less durable structures suggest a more mobile existence or, at least, reflect more mobile activities within the broader trends. Beyond the novel appearance of marked places in the landscape and the segmentation of village and building space, there was no unilinear trend through time in the techniques employed or the form of structures. Although in many places oval pit-huts were replaced by surface-level rectilinear structures, at some sites apparently progressive, more durable, materials were succeeded by less permanent ones as at Otzaki, where mud-block structures gave way to post-framed buildings.

Many of the techniques and materials apparent in northern Greece were also employed by people in regions to the north and the west. In neither of these regions, however, were present all of the techniques and materials in use in Greece. Nor were they in use from such an early date. Let us turn to the northern and western variations of people constructing their social environments.

WEST- AND SOUTH-CENTRAL BULGARIA

In west- and south-central Bulgaria, as in northern Greece, from the last quarter of the seventh millennium BC people built structures with timber posts covered in mud and clay. The rebuilding of structures and repetition of floorplans occurred over very long periods and many sites represent many hundreds of years of use. There is little, if any, evidence of short-term camps of temporary pit-huts or of villages that did not remain the focus for activity and occupation for extended periods; that is to say, the record is dominated by tell settlements.

Chavdar

In the western reaches of central Bulgaria, on a river bank, people built a village of timber, clay and mud buildings at the start of the sixth millennium

BC. This is the site of Chavdar (Georgiev 1973, 1981; Dennell 1978: 80–111). People may have chosen to focus their activities and ground their community in this place for several reasons. Most obviously, the river provided easy access to a water source. Indeed, during the first half of the sixth millennium BC the course of the river was much closer to the village than it is today; in the lower strata of the site appears a mixture of yellow and black clay layers documenting the ancient course of the river (Dennell 1978: 83). Furthermore, a low ridge of hills sheltered the village from northerly winds and, opposite the village, a small side-valley provided easy access to upland slopes for summer grazing (Dennell 1978: 76, 80).

Taken as a whole the region around Chavdar had very low agricultural potential. The village, however, was built in one of the few parts of the valley in which the widest range of resource zones were available: heavier riverine soils for grazing; forested slopes for hunting; and lighter loamy soils for planting (Dennell 1978: 100). In his analysis of Chavdar and two other villages in the region (Mirkovo and Chelopech) Dennell suggested that a prime factor conditioning village longevity and size was the ease of access to satisfactory amounts of arable land.

In other parts of central and south-central Bulgaria similar factors appear to have conditioned the selection of locations for establishing permanent villages: in the Valley of the Roses at Kazanluk and in Thrace at a range of locations (including at Azmak) people grounded their villages in places best suited to cultivation. At Karanovo people chose to build in an area between forested hill-slopes to the north and open grasslands to the south where diluvial fans graded into forest soils (Dennell 1978: 133, 135; Bökönyi and Bartosiewicz 1997: 392). While information available about site location is good for Chavdar and Kazanluk, it is less easy to understand the spatial layout of buildings, their orientations or spacings within these villages. More details are available for the Karanovo village (Hiller and Nikolov 1997).

Karanovo

At the beginning of the sixth millennium BC, people built rows of rectangular surface-level, post-framed one-roomed structures at Karanovo in south-central Bulgaria. Buildings were repeatedly repaired and rebuilt: the first horizon of structures at the site contained three episodes of rebuilding; the second horizon contained four; and the third two (V. Nikolov 1989, 1992a, 1992b).

The earliest buildings (from *Bauhorizont* 1)[3] were 7–8 m in length or width and most contained a hearth built along a wall. Buildings were constructed without any adherence to a common orientation and were relatively well spaced, at least 5 m apart (Hiller 1997b). In addition to a hearth the most completely preserved early building (*Haus* II.1) contained storage vessels, a grinding-stone and two clay platforms or benches placed on either side of the single doorway. An accumulation of stone debris outside the door marks, perhaps, an external activity area. More certain is the external hearth of *Haus* II.2 constructed in the second building phase (*Bauhorizont* 2). *Haus* II.2 was built exactly in line with a floorplan from the earlier level and suggests continuity from the earlier level. In this second phase of buildings a new structure (erected to the west) was laid out in the same orientation as the rebuilt *Haus* II.2.

The architecture of the following phase of Karanovo (*Bauhorizont* 3) reveals major changes in the organization of space. Two buildings contain three rooms and a third has a partially enclosed forecourt. Interiors contained similar features as before, although individual buildings contained more of each type; one of the three-roomed buildings has three hearths (one in each room), four storage vessels (two each in the north and central rooms) and two clay platforms (one on either side of the door in the central room). The amount of space kept clear between buildings was now reduced and a stone and post fence was erected, perhaps to separate the eastern three-roomed houses from other parts of the village. Despite these changes, the connection of both of the three-roomed buildings with the floorplans of buildings from the previous phase suggests continuity of community from one to the next village phase. The trend towards greater density of building and physical connections between phases continues in the next three generations of the village (*Bauhorizont* 4, 5 and 6) (Figure 2.3): indeed the two northern buildings were rebuilt through four successive phases of Karanovo and mark deep chronological roots to community residence.

With the recent publication of work carried out up to 1992 (Hiller and Nikolov 1997), Karanovo remains the only satisfactorily published village from this period in the region. We know only a limited amount about other sites such as Azmak where people built structures with floors made of mud, clay and plant material packed on to wooden substructures (Georgiev 1962, 1963, 1965, 1966). Some walls had been decorated with curvilinear designs. We must assume that other tell settlements were similar to Karanovo, Azmak and Chavdar.

Dennell's palaeoenvironmental work, now over twenty years old, remains the most detailed information on contexts of site location in south-central Bulgaria (Dennell 1978; Dennell and Webley 1975). Due to the sharp gradation of soil types over relatively short distances, the amount and distribution of arable land in both the Nova Zagora and the Chelopech region to the west were severely restricted (Dennell 1978: 136). It is likely that this would have had increasingly significant effects on people's perceptions of different parts of the landscapes and on preferences for locating, and retaining, village settlements in particular places. The creation of spatial boundaries and perhaps even the physical presence of villages themselves appear to have served to demarcate special parts of the landscapes.

oven
storage container
rubbish/debris and flint
postholes
utilised stone

0   5 m

N

Figure 2.3 Aggregation of buildings from *Bauhorizont* 4 at Karanovo in south-central Bulgaria (after Hiller and Nikolov 1997)

West- and south-central Bulgaria: conclusions

In west- and south-central Bulgaria, therefore, people were marking out and segmenting their social environments with some (but not all) of the materials and techniques that were in use in northern Greece. They built structures of timber, mud and clay but with neither stone foundations nor with mud-blocks. They built these structures in village aggregations and repaired and reconstructed them over long periods, creating traditions of community continuity which were anchored to particular places. With time, these villages rose out of the valley floodplains and formed substantial, monumental tell settlements. As is clear at Karanovo and as was clear in buildings further to the south, people also segregated and partitioned space within structures. Individual structures erected in the earliest phases (without regard to a common plan of orientation) were replaced with those attending to common arrangements of floorplans. In the materials they employed people restricted physical and sensory access to places, activities and people.

People selected particular places on which to focus long-repeating episodes of building and activity. This suggests that they perceived their landscape in terms of new spatial preferences. As Dennell's study suggests, one possible dimension of preference may have been the availability of arable land; other, yet unclarified, dimensions must have contributed as well to choices made over the suitability of locations for building aggregation. Overall then, the main trends of marking and segmenting which are documented for northern Greece are also apparent for southern Bulgaria from the beginning of the sixth millennium BC. To the west and north, however, there are important differences and to these we now turn.

THE WESTERN BALKANS AND THE LOWER DANUBE

A third major part of the Balkans which can be distinguished by the ways in which people constructed new social environments covers a wide zone from western Bulgaria, Serbia and south-eastern Hungary in the west, along both sides of the Danube through northern Bulgaria and southern Romania to the Black Sea coast in the east. In all of these areas people were building structures in aggregations in very similar ways. With the exception of the Danube Gorges, in all of these regions pit-huts and surface-level structures were constructed in a less durable manner than they were made in regions to the south. The long-term rebuildings of structures one on top of the other were not carried out: that is, there were no tell settlements. Furthermore, in the materials employed, people limited themselves to wood, mud and clay; the instances of mud-block or stone constructions are so few as not to warrant mention.

Western and south-western Bulgaria

In the middle of the seventh millennium BC, people dug a camp of pit-huts into the eastern bank of the Dzhubrena stream near what is now the modern town of Krainitsa in western Bulgaria (Chokadziev and Bakamska 1990). At the end of the seventh millennium BC and after a break in the village's life, people built a series of new surface-level structures (phases II and III). The floors of these buildings were made of beaten earth and their ovens were constructed with large stones which were covered with layers of clay plaster. Ovens were repaired and replastered in four major episodes.

Similar structures were built in the first quarter of the sixth millennium BC on a terrace on the right bank above the Pirinska Bistritsa at Kovachevo in south-western Bulgaria (Pernicheva 1990; Demoule and Lichardus-Itten 1994; Demoule et al. 1989). The village was rebuilt through three successive generations. The extent of the village covered 5 ha although it is not clear that all of this area was in use at one time. At least one building contained large storage bins made of coarse, poorly fired or unfired clay; one bin was almost 1 m high, had a flat quadrangular base 0.4×0.4 m and would have had a capacity of 100 litres (Demoule and Lichardus-Itten 1994: 576). As at other sites, in addition to surface structures, people dug pits into the ground and used them for burning and for rubbish disposal. To the south the village was bounded by the edge of the terrace and to the east by a ravine which had been cut by a small tributary of the Bistritsa. To the north-east an alignment of large stone blocks may have marked another boundary of the village (Demoule and Lichardus-Itten 1994: 565). Despite intensive surface survey in the region, Kovachevo remains one of the very few early villages in the middle Struma valley in south-western Bulgaria (Pernicheva 1993, 1995: 102).

A remarkably well preserved rectilinear surface structure has been found at Slatina in west-central Bulgaria dating to the second quarter of the sixth millennium BC (Figure 2.4) (V. Nikolov 1989, 1992a, 1992b). The structure was large (13×10 m) and had been rebuilt through two major phases of reconstruction; multiple layers of clay line a wooden-based floor and suggest a series of repairs or, perhaps, more frequent sequential episodes of reoccupation. The walls of the Slatina building were made of small posts (10–15 cm in diameter) woven with twigs and branches covered with mud and clay. The roof was supported by three larger posts (0.50 m in diameter) erected in the centre of the floor. Other buildings of this large village (perhaps covering over 8 ha) have yet to be thoroughly investigated.

The interior of the Slatina building was segmented into two rooms: a large outer one containing most of the finds and structural features and fixtures and a shallow room to the rear of the building. While the smaller, rear room contained assemblages of stone and bone tools and a footed storage container, the larger room contained almost all of the building's impressively preserved botanical samples and furniture.

In the southern corners of the outer room were two rectangular wooden structures (2×4 m) which the excavator has interpreted as beds. In the centre of the southern wall is the building's single external doorway and immediately to the west inside it was a hearth with an attached ash pit or receptacle. Some 3 m inside the doorway were four posts (25 cm in diameter) which probably served as a partition-screen blocking sight-lines into the building or acting as a wind- or rain-break. Along the western wall was a raised wooden platform and opposite it, on the eastern wall, was a loom. In the centre of the northern wall was a large domed oven (almost 2 m on a side) with an attached ash facility. Near the oven was a grinding-stone which appears, like the building's doorway, to have been shielded from the rest of the room by a post-framed partition or screen.

Concentrated in the north-eastern corner of the large room were four-teen clay-lined receptacles for plant stuffs; the largest was fixed into the

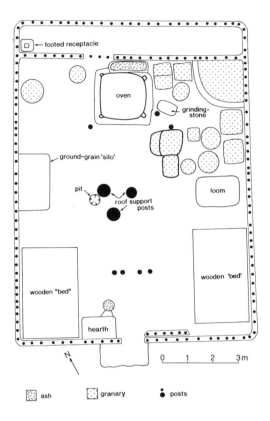

Figure 2.4 Rectilinear surface-level building from Slatina in western Bulgaria (after Nikolov 1992a)

corner and had an arcing front. Two other receptacles were placed in the large room's north-west corner. The amount of preserved botanical material is substantial: six of the receptacles contained a total of more than 200 kg of carbonized wheat, barley and beans (Docheva 1990). A large number of bone and flaked stone tools were in the room as well; over 3000 stone tools – mostly blades and debitage and few cores or retouched tools (Gatsov 1992: 99).

Without other buildings from Slatina to provide comparison, it is impossible to understand fully the local significance of this remarkable structure. In the larger regional context, however, Slatina offers important information at a level of preservation seldom encountered. In addition to the large number of plant-stuff receptacles, most important is the strong division of intra-mural space. The two post-frame partitions, the more permanent division of space into two rooms and the arrangement of permanent facilities such as the loom, the hearths, the grinding-stone and the 'beds' suggest that different activities were restricted to particular places in the building. Division of internal space segregated plant storage and processing to the northern part of the large room, textile production to the eastern wall, storage of ground-grain to the western wall, other storage of tools to the rear room and, perhaps, sleeping to the southern wall either side of the doorway. The constriction of all of these activities within the building, separate from the outside world of the rest of the village raises the demarcation and separation of community space to a level infrequently encountered to the west but more common at contemporary villages to the east and south. The large size of some building components, such as the roof-supports, the investment of effort in building internal features and the repeated desire or need to maintain or rebuild the structure suggest that people had a vested interest in maintaining the position and existence of this structure, what it contained and, thus, what occurred within it.

Serbia, south-eastern Hungary and south-western Romania

Towards the end of the seventh millennium BC, on a gentle slope running down to the Divostinski stream in south-central Serbia, people dug a series of pits into a strip of land bounded on two sides by springs. This was the beginning of the settlement of Divostin (McPherron and Srejović 1988). Nearby were deciduous forests of oak, elm and linden. Though heavy and intractable, and thus perhaps of little use for cultivation, the soil was fertile. The slope had a southern exposure and a hill to the west would have sheltered the village.

Three pit-huts mark the earliest phase (Ia) of Divostin. Spaced 3 and 10 m apart, the pits had irregular, mainly elliptical, shapes and were oriented without any apparent shared plan. Over the pits people erected tent-like superstructures made of small branches, twigs, mud and clay. Internal features of these pit-huts were limited to small hearths (0.5 × 0.5 m) built of clay and mud on stone bases and which were covered with a thin, smooth coating of an earth-sand-lime plastering (Bogdanović 1988: 36).

In the subsequent phase (Ib) new pit-huts were dug in a separate area and were spread out as much as 60 m from each other. The new pit-huts shared a common NE–SW orientation of their floorplans, were both larger and deeper than the earlier ones and were made of relatively more durable materials. In the centres of hut floors, people erected wooden posts and supported their bases with stones; the posts supported branch and twig superstructures (Figure 2.5). Some huts had more substantial walls of branches and twigs woven in and around alternating large (up to 20 cm diameter) and small posts; walls were covered with mud and clay. In addition to hearths some pits contained other internal features: a multi-layered stone construction in pit-hut 5; a round clay bank and a rectangular niche

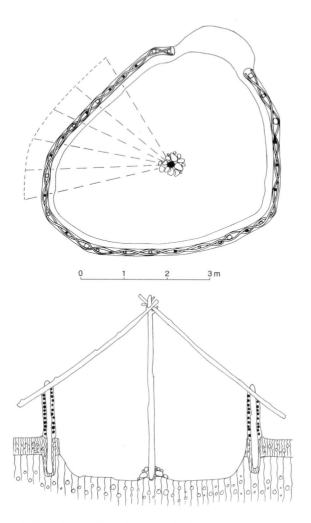

Figure 2.5 Pit-hut 4 from Divostin Ib (after Bogdanović 1988)

cut into the east wall of pit-hut 4. Perhaps these hut 4 features reveal a division of internal hut space into separate areas which were dedicated for separate activities. Features and activities also spilled outside of pit-huts; two small storage pits were dug into the ground near pit-hut 5.

The subsequent phase of Divostin (Ic) is marked by important changes in architecture. Buildings were constructed on ground level, had rectangular floorplans and post, mud and branch walls the bases of which were dug into supporting trenches (Bogdanović 1988: 74). Almost all the buildings contained hearths, simple artefact inventories and, often, layers of ash and charcoal; as in earlier phases, pits were dug although none appears to have been used for anything but burning and rubbish deposition. Hearths were also built in the spaces between the surface structures. Some limited evidence of separating one part of the village from another may be seen in a double trench and post-hole construction (Bogdanović 1988: 44). The village covered an area 325 × 300 m.

Divostin is characteristic of other Starčevo culture sites in the western Balkans. Pit-huts similar to those of Divostin Ia and Ib have been found at Banya, Vinča (Vasić 1931–4, 1932), Starčevo-Grad (Fewkes *et al.* 1933), Grivac (Gavela 1956–7, 1960) and, in the upper levels, at Lepenski Vir (Srejović 1969). Surface-level structures similar to those of the later Ic phase of Divostin have been found at Biserna Obala near Nosa (Garašanin 1958, 1959, 1960), at Starčevo-Grad (Milleker 1938), in Macedonia at Porodin (Grbić *et al.* 1960) and at Vršnik (Garašanin and Garašanin 1961). With the exception of Rudnik (which contained a three-roomed structure) almost all of these buildings were single-roomed (Bogdanović 1988: 88).

These camps and small villages were created on river terraces, as at Starčevo which overlooks the broad wooded and marshy Danube flood-plain. Other aggregations of buildings were constructed on low rises near swamps and marshes. At Divostin, the site rested on a gentle slope close to a stream and was positioned in a transitional zone between the environments of mountains and plains. People would have had access to both the, not distant, densely forested mountains and the more openly forested areas and steppe (Bökönyi 1988: 428).

In this western region of the Balkans, there is very little evidence that people reconstructed successive generations of buildings in exactly the same parts of camps or villages; there is very little vertical stratigraphy. The large pits that are such prominent features of Starčevo sites are relatively irregular in form and, in their construction, the use of relatively small posts for superstructure and walling (no larger than 10 cm diameter) suggests that they were relatively temporary fixtures. People appear to have stayed in one place for short periods. It may be most accurate to see people building in one particular place and using it as a base from which to make much shorter-term trips. At a larger scale, Whittle has suggested that the mobility of groups of people was tethered to these early Balkan sites (Whittle 1996: 34–5); people retained high levels of mobility but focused on a particular place as a base to and from which they moved.

Eastern Hungary

In eastern Hungary people were constructing new built social environments from the last quarter of the seventh millennium BC. Pits, if not clearly defined pit-huts, were frequent, often large and contained substantial quantities of artefacts. As in regions to the south and east, people dug these pits along the edges of terraces above floodplains or on islands within the plains. Again, as in neighbouring areas, people also constructed surface-level buildings. At Hódmezővásárhely-Kotacpart people built ground-level structures with clay floors and gabled roofs (Banner 1943). The majority of buildings consisted of a single, rectangular room built of post-framed walls made of branches, twigs, reeds, clay and mud; these were in use at Ludas-Budžak (Szekereš 1986), Tiszajenő (Selmeczi 1969), Szajol and Szolnok-Szanda (Kalicz and Raczky 1980–1; Raczky 1982) and Dévaványa-Katonaföldek. Individual buildings were similar in size (c. 8 × 4.5 m) to contemporary ones in neighbouring regions.

Once established, these camps were used for relatively short periods of time; there is little vertical stratigraphy and occupation must have shifted horizontally. As in neighbouring regions, tell settlement was absent. In their construction these buildings appear to have been less durable than were contemporary ones to the south in Serbia; walls were thinner and people used fewer posts to support them (Horváth 1989: 86).

The horizontal extent of areas of occupation ranged from 150–400 × 20–30 m × 300–400 × 30–40 m (Horváth 1989: 85), although it is unlikely that the entire areas were in use at the same time. The larger aggregations of buildings contained up to fifty buildings and more, arranged in one or two long rows; smaller sites were made up of as few as 5–10 structures. Some sites were more limited in overall size; the pit complexes and surface-level structures of Endrőd 119 in the lower Körös valley covered 75 × 50 m (Makkay 1992). In some cases buildings were widely distributed (in some instances 30–50 m apart) across an area of occupation but questions of structure contemporaneity remain. People built hearths in open areas, outside of buildings, perhaps more than they did inside structures; interior hearths are found at few sites: Tiszajenő, house 5 at Szolnok-Szanda, at Hódmezővásárhely-Kotacpart (Horváth 1989: 86). Outside as well as inside buildings, people dug storage pits and placed storage vessels in the ground; some pits were lined with plaster. In at least one instance (Nosza-Gyöngypart; Hováth 1989: 92, note 72) people dug ditches, perhaps in an attempt to separate one area of occupation from another.

The lower Danube

The relative impermanence of building technologies and materials evident in Serbia and eastern Hungary is also found to the east along the lower Danube in northern Bulgaria and southern Romania. From the middle of the seventh millennium BC in northern Bulgaria (but less clearly in southern Romania) people marked out particular parts of the landscape from others by digging small pits into the ground or by erecting rectangular, straight-walled surface-level buildings.

Northern Bulgaria

In north-eastern Bulgaria a series of open, horizontally spread sites were established on the gentle slopes of south-facing plateaux frequently in places where terrace edges were bounded by ravines or streams (Todorova and Vajsov 1993: 127); this is the case at Ovcharovo-platoto, Ovcharovo-zemnika, Ovcharovo-gorata (I. Angelova 1988, 1992; Angelova and Bin 1988), Pevets-lozyata and Polyanitsa-platoto (Todorova et al. 1983: 10–14; Todorova 1989a).

The buildings constructed on the plateau at Polyanitsa-platoto in the second half of the seventh millennium BC were small (4×4 m) and the entire spread of the thin layer of occupation and activity debris covered no more than 100×75 m. In the middle of the seventh millennium BC it is clear that people rebuilt structures through at least four successive generations of building at Koprivets (V. Popov 1993: 294; Stefanova 1996). Although excavations were of limited extent, hearths (perhaps extramural) were also uncovered at the site. People also built hearths and structures in caves, as at Devetki in north-west Bulgaria, from the end of the seventh millennium BC (Mikov and Dzhambazov 1960).

As was the case in western Bulgaria, Serbia and eastern Hungary, the lower Danube villages did not develop upwards into tell settlements as often happened further south, in southern Bulgaria and northern Greece. All of these early settlements were spreads of surface-structures or pit-huts such as Ovcharovo-zemnika I, where pits were spread over a large area (Todorova et al. 1983: 10–14). There are two important exceptions which suggest the beginning of vertically extending settlements at the end of the millennium considered in this chapter. The first of these is Ovcharovo-gorata.

In the middle of the sixth millennium BC at Ovcharovo-gorata people dug a series of small pits. Most were between 0.8 and 3.0 m in diameter but one was much larger (10–20 m long, 5–10 m wide and 0.6–2.0 m deep) (Nobis 1986; I. Angelova 1988, 1992; Angelova and Bin 1988). Succeeding these concentrations of pits and pit-huts were three generations of one-roomed, straight-walled, rectangular surface-level structures. New buildings were erected directly over the earlier structures and copied the earlier structures' orientations. Nineteen surface-level buildings, most of which contained hearths (and one of which contained a double-hearth), were constructed in the first, post-pit-hut, generation of the village. In the unbuilt space between buildings two hearths were found. In the following phase (horizon III) a similar number of buildings were built; one contained two rooms and all had hearths. In this phase many extramural hearths were also constructed. The final phase of the village was crowded with almost thirty buildings, all but six of which had hearths and all but one of which was single-roomed. The extent of the village was never any larger than 0.5 ha. Village space appears to have been held at a premium and preference for particular places for building may have caused the tight packing of structures.

59

The second exception to the absence of tell settlements in the lower Danube region was Samovodyane in north-central Bulgaria (Todorova and Vajsov 1993: 163; Ninov and Stanev 1991; Stanev 1979, 1981, 1982a and b). Here episodes of rebuilding superimposed structures one after another over a very long period. However, occupation of Samovodyane began quite late in the millennium considered in this chapter; Chapter 5 examines the development of lower Danube tells after 5500 BC and perhaps it is best to link Samovodyane to those phenomena. If not, then perhaps Samovodyane and Ovcharovo-gorata should be seen as a precocious manifestation of a style of building and a conception of expressing continuity of occupational space which had only been common up to this time in regions to the south.

Southern Romania

From the beginning of the sixth millennium BC in southern Romania, people dug shallow pits into the soil and covered them with thin-posted superstructures.[4] At Broneşti people dug a pit 2–3 m in diameter and lined it with a layer of clay. It was more common for people to build structures at surface level (Comşa 1971: 204). At sites such as Cleanov (Fiera), both surface-level and pit-hut forms appear to have been used at the same time, although the precision of the relative chronology is not clear. At Cleanov, people created a 4.0 × 2.5 m pit-hut near to several surface-level structures made of compacted mud mixed with plant material (Comşa 1971: 205).

At Valealui Zamen at Verbicioara early surface structures were rectangular in form; these were typical on sites of the developed Dudeşti culture and were found at the type-site where buildings had compacted clay and mud floors (Comşa 1971: 206). Inside the northern end of the structure at Dudeşti an oven had been built with a mixture of clay and sand. Walls of the building were made of interwoven branches and twigs which were covered with clay. Similar building techniques were employed at the site of Fundeni (Dolinescu-Ferche 1964). Almost without exception, these houses were single-roomed and no larger than 5 × 3 m; floors were often made of clay packed onto wooden planks. Some structures contained small platforms and small (12 cm diameter) grinding-stones. Although most buildings had only a single generation of building, in a few places such as at Dudeşti, Radovanu and Drăghiceanu people rebuilt structures horizontally displaced through successive village generations. At this time, nowhere in southern Romania did tell settlements develop (Dumitrescu et al. 1983: 94).

Camps and villages were constructed on terraces, 4–5 m above and overlooking river valleys (Dumitrescu et al. 1983: 92). More rarely people built on higher terraces, as at Radovanu, or on islands in lakes, as at Grădiştea Ulmilor (Comşa 1971: 203). Preference for location of building was influenced by proximity to water sources. The limited pollen work available, such as that for Radovanu, suggests that the environment around these camps and villages was transitional from forest-steppe to steppe (M. Alexandru reported in Comşa 1971: 204).

The horizontal extent of these sites varied through the successive phases of building or occupation. Some sites, such as Malul Roşu, were relatively small (50 × 50 m), some, such as Fundeni, were larger (100 × 100 m) and others, such as Cernica, were larger still, reaching several hundreds of metres on a side. The larger sites appear to be more frequent on those terraces which were naturally bounded by rivers on either side.

The western Balkans and the lower Danube: Conclusions

In many ways the character of early buildings, the techniques and materials of their construction and the relative absence of long-term rebuilding sequences distinguishes the western Balkan and lower Danube regions from northern Greece and south-central Bulgaria. There are, however, similarities between the ways in which people in both larger regions built their social environments.

Most obvious of these similarities is the marking off of parts of the landscape by constructing aggregations of buildings. In both of these larger regions people selected particular places in the landscape and marked them, in some but not all cases, with permanent constructions. In the west, people built structures in aggregations often with natural boundaries, such as the use of terrace edges at Kovachevo, or they constructed the limits to sites, such as the stone walls at Kovachevo or post-fences at Divostin. In both regions the walls of structures separated intramural from extramural areas of activities and interaction.

Although efforts to segment intramural space with the separation of rooms and the arrangement of fixed facilities for different activities are found in both regions, with the exception of Slatina these efforts were few in number in the west and north. In all of the north and western aggregations of buildings, as was the case in all regions of the Balkans, building materials and techniques provided excellent means of separating off individual units of built space from others. Building in wood, mud and clay succeeded in separating the interiors of individual structures from the open areas of camps and villages; the erection of trench and post-hole constructions, as at Divostin Ic, succeeded in separating one part of a camp from another. More infrequently, interior walls and partition-screens separated one room or area within a building from another. This is seen very clearly at Slatina, but also in the, admittedly infrequent, two-roomed structures in the third and fourth horizons at Ovcharovo-gorata.

There are significant differences between the north and west Balkans and the regions to the south. With the single exception of Samovodyane in north-central Bulgaria, the long traditions of building reconstruction, so striking in the tell landscapes of northern Greece and south-central Bulgaria are absent in the northern and western region. There appears to have been less concern physically to declare residential continuity than there was to the south. More frequent in the north and west was the regeneration of building by expanding sites horizontally in a relatively unconstrained manner. Compared to the deep expressions of tradition marked by tells, the thin spreads of pit-huts and surface-level structures give the western region an atmosphere of relative impermanence of occupation.

Also a stronger case can be made in the western regions for the development of architecture from semi-subterranean elliptical pit-huts to rectilinear surface-level structures, although it is impossible to determine whether the shift from one to the other was direct and immediate. Equally apparent, at least at sites such as Divostin, was the shift from relatively disorganized arrangements of pit-huts, dug into the ground without concern for a shared form or orientation, to a more unified strategy of pit digging and surface-structure building in which each architectural unit was oriented with respect to the directional arrangement of its neighbours.

The comparison of the north and western regions with those to the south highlights the distinctions in the degrees of permanence of building materials and in the efforts to build continuity into residence and occupation patterns. The social environments of the south can be characterized as permanent and pressing for continuity; those to the north as more temporary and less concerned with long-term occupation. These two attitudes to building are combined in two final areas of the Balkans: the Danube Gorges and north-west Anatolia.

THE DANUBE GORGES

Between the eighth and the sixth millennia BC people built durable stone-based structures in aggregations along the edges of the Danube on the banks and islands of what is now Serbia and Romania. Considerable attention has been focused on these sites as they are, in many ways, very different from other structures established in the surrounding regions (Srejović 1969; Radovanović 1996a; Whittle 1996).[5] Much of this attention has locked onto the early date at which some of these sites were established (from the end of the eighth millennium BC) and the absence in the first millennium and half of two of the traditional components of early settled life in the Balkans: pottery and domesticated foodstuffs. The present discussion is more attuned to the sites' importance as examples of local variations in the wider trends in the ways people actively built their social environments. Details of economy, material culture, burial and symbolic objects follow in Chapters 3 and 4.

Phase 1

In the Gorges, from the end of the eighth millennium BC (Radovanović's Gorges phase I)[6] (Table 2.1), people built structures and hearths with stone bases on thin strips of land between the shores of the Danube and the steep slopes which rose back from the river. In some places they erected structures on the slopes of the foothills or on the accumulations of ground deposited over time where small rivers flowed into the Danube; this is the case at Padina, Alibeg, Icoana, Veterani Terrace and Răzvrata. In other places, such as Vlasac, people built on terraces above the river, and at others such as Ostrovul Corbului, they built on islets (Radovanović 1996a: 61).

At Răzvrata people dug small oval pits in which they built circular hearths (Boroneanţ 1973; Radovanović 1996a: 122). Similar structures were created at Alibeg, Icoana, Veterani Terrace and Vlasac (Boroneanţ 1973; Radovanović 1996a: 117). At Padina, people used stone to build an amorphous structure (Jovanović 1969) and at Ostrovul Corbului they shaped a semi-subterranean dugout into a rectangular structure (Mogoşanu 1978; Radovanović 1996a: 122).

The two earliest structures at Vlasac took advantage of natural funnel-shaped hollows in the central part of the terrace (Radovanović 1996a: 120). More numerous, later constructions were built in two separate areas: one up- and one down-stream from the earlier ones. These later buildings also took advantage of natural hollows in the rocky ground which people

Table 2.1 Relative chronology of sites in the Danube Gorges (after Radovanović 1996a)

	7000 BC	6500 BC			6000 BC	5500 BC
Site	Radovanović's Phases (with site subphases)					
	1	2	3	4	5	6
Padina	A	A/A–B	A–B	B/I	B/II	B/III
Alibeg	I				II	
Vlasac	Ia	Ia–b	Ib–II	III		
Veterani Terrace	*					
Icoana	Ia–b		?		II	II
Răzvrata	I					
Schela Cladovei	I	I	II			
Ostrovul Corbului I	H.II	H.III–IV	H.V–VI			H.VII
Lepenski Vir		Proto	I/1	I/2	I/3	II
Hajdučka Vodenica	Ia	Ia	Ia–b	Ia	Ib	
Ostrovul Banului		IIIa	IIIa–b	IIIb	IIIb	
Kula			I		I–II	
Ostrovul Mare km 875				*	*	
Ostrovul Mare km 873						*

* indicates activity where there are no site-specific phase names.

modified into trapezoidal shapes by levelling the ground, plastering it with a mixture of crushed limestone, sand and clay and surrounding it with a line of crushed stones (Radovanović 1996a: 120). Round hearths were built on one side of the later Vlasac buildings; hearths contained burnt human bones. All of the early buildings at Vlasac contained significant concentrations of stone, antler and bone tools and animal and fish bones. Structures at Icoana also contained circular hearths as did the ones at Veterani Terrace, where people also used wooden posts in their constructions. There is little evidence for sequential reconstruction of buildings in this first phase of activity in the Gorges, although the rounded hearths in the rectangular semi-subterranean huts at Ostrovul Corbului were reconstructed three times (Radovanović 1996a: 122).

Phase 2

From the beginning of the seventh millennium BC (Gorges phase 2), many of the earlier sites remained in use. At new places of construction such as Ostrovul Banului and Lepenski Vir people built semi-subterranean pit-huts with oval floorplans. At Vlasac people built new buildings with trapezoidal floorplans. At Ostrovul Banului, people continued making circular hearths; some constructions used wooden posts as well as stone. At the new site of Lepenski Vir along a narrow strip of land between the river and the hills people built semi-subterranean oval structures into niches cut back into the hillside or in natural hollows (Srejović 1969; Radovanović 1996a: 119). Bases of some walls were made of stone and at the front of buildings, that is on the river-side, people used stone slabs to build rectangular hearths. In the narrower rear areas of buildings, dense concentrations of material culture accumulated. In this, the earliest phase at the camp ('proto-Lepenski Vir') the eight structures were spaced 5–12 m from each other.

Phase 3

In the first half of the seventh millennium BC (Gorges phase 3), people continued to build semi-subterranean pit-buildings with trapezoidal floorplans at Vlasac and at Lepenski Vir. After the use of the pit-huts at Vlasac, people constructed surface-level buildings on circular stone bases. Similar structures were created at new places, such as Hajdučka Vodenica and Kula. At Lepenski Vir (site phase I/1) buildings were separated into up- and down-stream aggregations (Figure 2.6). Upstream were three structures (building sequences 17–8–7–9, 30–29, and 58–53–47); 20 m downstream were eight structures (building sequences 41–38–37, 2–1, 50, and individual structures 3, 9, 40, 62, 63) (Radovanović 1996a: 106). The distinction between the up- and down-stream aggregations is amplified by a higher density of burials, altars and figurative material in the latter area.

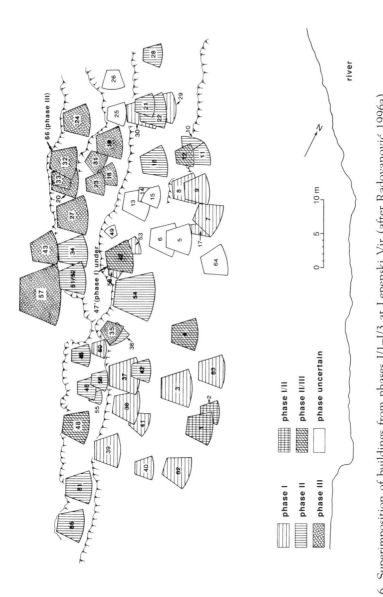

Figure 2.6 Superimposition of buildings from phases I/1–I/3 at Lepenski Vir (after Radovanović 1996a)

In both the up- and down-stream parts of Lepenski Vir, many buildings were repeatedly reconstructed. This is clear especially in the building sequences of structures 17–8–7–9 and 41–38–37. Such repetition suggests, if not permanent occupation, a greater continuity of use than was evident in earlier Gorges sites. A single building (no. 50) was built on a higher terrace and represents a third spatial element in this phase of the site. In all structures people built rectangular hearths with stone 'plaques'; most buildings contained places for ash disposal and stone thresholds (Radovanović 1996a: 104–6).

At Hajdučka Vodenica, a small area no more than 12 m in breadth was the focus of building activity. The structures had asymmetrical floors and rectangular stone hearths and thresholds. Hearths and amorphous constructions of stones were also built in the open areas of the site. At Vlasac three trapezoidal structures were built into naturally occurring funnel-shaped hollows, each structure positioned at least 5 m from the others. Floors and walls were plastered with a limestone mixture.

In the subsequent rebuilding of the site (Vlasac II), people abandoned the practice of using natural hollows, preferring to build along the border of a rocky plateau facing the river (Radovanović 1996a: 121). As at other sites, two clusters of circular buildings made with stone bases were separated into up-stream and down-stream areas (Radovanović 1996a: 121). Continuity of site-use is evident in the rebuilding of structures through at least two generations. Further downstream, at Kula, people built surface-level structures with trapezoid floorplans and rectangular hearths (Sladić 1986; Radovanović 1996a: 124).

Phase 4

From the middle of the seventh millennium BC (Gorges phase 4) several significant novelties in material culture appear in the Gorges: the introduction of pottery and important changes in lithic technology. Beneath these changes, however, ran currents of deeper continuities in many aspects of architectural technique and organization. People continued to build semi-subterranean structures with trapezoidal bases, as at Lepenski Vir and Padina, as well as surface-level structures with circular or rectangular stone bases, as at Vlasac and Hajdučka Vodenica. Continuity with the previous Gorges phase is especially clear at Padina, where one of the four new, phase 4, structures was positioned directly over a hearth from phase 3. Similar continuity is evident at Vlasac: seven of the new hearths appear in the same arrangement as those of the previous phase. The general method and materials of construction also remained the same; stone bases, several of which retained the earlier circular form, continued to be used.

The division of site space into concentrations of up- and down-stream areas also continued. At Lepenski Vir (site phase I/2) the earlier bipartite division of the village continued into phase 4, although buildings were distributed in a new way. Structures were built further upstream and increasingly away from the river's edge; some were now in a row on the middle terrace (Radovanović 1996a: 107). The largest building of the phase (no. 54) occupied the centre of the hamlet with other buildings constructed equidistant up- and down-stream. Two buildings, one each in the up- and down-stream aggregations (buildings 28 and 40), may have had special significance: both contain similar elements of figural art arranged symmetrically within the structures. With time, as space became increasingly crowded, people started building structures onto the upper terraces. Although the bipartite division continued, the previous symmetrical distribution of buildings began to break down (Radovanović 1996a: 107). However, continuity of the attachment of communities to particular places continues and is evident in the patterns of structure rebuilding; Radovanović identifies three major rebuilding phases and nine areas of superimposed buildings (Radovanović 1996a: 112).

Phase 5

At the end of the seventh millennium BC (Gorges phase 5) semi-subter-ranean structures with trapezoid bases continued to be built at Alibeg, Padina, Lepenski Vir, Ostrovul Mare km 875, and Kula. Often, massive stone blocks were used to build rectangular hearths (at Lepenski Vir, Padina III, Kula) which had clay linings or were bordered with clay and sand (as at Alibeg, Padina, Icoana, Ostrovul Banului, Ostrovul Mare km 875 and Kula). A number of hearths at Ostrovul Mare km 875 were built in the open areas outside of structures (Boroneanţ 1973).

The architectural layout at Lepenski Vir (site phase I/3) reveals signifi-cant changes at this time. Buildings were constructed closer together and were especially tightly packed further upstream (Radovanović 1996a: 109). One building (no. 57) was much larger than its neighbours; indeed it is the largest structure of any of the hamlet's phases. Rebuilding of structures carried on through four major phases of rebuilding and six individual foci for building superimpositions (Radovanović 1996a: 109, 112–13).

Phase 6

During the first half of the sixth millennium BC (Gorges phase 6) people continued building semi-subterranean and surface-level buildings with trape-zoidal bases. Hearths were made with large, specially arranged stones. Massive A-shaped stone supports were used in hearth construction at Padina (site phase B/III) and Lepenski Vir (II); alongside the hearths at Hajdučka Vodenica (Ib) ran stone-bordered channels.

After a hiatus in site use, Lepenski Vir (II) was rebuilt. The village now covered a larger area than in previous phases and people were building further away from the river on the terraces, which were reinforced by stone blocks (Srejović 1969: 42, 48, 77). Buildings were surface-level structures with trapezoidal bases; some were encircled with a ditch and posts reinforced by stone slabs (Radovanović 1996a: 120). Despite the hiatus in site use, continuity of place was maintained at Lepenski Vir; the central building of this phase (no. XLIV) was constructed directly on top of the central house (no. 57) from the previous phase.

Danube Gorges: conclusions

At first sight, the Gorges appears as a special place during the millennia of its early use. The particular natural environment of the area, the unique form of much of what people did there, especially the trapezoidal form of floorplans, and the early date at which these things appear tempt one to separate the Gorges from other developments in the Balkans. It is perhaps more appropriate, however, to investigate the Gorges phenomenon of building structures in terms of the patterns of spatial organization evident in other parts of the Balkans. By doing this the Gorges sites fit into the wider patterns of building social environments which define the other regions from 6500 BC.

In the Gorges and in other regions similar patterns of marking parts of the terrain and of separating places are evident. Perhaps the Gorges is unique only in the particular form, and perhaps the date, in which wider trends in human behaviour were manifest in a local variation. There are important similarities between spatial organization in the Gorges and that described above for other regions of the Balkans after 6500 BC.

As in other regions, within any one aggregation of structures, separate concentrations of buildings suggest that intra-village space was divided. At several sites people built structures concentrated in separate, distinct areas; one example is the distribution of early buildings at Lepenski Vir (site phase I/1), which created separate up- and down-stream concentrations of buildings. Radovanović suggests that each concentration contained a 'central place' marked by higher concentrations of buildings and ornamental art (Radovanović 1996a: 109).

In the subsequent phase of Lepenski Vir (I/2) buildings were again distributed in up- and down-stream concentrations. Again special roles have been proposed for a building in both the up- and down-stream groups (structures 28 and 40 respectively). In the early phase of Vlasac (Ia) as well, people created a bipartite separation of site space, although this distinction is marked, not as at Lepenski Vir by separate groups of buildings, but by focusing mortuary deposition in the upstream zone and building activity downstream (see the discussion in Chapter 4 for details). In Vlasac II two separate clusters of circular stone arrangements may represent another division of site space; the distinction between up- and down-steam areas continued in Vlasac III.

In addition to the separation of up- and down-stream areas at Lepenski Vir, each of the early phases (I/1, I/2, and I/3) contained a central structure: in I/1 building 50 was constructed on a higher terrace; in I/2 the large building 54 was built equidistant between up- and down-stream groups; in I/3 building 57 was the largest of any phase.

The distinctions between up- and down-river areas at these sites are matched by the ordered segmentation of space within individual buildings. For most building interiors the focus of the floorplan was a stone hearth; in many structures activity and deposition were structured in relation to the hearth. In the early buildings at Lepenski Vir the densest concentrations of material culture were discarded to the rear of the hearths. As is discussed in Chapter 3, similar patterns of deposition emerge with respect to the location of burials within buildings in phase I/2 and II at Lepenski Vir.

The arrangement of buildings across sites acquires further significance in light of the permanence of the structures. The widespread use of stone as a building material for the bases of building walls, hearths, post-supports and burial platforms, enclosures and conical constructions suggests a not insignificant investment of time and effort. Perhaps more importantly, at a more general, interpretive level, the widespread use of stone to define built space may be seen as a physical manifestation of people's long-term commitments to particular places, commitment irregardless of whether or not occupation was played out through continuous occupation or through a series of reoccupations over seasonal, yearly or longer cycles. The manufacture of building floors with durable limestone mixtures and the lining of hearths with clay, stone or sand layers at many sites in the later phases of the Gorges occupation, can be read as another measure of intended continuity of buildings and their internal features. Undoubtedly one reason for the permanence of building material may have been to prevent seasonal river flooding from obliterating traces of buildings; the desire to mark the intra-site divisions of social space in a permanent manner may have been another stimulus.

The sense of long-term commitments to particular river-side locations evident in the selection of building materials is heightened by the successive episodes of rebuilding and repetition. At the most general level, the long-term use of the Gorges sites, such as Padina, which went in and out of use over two millennia, documents a record of people repeatedly selecting the same place for their activities. At a more focused level, over much shorter periods, people rebuilt particular structures in exact, or nearly exact, replication of floorplans. Thus at Lepenski Vir, Radovanović has identified as many as four successive building subphases within the early (I/1) site phase; these are especially clear in the sequence of building numbers 17, 8, 7 and 9. The next major phase at the site (I/2) consisted of three major rebuilding subphases and site phase I/3 contained four major subphases (Radovanović 1996a: 113). At Vlasac (site phase II), circular stone structures were rebuilt twice. Continuity is also evident in sequential episodes of hearth rebuilding. In addition to the three successive generations of rounded hearths at Ostrovul Corbului, hearths were rebuilt at Padina (in site phase B/I) and at Vlasac (in site phase III).

Perhaps the most remarkable element of continuity and repetition in the Gorges sites is the dominance of a trapezoidal form for the floorplans of buildings. Buildings with trapezoidal floorplans appear both dug into the ground and as surface-level structures at a wide range of sites: Vlasac (Ia–b), Padina B (Sector III hor I–III; and Sector I hor I–II), Lepenski Vir I–II, Icoana II and Ostrovul Mare km 875 (Radovanović 1996a: 124). Of all the earliest Gorges sites (i.e., Gorges phase I), only at Vlasac were trapezoidal structures built; in the early phase of the site (Vlasac Ia), people created trapezoidal building floorplans by modifying the shape of natural hollows in the rocky ground. It is possible therefore that the trapezoidal floorplan developed as an exaptation of the local terrain. The dominance of trapezoidal buildings was not, however, complete; buildings also appear with oval and circular floorplans both as semi-subterranean pit buildings and as surface level structures; buildings with rectangular floorplans were also constructed (Radovanović 1996a: 124–5).

Thus, although the Gorges sites appear unique in some senses, they share many significant elements with the wider trend in building social environments which were spread across the Balkans. Undoubtedly the early date for the first Gorges buildings is important. Perhaps more telling, however, is the realization that the regular practice of repeatedly marking out particular places with repetitions of buildings did not occur until later stages of the Gorges occupation. The first evidence of regularly superimposed rebuildings of structures and hearths at sites such as Lepenski Vir (I/1), Vlasac (II), Ostrovul Corbului and Padina B/I did not occur until the middle of the seventh millennium (Gorges phase 3). The earliest appearance of intra-site separation of up- and down-river areas occurred at this time as well at Lepenski Vir (I/1) and Vlasac (II). This was the period of the Gorges sequence when other novelties appeared, especially the introduction of pottery and figurative art. Thus, while there were deep traditions in building technique and material which stretch to the ninth millennium BC, important changes in the ways in which people created their social environments suggest that the Gorges sites fit into the wider post-6500 BC developments in the continuity of marking out places and of separating areas of activities in permanent ways.

Set in the middle of this more fluid and mobile context in which people were building their social world in particular parts of the landscapes, the Gorges sites appear, at first glance at least, to be the manifestation of a very different set of phenomena. The widespread use of stone as a building material, the repeated selection of the same location for programmes of building (of aggregations as a whole as well as on individual buildings) and the strong sense of organized space (both within settlements and within buildings) all are similar to the longer traditions of the north Greek villages and, although to a lesser extent, the tells of south-central Bulgaria. The choice of a trapezoid for the shape of building floorplans (and the attachment of burial to structures) amplifies its apparent incongruence in the north and western Balkans. The early dates at which people started marking the strips along the Danube with structures and the formal and technological connections in lithics (discussed in more detail in Chapter 3) with earlier late Palaeolithic traditions suggest a depth to the social roots of Gorges communities that is not apparent in any of the other areas considered in these regions. Perhaps the local peculiarities of the Gorges architecture, art and attention to mortuary practice should be seen in the wider regional picture as discrepancies in form but not of principle. If this is the case, then the same patterns of marking places, dividing site space, segregating building interiors and boundary marking which permeated the rest of the regions can be promoted as the key to social and architectural activities. Perhaps the differences, at least in the particular form with which they built their physical environment, which make the Gorges special were differences of scale and not of type.

NORTH-WEST ANATOLIA AND TURKISH THRACE

While a detailed discussion of contemporary trends in the creation of social environments in western Anatolia and Turkish Thrace is beyond the intentions of this book, it is important to note contemporary similarities between what was happening in these Balkan regions and what was happening further to the north and west.

At the same time that social environments were being created in the Balkans by marking out particular places of living and building and by dividing space within camps and villages and within individual structures, similar things were happening in north-west Anatolia and Turkish Thrace.

In the last quarter of the seventh millennium BC, two different types of sites were being established and occupied in north-west Anatolia.[7] Although both types of sites share a common ceramic tradition (Fikirtepe wares; see discussion in Chapter 3), in other ways these sites were very different. The first type of sites, such as the type-site Fikirtepe, but also Pendik, Erenköy and Tuzla, were established on the eastern shores of the Sea of Marmara. There sites represent impermanent occupations of coastal areas in which activities focused on exploiting the rich local marine and terrestrial resource bases. Analysis of lithics suggests connections between these coastal sites and long-established pre-pottery traditions of micro to small bladelets, backed blades and geometrics (Özdoğan 1983, 1989a: 203).

71

Sites of the second type, such as Ilipinar, Menteşe, Iznik-Üyücek, Yenişhir II, Demirci Höyük, have a more permanent character. They were established and used over long periods. Ilipinar is one of the best studied examples (Roodenberg et al. 1990; Roodenberg 1993b, 1995; Thissen 1993b; Begemann et al. 1994).

Ilipinar

Ilipinar is located on the lower slopes leading down to a plain by Iznik Lake. At the very beginning of the sixth millennium BC people used trees, branches, mud and clay to build free-standing one-roomed structures. They built their village on an alluvial fan which graded out into the marshy lake plain; the village lay in a basin surrounded by mountains rising to 1000 m. Mountain slopes were forested and a low pass through the mountains led to the Sea of Marmara. Over 600 years, people built, repaired, rebuilt and reconstructed their village so that by the end of that time, there had formed a settlement tell 5 m high, covering 2.5 ha (Roodenberg et al. 1990: 63).

Four major phases of rebuilding can be detected for the first 400 years of the village's life. Throughout each major phase, people carried out shorter programmes of repair and rebuilding. In Ilipinar X, people constructed a 5 × 6 m building with timber-framed walls made from split wood. They built an oval hearth in the centre of the structure and dug two ash-pits near to it. In the building's north corner they placed a set of coarse mud-bins and in which they kept cereal; nearby was a large grinding-stone (Roodenberg 1993b: 253). The floor of one building from this earliest horizon reveals several episodes of building repair and reconstruction. Some structures in horizon VIII consist of 6 or 7 episodes of building (Roodenberg 1993b: 252).

In all of the phases of village rebuilding before the middle of the sixth millennium BC, mud and timber construction dominated architectural technique. Wall-posts were spaced close together and were set deep into foundation trenches (40–60 cm deep). In the second building phase of the village (Ilipinar IX) people used especially large, close-set posts to construct the walls (Roodenberg et al. 1990: 76). Smaller posts (5–6 cm diameter) formed a core to some walls and onto these builders applied alternating courses of mud and wooden laths to make a wall covering 5–20 cm thick. Other walls had thinner coverings (Roodenberg et al. 1990: 73). Central posts supported timber roofs.

In their form the Ilipinar buildings were very similar to the ones which people built in southern Bulgaria at Karanovo and Azmak: they were relatively small (5 × 6 m) with simple, one-room rectangular floorplans and some interior facilities but with only limited evidence of any effort to divide interior space into separate rooms (Roodenberg 1993b: 254–5). People split tree-trunks into wooden planks and lay them side-by-side to form the bases for buildings' floors. Attached to the exteriors of some Ilipinar structures were erected small 'sheds'. When people erected new buildings to replace older ones, they oriented the new floorplans in line with the older ones (North–South with a slight deviation to the west).

In the middle of the sixth millennium BC (Ilipinar VI) dramatic changes occurred in ceramic typology and economy (as discussed in Chapters 3 and 4). At this time people also changed the way in which they constructed their buildings: during the first 400 years of the village's life, people had built structures of timber frames; with Ilipinar VI people used sun-dried mud-blocks.

Non-ceramic sites

As noted in Chapter 1, there is also an intriguing series of early Holocene sites located in recent programmes of field survey in north-west Anatolia (Özdoğan 1989a, 1995; Gatsov and Özdoğan 1994). Some of these lithic scatters have been identified as evidence for a 'pre-ceramic Neolithic' in the region. One, at Çalca in the southern Marmara, is near the pottery Neolithic site of Karlidere-Çalca, which sits 200 m away on a small terrace (Özdoğan 1989b: 447–8; 1990: 347, figure 5). The surface finds at Çalca are concentrated over a 250×150 m area on a gentle slope which leads down to a stream (Özdoğan and Gatsov 1998). Although there is no evidence for any built structures, Özdoğan and Gatsov have argued that the strict spatial definition of the lithic concentrations is the modern surface level reflection of permanent buildings still hidden by alluvium (Özdoğan and Gatsov 1998: 214). Only further research, particularly excavation, at sites such as Çalca will allow us to understand their significance.

North-west Anatolia and Turkish Thrace: conclusions

There are many similarities between the ways in which people constructed their built environments in north-west Anatolia and the Balkans. The emphasis on long-term repetition of major building phases, the more frequent replastering and reflooring of structure interiors, the attention to continuous repair to buildings and the repetition of the orientation and form of floorplans all suggest a commitment to mark out a particular place within the plain of Iznik Lake. The construction materials used and the techniques with which walls were covered with layers of wood, clay and plaster and with which bases were dug into foundation trenches, again, suggest attention to preventing physical and sensory access to building interiors. Although people did not create separate rooms to segment space within buildings, the remains of the burnt structure from Ilipinar X suggest that different parts of the room were linked to separate activities such as the storage of grain, grinding and parching.

Perhaps the most intriguing component of north-west Anatolia at this time is the glimpse provided by the less permanent coastal sites and lithic scatters. Perhaps these, still little understood, places represent ephemeral parts of landscapes contemporary with the more permanent villages; perhaps they represent part of the non-built and non-permanent fluid landscape context in which the emerging and reconstructed built-environments derived much of their meaning as segregated and separate space.

CHAPTER CONCLUSIONS

One of the fundamental distinctions of the post-6500 BC Balkans was the building of social environments. With aggregations of pit-huts and surface structures people marked out particular places in the landscape. The aggregations themselves became the focus of communities of varying densities, sizes and durations. Camps and villages document the attachment of communities to place over both short- and long-term residence.

Aggregations of buildings also document new conceptions of group identity, cohesion and separation. At one level one can see the isolation of groups within villages and, to a less definite extent, in camps, from groups who lived beyond the village boundaries. At another level, within settlements, one can see the spatial separation of particular settlement areas. At a third level is the division of enclosed building interiors from more open extramural spaces. At yet another level one can see the segmentation of building interiors into separate activity zones and rooms. Evident on all of these levels and registered through the creation of physically tangible social environments is a clear commitment of people to place.

The shape of the people's commitments to particular places varied. There are distinctions between the relatively unconstrained camps and the more tightly bound, enclosed villages. There are distinctions in the organization of settlement space between the relatively simple and small pit-huts and the larger and more complex arrangements of multi-roomed village surface structures.

The chronological depth of people's commitment to place also varied. Thus, in terms of building materials and techniques distinctions of durability are evident between constructions made of stone and mud-blocks and structures built of large timber walls; further distinctions exist between these buildings and smaller structures made of thin posts and saplings. In terms of continuity of place, there are distinctions ranging from rather ephemeral pit-huts where hut space was created, used and abandoned perhaps over a season, to longer series of repairs to walls, floors and ovens and on to still longer sequences of rebuilding and superimposition of the floorplans of successive structures.

74

Also evident are distinctions within different degrees of community cohesion. Thus aggregations of villages suggest large units of community cohesion; forms, sizes and orientations of individual buildings share common patterns. Also however, it is evident that individual buildings could easily have served as physically bounded units for smaller, co-resident groups. Individual rooms and partitioned spaces within buildings suggest further, smaller spatial units of division and separation.

While aggregations of pit-huts and surface structures dominate the archaeological description of the Balkans after 6500 BC, and may have dominated the landscapes, it is critical to recognize that other more ephemeral activities were taking place as well. Even in the case of the monumental tell settlements, there is as much evidence for demographic flexibility as there is for actual permanence of residence as is often assumed (this is taken up in greater detail in Chapters 4 and 5, and see D. Bailey 1996b, 1997, 1999). I have no doubt, but little proof, that the size and composition of village communities shifted, expanded and contracted over seasonal, and longer, periods. The case is for a more mobile Balkans during this millennium (see Whittle 1996) and it can be made most strongly for camps of pit-huts. In this sense, these landscapes were fluid, only occasionally punctuated by islands of visible and recordable permanence.

The distinctions in structure size, form, building material and technique as well as the varying degrees of separation and division of space suggest more general contrasts in community organization between the camps of pit-huts and the villages of surface structures. These issues are taken up in later chapters, especially in Chapter 8.

SUMMARY

In this chapter I have described the emergence of the built environment between 6500 and 5500 BC and its variation in form and material through the different regions of the Balkans. The construction of buildings and their aggregations created the potential to ground interpersonal relationships in explicit ways that had not been utilized before. This was a fundamental shift from long existing ephemeral kinship links and alliances to more durable, but at the same time more inflexible, connections between people, connections which were moderated by the physical bounding of these people to place. In the next chapter, I examine the two other important innovations of the post-6500 BC Balkans, pottery and expressive material culture, and, in doing so, introduce some of the processes, activities and objects which filled these newly defined places.

3

NEW DIMENSIONS OF MATERIAL CULTURE

Pottery containers and other forms of expression (6500–5500 BC)

In addition to the emergence of buildings and villages, two important developments which distinguish the post-6500 BC Balkans from previous millennia were the adoption of ceramic pyrotechnology to make a wide range of containers and other objects and an increase in the number and types of visually expressive items. While the new technology accounts for much of the massive increase in the number and range of objects made after 6500 BC, many were made from materials and with technologies which had deeper continuities with local traditions. In this chapter I consider two major categories of these new things: ceramic vessels and intentionally expressive or symbolic objects made from ceramics, bone, antler and stone. Both categories shared a similar position within the new ways of living which emerged across the Balkans from the middle of the seventh millennium BC; both were the symptoms and mechanisms of new strategies of making explicit and tangible the relationships among individuals and groups and between people and places.

POTTERY

The making and decorating of pottery has been the predominant focus of research carried out on the later prehistory of the Balkans. Grand descriptive schemes and detailed regional variations overwhelm the literature. Attention is directed at diachronic developments in vessel form, the methods and styles of decoration and variations in shape and decoration within and across regions. As such, pottery analyses have formed the basis for the culture-history approach which, almost exclusively, dominates Balkan prehistory.

Within these traditions of research (or perhaps it is better to say alongside them) very little attention has focused on how or why pottery developed in the Balkans as and when it did or how pottery worked within the camps and villages of the period. Among the exceptions is Karen Vitelli's work on the ceramics from the Franchthi cave (Vitelli 1989, 1993a, 1995). For later periods Tim Kaiser has asked similar questions of the ceramics from the sites of Selevac and Opovo (Kaiser 1990). The present chapter draws on Vitelli's work as well as that of Kotsakis and his colleagues for the Sesklo material (Kotsakis 1982; Wijnen 1993, 1995) and Thissen's on the north-western Turkish material (Thissen 1993b). As yet there is little, if any, work that takes this perspective on the ceramics from sites in Bulgaria and Romania, although some recent efforts have focused on early monochrome horizons in northern and western Bulgaria (Todorova and Vajsov 1993; Stefanova 1996). Much of the discussion which follows, therefore, is based on Neolithic material from Greece; indeed examination of the Franchthi cave work pulls our attention disproportionately into southern Greece. Until future work begins to ask behavioural, in addition to descriptive, questions of more northern material, there will be no alternative but to rely on the Franchthi and Sesklo studies.

Working within these restrictions, this chapter argues that early pottery developed in two stages in many different parts of the Balkans. Furthermore, it suggests that these two stages represent differences not only in the technology of making pots but also in the uses to which people put pots as well as how people perceived ceramic vessels, potters and the processes of potting itself. The chapter also suggests that these early developments in the millennium leading up to 5500 BC set the stage for increasingly dramatic and complex forms and decorative schemes which characterize the succeeding 1000–1500 years and which became major components in the expressions of personal and group identities.

Early pottery in Greece

Although there is sporadic evidence for making objects of fired clay from upper Palaeolithic contexts (e.g., the ceramic figurines from Dolní Věstonice), the more widespread and regular adaptation of ceramic pyrotechnology did not occur until the middle of the seventh millennium BC. Early pots were small and few in number; decoration was scarce. In Greece early Neolithic pottery appears in the form of bowls produced with a simple technology (Demoule and Perlès 1993: 377). Pots were fired at low temperatures (below 650°C) in an oxidizing atmosphere (Maniatis and Tite 1981). The striking developments and innovations that mark out early Greek pottery did not appear until later pottery production (i.e., at the beginning of the sixth millennium BC) when shapes became larger and more complex, firing temperatures increased and decoration was more common and appeared in regional styles. There are many intriguing components within this apparently simple development.

'Pre-ceramic' sites?

There is disagreement over the first appearance of pottery in northern Greece. Earlier suggestions that a pre-pottery or aceramic period preceded a full pottery Neolithic at Argissa (Milojčić 1960, 1973) and Sesklo (Theocharis 1958, 1973) have received recent dismissals (Demoule and Perlès 1993; Runnels 1995; Gallis 1996; Özdoğan and Gatsov 1998) which have affirmed earlier work (Nandris 1970; Bloedow 1991, 1992–3). The supposed aceramic levels are almost indistinguishable from the full-pottery post-6500 BC contexts, contain a rich and well-made bone industry, ground-stone tools, pressure-flaked lithics, ceramic anthropomorphic figurines and other objects, such as ear-studs, which were common for the later period (Demoule and Perlès 1993: 368). At the top of these aceramic levels appear a few sherds; these are traditionally interpreted as post-depositional intrusions from the younger, overlaying levels of the full-pottery Neolithic.

Karen Vitelli has argued that these early sherds are not intrusions but evidence of an initial period of pottery use when fired clay vessels were rare objects which people held as precious. In her work on the Franchthi material, Vitelli studied the small assemblage of pottery (twenty-five sherds in all) from the aceramic deposit (Vitelli 1993a). She suggested that these sherds represent a temporary use of the cave at a time when pots were infrequently made and used. In this phase people valued highly the few pots which did exist and would have repaired and curated them. Indeed, several of the sherds from the early levels were pierced with holes which Vitelli suggests are evidence of attempts to repair vessel fractures (Vitelli 1989: 26).

Traditionally, aceramic contexts have been found at sites in northern Greece such as at Sesklo (both in area C and in the lowest part of the area A's stratigraphy) and at Soufli Magoula (in three separate aceramic layers). Perhaps these should be viewed as Vitelli does the Franchthi deposits, as evidence of an initial phase of pottery use when ceramic vessels were rare, highly valued, carefully handled and thus only infrequently discarded.

Early potting at Franchthi

As the aceramic period Franchthi sherds were made from the same fabric which dominated the site's early Neolithic pottery, Vitelli's in-depth analysis of the more numerous pottery from this level (phase FCP1)[1] provides important information about the early process of pottery production and the people who may have produced and used pottery, as well as about the uses to which people put that pottery (Vitelli 1993a). Vitelli noticed that FCP1 pots varied greatly in the thickness of their walls, the angles of their rims and in the curvature of their profiles (Vitelli 1993a: 213). Also, the early sherds bear traces of direct fuel firings, perhaps events which may have included only a few pots at a time in fires that people might also have used for cooking or other non-pottery-related activities (Vitelli 1993a: 207).

Early pots at Franchthi were small and made in very limited numbers. Taking into account the weight of typical vessels, the total weight of pottery recovered, the percentage of the site excavated and the duration of site use, Vitelli calculated that FCP1 potters produced no more than 12–13 pots per year (Vitelli 1993a: 210). Assuming that variations in ware-recipes correlate with different pot makers, she suggests that no more than five potters worked in FCP1 times. The unintentional asymmetries and the inconsistencies in form which mark all of the FCP1 pots suggest that these potters were inexperienced, perhaps only occasionally making pottery, never often enough to obtain any rhythm in their work (Vitelli 1993a: 210).

Vitelli argues that previous definitions of Greek early Neolithic pottery as coarse or crude are mistaken. Early Neolithic pottery surfaces were burnished and, as burnishing was the most time-consuming stage of pottery making, Vitelli suggests that the apparent crudeness of early pots is a reflection of potters possessing insufficient knowledge and experience and not of their making insufficient effort. These pots were made to a standard recipe with significant investment of effort and time, but by novice potters (Vitelli 1995: 59).

Vitelli also argues that the first potters may have been the members of communities who were skilled in gathering plants (Vitelli 1993a: 217). Similarities between the knowledge required to find, harvest and process plants for nutritional and medicinal uses and the skills required to find, extract and process raw clay suggest that the same people may have carried out both tasks (Vitelli 1995: 61–2). Access to esoteric knowledge of sacred plants and about a new medium, clay, may have set potter-gatherers into a special social category (Vitelli 1993a: 253). Perhaps people perceived that there was a special relationship between pottery and the mystical or magical. Perhaps people perceived potters to be capable of manipulating the supernatural, of having preferential access to supernatural powers and of imbuing their pots with such powers (Vitelli 1993a: 253). They may have identified the source of the magic in the power of fire to transform matter; the abilities to manage, control and manipulate pyrotechnology may have invested particular people with additional special powers. People may have believed that similar powers had been invested in pottery itself.

The significance of early pottery may not therefore have been a functional matter but an imaginative, social and perhaps magical one; potters thus may not have been perceived as mere labourers, but as special members of a community. Perhaps this perspective helps us understand why pottery became, eventually, the prime material for expression and display over the next three millennia; the message of and on the pot was powered by the intangible magic and mysticism of the medium.

Early pottery use

With respect to the function of the earliest ceramic vessels, Vitelli argues that it is a mistake to focus on food preparation. She shows that early pots do not possess the characteristics that would associate them with food warming or cooking: they lack soot deposits, were made from fine-grained fabrics which would have been unsuited to frequent reheatings, lack ring-bases and have well preserved burnished glosses on their surfaces (Vitelli 1989). Furthermore, Vitelli suggests that there would have been a wide range of successful non-ceramic means of preparing food in use before (and during) the development of ceramics (Vitelli 1993a: 215). It is safer to assume that food preparation (or storage – due to small pot size and rarity of examples) and pottery were not inherently associated (Vitelli 1989; 1993a: 214).

If pots were part of food consumption, then their size suggests that they may have been used in the feeding of small groups or that the contents of any one pot may have been only a small part of what was being consumed. Instead of a major role in food preparation, Vitelli argues that early pots may have served as containers for special plants such as medicines, poisons and mind- or mood-altering potions (Vitelli 1993a: 253). The shapes of pots suggest that they may have been used to display their contents. Thus the pedestalled saucers and flaring basins at Franchthi appear to have been designed to display as much as to contain. The majority of pots made of 'Urf' ware (a fine-ware which came to dominate later assemblages of cere-monial forms) were bowls which would have been appropriate as serving or presentation vessels (Vitelli 1993a: 216). In the centre of the interior of many of these pots were traces of burning and marks left from scraping; these may be the result of removing resinous remains of substances after they had been burned in the vessel. Vitelli suggests that these marks docu-ment the use of the pots for burning incense, aromatic gums and other substances which had psychoactive or medicinal properties. Perhaps these events were part of special ceremonial occasions; perhaps the limited number and sizes of the FCP1 pots represent a limited use of ceramics, perhaps restricted to special occasions.

Development in pottery in Greece at 6000 BC

The early pots and their surrounding social and functional contexts and consequences are set apart from later potting that marks the beginning of the local middle Neolithic at the start of the sixth millennium BC. Although the special power invested in the character of pots and of potters may have remained in force, there were significant developments in the Greek sequence at this time. Potters used different fabrics for different purposes (Wijnen 1995: 154; Vitelli 1989) and were making larger and more complex shapes such as simple carinated forms, pyriform vases, pedestalled basins and collared jars (Demoule and Perlès 1993: 381). Firing temperatures were higher and more consistently controlled (above 800°C) (Maniatis and Tite 1981) and larger collections of pots were fired together (Vitelli 1993a). Decoration was more diverse, employed varied surface treatments, such as painting, scraping and incising, and covered most of the pot surfaces. Regional styles emerged: brown-red geometric patterns on white/cream backgrounds in Thessaly; brown-red motifs on a light slip in western Macedonia (Demoule and Perlès 1993: 381). Such regionality suggests that pottery may have taken on an increasing role in strategies to express differences and similarities within local and regional social systems (Perlès 1992).

Compared to the early Franchthi pottery, the shapes of vessels made in the FCP2 phase were more symmetrical and regular. Fewer wares were produced but within each ware a broader variety of shapes was created and a wider range of firing temperatures employed (Vitelli 1993a: 210). Saucers and basins, rare in FCP1 contexts, were now more common. Potters were producing sharply angular vessels often with tall bases or pedestals (Vitelli 1995: 55). Some surface decoration was superbly finished; a quarter of pots were painted although no two pots bore the same pattern (Vitelli 1995: 56).

Vitelli argues that compared to the earlier phase fewer potters were at work in Franchthi in FCP2 but that they were potting more frequently; more pots were being produced (125–150 per year). The impression one receives from Franchthi is that these later potters were showing off their skills, producing vessels with sharply angular profiles and frequent contour changes (Vitelli 1993a: 24). The vast majority of pots, however, still were not used for cooking: none of the hundreds of thousands of sherds which Vitelli examined from FCP2 contexts had carbon-sooting in places which would suggest that the pots had been used repeatedly on a fire (Vitelli 1989: 24).

Also at this time, a new division between fine and coarse wares appeared and it is these first coarse-wares which show uses of pots for cooking, although they make up no more than 10 per cent of vessels (the use of pots for cooking does not increase dramatically until the second half of the sixth millennium BC) (Vitelli 1993a: 252). Cooking pots were deep, round-bottomed bowls made in heavily gritted fabric and fired at low temperatures with unburnished, blackened interior and exterior surfaces. The increase in non-plastic inclusions in the fabric would have improved the chances of pots surviving repeated exposures to temperature changes inherent in cooking (Vitelli 1995: 57). Downward-angled lugs were placed high on vessel bodies and would have provided a point from which sticks could be used to lift the vessel from a fire. The lower parts of pot surfaces bore traces of repeated exposure to hot, oxidizing flames and coals; that is to say they were light-surfaced or mottled (Vitelli 1989: 24). Cooking pots were not large (c. 4-litre capacity) and so may have been used to prepare food for a limited number of, Vitelli suggests, special people.

Thus at Franchthi, at least, the position of pottery as a social and symbolic element of material culture remained predominant over its use in purely functional terms. Over the longer term, the production of pottery shifted from one based on inexperienced individuals making simple forms to specialized production of high-risk shapes intended for highly visible social or symbolic roles. All of these changes suggest that from the beginning of the sixth millennium BC the role that pottery played within communities had changed.

Social pots in northern Greece

The effort which Vitelli invests in shifting the significance of early pottery from the technological and functional to the social is supplemented by other work on early pottery from northern Greece. Paul Halstead has argued that pottery was one of the powerful and important elements which people used to build alliance networks among groups of early agricultural communities based at separate villages (Halstead 1989b). Halstead argued that these village economies were based on the cultivation of cereal and pulse crops and that this would have been inflexible in times of drought or other, unexpected, inclement weather. To reduce risk, these communities negotiated networks of alliances with neighbouring villages. In difficult times these alliances would have served as a safety net providing support and necessary foodstuffs.

Halstead's model suggests that the alliance networks were founded on regular meetings and sharing of food and drink, perhaps even feasting. Meetings would have taken place around the ovens, hearths and food preparation areas located in the open spaces between buildings at sites such as Achilleion. Food and drink would have been served in and on the dramatically painted pottery. Again, as in Vitelli's arguments, the importance of pottery vessels rested in their capacity to function as part of a social, though admittedly partly economic, ceremony. If pots in general were held to contain special, perhaps implicit magical qualities, then their use in important alliance maintenance ceremonies would have been all the more powerful.

Sesklo

At Sesklo the earliest pottery (from the middle of the seventh millennium BC) was undecorated, but had well smoothed surfaces, and was made of not very striking colours, in simple, small or medium-sized vessels (Wijnen 1993: 321). In the subsequent phases of the site (6400–6250 BC) pots were of similar sizes but decoration appeared, although rarely, as plastic, impressed or painted treatment (Wijnen 1993: 321). These trends continued in the subsequent phase with the appearance of red-coloured pottery. Pottery production technologies developed from a reducing or neutral atmosphere in the first phase to a neutral or oxidizing one in the second to a mostly oxidizing one in the third (Wijnen 1993: 323). Potters exploited a variety of local clay beds and early potting was a local activity with little evidence of imported vessels (Wijnen 1993: 322).

As Vitelli suggested for the early Franchthi ceramics, so Wijnen argues that early pottery production at Sesklo may be characterized as a period of experimentation and adaptation setting the technological stage for more dynamic developments in subsequent phases (Wijnen 1993: 323). The function of early Sesklo pots is unclear although Wijnen has suggested that the storage of special goods may have been one use (Wijnen 1993: 324). Analyses of pottery from other sites, including Achilleion and Anza, suggest that pottery vessels were not used near fire but were used for storage or for display (Gardner 1980).

As noted in Chapter 2, the physical division of sites into different areas, as seen in Sesklo A and B, by the use of a wall was amplified not only by differences in the areas' architectural techniques and building layouts but also by differences in ceramics (Kotsakis 1982; 1995; Maniatis et al. 1988). Kotsakis has argued that the higher frequencies of painted pottery at Sesklo A (12–22 per cent versus 1–8 per cent at Sesklo B) reflects a greater use of prestige pottery in displays (and not in the preparation of food) in this part of the village. As at other sites, the shift from the early to middle Neolithic was marked by the development of pottery technology at Sesklo as well. This included moves towards more specialized and controlled pottery technology: increasingly consistent use of specific clay-beds, a preference for clay which fired to particular colours, such as red, increased control over firing temperature, the use of higher temperature firings (above 800°C) and the use of higher quality, better adhering slips (Maniatis et al. 1988; Wijnen 1995: 150–2). Again, the use of pottery as one of the ways in which people defined themselves in relation to others, especially those who lived nearby in other parts of a settlement area or in neighbouring villages, would have had added potency if the medium of pottery was fuelled by an implicit role of pottery as mystical and magical.

Achilleion

At Achilleion the pottery from the earliest contexts (phase Ia) was very simple and often crudely made. Vessels have irregular dimensions and shapes. Firing conditions were poorly controlled (Winn and Shimabuku 1989b: 77) and very little care was given to treating vessel surfaces. Early attempts at slipping pots (in phases Ib and IIa) produced a 'crackly' slip and peeling paint

(Winn and Shimabuku 1989b: 81). During these phases, however, improvements are evident in abilities to levigate the paste used in pottery production and to slip and fire pots. As at Franchthi and Sesklo, early pots at Achilleion were produced during a period of experimentation when potters possessed unperfected knowledge of pot-making (Winn and Shimabuku 1989b: 78). With Achilleion IIb and successive phases, ceramic production was marked by technological innovation in uses of temper and vessel surface finish. More carefully made red-painted thin wares and red/brown on white decoration show greater care in the preparation of vessel surfaces, which were finely smoothed and some of which had been slipped with white on both interiors and exteriors (Winn and Shimabuku 1989b: 95).

Almost all of the early Achilleion vessels were hemispherical (Winn and Shimabuku 1989a: 32–3) (Figure 3.1). Larger pots (with rim diameters 16–30 cm) dominated the earlier phases (Ia–IIb); smaller pots (6–15 cm diameters) appeared from IIb onwards; and the smallest vessels (less than 5 cm diameters) only appeared towards the end of the village's life (Winn and Shimabuku 1989b: 89). Petrographic analysis suggested that the Achilleion potters were exploiting a single clay source (Ellis 1989: 165).

Pyrotechnology developed gradually from no control over atmospheric conditions in phase I pottery to conditions ranging from complete oxidization to complete reduction in phase II and afterwards (Ellis 1989: 165–7). By the later phases, such as IVa, the percentage of pottery which was incompletely fired had decreased from high levels in phase Ia (40 per cent) to less than 10 per cent (Winn and Shimabuku 1989b: 77, table 5.2). The repertoire of decorative techniques also increased through the site's phases to include a range of different slips (Ellis 1989: 169). Bowl shapes predominated throughout the life of the village, being especially popular in the earliest Ia phase. The proportion of open shapes decreased with time; closed forms peaked in phase IIa, when they account for almost a half of all pots (Winn and Shimabuku 1989b: 87). Phase III contains fine-ware vessels with high necks and S-shapes, a trend that grows in popularity until the end of the site's life (Winn and Shimabuku 1989b: 85). Thinner-walled vessels appeared eventually; those with walls 0.35 cm thick or less appear first in small quantities (1–2 per cent) in phase IIa but account for 20 per cent in the later phases (IVa) (Winn and Shimabuku 1989b: 82).

Thus at Achilleion, as at Sesklo and Franchthi, pot making developed from an early stage of experimentation and inadequate understanding of pottery creation to later stages when potters possessed better controls over firing conditions and were able (and desired) to treat vessel surfaces in increasingly refined and decorative fashions. Earlier pots were larger and mainly hemispherical open bowls; later pots include very small vessels (Figure 3.2) as well as more complicated closed forms such as S-shaped jugs and high-necked pots. It would be easy to suggest, but difficult to prove, that the trends at Achilleion represent a move in pottery use away from

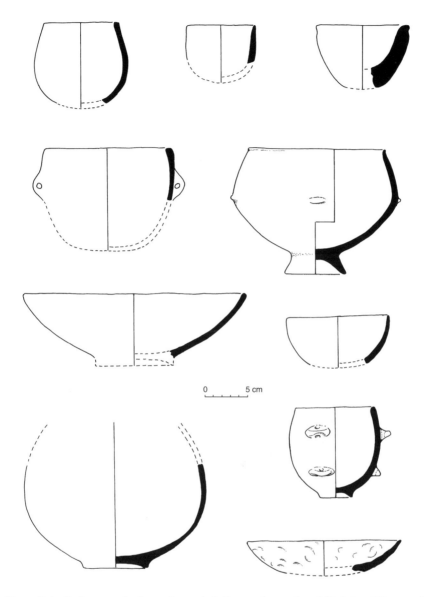

Figure 3.1 Early ceramic forms from Achilleion phases I and II (after Winn and Shimabuku 1989b)

open display and sharing within and among groups and towards more closed storage or the restriction of pot contents. One could read the emergence of very small pots in the late phase of the village as an indication of the rise in importance of consumption or storage based on individuals. Perhaps

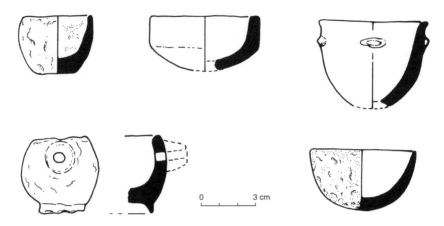

Figure 3.2 Small pottery vessels from Achilleion phase IVb (after Winn and Shimabuku 1989b)

it is more prudent to recognize, in these trends, a general shift in the use and meaning of pottery vessels from original purposes.

Nea Nikomedeia

The patterns evident at Franchthi, Sesklo and Achilleion are not found everywhere in northern Greece. Early pottery produced at Nea Nikomedeia appeared in greater quantity and more frequently than it did at Franchthi (Yiouni 1996: 185). Direct comparisons between the two sites, however, may be misleading. Nea Nikomedeia was a very different site in terms of length of occupation and economic activity (Yiouni 1996: 185). Nea Nikomedeian pots appeared in three main shapes: closed, open and necked jars (Yiouni 1996: 92). The predominant shapes (33–43 per cent of all forms) were closed, including jars with necks and hole-mouths. The Nea Nikomedeia inventory also contains a number of large vessels. The biggest were hole-necked and necked-jars; other large vessels were deep forms with rim diameters up to 32 cm and heights reaching 60 cm. Capacity of these pots was as much as 85 litres (Yiouni 1996: 191–2). Over the three phases of building at Nea Nikomedeia there was little change in ceramics (Yiouni 1996: 104) and there is little evidence for the initial experimental stages documented at other sites in the region.

Early potting in parts of the Balkans other than Greece

The study of the evidence of early pottery from other regions of the Balkans is much less detailed than it is for the Franchthi or Sesklo material. In addition to the Greek material, there are at least two other broad regional variations in early ceramics: the north-west Balkans; and the lower Danube.

The north-west Balkans

In the north-west, at Starčevo-Körös-Criş culture sites, painted pottery was rarer than it was to the south. Where it appeared it was black-on-red and white; decoration consisted of incised, impressed and roughened wares. For Starčevo culture contexts, predominant among the earliest pottery, at the end of the seventh and the beginning of the sixth millennia BC, was 'barbotine' decorated ware in which vessel surfaces were coated with a rough application of clay which was streaked with a finger or a stick so that ridges were raised (Manson 1995: 66). Unpainted, fine burnished monochrome wares were also common; incised, finger-impressed and applied decoration appeared on both coarse and fine-ware.

Painted pottery (white and dark colours sometimes with linear or curvilinear motifs) appeared in classical Starčevo assemblages (Manson's Starčevo phase II in the first half of the sixth millennium BC) (Manson 1995: 67). Coarse-ware still predominated although the percentage of fine-ware increased. Barbotine was still the most frequent type of coarse-ware surface finish although there were slightly higher proportions of vessels with incised, impressed and applied decoration. After painted pottery's appearance, with white and dark colours with rectilinear and curvilinear motifs, in the early part of the phase, it deceased in the second half of the phase (after 5600 BC); white painted wares disappear altogether (Manson 1995: 67). In the following Starčevo phase (Manson's Starčevo III, the second half of the sixth millennium BC), barbotine continued to dominate the coarse-ware; fine-wares increased in frequency as did ceramics decorated with impressions, appliqués and incisions. Darker painted wares continued. More pots were made with high pedestals and in biconical shapes.

As with the development of potting at sites to the south, at Achilleion, Franchthi and Sesklo, the control and standardization in Starčevo potting technology increased through time (Manson 1995: 73). In his analysis, Manson identified a shift from the use of organic to the use of mineral tempers in pottery production. Following Skibo et al. (1989), Manson argued that this shift in fabric was a symptom of greater residential stability among the later Starčevo communities. Skibo et al. had suggested a link between organic tempered pottery and greater group mobility: pots with organic temper are lighter, are thus more easily transported, and are more quickly made. Perhaps more significantly, pots with mineral inclusions are better survivors of direct high temperature heatings of contents which would have been required when cooking starchy foods such as seeds (Manson 1995: 72). The maximum firing temperature would have ranged from 500–600°C and not higher than 750°C (Manson 1995: 71; Maniatis and Tite 1981).

In the Starčevo phases at Divostin potters produced a limited range of shapes, mostly jars and bowls. Most of the latter were fine-ware vessels. Most decoration occurred on bowls. Organic-tempered wares would not have been fired above 500°C (McPherron and Christopher 1988: 472, table 20.4).

The Danube Gorges

In the Danube Gorges the earliest pottery appears, sporadically, at Hadjučka Vodenica I in the middle of the seventh millennium BC (Gorges phase 3), when a few unspecified sherds appeared in an early context (site horizon Ia). More sherds were associated with later (horizon Ib) stone structures. During the site's subsequent phase (horizon II), monochrome reddish- or yellowish-grey, sometimes burnished, wares tempered with sand appeared and are characteristic of Starčevo-Criş culture inventories (Radovanović 1996a: 323). In the second half of the seventh millennium BC (Gorges phase 4) pottery became a more frequent element in Gorges communities. Fragments of fine monochrome coarse-ware and pinched and impressed ornamented ware appeared at Padina (B/I) (Radovanović 1996a: 340). At Lepenski Vir (site phase I/2–3) small numbers of sherds of buff and red-burnished monochrome pottery were found in a number of the buildings (Radovanović 1996a: 330). At the transition from the seventh to the sixth millennium BC (Gorges phase 5), fine monochrome wares continued from the previous phase but larger vessels were more numerous. Shapes included amphoras with thick walls, globular cups and small legged-plates, the so-called 'altars', with triangular or circular legs (Radovanović 1996a: 340–1). This last form suggests a special or at least non-cooking use perhaps for burning materials as suggested by Vitelli for medicinal or magical purposes. At Alibeg II, Starčevo-Criş coarse-ware pots were in use at this time as well (Radovanović 1996a: 280). In the first half of the sixth millennium BC (Gorges phase 6) biconical vessels appear at Padina (B/3) along with amphoras, globular amphoras, a deep conical bowl, a ring-footed bowl and a larger bowl with a rectilinear rim. One building (no. 18 in sector III) contained eight complete pots. Fine monochrome reddish and buff wares continued and coarse-ware was made with sand as well as with chaff tempers; better-quality black-grey ware also appeared.

Pottery was in use at other Gorges sites as well. At Cuina Turcului, pottery was found in all of the Starčevo-Criş levels; ceramics of the later phases, which correspond to Starčevo III/IV, revealed, as Manson suggested for other Starčevo assemblages, a decrease in the use of organic temper (Radovanović 1996a: 319). At Kula (site phase III) a few sherds of chaff-tempered Starčevo wares come from large vessels (Radovanović 1996a: 327). In the first half of the sixth millennium BC, at Ostrovul Mare 873 early pottery was found in and around buildings (Radovanović 1996a: 333).

At Schela Cladovei, Starčevo-Criş wares come from the later levels (Radovanović 1996a: 344). At Stubica after the middle of the seventh millennium BC shallow and large bowls and bowls on high pedestal bases were made of reddish-grey monochrome ware with thick walls (Radovanović 1996a: 345). At Velesnica abundant coarse and unpainted fine-ware was found in early Neolithic contexts (Radovanović 1996a: 346).

At Lepenski Vir, the later horizons, Srejović's phase III, contained large amounts of Starčevo pottery. In IIIa deep globular, semi-globular and conical bowls and oval plates were made from coarse- and fine-wares decorated with fine burnishing with brown and black spots, red, brown or white paint, barbotine finishing, impressing and incising; painted wares were decorated with fishnet, triangular or other linear motifs. In IIIb, forms include footed bowls with ring-like or conical pedestals, deep carinated bowls, globular vessels with short cylindrical necks and lug-handles, and pithoi made predominantly of coarse-ware with surfaces treated with barbotine or with impressions arranged into triangles or trapezoid motifs; some brown-painted ornament was also used (Radovanović 1996a: 330).

The appearance of pottery at Gorges sites is important as it allows us to witness the appearance of the new technology in the context of longer continuities of community residences. Pottery appeared at these sites at an important time, the middle of the seventh millennium BC, in the Gorges sequence. Two themes define the Gorges in this period. On the one hand, the new elements of ceramic technology appeared at the same time as there occurred an increase in the participation of Gorges communities in larger regional networks of relationships with other communities. On the other hand, important continuities in the maintenance of existing traditions of architecture and burial ran alongside the innovations in material culture and the expanded networks of extra-regional contacts (Radovanović 1996a: 41).

Northern and western Bulgaria and southern Romania

In northern and western Bulgaria the earliest pottery is dominated by monochrome wares and dates from 6400–6200 BC at Polyanitsa-platoto (Todorova and Vajsov 1993; Todorova 1995a). Monochrome wares have now been found at an increasing number of sites: Cherven I, Orlovets I, Pomoshtitsa and Koprivets (V. Popov 1994; Stefanova 1996). At Koprivets monochrome pottery is beige, grey-beige, grey-brown and red-brown; it appears as both slipped and unslipped, smoothed and burnished. Bowls and jars are the most frequent shapes (V. Popov 1994: 295). The monochrome pottery at Koprivets was found in two successive cultural levels which contained no associated buildings or hearths. Stefanova has argued that no monochrome assemblages have been found in buildings, all coming from pits and unidentified structures of stones and sherds (Stefanova 1996: 19).

Monochrome phases were also present at the lower of three levels of Krainitsa in western Bulgaria (Chokadziev and Bakamska 1990). At Krainitsa the monochrome layers contained pit-huts but, again, no evidence of surface-level structures. Vessels were spherical, semi-spherical and tulip-shaped bowls, jars and plates in beige to dark-brown colours and with smoothed and burnished surfaces (Todorova and Vajsov 1993: 99). A hiatus separates the monochrome layer from the site's subsequent two cultural phases which contained white-painted pottery (Stefanova 1996).

Monochrome wares also dominated at Pomoshtitsa in north-eastern Bulgaria (Stefanova 1996: 17). Again, bowls, jars and plates were common forms. The pottery is dark red, red-brown and brown-black, slipped or unslipped, well finished and sometimes burnished (Stefanova 1996: 17). At Koprivets, Pomoshtitsa and Krainitsa the early levels that contained mono-chrome wares were followed, immediately at the first two sites, by levels dominated with white-painted wares; indeed, at Pomoshtitsa there were a few white-painted sherds in the upper part of the trench. Stefanova (1996: 16) has suggested that occurrences of monochrome and white-painted pottery assemblages were contemporary in the earliest stage of the Neolithic; this appears to have been the case, to a limited extent at least, at Eleshnitsa, where monochrome pottery appeared together with a few white-painted vessels (Nikolov and Maslarov 1987).

White- and then red-painted ceramics define the local Bulgarian early Neolithic A (6200–5700 BC) and are especially evident in the country's western regions, as is seen at Gulubnik, in the upper levels of Krainitsa and at Kovachevo. At Kovachevo white-painted pottery was produced in conical and rounded dishes, deep spherical vessels and beakers with a variety of neck forms (Pernicheva 1990: 102). Bowls appeared in a variety of shapes, including ones with S-shaped profiles (Demoule et al. 1989: 36); the most characteristic were hollow-based, open bowls. The white-painted decoration appeared in geometric motifs (triangles, zigzags and spirals).

It has been suggested that the monochrome wares were made with organic inclusions while the later white-painted wares were produced with mineral inclusions such as fine sand and tiny pebbles. If this is the case, then one could draw similar conclusions for northern Bulgaria as Manson suggested for the Starčevo pots and which may also have been the case at Divostin. Perhaps in all of these instances, the early organic-tempered pottery was produced by relatively mobile communities, and hence the pit-dwellings at the northern Bulgaria monochrome pottery sites, for purposes other than cooking. The mixture, albeit of very few sherds, of monochrome and white-painted wares, the direct succession of levels dominated by the former ware with those of the latter and the very close similarity of vessel shapes made in both wares, especially at Eleshnitsa and Slatina, suggest that mono-chrome phases represent an earlier period of pottery use during which ceramic methodology developed for particular purposes, perhaps storage and display, and that the white-painted phases represent a direct development of ceramics into phases when the use and role of pottery had changed, perhaps to food preparation in addition to storage and display. As in the Greek sites, once again there emerges the pattern of a shift from the initial, perhaps experimental, production and use of pottery to a later and different technology and use.

In southern Romania, information about ceramics from the millennium before 5500 BC is limited. On the one hand, the Starčevo sequence can be extended into Criş with many of the same technical and stylistic development overlapping both culture groups. This holds for south-western Romania. For south-central and south-eastern Romania the solution is less simple or satisfactory due to the absence of uncovered sites. One could argue that the patterns revealed south of the Danube, such as the monochrome sequences of Koprivets and other sites, may have been repeated to the north. As was suggested in the discussion of the built environment in Chapter 2, it may be satisfactory for the present to refer to the early phases of the succeeding, Dudeşti culture for remnant traces of the missing, earlier potting tradition. This solution makes sense, as in other aspects of Dudeşti sites there are significant similarities with sites in northern Bulgaria, especially the absence of significant surface-level structures. Dudeşti ceramics appeared in coarse, medium and fine wares and in the early Dudeşti pottery, that is the Malul Roşu or Dudeşti I phases, there are few distinctions from Starčevo-Criş ceramics.

North-west Anatolia

In north-west Anatolia pottery appears to have been a local development and is best seen in Fikirtepe culture sequences (Özdoğan 1989a: 204). The earliest pottery appears within sites where the lithic traditions document local connections with pre-pottery traditions (Özdoğan 1989a: 203). At Fikirtepe and Pendik potting seems to have arrived fully developed from the south. At the Yarimburgaz cave, however, the development of pottery appears to have been a local phenomenon; the composition of the ceramic assemblage is very different from any other culture group (Özdoğan 1989a: 204). Yarimburgaz, like the Gorges sites, contains a sequence of pre-pottery site-use into which pottery was introduced and adapted. While the pre-pottery layers begin from the end of the ninth millennium BC, the earliest pottery bearing context (layer 5) dates, as it does in the Gorges, to the middle of the seventh millennium BC. Layer 5 contains only a few sherds with little decoration; red- and dark-burnished wares are most distinctive (Özdoğan et al. 1991: 69). In the next horizon, layer 4 dating to the last quarter of the seventh millennium BC, pottery was in much greater use. Shapes include curved or straight-sided open bowls, necked jars and hole-mouth cups. The short-necked jar, with the neck tapering towards the rim, a globular body and a large flat base was the most frequent form; closed shapes were more frequent than were open ones. Necked jars were almost all decorated with complex geometric designs and 10 per cent of other sherds were decorated by incisions, grooves or impressions (Özdoğan et al. 1991: 70–1). Parallels have been drawn with the sequences to the west at Karanovo I and Chavdar IV (Özdoğan et al. 1991: 84).

After a gap in the Yarimburgaz sequence, the ceramic sequence in layer 3 (the first quarter of the sixth millennium BC) reveals significant changes in wares, shapes and decoration. The range in pottery form is more diverse. With respect to dominant wares, black-burnished sherds replaced the earlier red- and light-coloured wares. A significant proportion of very thin-walled, eggshell wares appeared. Open shapes now predominated; bowls were smaller than previously and carinated bowls were being produced. Decorated sherds make up a larger proportion of all ceramics (almost 20 per cent); deep incisions, grooves, excision and impressions continue. Linear motifs replace the earlier complex geometric ones (Özdoğan et al. 1991: 73).

At Ilipinar, the early phases (Ilipinar X) contained monochrome wares which are also seen at Fikirtepe and Pendik (Roodenberg 1993b: 256). Ilipinar X vessels include a few bowls, some lids but no jars. S-shaped bowls are present and some have globular or squat bodies. Very few pots were decorated; the decoration which did appear occurs only on what are probably imported wares (Roodenberg et al. 1990: 82–3). With Ilipinar IX, organic tempering came to an abrupt halt and some pots had thinner walls (Roodenberg et al. 1990: 76, 84). Open shapes now prevailed and the s-shaped pot was the dominant form. Few pots were decorated (1.7 per cent of sherds analyzed) and what decoration did appear was made with impressed, incised and plastic techniques (Roodenberg et al. 1990: 83). Lids were popular and sieves appeared, as did miniature pots. In the second quarter of the sixth millennium BC (Ilipinar VIII) the proportion of pots with surface decoration was still limited (1.5 per cent), although excision appears as a new technique. The quality of burnishing and overall surface finish increased. Lids were very common; sieves and miniature pots continued (Roodenberg et al. 1990: 86). Roodenberg and his colleagues suggest parallels in the use of impressed decoration between Ilipinar IX–VIII and Anza Ib–II (Roodenberg et al. 1990; Roodenberg 1993b: 256).

Continuity in fabrics accompanied continuing increases in the quality of vessel burnishing. Also, with time, pots were harder fired. The quality of pottery improved. S-shaped, squat, carinated pots became more frequent and jars, previously rare, became a common part of the inventory. Miniature pots, lids and sieves were now few in number (Roodenberg et al. 1990: 88). With Ilipinar VI (the middle of the sixth millennium BC) continuity is seen in technological and fabric similarities with the previous horizon. There were, however, significant changes: the repertoire of vessel forms was extended with more open forms in use. S-shaped vessels with a small mouth (average diameter 13 cm) and the use of two opposing strap handles were new as were carinated bowls with large mouths (over 30 cm diameter). New, but rare, elements included carinated open bowls with sharp carinations and square vessels; s-shaped carinated bowls dominate (Roodenberg *et al.* 1990: 89). Potters experimented with new techniques of decoration: painting surfaces, using slips in colours different to the fabric, black-topping (by employing new firing techniques), applying geometric motifs and using new grooving techniques (Thissen 1993b: 296). Layer V (in the fifth millennium BC) marks a major break in the sequence with new shapes and wares deposited in pits (Roodenberg *et al.* 1990: 90). Thissen has suggested that from layers IX–VI, potting at Ilipinar was carried out by a particular, limited group of people (Thissen 1993b: 298). The trends at Yarimburgaz bear strong resemblance to those in the north Balkans.

Pottery: summary and conclusions

A strong case can be made in almost all of the regions for a preliminary stage of pottery making which was experimental in nature and during which pottery was made infrequently, in small quantities by non-specialist potters and was used, perhaps, mainly for special purposes linked to ceremonies, feasts or other purposes of a non-functional nature. With time, pots were used for a wider range of purposes, including cooking but also involving ceremonial or social display of vessel contents. Also with time, potting skills, including control of higher temperatures and making increasing complex, high-risk shapes, improved. More pots were produced, probably by specialist potters. The suggestion that the initial creation and uses of pottery were linked to special people and special contents, such as medicines or narcotics, has important consequences for the power of pottery as an expressive medium both in its early forms and in later manifestations and developments.

Fired clay technology: implications

Even without any mystical undercurrents, fired clay was a particularly dynamic medium and is symptomatic of other changes evident in people's lives after 6500 BC. As employed as a container technology, fired clay had obvious advantages over more permeable and perishable materials: in comparison with the contemporary alternatives of wooden bowls and leather, reed and fibre bags and baskets, ceramic vessels offered much superior properties both for keeping out things such as rodents, bugs and the elements and for keeping in other things such as liquids as well as loose solids such as plant materials.

Ceramic pots were important fields within, upon and with which there existed an almost unlimited potential expression. Although the potential for formal and decorative variation was almost unlimited, the similarities among pots of any one region are very striking. The greatest benefit of the deep academic tradition of identifying, recording and mapping the distribution of styles in ceramic decoration is the ability to recognize that once pottery making had progressed beyond its initial experimental stage, people decorated pots within relatively restricted similarities or dissimilarities in patterning and method of application. Whether people were conscious of the effects of such similarities or not, they served to project atmospheres of community cohesion across regions within the Balkans. In some regions these atmospheres were highly charged, as in the evocative painted wares of northern Greece; in other regions, such as the lower Danube, the expressive power was more muted. Pots may not have been people, but people used pots as one of several media in their attempts to define themselves and their communities.

It has been suggested that the Balkan Neolithic is best understood as the age of clay (Stevanović 1997); this indeed is the case as much for the production of ceramic vessels as for the contemporary creation of buildings from combinations of clay, wood and mud discussed in the previous chapter. All of these issues surrounding the significance of the adaptation of ceramics are taken up in Chapter 8, where larger patterns and longer-term trends are considered together.

With respect to the origins of pottery making in the Balkans, at some sites, where the experimental stage is clearest (Franchthi, Achilleion, the early monochrome sites further north), potters developed techniques and abilities on a local scale through experimentation. In such cases it is perhaps best to envisage local people adapting and adopting ceramic technology in many different places at roughly the same time. At other sites, however, as at Nea Nikomedeia, the earliest pottery appears in a developed, post-experimental form. For these sites perhaps it is best to envisage potting skills already in the possession of the earliest villagers.

Considering the potential for the almost limitless range of three-dimensional forms which could have been made out of clay, it is perhaps surprising that most objects fall into one of three categories: vessels, ornaments and representational figurines. Indeed the post-6500 BC Balkans witnessed a dramatic increase in the creation of expressive material culture made of fired clay as well as of other materials. It is to this broader category of material which this chapter now turns.

OTHER FORMS OF EXPRESSIVE MATERIAL CULTURE

While ceramic vessels provided a very powerful, durable medium of versatile form and potential for decoration, other important innovations in material expression emerged in the Balkans after 6500 BC. Of these the most striking was a range of material objects created in forms which were easily recognizable as representational. This category contains the many thousands of anthropomorphic figurines and the less numerous anthropomorphic and anthropographic pots, zoomorphic figurines and, much rarer, miniature representations of buildings, furniture and tools. Almost all of these representational objects were made of fired clay; the contemporary figurative boulder sculpture from the Danube Gorges sites are examples of a similar process manifest in other materials.

Representational material culture

After 6500 BC people living in the Balkans started making miniature figurines and models of animals, furniture, buildings, tools and, most frequently other human beings; more rarely, they made pots in human shapes or decorated vessels with human and animal images. The making of miniature representations of people, animals and other things was a striking novelty in the Balkans after 6500 BC.

Representational objects appeared across the region at the same time. Thus, in the Danube Gorges, although people had been building structures and burying the deceased since the eighth millennium BC, the earliest representational creations did not appear until the middle of the seventh millennium BC in Gorges phase 3 or, more probably, in a stage transitional to phase 4. At this time at Lepenski Vir (late site phase I/2 to early phase I/3) people shaped and hammered a sandstone boulder into a recognizable human face with forehead and eyes but with a fish-like mouth (Radovanović 1996a: 146). In the second half of the seventh millennium BC, in phase I/2 at Lepenski Vir, representationally worked boulders became more frequent; four of twenty decorated boulders from this phase of the site had representational decoration. Images included a vulva-like shape and a figure with a fish-like mouth (Radovanović 1996a: 143–4). The boulder-sculptures were placed inside buildings and were positioned with particular reference to ash-pits or hearths and, usually, away from the buildings' open frontage and the riverside.

Anthropomorphic figurines

At the same time as people in the Gorges were hammering and pecking the surfaces of limestone boulders into human and fish forms, people at other sites in the Balkans were modelling, decorating and firing miniature clay representations of humans (Figure 3.3).

In northern Greece, anthropomorphic figurines were very numerous (Hourmouziadis 1974; Marangou 1992; Gallis and Orphanidis 1995;). At Achilleion, almost 200, mostly fragmentary, zoomorphic and anthropomorphic figurines were recovered during the limited excavations of the

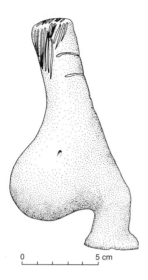

Figure 3.3 Anthropomorphic figurine from Vinča (after Todorova and Vajsov 1993)

village (Gimbutas 1989c). The majority (96 per cent) were anthropomorphic and their frequency increased with time through the site's four phases: 4 per cent, 21 per cent, 21 per cent, 54 per cent respectively (Letica 1988: table 7.1).

The makers of the early Achilleion figurines (the second half of the seventh millennium BC) emphasized the buttocks and hips by exaggerating the modelling of these areas and making horizontal incisions upon them. One, more visually striking, figurine was made of polished black greenstone and had perforations at the hips and a slit in the pubic area. In the next phase of the village, during the last quarter of the seventh millennium BC, the creation of similarly simple anthropomorphic figures continued; on some, more particular features were emphasized. In addition to the attention given to the buttocks and the marking of the pubic area with incision, one figurine has legs raised and spread with vagina exposed. Hands and fingers were marked by modelling or incision. In some cases hands were placed on the chest; in others, hands held a bulging abdomen. Increased attention was also focused on the face: diagonal incisions depicted eyes; modelling formed noses and mouths. On some, long rod-like necks supported the faces. Some figurines were slipped in red although these remain otherwise featureless.

At the end of the seventh millennium BC at Achilleion (phase III) attention to hips, pubic areas and the placement of hands on abdomen continued. Emphasis on the head and face also continued with strikingly prominent noses modelled on several figurines and very long necks supporting both detailed faces and featureless heads. Several leg fragments reveal

96

decoration with red paint applied over a white slip. In the final phase of the village, during the first centuries of the sixth millennium BC (Achilleion IV), most of these trends continued; hips, buttocks, pubic areas, hands and arms were frequently accentuated. In addition, greater detail addressed facial and head features (Figure 3.4); headbands, hair-knits, coiled headdresses or hair were modelled or incised and in one case painted red. On other figurines short lines were incised under the eyes; lips and a beard were represented with paint (Figure 3.5). On others necklaces and shoulder decoration were marked with incisions and, in one instance, with red paint on a white slip.

In the western Balkans at Divostin, in and around the pit-huts dating to the end of the seventh and the beginning of the sixth millennium BC (site Phase I), seventeen anthropomorphic figurines were found (Letica 1988). Some of the pit-huts contained concentrations of figurines: hut 4 had six. Most of the Divostin anthropomorphs were small and simple; for the most part modelling produced mainly schematic representation of the human form. On one figurine however, incision and modelling marked more realistic eyes, eyebrows and hair. Other similar anthropomorphs have been found at the neighbouring Starčevo sites of Grivac and Banja.

Like the Starčevo figurines, those from Körös contexts further to the north have similar attention paid to the buttocks-hips-pubis area with relatively featureless faces (see Whittle 1998). Similar patterns are evident in Criş culture figurines, which have well developed buttocks, cylindrical heads, faces with horizontal incised eyes, impressed mouths, and modelled noses as well as short stubby arms and incisions in the pubic area (Todorova and Vajsov 1993: 184).

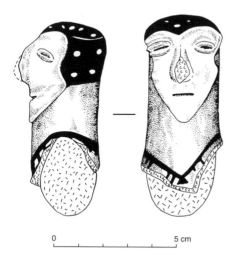

0   5 cm

Figure 3.4 Fragment of anthropomorphic figurine with painted head covering and neck detail from Achilleion phase IV (after Gimbutas 1989c)

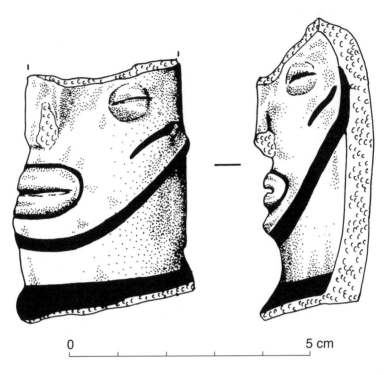

Figure 3.5 Fragment of anthropomorphic figurine with painted facial features from Achilleion phase IV (after Gimbutas 1989c)

The earliest figurines in Bulgaria appear at Krainitsa in the middle of the seventh millennium BC and, as in the other regions, have very vague connections to the human form. Attention to the modelling of buttocks and breasts is seen in the figurines from Chavdar IV and V as are the modelling of noses and the incising of eyes (Todorova and Vajsov 1993: 200). Similar forms were found at Gulubnik, Sapareva Banya and Gradeshnitsa–Malo Pole. In a few cases hair was depicted by incision; in others tightly packed incised lines depict clothing. In a very few cases, as at Gradeshnitsa–Malo Pole, arms were perforated at the shoulders perhaps to enable suspension or perhaps for the attachment of some, perishable, material used to decorate the figure. At Karanovo, one figurine has breasts modelled and an indistinct impression or small horizontal incision in the pubic area.

Three unusual rectangular anthropomorphic 'plaques' come from Pernik and Gulubnik (Figure 3.6) (M. Chokadziev 1981; Todorova and Vajsov 1993: 195). The plaques are small flat ceramic objects with linear incisions on front and rear surfaces; on the front, incisions mark eyes and, perhaps, hair and clothing. Noses are modelled and the incision continues onto both

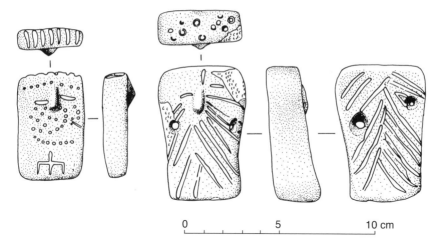

0   5   10 cm

Figure 3.6 Anthropomorphic plaques from Gulubnik (after Todorova and Vajsov 1993)

sides and the rear of the plaques. On the two Gulubnik anthropomorphic plaques incised lines or impressed circles on the top surface of each may represent hair. The arrangement of parallel incised lines on one of the Gulubnik examples is strikingly similar to patterns found on some of the contemporary clay sealing-stamps (which are discussed below). The other Gulubnik plaque has two perforations which, again, probably were used for suspension or for attaching addition decoration. A similar plaque, though without perforations or top surface marks, comes from a Criş context at Méhtelek in Hungary (Kalicz 1983).

At the end of the seventh and the beginning of the sixth millennium BC many figurines were made with flat heads and wide lower parts. The anthropomorphic form was simple with wide heads, modelled noses and stubby arms sticking out at right angles from the shoulders. Faces were simple with horizontal incisions for eyes and small modelled noses. Buttocks and hips were emphasized in width (Figure 3.7). At Kovachevo, in western Bulgaria, female figurines were made with stylized faces but careful modelling of sexual features. There were also local variations: in northern Bulgaria, figurines had very plain torsos, chests, shoulders and heads but massive hips and legs with dense concentrations of sweeping curvilinear parallel incisions. In the main however, modelling and incising of facial features, short stubby arms and occasional perforated shoulders were common.

In Bulgaria, in the middle of the sixth millennium BC, continuities of figurine modelling and decoration were supplemented by trends seen in other regions. Cylindrical-shaped heads have been found at Yasatepe, Karanovo and Drama; faces have diagonal slits for eyes, modelled noses and

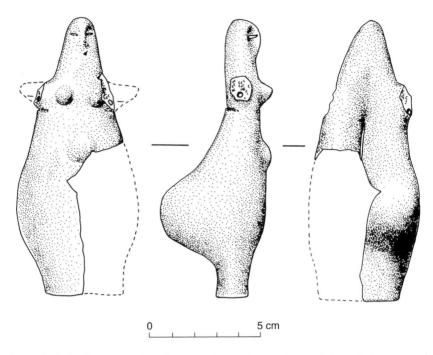

Figure 3.7 Anthropomorphic figurine from Samovodyane (after Todorova and Vajsov 1993)

breasts. Some have incised patterns around the tops of their heads perhaps representing hair, scarves or hats. One from Karanovo has modelled breasts, three bumps in the pubic region and painted decoration on the head-top, waistband and one leg. In some cases, ears were perforated. At Kurilo, simply shaped heads have very pointed noses but few other facial features (Todorova and Vajsov 1993: 179–80).

North of the Danube, the evidence is less clear. If, as suggested above for ceramics and buildings, one relies on the slightly later Dudeşti assemblages, patterns similar to those to the south and west emerge. Early Dudeşti figurines (Dudeşti phase II) were simple in form with few characteristics beyond the most basic human form as is seen in the four figurines at Drăghiceanu (Păunesu 1964; Comşa 1971: 234, figure 29). Later Dudeşti figurines (Dudeşti phase III) have more detailed form and decoration. One of two figurines found in hut 2 at Cernica has modelled breasts but no facial features other than a bulbous nose. Perforations through the arms and perhaps the neck may have been used for suspending the figurine or for attaching decorative materials (Morintz 1963; Comşa 1971: 236, figure 31).

Overall, then, the early anthropomorphic figurines from across the Balkans share a common simplicity of form. Where special attention is devoted to particular parts of the body, it focuses on the head, the breasts or the buttocks, hips and pubis. The amount of attention devoted to depicting body parts and details of those parts (e.g., hair or hats) increases with time.

Anthropomorphic and anthropographic pots

Much less frequent than anthropomorphic figurines were pottery vessels made in a human shape or decorated with human imagery. On some Körös and Starčevo vessels, potters placed human shapes in simple relief (Banner 1937; Kalicz 1970). These pots appear through the millennium from 6500 BC. An early example is a high-necked pot from Chavdar which has facial features incised or impressed near the rim. A similar vessel from slightly later contexts at Kazanuluk is a high-necked, rounded-bottom pot, with modelled nose, eyes with eyebrows in relief and modelled breasts and, perhaps, a vulva as well as arms and hands which meet in the front of the body. A simpler form from Slatina has a face painted near its rim; a vessel of similar shape but with eyes depicted with modelling comes from Gradeshintsa–Malo Pole (Todorova and Vajsov 1993: 214–5).

The other variant of vessels with human forms (in Bulgaria at least) consists of anthropographic pots. These have simple human-shapes (stick-figures) applied in relief to the sides of vessels; examples come from Azmak and Chavdar VI. On the Chavdar pot, the figure has one hand raised and the other reaching towards the pubic area which, in turn, is marked by a single incision.

Interpretation of anthropomorphic imagery

Paradoxically, despite their ubiquity and evocative appearance, it is difficult to write about the social or even, in some cases, the depositional contexts of anthropomorphic figurines. Limitations of some excavation and recording methodologies, the location of many figurines in private collections and the over-exuberance of popular, imaginative, interpretations combine to provide little substantive detail. There are, however, a number of generalizations that can be drawn.

First, anthropomorphic figurines were numerous; the excavation of some sites produced hundreds and estimates of the total number of figurines produced between 6500–5500 BC realistically reach the tens of thousands. Second, although there are exceptions, almost all of the early anthropomorphic figurines were made in clay, the new transformative, potentially magical and mystical medium of the post-6500 BC Balkans. Third, the proportion of figurines identifiable as female is not as overwhelming as is frequently claimed: all figurines do not represent women; in fact many have no recognizable sexual characteristics. Fourth, where sex is depicted, it is very seldom, if ever, male, although Whittle has recently argued that the long cylindrical necks and bulbous buttocks and hips of Körös-Criş figurines should be viewed as erect penises and that designation of sexual identity is double, dual or ambiguous (Whittle 1998: 140); similar arguments have been made for Greek 'rod-headed' figurines (Kokkinidou and Nikolaidou 1997)). Fifth, figurines are exclusively found and thus presumably used and, if not necessarily but probably, made in village and building areas. Sixth, there is no recognizable standard schema for figurine decoration: incision, modelling and painting occur with great variety. Seventh, although there is no standard decorative schema, it is clear that particular common areas of the body received the majority of attention: the face and the hips-buttocks-pubic area. Eighth, the proportion of decorated and more detailed figurines to undecorated ones increased over the 1000 years considered in this chapter and continued to increase in the succeeding 1500 years (see Chapter 6).

The literature on the meaning and function of anthropomorphic figurines is vast. Most of it agrees in seeing a ritual, religious or at least spiritual function for anthropomorphs (Kalicz 1970; Gimbutas 1974, 1982; Vajsov 1984; Todorova 1986; Talalay 1993; Todorova and Vajsov 1993; Comşa 1995). A smaller, but growing, body of research has questioned these traditional interpretations by attacking their implicit assumptions or by looking in more detail at figural material in its archaeological and social contexts (Ucko 1962, 1968; D. Bailey 1991, 1994a, 1996a; Biehl 1996; Haaland and Haaland 1996; Hamilton 1996; Marcus 1996; Whittle 1998: 140–1). Other studies have focused on the academic and social contexts of the traditional goddess school (Meskell 1995). There is neither the room nor the intention to replay these arguments here.

Perhaps the next step in interpretation is to recognize that the essence of the production and use (including the possibility of intentional breakage and special deposition) of anthropomorphs rested in the new ways in which people were defining and identifying themselves and others within and beyond their communities. This makes sense for several reasons. The early figurines were simple in form and decoration; representation was more often on the level of the general human than of any particular individual (as appears in the succeeding millennium and a half). For the Körös-Starčevo figurines, Whittle has suggested that the lack of particularities evokes a sense of anonymity in figurine representation (Whittle 1998: 140). Human-ness was the focus of attention more than was any individual persona. The emphasis which was made, however, was placed on particular parts of the body, such as the hips-buttocks-pubis, and on particular gestures, such as the placement of hands on the chest and abdomen. These early figurines draw attention to characteristics shared by at least part of village populations, perhaps to do with childbirth and reproduction, and to human activities; thus Whittle has followed Banner's earlier suggestion

(1937: 41) that the attention to arms may have referred to dancing (Whittle 1998: 139).

Towards the middle of the sixth millennium BC more detailed figurine ornamentation appeared in an increase in the use of painted decoration and the greater detail of facial and head features. These figurines appear to be more particular representations of specific individuals. Perhaps the unusual anthropomorphic plaques, with their potential parallels with stamp-seals also suggest that human figurines were increasingly used in rituals and ceremonies in which people expressed claims to personal identities. The perforations of ears on some figurines, arguably for the attachment of additional decorative items, foreshadows the more dramatic increase in density and variety of figurines which emerged in later millennia (see Chapter 6).

The use to which figurines were devoted is less straightforward. Perhaps their act of representing the human, whether general or particular, was their main function. The perforation of many figurines suggests that some figurines were worn as pendants (this is a use which is attested in later figurines, as at Selevac – discussed in Chapter 5). Perhaps most important is the association of figurines with built structures. Although figurines (usually broken) also appear frequently in rubbish pits within village confines, the connection between human representation and the built environment suggests that the two processes may have worked, in part at least, in shared systems of signification.

If the pit-huts and the surface dwellings of the post-6500 BC Balkans are understood in terms of new definitions of community composition, then the position of anthropomorphs within these new enclosed spaces may suggest that they were part of the ceremonies and processes by which these new social units were created and maintained. As suggested in Chapter 2, the negotiation and maintenance of household identity and membership, as well as village membership, involved rituals and expressive displays performed in order to visibly mark the physical incorporation of individuals into house-based co-residential groups. The additional role of burial within these rituals will be stressed in Chapter 4. Perhaps the fashioning, decoration and inclusion, and perhaps ritual breakage, of anthropomorphs was another element in the wider set of ways in which household composition was established, maintained and, perhaps, broken down. If the emphasis on hip-buttock-pubis and breast is taken as referring to pregnancy and birth, then figurines may have played one part in visible rituals or ceremonies through which the membership of the newborn or, perhaps more likely, the producer of the newborn was incorporated into the household. If the positioning of hands and arms do indeed represent dancing perhaps they refer to ritual ceremonies that surrounded the required expression of household membership.

Zoomorphic imagery

While anthropomorphic imagery was widespread in the Balkans after 6500 BC, other representational objects were in use less frequently. The appearance of the boulder objects with fish features in the Gorges has been noted; in other regions, other animals were more regularly depicted in clay miniatures.

In Greece zoomorphs were in use from the early Neolithic (Toufexis 1995). Most are representations of cattle and ovicaprids, although a very few may represent dogs or pigs. Some represent pack-animals, as do two from Itea, north-east of Karditsa, and some are perforated for suspension (Papaxatzis 1983: 35–43; Hellström 1987: 79; Toufexis 1989). Zoomorphs were used at Achilleion from the early levels (phase Ib) and little formal variation extends beyond that required to depict generally indistinguishable quadrupeds; tails were modelled on the rears of some. One zoomorph had a perforation through its back (Gimbutas 1989c). In the early levels of Divostin eleven zoomorphic figurines appeared in the same contexts along with anthropomorphs; two of the zoomorphs were found in hut 4 in close association with four of the anthropomorphs (Letica 1988). All of the Divostin zoomorphs are quadrupeds and among them there is little distinguishing decoration: heads, tails, ears and, in a few cases, snouts were modelled. Eyes were marked with jabbed impressions (Letica 1988: table 7.1). Quadruped, horned figurines have also been found in Körös contexts as at Szolnok-Szanda (Kalicz and Raczky 1980–1). Zoomorphs also appear, though again more infrequently than anthropomorphs, in the early phase of Kovachevo as well as at other Bulgarian sites dating to the first half of the sixth millennium BC. A quadruped with snout and tail and with a large cup modelled on its back was found at Gulubnik in western Bulgaria and is comparable to the representations of pack-animals from Greece. Also at Gulubnik were found an indistinct quadruped, suggested to be a wild boar, and the head of an animal interpreted as a jaguar (Todorova and Vajsov 1993: 211–15). At Kurdzhali in southern Bulgaria, a polished stone zoomorph, perhaps a frog or, more radically, perhaps similar to the spread-legged anthropomorphs from Achilleion, is similar to one found at Kovachevo and has similarities with a green jasper zoomorph found at Ilipinar (level IX) in north-west Anatolia (Pejkov 1986; Pernicheva 1990; Roodenberg 1993b, 1995).

North of the Danube quadruped zoomorphs have been found at Dudeşti culture sites, as at Dudeşti itself and at Drăghiceanu (Comşa 1971: 237; Păunescu 1964). As in the south, zoomorphic form and decoration lack the diversity or detail that were invested in contemporary anthropomorphic figurines. Among zoomorphic figurines the schematic dominated over the naturalistic (Toufexis 1995: 167)

Zoomorphic vessels were also in use, although much more infrequently than the zoomorphic figurines: the most spectacular is a large vessel in the form of a deer found in a Karanovo I context at Muldava (Todorova and Vajsov 1993: 214, figure 146). In Greece zoomorphic relief figures were attached to the handles of vessels or served as the handles themselves (Theocharis 1967: 150). A stick-figure of a deer was applied to a Criş culture pot found at Dudeşti-Noi (V. Dumitrescu 1972: plate 37:4). Zoomorphic relief decoration of pottery surfaces has been found in Körös contexts as well: a deer from Csépa and Hódnezővásárhely-Hámszáritó, and a horned animal from Hódnezővásárhely-Kotacpart (Kalicz 1970). Similar, though less frequent, surface representations occur at Starčevo sites (M. Garašanin 1979; and see Whittle 1998 for discussion).

Interpretation of zoomorphic imagery

Traditionally, interpretation of zoomorphs has followed that of anthropomorphs and similar limitations attend. Although there are important similarities between the two forms of miniature representations (both are made almost exclusively of fired clay, both are found mostly in building contexts), there are important distinctions. Zoomorphs appear less frequently than anthropomorphs; Toufexis suggests that, for Greece, anthropomorphs outnumbered zoomorphs 9 to 1 (Toufexis 1989). Furthermore, zoomorphs were decorated much more rarely and with much less detail than were anthropomorphs.

While one of the significances of anthropomorphs can be sought in the establishment and maintenance of household membership, it is unclear if one can conclude the same for zoomorphs unless one expands the boundaries of household membership to include animals as well as people. Were zoomorphic miniatures also participants in ceremonies and ritual displays which, perhaps, legitimated the incorporation of animals into households?

It is perhaps significant that the range of zoomorphic form is limited. Almost all zoomorphs are representations of quadrupeds and almost all of these depict horned animals. Claims for birds and snakes (as by Gimbutas 1989c: 179) are based more on modern imagination than on recognizable morphological similarities and thus deserve to be discarded. However, the overall general level of formal and decorative attention depicted by the early anthropomorphs may have parallels in the similar restriction on formal variation and the almost complete absence of surface decoration among zoomorphs. If the early anthropomorphs represented a more general sense of human-ness, perhaps the zoomorphs represented a similarly general sense of animal-ness or cattle-ness. If so, it is difficult to understand why individual zoomorphs did not develop to include more particular patterns of animal individuality in modelling and surface decoration. Zoomorphs appear never to have developed beyond the relatively generic representation of cattle or ovicaprids.

The emphasis on fish imagery in the Gorges requires similar consideration. Radovanović has suggested that fish may have had a greater ideological than economic significance for the people of the Gorges (Radovanović 1996a: 40–1). The representation of water-motifs on some of the Gorges sculptures and the alignment of burials and buildings with respect to the river's course add weight to the suggestion that people perceived the river itself, as well as its living contents, in terms of a particular identity. The same probably holds for the relationship between the horned quadrupeds and the people living in their villages. Some animals may have had a particular identity which required visual expression; perhaps the relationships among such animals, people and the new social institutions such as houses, households and villages required legitimation through ritual or ceremony. Perhaps, just as fish and the river played an important role in the ideology of Gorges populations, so also did grazing animals and grazing land play a role with the early Balkan villagers. The importance of grazing (and arable) land is addressed in Chapter 4.

There are many unknowns in these relationships between animals and people: what, for example, were the particularities of animal management in relation to the household and the village? Perhaps human perceptions of animals, at least between 6500 and 5500 BC, did not develop beyond relatively simple ideas about animals such as cattle and sheep and goats. Such perceptions may only have developed in later millennia when these animals took on new roles in primary, but perhaps more importantly, in secondary production (see Chapter 5) and when cattle attained a much greater position within people's perceptions of status, prestige and identity. Perhaps it is best to understand both anthropomorphic and zoomorphic imagery against the broader backdrop of post-6500 BC changes in the ways people lived their lives and chose to express relationships and identities through new media.

Other representational material culture

In addition to human and animal representations, miniature clay figures of buildings and furniture and, in a few cases, tools also appear in village contexts after 6500 BC. None of these categories of artefacts appear in frequencies similar to those of anthropomorphs and few in frequencies similar to that of zoomorphs. Most numerous are finds of furniture.

Although there are examples of miniature sloped-back chairs and bench-seats, as at Achilleion in phases II and IV respectively (Gimbutas 1989c: 204), the overwhelming majority of clay representations of furniture are miniature, triangular or rectangular tables. Almost all are heavily decorated with rectilinear patterns of incision or paint. They appeared throughout the Balkans from at least the end of the seventh millennium BC, as seen at Karanovo where three triangular examples have been discovered, and they continued in use into the local later Neolithic as seen, after 5500 BC, at Hotnitsa and Samovodyane in Bulgaria (Todorova and Vajsov 1993: 215–19). Often described as 'cult-tables' or 'altars', there is nothing in their form, decoration or deposition that suggests that they were used in any activities more special than the uses to which any small, open, footed dishes or plates would have been used. The distinction is that they were made in the form of three- or four-legged tables.

The archaeology of furniture is an almost unresearched topic in Balkan prehistory. In most cases, descriptions of furniture are limited to relatively permanent, fixed features within structures: hearths or ovens, grain-bins, grinding-stones and clay platform-benches. The excavation in the Gorges provided detailed discussions of hearths and stone 'altars'. The excavations of the Slatina house revealed a range of furniture which included platforms as well as wooden bed-structures. As is discussed in Chapter 5, the division of interior building space becomes an increasingly evident feature of village architecture in the fifth millennium BC. The fact that there is little evidence of furniture such as chairs, stools and tables may rest more with excavation strategy and the absence, in most cases, of rigorous attention to collapsed daub of building walls and roofs. In addition to the miniature tables and the occasional chairs or stools, which may be mainly an association of anthropomorphs, there are few other miniature representational objects. An axe made of fired clay was found at Achilleion (phase II).

NON-REPRESENTATIONAL, VISUALLY EXPRESSIVE MATERIAL CULTURE

In addition to representational material culture, a (numerically) significant body of non-representational but visually expressive objects appeared in the Balkans after 6500 BC. Again examples come from sites across the region, including those in the Danube Gorges. As with the representational objects, clay and stone were employed to make pendants and sealing-stamps. Other raw materials, such as bone, teeth and antler, malachite and shell, were also used to make pendants as well as rings, beads and bracelets. There is also good evidence for the importance of pigment preparation, potentially for decorating the human body. With the exception of the sealing-stamps, the creation of many of these objects and the use of these materials had deeper roots of use in earlier millennia (see Chapter 1). If there is a distinction which separates the post-6500 BC non-representational materials from earlier manifestations it is the frequency and density in which these material symbols appear in the archaeological record. However, increased frequency may be no more than a symptom of the increase in the numbers of recognizable (and thus excavatable) places of permanence within which people were living their lives in new, less impermanent fashion. It is useful to consider the non-representational materials in the following categories: ornaments, sealing-stamps, decorated objects and tools and decorative raw materials.

Body ornaments

Objects of use for ornamenting the human body were made from a wide range of materials in a limited range of forms such as pendants, beads, rings, bracelets and studs. Pendants, that is to say, perforated objects larger than beads, were made from stone, bone and shell. In the early levels of Lepenski Vir pendants were made of limestone, calcite, marble and crystal limestone. At Vlasac, in Gorges phase 3, a pendant was made of animal tooth, perhaps a boar. In phase 4, five animal-tooth pendants were used at Vlasac (Srejović and Letica 1978a). At Divostin (site phase I) three pendants were made of bone or tusk and one of shell and a small pendant (12 mm high) was made of malachite. At Kovachevo a variety of pendant forms appear fashioned in a range of materials. At Achilleion pendants appear through at least the last three of the village's four major phases and most were made of bone, although one was of alabaster. The latest phase of the village contained the highest concentrations of bone pendants.

Beads were made from a wider variety of materials. At Alibeg in the Gorges (phase 5) two flat bone beads were painted red (Boroneanţ 1973: 23, plate XII-4). At Divostin beads were made of white limestone, red fired clay, green serpentine and, provocatively, the copper carbonate minerals malachite and azurite (Glumac 1988). Malachite has also been found at other Starčevo sites such as Obre I and Zamjovac (Gimbutas 1974; Glumac 1983). In the Gorges the late phases of Lepenski Vir and Cuina Turcului contained beads made of malachite and azurite in the former and white calcite and sandstone in the latter. At Achilleion beads were found in all phases and were made of *Spondylus gaederopus* (and other shell), bone, greenstone and clay. Variety in form (oval, annular, trapezoidal, cylindrical) and material increased in Achilleion III and the richest concentrations, as with the pendants, were found in phase IV (Gimbutas 1989d: 252). In addition to beads and pendants, shell and marble, at Kovachevo at least, were used to make bracelets; rings were made of fired clay, bone, shell, green serpentine and white limestone, especially as seen at Divostin.

A large number of other objects useful for body ornamentation, particularly ear, nose or lip studs, were also in use across the Balkans. In the earliest levels of Achilleion people used greenstone studs perhaps as ear or lip plugs; greenstone and marble studs also appear at Sesklo, Nea Nikomediea and Argissa (Gimbutas 1989d: 251–2). At Divostin twenty 'lobates' (that is small oval forms with one widened end which may be better understood as unpierced pendants) made of fine Starčevo ceramics and fine-grained white stone were recovered (McPherron *et al.* 1988b). Similar objects have been found at Banya and Grivac.

The range and frequency of these ornaments suggest a widespread use of several materials to make pendants and beads especially but also studs, rings and bracelets which would have been worn by people. In many ways, the creation and wearing of these objects were the continuations of much longer and deeper traditions which extended back at least to upper Palaeolithic times (see Chapter 1). Obviously the use of fired clay was a novelty, but the use of bone, antler, animal teeth and stone was nothing new.

Sealing-stamps

More of a novelty was the appearance in the Balkans after 6500 BC of sealing-stamps (Makkay 1984; Todorova and Vajsov 1993: 233–4). Stamps were made of clay and stone with flat bases upon which designs were incised, impressed or depicted in relief; many had a small non-descript, sometimes perforated, handle on the top. Designs on stamp bases varied and include arrangements of small circles and dots, multiple zigzag lines, concentric circles and spirals, concentric rectilinear forms, maze-like interlocking rectilinears and straight or inward pointing V-shaped lines.

There are potentially important patterns in the appearance of very similar stamp-designs at different villages: on the one hand, some identical or very similar designs appeared at separate sites; on the other, some sites contained many different stamps. One of the most frequently repeated designs consists of parallel bands of one, two or three zigzag lines. Stamps with this design have been found at more than twenty sites: in Greece at Argissa, Sesklo, Nea Nikomedeia (three examples); in southern and south-central Bulgaria at Kurdzhali and Karanovo; in western Bulgaria at Sapareva Banya, Azmak, Chavdar V, Kazanluk, Kovachevo, Slatina (two examples) and Gradeshnitsa-Malo Pole; along the lower Danube at Maluk Prezlavets and Zobanu (Romania); in the western Balkans at Hódmezövásárhely-Bogzapart, Belushina Belushka tumba, Endröd-Súokerest, Turkebe-Liukashkhalom (Hungary), Gradovats-Vinogradi (Yugoslavia) and Rug Bair; and at Burit-Peskori in Albania and Anzabegova in Macedonia (Makkay 1984; Todorova and Vajsov 1993).

Another frequently reoccurring stamp design consisted of interlocking rectilinear lines forming a maze-like pattern. Sealing-stamps with close variations of this design have been found at a dozen sites across the Balkans: in Greece at Nea Nikomedeia, Pirassos, Tsangli, Filia, Sesklo and Nessonis; in the western Balkans at Tečić in Serbia and at Endőd-Súokerest; in western Bulgaria at Pernik; in southern Bulgaria at Kurdzhali; and in the lower Danube at Perieni-Pupa Roshkanilor in Romania. Stamp-designs consisting of parallel lines similar to the anthropomorphic plaque from Gulubnik noted above are found on stamps from Chavdar V, Tsakran de Fieri (Albania) and Sentesh-Yakshorerpart (Hungary).

How are we to understand the occurrence of sealing-stamps with identical or closely similar patterns in separate villages? Do the similarities document a common system of exchange or are they evidence of control over production and distribution? Halstead has suggested that some degree of connection between sites is marked by the distribution of the similar seals at four sites in different parts of Thessaly: Nessonis in north-east Thessaly, Pirassos in the south-east, Tsangli in central-southern, and Filia in south-west Thessaly (Halstead 1989b). Perhaps it is possible only to suggest that, like styles of ceramic decoration, so also did the marking of some, long perished, items with stamped impressions serve to express connections or commonalities of activities between different communities. The absence of sealings makes further discussion difficult.

Another pattern of potential significance is the frequency of stamps at individual sites. Excavation at most sites has produced small numbers of stamps, from one to four per site. At some sites frequencies are greater; nine sealing-stamps were found at Nea Nikomedeia; four come from Sesklo. Were these villages places in which some special commercial activities took place? Again the absence of sealings makes progress difficult; the probability that many stamps may have been lost from other sites, due to the absence of sieving during excavation, makes conclusions about site-specific frequency dangerous.

A better understanding of the significance of the patterns of distribution and frequency of stamps rests with a better understanding of how people used these objects. What was being stamped and for what purpose? Suggestions of ownership or a role in a redistributive network as suggested elsewhere for later periods, such as for the Mycenean and Minoan palace centres, may be over-ambitious. At present one can assume no more than that the stamps were used on some perishable materials.

Perhaps it is only possible to understand the use and meaning of stamp-sealings in general terms of expressing and marking identities in a new permanent fashion, a permanence of the stamp at least, and that parts of the system of symbols used were shared at villages which were spread within and between regions. Whether the identity expressed referred to an individual, a household or a village community or whether the declaration of that identity referred to some quality or characteristic of the material being stamped is, perhaps at present at least, a moot point. Perhaps it is sufficient to record that frequent efforts to mark identities of people or things were made in many different regions using broadly similar designs.

Decorated objects and tools

Another category of non-representational but visually expressive material consists of objects or tools decorated with incised, engraved, hammered or painted ornamentation. The materials are the same as those used for producing beads, pendants and studs (i.e., bone, antler, animal teeth, stone), although in some cases larger stones, boulders and architectural features were decorated. A great deal of this material has been recovered from the Gorges sites and this is perhaps significant as many of these materials, methods and designs have deep connections with late Pleistocene and early Holocene activities.

Implements made of bone, antler and animal teeth were ornamented with incisions forming zigzags, hatching or net-like grids (Srejović and Letica 1978a: 105–9; Srejović and Babović 1983; Radovanović 1996a: 283). In Gorges phase 1 a building at Vlasac contained a piece of deer antler ornamented with incised motifs of cross-hatched rhomboids and a net pattern. Two bone tools bore incised decoration (Srejović and Letica 1978a: 27–8).

The Gorges sites also contained many pebbles, boulders and architectural elements made of stone which had been decorated by engraving or treatment with ochre. Red-ochre, painted pebbles were found at Vlasac I–III and Ostrovul Banului I-II; pebbles with geometric engravings come from Veterani Terrace and Vlasac I; zigzag and wave-like motifs were engraved on stones from Lepenski Vir, Vlasac Ib and Hajdučka Vodenica I–II (Radovanović 1996a: 283). Pebbles with hollowed-out cup-marks were found at Padina (A/A–B) and at many other sites in all phases of the Gorges (Radovanović 1996a: 277, 280).

A boulder decorated with a net-like pattern was found in a building at Vlasac Ia (Srejović and Letica 1978a: 17; Radovanović 1996a: 157). In Vlasac II (Gorges phase 3) boulders were decorated with red paint (Srejović and Letica 1978a: 41). Irregularly shaped or rounded stones with circular hollows at one or both ends are often termed 'altars' but may more accurately be considered as ornamented architectural elements. Many of these were decorated with hammered motifs of meanders, rows of interconnected concentric circles or, perhaps, patterns resembling fishbones (Radovanović 1996a: 145). These ornamented, but non-representational, boulder and stone objects appear to increase in frequency with Gorges phase 3 and, overall, account for the majority of rock-art in the Gorges sites. In fact they outnumber the more famous representational boulder sculptures: in phase 3, 94 per cent of the decorated large stones are non-representational; in phase 4, 80 per cent; in phase 5, the percentage is down to only 17 per cent.

Radovanović suggests that these ornamental activities in the Gorges continued an earlier Epi-palaeolithic tradition. Although the evidence for late Pleistocene activities in the Balkans is not extensive, there are clear similarities with the zigzag incision on the bone piece from Bacho Kiro (Kozłowski 1982a; Marshack 1982).

Decorative materials

Frequent finds, especially in the Gorges, of raw and processed materials used to decorate buildings, people and other objects suggest continuations of longer traditions of expressive activities in the Balkans. Graphite has been found in very early contexts in the Gorges: pieces of the material come from pre-phase 1 contexts (c. 12,000 BP) at Climente II. At Cuina Turcului II, Ostrovul Banului I and II and Vlasac I–II, blocks of graphite were also found; the Vlasac examples came from a burial (Radovanović 1996a: 280). In addition to their use in making beads, the malachite and azurite at Divostin may also have been ground to make pigment (Glumac 1988: 457).

Interpreting visually expressive material culture

The ornaments, sealing-stamps, decorated tools and architectural elements and the decorative materials themselves amplify the patterns evident in the anthropomorphic and zoomorphic figurines. Although the non-representational objects had deeper continuities with previous millennia of behaviour, together with the new phenomena of figurines and anthropomorphic and zoomorphic pots and vessels with human and animal representations on them, they suggest that new, more dramatic efforts were being made to declare and maintain relationships among people, animals and places.

In Chapter 2, it was proposed that one of the major novelties of the post-6500 BC Balkans was the construction of physically marked and arranged social environments in which people defined social relationships in tangible, permanent ways. The modelling, firing and display of figurines and the making and wearing of non-representational expressive objects suggest that efforts to define individual identities were a major component of material life in the villages of the Balkans.

After 6500 BC people in the Balkans were living within a new semiotics of identity (to borrow David Pollock's term; Pollock 1995: 581). Figurines, styles of pottery surface treatment, decorated elements of buildings and objects of personal ornamentation combined into new semiotic systems through which people disguised, transformed and displayed identities. At one level the systems were co-ordinated around the household; at another they were co-ordinated around aggregations of households at the level of the village as an extra-domestic community.

People expressed identities both through direct representation such as figurines and through indirect representations such as the decoration of pottery and buildings and the use of sealing-stamps. Through all of these objects and processes people signalled particular identities grounded in particular places. Undoubtedly, not all people had the need to express identity, nor did all need to express identities via visible, tangible, permanent objects. Further differing levels of identity are evident, ranging from public to private as well as from the transient to the more permanent.

Permanent physical expressions of identities provided a very powerful way in which people could attempt to stabilize otherwise untethered and shifting identities; equally, people could have used them in attempts to transform or contradict existing identities. Different manipulations of the materials and objects that were employed to establish or transform identities also could have been invoked to destroy and devalue them. Thus ceremonies in which figurines were displayed and introduced into buildings in order to declare an individual's membership within a household could be inverted by other ceremonies in which, for example, figurines were ceremonially broken in order to negate membership. Similar inversions will be proposed in Chapter 5 as one explanation of the destructions of buildings in many villages.

Thus, in order to investigate what a figurine meant or how it functioned or to examine the patterns of stylistic variation of pottery decoration, it may be more fruitful to rephrase research in terms of how these objects and practices were employed in ceremonies to establish, transform and negate identities. The significance of making and using an anthropomorphic figurine might lie in its inclusion in some, probably untraceable, event of identity expression. Perhaps the overtly female figurines were linked to the maturation of young women or, in other cases, to other ceremonial events related to people and different stages of their physical growth and ageing and their reputation or position within a household or within a larger community.

I have suggested elsewhere that the emergence of human figurines in the Balkans was one of many symptoms of a new way of seeing (D. Bailey 1996a). Part of these symptoms was the firing of pottery; other symptoms revolved around the construction of restrictive physical boundaries to the relationships between people and between activities. Eventually, these symptoms developed within an intensification of this new way of seeing that revolved around more extended systems of expression and the display of identities. These issues are taken up again in Chapters 5 and 6.

CHAPTER CONCLUSIONS AND SUMMARY

In this chapter I have argued that the adoption of fired clay technology and the creation of many different representational and other visually symbolic artefacts complemented contemporary developments in building new social environments. In some respects, these technologies and artefacts were new elements in the social landscapes and the community architecture of the Balkans; thus the making of ceramic vessels and the fashioning of human and animal representations. In other ways, links with earlier practices are evident; thus the decoration of the human body and the wearing of personal ornaments. It is even possible to suggest connections between the new and the old; perhaps the depiction of selected body parts on anthropomorphic figurines was an extension, though amplified in terms of tangible durability at least, of earlier body painting and ornamentation.

I have stressed the connections between early potting, special ceremonies and rituals and have argued against traditional suggestions that early pots were used for cooking. Early potting was probably carried out by a limited number of relatively inexperienced potters whose ceramic activities may have complemented their other, perhaps special, activities such as gathering and dispensing medicinal or intoxicating herbs. The earliest pots were as much, if not more, about displaying their contents than they were about containing them. In the development of potting technique and use, more potters were involved and their control over the science of ceramic pyrotechnology increased. At the same time, at some sites more closed shapes as well as smaller vessels were in use. In some regions, especially to the north and west, one element of the shift from the early experimental stage of pottery making was a shift from organic to mineral tempering; this accompanied a shift from more mobile to more stable, permanent communities.

Anthropomorphic figurines and other material expressions of human characteristics appeared and were formed and decorated to focus attention on faces and hips, buttocks and the pubis. Attempts to understand the content of particular identities, that is to ask who was represented with what visual symbols and for what reasons, are not straightforward. The argument that people may have perceived early potters and gatherers in a special way that differentiated them from other members of their communities suggests, at the very least, that some people were engaged in new activities that identified them in terms of their skills and knowledges and thus distinguished them from others. Identification of differential skills and knowledges was not something new; Pleistocene gathering and hunting, knapping and fishing as well as a range of other skill- and knowledge-based activities surely would have set particular individuals apart from others (see Sinclair 1998). What is significant about the post-6500 BC expressions of identities is their material manifestations: identities were being expressed more frequently and in more durable and representational ways.

It was suggested in Chapter 2 that the creation of built social environments was, at least partly, about the establishment of grounded identities for people in particular parts of landscapes as well as for the distinction between different people or groups of people within communities. The use of pottery vessels to display, to contain and to incorporate things in households and within villages and the use of visually expressive objects to declare links between people and animals to particular households, villages, or both, elaborate the processes of constructing new arrangements of people in places.

114

Links were established through rituals and ceremonies which were focused on declaring or negating membership within activity- or co-residence groups. Other links existed between village groups; the similarities in styles of ceramics and figurines as well as sealing-stamps were spread across broad regions and suggest expressions of group or individual identities at an institutional level, perhaps involving village communities.

Three other sets of activities revolved around people, their identities and their places in post-6500 BC Balkans: burial; patterns of human exploitation of plants and animals; and lithic acquisition and working. These subjects are addressed in the following chapter.

4

CONTINUITY OR CHANGE?

Burials, lithics, plants and animals
(6500–5500 BC)

The firing of clay to make pots, figurines, and other representational or
expressive material culture and the construction of new social environments were major novelties in Balkan life after 6500 BC. Contemporary
changes in the treatment of the dead and the production of flaked-stone
tools, however, were less dramatic. The traditional defining characteristic
of Neolithic life, the cultivation of plants and the breeding of domesticated
animals, may be better understood in terms of continuity than of novelty.

TREATMENT OF THE DECEASED

The claim that formal, archaeologically recognizable burial was more
frequent after 6500 BC rests uncomfortably on the fact that there are very
few known Epi-palaeolithic sites with which to compare the many Neolithic
ones. If we appear to know more about burial after 6500 BC it is because
people were doing important new things with buildings and because one
of those things was the occasional interment of the bodies of deceased
individuals around or under these structures. What is clear is that, with the
exception of the Danube Gorges, inhumation occurred infrequently at this
time in the Balkans. When it did occur it involved little more than simple
placement of the body into the ground without numerous, if any, grave-
goods. Variation in burial method is evident across three regions: the Danube
Gorges; south-central and southern Bulgaria and the western Balkans; and
northern Greece.

The Danube Gorges

One of the many remarkable elements of the Danube Gorges sites is the
evidence for formal disposal of the deceased. For all periods represented
from the nine sites for which detailed information exists the Gorges sites
contain the remains of almost 600 individuals.[1] Of these, almost half (256)

are represented by disarticulated bones or disturbed skeletons (Radovanović 1996a: 161). Of the 331 individuals recovered, the overwhelming majority come from three sites: Lepenski Vir (146), Vlasac (119) and Padina (75). Of the other sites, only two have more than seven burials: Hajdučka Vodenica (with 30) and Schela Cladovei (with 20 graves accounting for 33 individuals). From these five sites then, several patterns emerge.

Gorges phase 2

People started burying individuals at the end of the eighth and the beginning of the seventh millennia BC at Vlasac (Srejović and Letica 1978a, 1978b; Radovanović 1996a: 187–219) and Schela Cladovei (Boroneanţ 1973; Radovanović 1996a: 222). There is also evidence of burial at Lepenski Vir (in the proto-Lepenski Vir phase) as seen in burial no. 60, an adult male buried without any grave-goods (Radovanović 1996a: 176). Other early Lepenski Vir burials are considered below with Gorges 'phase 3'.

At Vlasac, fifty-eight individuals were placed in forty-nine graves. For the most part, the early Vlasac burials were deposited in groups outside of the areas of building. In the central part of the site, burials were concentrated to the rear of the site or at the border of the rocky plateau and thus exploited the natural hollows of the terrain for use as 'tombs'. In the upstream part of the site, burials concentrated around one of the buildings.

In the early Vlasac burial treatment, both men and women were interred, although men were interred twice as frequently as women (Nemeskéri and Szathmary 1978: 285–425). A complete range of individuals of different ages are present but adults and older individuals (twenty-five years and older) were twice as frequent as younger ones (Radovanović 1996a: 188, 197). Three male, two female and one child's burial were cremations: the child's was associated with the hearth of a building. Of the forty-nine early burials at Vlasac, twenty-three (47 per cent) contained grave-goods including stone (such as flint, quartz, red limestone and pebbles), animal parts (such as animal bones, a bone awl, an ornamented bone, antlers, fish teeth, and a tool made from a boar's tusk), shell (a bracelet of snail shell beads) and decorative materials such as ochre and graphite (Radovanović 1996a: 199–201). No clear relationships appear among the frequency or types of grave-goods and the age or sex of the deceased.

The recurrence of graphite and ochre in burials (fourteen of the twenty-three burials with goods) and the two bracelets reveal that over half of all burials with grave-goods contained objects that would have been useful in making visual expressions of personal or group identity. If the fish teeth were perforated and thus attachable to clothing or worn as pendents or beads then another four of the burials, accounting for 78 per cent of the early Vlasac burials, contained objects of personal ornamentation.

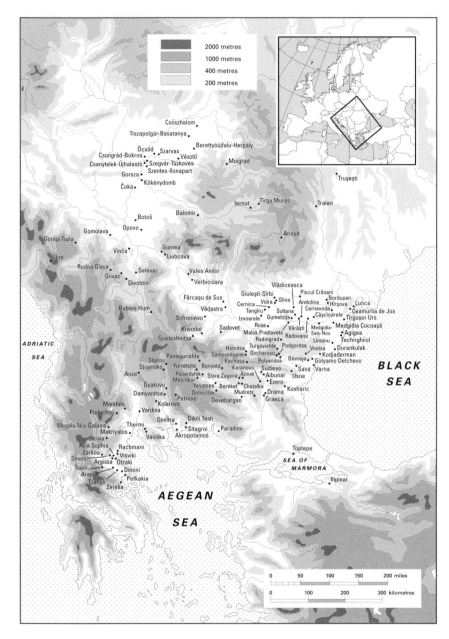

Figure 4.1 Key sites discussed in Chapters 4, 5 and 6

The evidence from Schela Cladovei is less clear or complete: thirty-three individuals were buried, most of whom were placed around a hearth. Some burials contained traces of ochre and one body was found with five bone points. One burial was a partial cremation.

Gorges phase 3

During the first half of the seventh millennium BC, burials were deposited at Vlasac, Lepenski Vir, Padina (Jovanović 1974, 1984b; Mikić 1981: Radovanović 1996a: 170–74) and Hajdučka Vodenica (Jovanović 1966, 1984a; Radovanović 1996a: 219–22).

At Lepenski Vir (site phase I/1), twenty-five individuals were buried during this period (Radovanović 1996a: 175–9). Of these the majority (twenty, 80 per cent) were less than 12 years old and of these most (80 per cent) were less than 3 years old. Four of the five individuals aged over 25 years were male. None of the youngest group were interred with any grave-goods but two of the 3–12-year-olds were; one burial contained a necklace of limestone and snail-shell beads as well as flaked stone and animal bones. The burial of an adult female contained a human mandible, although this may mark a separate burial interred late in phase I/1. All but one of the children and infant burials were placed under the floors of buildings; most of the adult burials were placed between buildings with their bodies perpendicular to the river.

At Vlasac (site phase II) there is evidence for a change in burial treatment at this time. While some burials were similar to those from the previous phase (and have been included in that analysis above), others were closer to the pattern of later burial treatment (and are included in the analysis below for Gorges phase 4). During Gorges phase 3 burials were clearly oriented in relation to buildings, and often placed between structures. In some cases, as at Lepenski Vir and Vlasac, child burials were placed between buildings. At Padina (site phase A2 or A-B) the earliest burials were arranged in relation to the axis of a stone construction. All of the other Padina burials have been associated with the later types from Vlasac and are included in the discussion below.

Gorges phase 4

During the second half of the seventh millennium BC burial continued at Vlasac (site phases II/III and III), Lepenski Vir (I/2), Padina (B/I) and Hajdučka Vodenica (Ia-b). The later type of Vlasac burials is represented by fifty-four burials containing sixty-one individuals. Burials of males outnumbered those of females which, in turn, outnumbered those of children (46, 33 and 21 per cent respectively). Individuals over 25 years of age outnumbered younger ones by three to one. Cremation only appears in one instance in the burial of a male of indeterminate age.

119

Of the sixty-one individuals from Vlasac only sixteen (26 per cent) were buried with any grave-goods. The practice of interring particular animal parts in the earlier burials continued in use (a boar's tusk tool, antler tools, ornamented bone, fish teeth and bones) and parts of new animals, such as dog mandibles, were added. Ochre continued to be used as did a necklace and snail-shell beads. Grave-goods which could have been used for personal ornamentation were deposited in over half (56 per cent) of those burials which contained grave-goods. The most striking new grave inclusion is human bone: male mandibles were placed in two burials both of which were graves of adult females; a skull from a male was placed in the burial of an adult male (Radovanović 1996a: 211–17).

At Lepenski Vir (site phase I/2) twenty-two individuals were buried during this period. As in the site's previous phase, the majority of burials (fifteen, 68 per cent) were of individuals under the age of 25. Of these most (80 per cent) were under three years of age. Among the six adults, four were female; female mandibles were also found in hearth constructions. All but four of the burials were placed within buildings. Only three burials (an adult male, a juvenile, and an elderly female) contained grave-goods: the juvenile male burial contained the skull of a large bovid as well as other animal bones and flaked stone; the elderly female's contained a bone awl. Orientation of burials within the site was dominated by those placed parallel to the river (Srejović 1969; Zoffmann 1983; Radovanović 1996a: 174–87)

There is less precise or complete information about age and sex for the fifty-one individuals interred at Padina at this time. Over half (59 per cent) contained grave-goods, including bone tools (such as awls), flaked stone, animal bone, antler and human bone (a mandible). Many of the burials with grave-goods were inhumations made under stone constructions. At the rear of the site, a child's skull was placed under another stone construction.

Thirty individuals were buried at Hajdučka Vodenica (Jovanović 1966, 1984a; Radovanović 1996a: 219–22) and have been associated, chrono-logically, with the later Vlasac types. As with the Padina burials, there is little detailed information of sex and age. Twelve of the burials (40 per cent) were made within a circular stone construction; only three burials (10 per cent), each of which was made with a special stone construction, contained grave-goods: antler in one, a stone axe in another, a herbivore mandible in the third.

Gorges phases 5 and 6

At the end of the seventh and the beginning of the sixth millennia BC (Gorges phase 5) burial continued at Vlasac, Padina, Lepenski Vir and Hajdučka Vodenica. At Lepenski Vir (site phase I/3), twenty-three individuals were interred. As in previous phases of the site, younger individuals were more frequent (52 per cent) and most of these (92 per cent) were under 3 years of age. Of the six adults who could be sexed, four were male. Five individuals (22 per cent of the total) were buried with grave-goods. One of the child burials contained a human mandible and animal bones; an adult male burial was associated with the skull and antlers of red deer; an unsexed adult was buried with a dog mandible. All but four burials (83 per cent) were placed within buildings.

During the first half of the sixth millennium BC (Gorges phase 6) burial took place at Lepenski Vir (site phase II) and Hajdučka Vodenica (site phase Ib). At Lepenski Vir, thirteen individuals were buried. All were adults, all were positioned parallel to the river. Eight of eleven sexable individuals were female. Almost half (46 per cent) of burials contained grave-goods; all are female. Grave-goods include red-deer antler, bovid vertebrae, bone tools and necklaces, including one made of ninety-three limestone beads (Srejović and Babović 1983).

Gorges burial: conclusions

The frequent inhumation of burials in the Gorges sites provides a significant body of information about early treatment of the deceased and about the development of burial during the period of the most significant changes in the Gorges (that is Gorges phase 4 and after) and across the region. Taking the Gorges as a whole over the millennia it was in use, there appear to have been few hard and fast rules governing age of deceased or distributions of grave-goods. There are general trends, however, especially in the association of burials with buildings or stone constructions (except for the earliest burials) and with the association of younger individuals with burials in buildings. Another important, though perhaps not surprising, pattern was the orientation of burials either perpendicular to or parallel with the river and the occasional inclusion of the bones or teeth of fish with the deceased. While some phases of some sites suggest that the majority of burial treatment was directed at younger members of the community (Vlasac phase 3, Lepenski Vir phases 4 and 5), other phases of other sites suggest that adults drew most burial attention (Vlasac early and phase 4, and Lepenski Vir phase 6). Concerning grave-goods, two patterns appear: fewer grave-goods were used with time (except for the final phase of Lepenski Vir); and objects of personal ornamentation predominated. If there was a rule to mortuary behaviour in the Gorges then it was one of variation.

Southern and south-central Bulgaria

While the Gorges record of mortuary behaviour provides a high concentration of detail about how people disposed of the deceased, more disparate information comes from burials in other parts of the western Balkans and from southern and south-central Bulgaria. The depth of detail and the reliability of analyses of this broader body of mortuary information are variable at best.

In southern and south-central Bulgaria, at the beginning of the sixth millennium BC, that is within Karanovo I culture contexts, most inhumation focused on children or babies (Buchvarov 1994). Burials were placed in the periphery of settlements, between buildings or under the floors of buildings and, in some cases, under the building's oven. Some burials were inhumed with ceramics as grave-goods. At Kovachevo the burials of three children were recovered. Two of the burials were of very young individuals: one was 2–3 months old and another was 11–12 months (Demoule and Lichardus-Itten 1994: 577). Although there was no common burial rite at Kovachevo, each of the children was buried near a building. Fragments of human bone were also found in other parts of the site. At Azmak and at Karanovo young infants were buried under the floors of houses (Todorova and Vajsov 1993: 222).

At Kurdzhali in southern Bulgaria five early Neolithic burials have been excavated (Pejkov 1978: 16–17; Boev and Kavgazova 1983; Buchvarov 1994: 263–4). Of those that could be identified, two were children under 10 years of age and two were women (one 25–30, the other 60 years old). Four of the graves contained grave-goods: ceramic vessels, bone beads, flint tools, bone awls and stone balls. One of the women's graves was placed under the floor of a building and two of the graves may have been 'fenced off' with lines of stones.

At Karanovo twenty-seven burials have been recovered from the site as a whole (Buchvarov 1994: 264–5). Five individuals were interred in Karanovo I contexts. Four of these were children; one was a 50–55-year-old man (Boev 1963). At Azmak, burials (mainly of infants and children) were found in all of the Neolithic levels (Georgiev 1963, 1966; Buchvarov 1994: 264). At Karanovo seven burials come from Karanovo II contexts. Three of these were children, one was a 20–40-year-old woman, one was a 14–15-year-old male and one was a male of unspecified age (Georgiev 1957). One of the children's burials was placed under a hearth. A collection of children's bones was found under the floor of one building; the mandibles and most of the children's skulls had been detached from their bodies (Buchvarov in press). The only evidence of grave-goods comes from the woman's burial in which had been placed seven snail-shell beads and two bone pins.

Nine individuals were recovered from Karanovo III contexts: five of these are unsexed and unaged; of the others, two were women and two were unsexed 'youths'. One of the youths was buried under a building floor near an oven; the other youth was buried without its skull (Buchvarov 1994). At Yasatepe, also in Karanovo III contexts, an adult female was interred near one of the buildings and a pottery dish was placed next to the body. Near to the woman's burial, a thigh bone and part of a male skull were found (Detev 1959; Buchvarov 1994: 265). At Rakitovo (although from an unclear chronological context), an infant was buried in a pot placed in a pit under a building floor. A piece of ochre and flaked stone had been placed in the pot with the skeleton (Buchvarov 1994: 265–6).

Western Balkans

The trend of linking burials with buildings that is evident in both the Gorges and in southern and south-central Bulgaria is also found in the western Balkans. Burial within village boundaries occurred at Vinča where nine individuals were discovered (Schwidetzky 1957, 1971–2) and at a range of other sites of the Starčevo-Körös-Criş culture complex. At Golokut two individuals were buried inside pit-huts. In one of the burials, that of a 50-year-old woman, the skull of an auroch was placed on the deceased's right hand and a scapula on her knees (Petrović 1987, 1990a; Zoffman 1987a; Borić 1996: table 1). At Zlatara three burials have been excavated. In one a middle-aged women was interred with the antlers of a red deer. In another an adult male was buried with a young child in an elaborate stone grave construction. Quartzite and animal bones accompanied the deceased (Leković 1985: 160–1). At Nama four individuals were buried within one pit-hut and a pottery vessel was placed by the head of one of the adults (Iskra-Janošić 1977, 1984). At Tržnice three adults and a child were buried together; the child wore a shell pectoral (Borić 1996: 73). At Obrež burials of children were made under the floors and inside buildings (Raczky 1982–3). At Divostin a 31–35-year-old pregnant female was 'casually' interred. A child's body was also buried and scattered human bone was found across the site: nineteen long-bones, six skull fragments and several tarsals and phalanges (Zoffman 1988).

Northern Greece

In northern Greece people treated the deceased in a fashion similar to the other regions. Burials were often made in shallow pits outside buildings or under their floors (Hourmouziadis 1973). At Nea Nikomedeia a woman was buried with a child (Rodden 1962). At Prodromos, two or three successive deposits of disarticulated skulls and long bones were found under the floor of a building (Hourmouziadis 1971). At Soufli Magoula a series of cremations were made in pits; burials consisted of a concentration of human and animal bone, pots and traces of burning. One cremation contained a stone axe (Gallis 1975, 1982).

Burial: conclusions

The evidence for burial after 6500 BC, therefore, illustrates the correlation of bodies with village areas and in many cases with particular buildings.

The deceased include young and old, male and female, although the number of children's burials is striking. The range of grave-goods was limited. It is difficult not to conclude that inhumation was infrequent and it is difficult to read any significance into patterns of age, sex or differentials of grave-good distribution except perhaps the large proportion of children's graves. The occasional inhumation of body parts or dismembered skeletons is found in all of the regions and the fact that unassociated fragments of human bone were distributed across some sites suggests that whatever the criteria for formal inhumation consisted of they did not apply equally to all people. Although the evidence for pre-6500 BC burial is very poor, there is no reason to assume that any dramatic changes occurred in this aspect of human existence.

FLAKED STONE TOOLS

If the apparent changes in the appearance of formal burial after 6500 BC are less an independent sign of innovation than they are an accompaniment of the new built environment, what can one conclude about contemporary developments in the manufacture of flaked tools? The vast majority of analysis of Balkan lithic material has focused on changes in the technology and typology of flaked stone in attempts to decide whether the origin of the post-6500 BC Balkan life was an event of indigenous development or colonization. Comparatively little work has examined the ways in which lithic tools were made, although more work has focused on sourcing raw material. Even less attention has been directed at the ways in which lithic tools were used and the distribution of events of manufacture, use and discard within a site, let alone on any smaller scales such as within an activity area or individual building. There are important exceptions to these general trends in lithics work and this section will rely on them (e.g., Perlès 1988, 1990; Gatsov 1993).

Transitions and continuities

Significant changes in the lithic assemblages of the Balkans accompany the suite of other materials and activities which appear after 6500 BC. Two important developments were the appearance of large, standardized blades produced with pressure flaking and an increase in the time and labour invested, and knowledge required, for acquiring particular raw materials for flint-working. As with so many other trends, there is no blanket application of these changes across the regions or through time. As in other spheres of post-6500 BC life, if there is a rule it is one of variety both across and within regions. This is especially so in the case of transitions from Mesolithic to Neolithic assemblages; contemporary sites contain evidence alternatively for a gradual development from local traditions and for a sharper break and the introduction of new forms and conceptions of lithic production.

Kozłowski has suggested two major periods of change in lithic technology in the Balkans (Kozłowski 1989). The first occurred in the middle and last half of the ninth millennium BC. At this time blade technology was replaced by flake utilization of unworked tabular flint and chunks as roughouts for tool production. Microliths (geometrics) were replaced by notched and denticulated tools, scrapers and end-scrapers. These changes were particular to the Balkans; in other parts of Europe geometric microliths increased in frequency. Kozłowski's second major change occurred around the second half of the seventh millennium BC and separates the non-ceramic phases of Balkan prehistory from the ceramic ones. With the ceramic phases, a very sharp increase in the proportions of large blade blanks occurred. The investigation of differences or similarities between the non-ceramic and ceramic phase lithic assemblages is important and can be examined in three key areas: the Danube Gorges, northern Greece and north-western Anatolia.

The Gorges

In the Gorges significant changes in lithics occurred in the second half of the seventh millennium BC. As with the introduction of ceramics and representational material culture, new activities, materials and ideas emerged at this time to run alongside longer-running trends in architecture and burial, which showed less change. In Gorges phases 1–3 elements of a local Epi-palaeolithic lithic tradition were present: high proportions of end-scrapers and retouched bladelets (Radovanović 1996a: 233–51). With Gorges phase 4, however, significant changes occurred. Local raw materials, such as radiolarites and flints, were replaced by waxy flint obtained from more distant sources such as north-west Bulgaria. The shift to extra-local sources suggests that the Gorges communities were now participating more intensively in a larger regional network of contacts (Radovanović 1996a: 41). Blades were produced from well prepared cores and replaced existing flake and splintering techniques; elongated retouched blades replaced irregular scrapers and retouched flakes (Kozłowski 1989: 133).

Another important sequence providing evidence across the period when ceramics appeared in the Balkans is the Odmut cave in south-western Montenegro (Srejović 1977; Kozłowski 1989: 132). Odmut contains eight major layers dating from 8100–5200 BC and covering both non-ceramic (layers Ia and Ib) and ceramic phases (layers IIa and IIb), the latter containing monochrome Starčevo pottery with barbotine roughened surfaces (Marković 1977: 10). There was no archaeological hiatus between the ceramic and the non-ceramic uses of the cave and the sequence reveals similar patterns in technology with a 'stable' set of tools, although the number of parallel-sided blades with regular cross-sections represent a gradual perfecting of blade technology through time (Kozłowski 1989: 132).

Franchthi and northern Greece

In addition to the Gorges sequences and that at Odmut, a third bridging site is Franchthi in southern Greece (Perlès 1988; 1990). Here the lithics of the initial Neolithic contain both 'Mesolithic' and 'Neolithic' elements: notched, denticulated and marginally flaked tools; and less numerous well-made regular blades and bladelets respectively. The lithic assemblages of early ceramic Franchthi were 90 per cent Mesolithic in character and contained some geometric microliths (trapezes) as well as rarer transverse arrow-heads characteristic for the later Mesolithic. However, these early ceramic-phase trapezes are distinct from their Mesolithic predecessors: the former are more elongated, symmetrical and manufactured from well made narrow obsidian or flint blades and probably were produced with pressure flaking. These were distinct from the Mesolithic trapezes which were short, asymmetrical and made of flakes or irregular blades (Perlès 1988: 483). Thus, at Franchthi, although there is continuity in form between ceramic and pre-ceramic phases, these is an important distinction between two completely different production sequences using different techniques.

Perlès has studied other early ceramic-phase lithic assemblages. In the material from the early Neolithic levels at Argissa in northern Greece, Perlès found a greater proportion of 'Neolithic' elements (especially sickle blades, which were not present at Franchthi) produced through a system geared towards making highly standardized, high-quality blades via pressure flaking (Perlès 1988: 484). There were no Mesolithic elements; although trapezes were present, they were very rare and had been made in a non-Mesolithic way, as they had been at Franchthi.

For Perlès, the distinction between the Mesolithic and Neolithic lithic assemblages rests in a difference in the conception of lithic production (Perlès 1988: 484). With Mesolithic lithic production, minimal core preparation was undertaken, there appears to have been no standardization in form and production of flake tools was quick; working edges could be adapted to fit needs and tasks as they arose. Within the early ceramic Neolithic conception of production, time and effort were invested in earlier stages of the process: that is, particular qualities of flint from particular sources were selected and acquired and cores were specially prepared. Standardized, regular blades and bladelets were the result. Neolithic investment was made earlier in the process when the blades and bladelets were being produced (Perlès 1988: 484–5). In Mesolithic lithic working, the investment was placed in post-production adjustments to form and edges as needed and as tools were used. Perlès concluded that while this new conception of lithic production was in full force at Thessalian sites such as Argissa, it was only partially in force at Franchthi and at other sites, such as Sidari, with characteristically Mesolithic sequences.

Perlès suggests that the cause of these differences did not necessarily rest in functional terms. Perhaps, although she may not agree, the changes in lithic technology were similar in scale and development to the contemporary experimental adoption of ceramics. The theme, which applies to both processes, was of variation between regions and, undoubtedly, within regions as well. It is also significant that sites such as Franchthi and Odmut represent locations and foci for human activities very different from the early villages such as Argissa. Thus the distinction between the more 'Neolithic' Argissa lithic assemblages and the more gradual and continuous 'Mesolithic' lithics of Franchthi and Odmut may reveal more about the types of activities which occurred at these sites than it does about any conflicting processes of neolithization.

North-western Turkey

As there was variation between the character of the lithic assemblages at Franchthi, Odmut, in the Gorges and from the early Thessalian sites, other variations between lithic assemblages have been noted between different early sites in north-west Turkey. As in Greece, the lithic assemblages at some sites suggest links to deeper local traditions of flint-working while those at other sites suggest a major break. Thus there is evidence for a continuity between the pottery Neolithic and the Mesolithic in the eastern Marmara and in the lake district of the southern Anatolian plateau.

In the eastern Marmara region, the lithic assemblages of late Mesolithic Ağaçli group sites, which date no earlier than the eighth millennium BC, are characterized by pressure-flaked micro-blades and specific Gravettian elements (Gatsov and Özdoğan 1994). In distribution, Ağaçli sites are limited to coastal locations; the eponymous site consists of nine main clusters of material located on a hill between two streams not far from the present shoreline of the Black Sea.

The most prolific Ağaçli sites were located on fossilized reddish sand-dunes on the Black Sea coast as seen on a small dune by the Dardanelles at Tepecik, at Musluçeşme by the Manyas Lake and on a high terrace overlooking an inlet by the Sea of Marmara at Harmidere. These sites may well have been linked to the exploitation of aquatic and marine resources. No similar examples have been found in inland areas even where, as in Turkish Thrace, extensive survey work has been carried out (Özdoğan 1991: 347; Gatsov and Özdoğan 1994: 100–1).

Gatsov and Özdoğan's analysis of a sample of the lithics from the Ağaçli suggested that blades and bladelets were made here and that cores were discarded as they reached the end of their usefulness (Gatsov and Özdoğan 1994: 103). The same patterns were found at Gümüşdere, which

127

is also on the Black Sea coast 5–6 km from Ağaçli (Gatsov and Özdoğan 1994: 106–7).

The lithics of the subsequent earliest pottery Fikirtepe culture sites on the coast, as at Pendik and Fikirtepe itself, have connections with assemblages from the local pre-pottery Ağaçli sites: micro-blades, keeled scrapers, backed bladelets. Unlike the Ağaçli phenomenon however, Fikirtepe sites also appear in inland locations as at Ilipinar. While the ceramics at both inland and coastal sites are identical, the lithic industries are completely different (Özdoğan and Gatsov 1998: 213). This is most clearly seen at the small inland site of Çalca Mevkii located on a high plateau in the southern Marmara. The site contains Fikirtepe pottery but a lithic assemblage that is distinct from that of the coastal Fikirtepe sites. The Çalca Mevkii lithics are dominated by large blades and blade segments (Özdoğan 1989b: 447–8; 1990: 347, figure 5; Özdoğan and Gatsov 1998: 214). A major concentration of lithic working was found 200 m from the main focus of the pottery Neolithic site; cores are in their final, or at least advanced, stages of exploitation; both blade and flake cores were discarded (Özdoğan and Gatsov 1998: 221).

The early Neolithic sites in north-western Turkey did not contain the Epi-gravettian elements that were characteristic of the Ağaçli group (Özdoğan and Gatsov 1998: 213). The assemblages of pottery Neolithic sites such as Hoca Çesme, Aşaği Pinar have large blade segments and the larger 'Karanovo I-type' blades, although there is also an unstandardized character to some of the assemblages (Özdoğan and Gatsov 1998: 213). The Ağaçli assemblages were completely different from those of succeeding sites in the east Balkans, such as Karanovo and Azmak (Gatsov and Özdoğan 1994: 110), which are characterized by heavy macro-blades and tools with semi-steep and steep retouch.

Thus in north-western Turkey, in the case of the Fikirtepe phenomenon, there were two different types of sites connected by a similar style of pottery but distinguished by different lithic industries. One type of site is coastal, in areas where marine and aquatic resources were exploited; the lithic assemblages of these sites had connections with long-standing local traditions. The second type of site was located inland and had lithic assemblages characterized by classic Neolithic elements.

The recent work on the early north-west Turkish lithic scatter sites is important, as it provides a new and more detailed picture of late Mesolithic activity and the transitional early ceramic sites. It is perhaps appropriate to use them as a context for understanding the lithic scatters at sites such as Pobiti Kamuni in north-eastern Bulgaria that were introduced in Chapter 1. The scatters at Pobiti Kamuni mark the locations of flint-working and were in use over very long periods of time, from the Palaeolithic to the Bronze Age (Margos 1961; Gatsov 1982, 1984a, 1984b, 1995). Although the surface material is a mixture from across this span, some of the cores

128

can be isolated and dated to a period between the ninth and the seventh millennia BC (Petrobok and Skutil 1950; Gatsov 1995: 74; 1982: 113). Gatsov has suggested that the formal similarities in backed forms connect the Pobiti Kamuni material with that found in the Gorges, as at Cuina Turcului, Lepenski Vir and Vlasac (Gatsov 1982: 120). Other formal analyses connect Pobiti with later sites: similarities in end-scrapers, including microlithic ones, suggest links with the assemblages from the later sites of Usoe and Golyamo Delchevo, which are discussed in Chapter 5 (Gatsov 1982: 126). There are also similarities with Dudeşti assemblages from southern Romania. Perhaps Pobiti Kamuni, or at least those of its lithic scatters that can be dated to the millennium under consideration, should be understood in the same way as are the lithic sites in north-western Turkey: as foci for activities distinct from, but contemporary with, ceramic sites.

The western Balkans

In western Bulgaria, the lithic assemblages of early ceramic sites contain developed macro-blades (Gatsov 1995: 76). Tools were made from high-quality yellow or wax-yellow flint and were produced away from the village sites (Gatsov 1993: 44). Thus although macro-blades were characteristic of both the Gulubnik and Pernik assemblages, no cores or rejuvenation flakes have been found at either site, nor, Gatsov suggests, are they found at any of the other excavated sites in western Bulgaria (Gatsov 1993: 44; 1995: 76).[2] At some sites, quartz was worked on site; indeed at Kovachevo quartz was much more abundant on site than was flint. Significantly, at the end of the local early Neolithic (5600 BC) the use of high-quality flint and the production of macro-blades disappeared (Gatsov 1995: 76)

It is of interest to compare the west Bulgarian patterns with the evidence from Starčevo contexts, especially as studied at Divostin I. Flaked stone tools at Divostin were made at the site from local pebble flints and cherts collected from nearby stream-beds; similar patterns are clear at Banya, Grivac and in the Starčevo levels at Lepenski Vir (Tringham et al. 1988). At Divostin, flint-working was adventitious with little modification or retouching. There was no standardization of core shapes. Few blanks were present; but large amounts of quartz wastage were. Classic, long, parallel-sided blades were not found, perhaps due to the limitations of the raw materials in use. The rate of used to unused blanks was very high and may suggest that raw materials were difficult to obtain or it may be a further reflection of the limited effort invested in the early stages of lithic production. The majority of blade blanks were made from locally available pebble-flints and cherts (Tringham et al. 1988: 205).

The reliance on working local materials in an immediate fashion seen at Divostin is a characteristic of other Starčevo sites such as Grivac, Banya,

Anzabegovo, Lepenski Vir III. Starčevo-Körös sites in the Hungarian Plain are poor in lithics (Whittle 1998: 138; Kertész 1996). In a few exceptional cases some lithic material appears to have been perceived in an extraordinary sense. At Endrőd 39, for example, a hoard of flint contained 101 blades made of non-local raw material probably of north-west Bulgarian origin (Kaczanowski et al. 1981). An even larger concentration of hoarded blades was found in the large building at Nea Nikomedeia.

If the majority of lithics of the Starčevo and Körös sites represent immediate, expedient tool production using locally available, poor-quality materials, then this further strengthens the interpretation of these sites as temporary collections of impermanent huts, very different from the surface-level structures found to the south and east (e.g., the use of non-local flint in western Bulgarian sites). The characteristics which link the Starčevo lithic assemblages to those of the Gorges with their traces of deeper local traditions may also be relevant for other early ceramic Neolithic groups where the introduction of pottery accompanied almost no change in the technology of stone tool manufacture (e.g., in the Bug-Dneister and Sursk-Dnieper groups in the north-western Black Sea zone) (Kozłowski 1989: 136).

Gatsov's study of patterns of lithic exploitation at the west Bulgarian sites documented how distinct, in both the types of tools produced and the types of raw materials exploited, these assemblages were from the Starčevo industries dominated by local lithic resources (Gatsov 1993). At Pernik and Gulubnik the large blades had been produced at non-local outcrops (Gatsov 1993: 44). Blades were made of yellow-wax-coloured flint, which comes from outcrops in north-western Bulgaria. Gatsov concluded that the perfection of the production of macro-blades in the early sites in this region was linked to the processes of acquisition (Gatsov 1993: 41). In terms of lithics the west Bulgarian sites had more in common with sites to the south (i.e., in Thessaly) and little, if any, similarity with the Epi-gravettian traditions seen to the north in the Gorges (Gatsov 1993: 48).

Lithics: conclusion

If anything, the differential industries of lithics at late Mesolithic, transitional and early Neolithic sites support the case of variability in the types of lithics associated with early ceramics. The traditionally acknowledged Neolithic lithic signature of macro-blades may only be a character of established, relatively permanent villages of surface-level buildings. Sites of other character, especially caves but also collections of pit-huts, appear to contain a less dramatically altered lithic composition and the continuation of many traditionally Mesolithic forms. However, as Perlès has argued, the main element of change may have been the approach to lithic production and not necessarily the forms in and of themselves.

Therefore, it may have been that the significant change in lithic production after 6500 BC was not the appearance of macro-blades, although this may have been one symptom of the larger change; the major change may have been a shift away from a reactive and adventitious production and refinement of tools on the spot as necessary, towards a proactive and foresightful system of acquiring appropriate high-quality raw materials, shaping blade cores and perhaps even producing the majority of blades at a distance from the place and time of eventual use.

PLANTS AND ANIMALS

Archaeologists have assumed since Childe's revolutionary work in defining the Neolithic that the significant element of change in south-eastern Europe was the shift to food-production, particularly the breeding of domesticated grazing animals and the cultivation of cereals. The faunal and floral records confirm the appearance of these species and activities from 6500 BC.

Less well understood is the significance of the adaptations of non-indigenous domesticated species and the adoption of the technologies of animal and plant domestication. A more accurate view may be that the significance of changes in plants and animals lies not with any nutritional or purely economic advantage potentially provided by these new species; rather the significance may lie in the organizational requirements and the social consequences of exploiting these new species and employing these new technologies.

Limitations of the data

There are significant limitations to the potential for synthesis and understanding of the role of plants and animals in the communities of the post-6500 BC Balkans. Some limitations are methodological; others, equally importantly, are theoretical and concern questions of what bones and seeds represent. In attempts to identify the primary cause of post-6500 BC changes in the Balkans, the continued acceptance of the importance of the shift from food-gathering to food-producing has had two important, and largely unhelpful, consequences. First, it has been assumed that the importance of plants and animals was economic, that is that they were seen by people primarily as sources of human nutrition. Because of this there has been little attention focused on what animals may have meant to people in non-economic terms. Second, and perhaps as a consequence of the assumed primacy and simplicity of the economic role of plants and animals, archaeologists have paid little attention to the contexts of deposition of plant remains and bones and thus have not addressed the potential variations in the uses of animals and plants between or within sites.

In some cases, the analysis aims no higher than recording the presence/ absence of species at sites. In many projects, bone and seed specialists are added on as short-term components and are excluded from the formulation of overall project research designs. In most cases little attention is devoted to regular sampling; dry sieving remains an irregular practice; wet sieving is found at few excavations. In almost every case there is little attention to the behavioural contexts in which faunal and floral remains are found. In addition to these problems, attempts at the interpretative synthesis of existing analyses are impeded by variations in the ways in which data are presented. Some present data as counts of bones, others as Minimum Number of Individuals; few offer estimates of meat yield. Almost no attention is directed at reconstructing grazing patterns or cultivation techniques.[3]

One of the most significant current limitations to floral and faunal analyses is the misconception of what seeds and bones on sites represent. Despite Dennell's seminal study of southern and western Bulgarian tells (Dennell 1978), there has been very little detailed attention devoted to the importance of the context and the potential variabilities inherent in different assemblages of economic material. Patterns of finds represent events of deposition influenced by taphonomic and post-depositional factors; they seldom represent events of consumption.

Because of these problems it is very difficult to offer the level of detailed, region-by-region, synthesis that is possible for other topics, such as pottery or architecture. It is clear that a new suite of plants and animals was in the hands of the new camp and village communities of the Balkans after 6500 BC. The following discussion approaches the floral and faunal records of these new elements by addressing the social contexts of the changes which took place. Special attention is given to the ways in which people exploited plants and animals.

Grazing patterns and new animals

New animal species enter Balkan lifestyles after 6500 BC. Significant was the appearance of sheep and goat. New technologies for directing animal breeding also appeared for the first time; these technologies were applied to indigenous species such as cattle, pig and dog as well as to the non-indigenous animals. These changes introduced new components to Balkan life and included new types of meat as well, eventually, as wool and milk. In other important ways, however, the practice of exploiting animals for meat and blood, antler and bone represented a continuity with earlier millennia; the eating of meat from herbivores was nothing new.

What were new, however, were the packages in which that meat was available. It is perhaps not surprising that the new non-indigenous element (sheep and goat) fit into the range of domesticated animals between pigs and cattle in terms of body size and, perhaps, in rates of reproduction and maturation. Thus the importance of sheep and goat may have been their particular ability to fill a social as well as an economic niche between the larger animals, such as the domestic and wild cattle and the red deer, and the smaller parcels of meat provided by wild and domestic pig, dog and a wide range of fish, birds and other wild species.

In addition to potential consequences of animal size, it is important to consider the seasonal patterns of activities that can be linked to each of the main animal species and the consequences these patterns had for variations in human behaviour, especially with respect to mobility and sedentism but also to the practicalities of consuming meat. Key variables of animal behaviour include species-dependent feeding requirements, breeding seasons and consequences of animal slaughter. All of the new patterns of grazing, animal mobility and overwintering to be discussed here must have run in parallel with other patterns of activities, such as the continued importance of hunting, foraging and fishing.

Feeding requirements

In terms of feeding requirements, the grazing and browsing patterns of cattle, sheep and goat were complementary and would have contributed to an effective package for exploiting naturally available vegetation. Because they have no upper incisors, cattle prefer grasses and eat plants that they can tear from the ground with their teeth and tongues; they are not suited to pastures with woody plants. Sheep prefer herbs. Goats on the other hand eat anything, although they prefer woody plants. Pigs are less particular even than goats. Red deer depend on a bulky diet of grasses, herbs and shrubs (Barker 1985: 171; Gregg 1988: 102, 123). The grazing preferences of different animals suggest it was necessary for people to move at least two of the key species of animals, ovicaprid and cattle, to preferred grazing lands at different times of the year.

The emphasis on movement of grazing species assumes that fodder crops were not cultivated. Dennell has suggested, however, that for the Bulgarian sites some of the grain and pulse harvest and all of the straw and husks were used as fodder, perhaps for overwintering animals in or near villages. Mortality profiles show that each of the post-6500 BC species was kept beyond their first winter, although the proportions of one age-group to another and of age proportions between different species' populations varied between sites and between regions. For some animals, such as pigs, slaughtering decisions were taken to relieve villages from supporting the entire population of domestic pigs through the winter. Sheep were slower in maturing than were pigs (up to three years before they reach their full size) as were cattle; thus both ovicaprid and cattle present potential feeding problems if they were overwintered with the support of village resources. In some regions with milder (but wetter) winters, such as the southern

Balkans, overwintering probably may not have presented a major problem; in other, northern regions, provision of winter fodder may have been one of the important stimuli for plant cultivation, especially perhaps of barley.

Animal mobility

Regardless of the role, if any, of fodder in animal sustenance, it is clear that a major component of human management of domesticated animals after 6500 BC was the movement of ovicaprids and cattle to satisfactory grazing areas. Some animals required little or no human management. Obviously this includes wild animals, although the grazing and territorial incompatibility of red deer and ovicaprid is of note and may have influenced strategies both of hunting and of moving flocks; in the spring, red deer migrated out of the lowlands to their upland summer ranges; in winter they moved back to the protected lowlands (Barker 1985: 171). Pigs could have been allowed to roam freely over stubble or in woodland for most of the year with minimal attention except, perhaps, during farrowing and then for slaughter in the autumn (Barker 1985: 36).

The environmental knowledge required, such as location of pastures or ability to read seasonal stages, would have been no more complex, or different, from that required for foraging, hunting and gathering activities of previous millennia. Knowledge of animal grazing preferences had been an important element of late Pleistocene and early Holocene foraging and hunting strategies. The link across the millennia provided by the continuing exploitation of red deer would have been direct and the success of ovicaprids and cattle mobility rested on similar principles of knowing the eating and breeding requirements of different species and understanding how to satisfy those requirements with available land resources during the different seasons. Indeed, patterns of grazing of domesticated animals after 6500 BC could be seen as nothing more than the insertion of new species (in the case of sheep and goat, at least) into long existing mobility strategies.

Soils and grazing

Grazing potential varies across the landscape in accord with differences in soil character and thus with vegetation type and its availability during different seasons. The potential to retain moisture is one of the most important factors in accounting for the fertility of different soils. Soils that retain sufficient moisture after the winter thaw or wet periods would have supported plant growth, and thus allowed grazing, late in the summer when other, less water-retentive, soils had become too dry to support suitable grazing plants. Good grazing would have been found on riverine soils where moisture retention was high due to impeded natural drainage; equally good grazing would have been available on clays found along rivers and streams

(Dennell 1978: 70). These *smolnitsas* and *chernozems*, rich in nutrients and stable in structure, are some of the most fertile soils in the Balkans. Although they were too heavy for unmechanized ploughing, and indeed were not cultivated until the middle of the present century, they would have been ideal for grazing livestock (Barker 1985: 86–7). Where such water-retentive soils were present and accessible, grazing could have taken place on a year-round basis.

In areas where soils were less moisture-retentive, late summer grazing would not have been possible. Animals would have been moved to other, probably upland, areas where pastures, which were inaccessible in the winter due to low temperatures and snow cover, would have provided good grazing from spring to late summer (Dennell 1978: 70). In some regions, as around Chavdar and Kazanluk in Bulgaria, the differential distribution of grazing soils would have meant that some animals, such as pigs and cattle, could have browsed in the valley lowlands while others, such as sheep and goat, would have been taken to upland pastures (Dennell 1978: 129).

The pattern of seasonal grazing in the Nova Zagora region in south-central Bulgaria around sites such as Karanovo would have taken advantage of early spring vegetation of the foot hills and parts of the lowlands that dried earliest. As the year proceeded and these areas became parched, grazing would have shifted to areas of lower elevation that dried out later in the spring and summer (Dennell 1978). Dennell has gone as far as to suggest that smaller outlying sites may have functioned as seasonal grazing settlements (Dennell 1978: 136–7).

Browsing, on the other hand, occurred in areas with extensive tree-growth and provided large proportions of food for red deer, cattle and pigs (Dennell 1978: 70). In the vicinity of Kazanluk, for example, there would have been a greater availability of browse; perhaps this is why deer, cattle and pig account for 70 per cent of meat consumed at the village (Dennell 1978: 129). In addition to providing nourishment, the regular movement of grazing animals to different pasture areas had added benefits. Risks of bacterial and parasitic diseases such as foot-rot and liver-fluke, which are common in flocks kept in enclosed wet pastures, would have been much reduced (Barker 1985: 41).

Breeding and birthing

With respect to breeding and birthing schedules, one can assume that human intervention, or at least observation and perhaps assistance, was required if not necessarily during insemination, then probably in the later stages of gestation, at birth and during weaning. This may have been especially necessary with pigs, to prevent sows eating their litters; increasingly it would have been the case when cows and goats came to be exploited for their milk supplies.

As it is linked to the shortening of the length of daylight, ovicaprid breeding is season-specific. Conception in autumn with birth in late winter or early spring would have allowed lambs to take advantage of new spring growth of vegetation within weeks of their birth (Gregg 1988: 111). Pigs, perhaps the most prolific breeders of the new domesticates, rut in late autumn; sows farrow in early spring (Barker 1985: 36; Gregg 1988: 119). Cattle have no specific breeding season, although a late winter/early spring calving would fit into a system of overwintering in the later stages of gestation (Gregg 1988: 103–4).

Slaughtering: potentials and consequences

While archaeologists have focused much analytical attention on distinguishing and interpreting age and sex mortality profiles for faunal assemblages, less work has addressed other dimensions of animal slaughter that may allow more important insights into the consumption consequences of these animals. The three main species (ovicaprid, cattle and pig) have very different characteristics of yield; differences in yield suggest that the slaughter of an animal of each of these species would have had different social, as well as economic, consequences.

At one end of the spectrum, pigs are small, and require little investment in time, effort or fodder. Pigs were trash-compactors, converting village rubbish and mostly inedible forest products into meat (Bogucki 1993: 497). Slaughtering a pig would have had few consequences. Killing one pig would not have affected the total resource of pig population. Any one animal represented a small part of the total number of pigs available; rapid reproductive rates would have replaced the loss with little delay. Furthermore, and perhaps most significantly, in terms of consumption, the small body size of a pig would have meant that the meat obtained from the slaughter of a single animal could have been easily consumed by a relatively small group of people, perhaps a small activity-connected or kin-related group such as a household.

Like pigs, sheep and goat were also small and could have been culled one at a time without any great detriment to the overall size of the flock. As Bogucki puts it, both ovicaprid and pigs lend themselves to short-term liquidation (Bogucki 1993: 497): single animals can be killed one at a time leaving the rest of the flock intact. Furthermore, as with the slaughter of a pig, culling a single sheep or goat would have produced an amount of meat that could have been completely consumed by a similarly small group of people.

Unlike pigs, however, each sheep or goat represented a not insubstantial investment in maintenance and, perhaps, fodder over a significant period of time (two to three years in most cases). Thus, although the meat yield would have been similar, the slaughter and consumption of a sheep or goat probably meant something different to a community from the slaughter and consumption of a pig. The difference may have rested as much in the perception of sheep and goat as relatively exotic animals that had no local wild breeding stock to maintain and support as much as it rested on a purely economic conception of time, labour and fodder invested.

Like sheep and goat, a cow or a bull represented a significant investment in the maintenance of an animal over a not insubstantial length of time. Unlike both pig and sheep or goat, however, cattle are very large animals. By concentrating the investment of time and labour into the growth and maintenance of a cow or bull, people would have engaged in a relatively high-risk strategy, relative to similar investments of time and labour in sheep or goat. With sheep and goat, the risk of failure due to disease or death was spread across a herd; with a cow or bull, investment was concentrated in a single larger animal. The trends in keeping sheep and goat in the more arid, southern regions of the Balkans may have been a symptom of people's desire to spread the risk in a less forgiving climate (Barker 1985: 42).

In addition to the potential risk of focusing time and labour on an individual cow or bull, the large body size of cattle meant that slaughter would have presented significant problems of consumption. If animal meat was not to be wasted, and Dennell's work on the condition of bones at Chavdar concluded, for that village at least, that people used animal carcasses very thoroughly (Dennell 1978: 111), then a larger number of people must be involved in the act of consumption than were involved in the consumption of a pig, goat or sheep. The consumption of a cow or bull therefore would have been an extra-domestic event involving a larger number of people, including some from more than one activity, co-residence or household group (Russell 1998).

Therefore, just as people and places were developing new identities after 6500 BC, so also perhaps animals, both the new and long-established species, were taking on new identities related to their role in social activities such as herding, grazing, breeding, overwintering and also in events of consumption, such as feasting. Perhaps it is not surprising that people also were beginning to model miniature clay figurines of particular species at this time and perhaps it is even less surprising the species represented almost exclusively was cattle, or at least generic, horned quadrupeds.

Cattle versus ovicaprid communities

The differences in the ways in which different species needed to be fed and, most especially, the different social consequences of their slaughter offer an avenue into understanding the potential differences between villages with faunal assemblages with different dominant species.

Halstead has noted that the principal constraints on plant-growth change as one moves from the southern Balkans into the Balkans proper, that is into Bulgaria and on to the north and north-west (Halstead 1989a). The southern region has a winter precipitation, is warmer and is less continental than the northern one, which has year-round precipitation. On the one hand, these differences would have had important consequences for cereals and pulses, which would have suffered under the shorter growing seasons, the late frosts and the destructively wet summers (Halstead 1989a: 26). Similar consequences would have applied to decisions of animal management. Sheep and goat may have been easier to keep in the drier hotter conditions of the southern Balkans, where pasture may have been poor and water scarce, although less so in the winters (Barker 1985: 42). In the southern regions, the new animals and crops were being grown in a climate not unlike that of their regions of origin. Similar growing conditions may have prevailed in southern Bulgaria.

Overall, therefore, it is possible to detect a distinction between areas in which cattle dominated, or at least where they were the most frequent element in faunal assemblages, and those in which ovicaprid remains are the most numerous. Achilleion is an example of the latter pattern. There sheep dominate the faunal assemblages of domesticates of all four phases, ranging from 58 per cent in phase I to 41 per cent in phase IV (Bökönyi 1989b). Similar examples can be found at other sites in northern Greece, in north-west Anatolia where ovicaprids dominate the early phases of Ilipinar (Buitenhuis in Roodenberg *et al.* 1990: 113–4; Buitenhuis in press) and in south-western Bulgaria where they dominate at Kovachevo (Ninov 1990).

In the north Balkans, however, the range of subsistence strategies would have been more varied; by foraging and by varying strategies of stock management and mobility, people would have offset any of the problems imposed in cropping by the harsher winters and summer rainfall (Halstead 1989a: 32). Solutions to problems posed by climate were found in dispersed, temporary settlement: what Halstead calls short-lived drifting occupation (Halstead 1989a: 40). Northern climate and vegetation would have better suited cattle and pigs than it would sheep and goat (Barker 1985: 147). The pattern, according to Halstead, is of crop-dominated subsistence in the south, including the large villages of south central Bulgaria, and cattle-cum-foraging dominated subsistence to the north (Halstead 1989a: 38). The cattle-dominated faunal assemblages ranged from north-western Anatolia (at least in some of the Fikirtepe culture sites), through southern Romania (in Criş and Dudeşti sites), the western Balkans (in Körös and Starčevo sites), the south-central Bulgarian sites (as at Kazanluk) and to the Gorges, where early faunal assemblages are dominated by red deer and cattle or pig.

Thus the distinction between communities that maintained and consumed cattle from those that maintained and consumed sheep and goat may be important for understanding community structure as seen in the events of consumption. For example, it is possible to argue that cattle-based communities engaged in more open, larger networks of individuals and groups while those based on ovicaprid, focused on small individual units, perhaps centred in and around individual buildings. Is it not significant, therefore, that those communities with faunal remains dominated by cattle are those to be found to the north and are those which built and lived in and around pit-huts, an architecture well suited to a more mobile lifestyle? And conversely, that the sites dominated by sheep and goat are found mainly to the south and have more substantial surface-level architecture of a more exclusive nature?

New plant species and technologies of cultivation

As with animals, so did new plant species enter Balkan lifestyles after 6500 BC. People grew new species of plants, many of which were originally of foreign origin: wheat, barley and legumes. Two wheats (emmer – *Triticum dicoccum* – and einkorn – *Triticum monococum*) were the most commonly grown and of these emmer was most frequent. Both emmer and einkorn were robust strains of wheat: emmer could tolerate and thrive in a wide variety of soils and climatic conditions and made few demands on the mineral and chemical properties of the soil (Barker 1985: 44); einkorn was resistant to cold, heat, drought and fungoid diseases. Both emmer and einkorn were hulled wheats and thus required particular extra processing stages, the significance of which is discussed below. Other wheats also appear: spelt was resistant to fungus, damp and the cold (Barker 1985: 44). Naked wheats, such as durum, were also grown. Hulled barley (*Hordeum vulgare*) was also a common crop.

With wheat and barley, a third staple crop were legumes, especially pulses and grasses. Among the pulses, peas, beans, vetch and lupins appeared frequently; of the grasses lucerne and clover were common (Barker 1985: 46). Legumes would have complemented wheat in the human diet. Although they lack the essential amino acids trytophan and methionine that are present in wheat, legumes are a good source of plant proteins for the human diet. Furthermore, peas and lentils both contain high levels of two other amino acids, isoleucine and lysine, that are not abundant in wheats. Peas and lentils are both cool-weather crops and have relatively short growing seasons. Perhaps more important than their contribution to human nutrition, legumes helped to release nitrogen into the soil (Gregg 1988: 74). Thus, while a variety of different plants were grown at different sites, emmer, barley and legumes were the staples of equal importance (Dennell 1978: 89–90, 162). These three species were the only ones found in large homogeneous samples at Chavdar where adequate recovery and sampling was carried out. That these species were found in large homogeneous samples suggests that they had been prepared for storage or consumption (Dennell 1978: 89–90).

Patterns of plant cultivation and processing

Perhaps more important than the presence and absence of different species at different villages were the ways in which plants were grown and the scales of their cultivation. Methods and scales of cultivation varied between villages and between regions. In some instances garden horticulture was practised; people cultivated small plots of wheat, barley, legumes or, most likely, one, two or all three species together. Placement of plots probably took advantage of existing open, unforested parts of the terrain. Probably individuals or small groups of people tended these plots; consumption of plants grown on any plot would have been limited to the same small group. This scale of garden horticulture would have had limited physical effects on the land beyond those that accompanied the turning of the soil, planting of seeds and the tending, weeding and harvesting of the crop. Cultivation of a garden plot could have occurred as a one-off event with people moving (perhaps for reasons unrelated to plants), perhaps after a single growing, to another area.

Greater investments of labour and longer commitments to particular parts of the terrain would have been required in swiddening, in which larger areas of land were put under cultivation perhaps after brush and trees had been cleared. In such a scheme, cultivation may have taken place for longer periods, perhaps over several years in succession in one place. As with garden horticulture, so also with swiddening the emphasis would have remained on mobility with relatively low investments of labour and time made in the land and an impermanent relationship maintained between people and the areas they cultivated.

Garden horticulture and swiddening were flexible adoptions of cultivation technology. Both allowed group movement as and when necessary; neither tied people to a particular place for long periods. Both techniques would have succeeded in socially open landscapes in which new areas were readily accessible and available for planting and through which people could have moved without restriction. Undoubtedly, in both garden horticulture and swiddening, planting was only one of many different ways of obtaining food, in addition to foraging, hunting, gathering and fishing; the proportion of time and effort devoted to any one method could easily have varied in response to social or environmental cycles and catastrophes without precipitating any overall crisis in human survival. These were flexible systems of food gathering and producing which entailed very limited, if any, lasting connections between people and parts of the landscape.

However, if any one of the variety of food sources acquired a new and elevated status (either economic or social) and thus became the focus of greater attention and investment of labour and time, then flexibility would have been reduced. If the cultivation of cereals and legumes took on this new status, the consequences would have been dramatic. The elevation of the three staple crop species is what marks out the post-6500 BC Balkans.

Intensity of cultivation

There is little evidence for very dramatic increases in the intensity of cultivation until after 5500 BC (see Chapter 5), when cattle were used as animals of traction to pull simple ploughs, or ards, and when people may have started, gradually, clearing increasingly larger areas of land for use in cultivation. Studies of pollen cores and sedimentation suggest that the impact of the earliest cultivators was minimal and short-term (Willis 1995: 15); the first major clearance of the wooded landscape did not occur until several millennia after the first appearance of cultivated plants, that is, not until after c. 4000 BC. Thus, the earliest exploitation of domesticated crops did not entail intensive human alteration of the landscape such as large-scale tree clearance or ploughing. Willis's work adds weight to earlier conclusions by Halstead and others that the impact of early farmers was low and any clearance of the landscape was a gradual process (Halstead 1987: 81). Indeed Halstead has argued for small-scale intensive horticulture (1989b). Quite probably, the early cultivation of crops appeared in many different places as local adoptions among communities whose subsistence base was oriented principally towards foraging (Voytek and Tringham 1989; Chapman and Müller 1990; Dergachev et al. 1991; Zvelebil and Dolukhanov 1991; Gatsov and Özdoğan 1994; Edwards et al. 1996: 120). In the first millennium of cultivation there is little evidence for any agricultural equipment other than simple stick and antler digging tools, mattocks and hoes.

Running alongside the evidence for gradual, small-scale cultivation in some regions is evidence of more intensive planting activities. The finds, admittedly infrequent, of large quantities of plant remains, as in the Slatina house that contained over 200 kg of carbonized seeds, suggest that at some sites people were engaged in more intensive agriculture than was entailed in garden horticulture or swiddening. Without the implementation of animal-traction ploughing, early cultivators could have, perhaps gradually, increased their output in a number of different ways. One possibility would have been to reduce the time during which areas of planting were left fallow between cultivation in swiddening schemes. Other people may have taken advantage of animal manure to fertilize cultivated land. Many communities would have been established in particular places in order to take advantage of naturally irrigated river and stream floodplains. A more radical way to increase yield would have been to reduce the number of cultigens grown at one time in one place through monocropping. It is perhaps not a coincidence that cereal grains respond well to efforts to intensify cultivation; they permit, for example, multiple plantings within a single year. Any or all of these efforts may have been made. The evidence of larger concentrations of seeds and the presence of grinding-stones in many buildings from their earliest phases suggests, as seen at Slatina, that larger-scale cultivation was practised at many contemporary sites.

Locations of sites with reference to soils

One of the few indicators suggesting that the scale of at least some cultivation was more intense than small plot horticulture or swiddening was the location of early villages in arable and fertile micro-zones. When people decided to establish more permanent places for living after 6500 BC, in many cases they chose to do so in places ideally located for cultivation. The distribution of soils of different character and suitability for cultivation varied across the landscapes of the Balkans. In the uplands in areas of steep slope and excessive natural drainage, many soils were shallow, stony and relatively unfertile. The erosion of these upland soils led to build-ups of diluvial fans and the formation of shelves on the edges and in the bottoms of river valleys. These fans and shelves, well drained and moderately fertile, would have been good areas for cultivation (Barker 1985: 87). It is on these fans that many early villages were established.

In the early 1970s Dennell made a detailed study of the locations of villages in three regions of western, southern and central Bulgaria (Dennell 1978). Dennell examined the location and character of early villages in relation to the types, arability and fertility of surrounding soils. He discovered that the emerging tell settlements grew in carefully selected areas of arable and fertile land. The people who established these villages chose to do so in the places they did with the benefit of a detailed knowledge of the varying potentials of different parts of the valleys. Taken as a whole, the Chelopech region, in which people established the village of Chavdar, was of low arable potential; much of the soil was too heavy to till or too stony to cultivate. The people who established Chavdar did so by selecting, within this large region, one of the very few areas of good arable land (Dennell 1978: 78).

Dennell also examined the relationship between the duration of tell village existence (as measured by tell height) and the amount of fertile arable land within 2 km of the village. A clear pattern emerged. The larger sites (both in area and in continuity of occupation and re-occupation) developed in areas with larger amounts of potentially arable land; smaller sites were associated with areas dominated by land better suited to grazing (Dennell 1978: 137). Thus, in central and south-central Bulgaria at least, the fertility and arability of the soil were major factors in the location of villages and in their long-term existence.

142

In northern Greece, van Andel has carried out detailed soil studies around the tell of Platia Magoula Zarkou (van Andel *et al.* 1995). He concluded that the choice of location for the village was intended to take advantage of the regular seasonal flooding for re-nourishing the soils for cultivation; the village began and grew in an active, fertile, arable flood-plain. A similar relationship between the benefits of river flooding and early village location is clear at Chavdar, where the early phases of the village's life were regularly affected by the flooding of the nearby Topolnitsa River (Dennell 1978).

Cereal processing

In addition to the connection between early villages and arable, fertile and regularly re-nourished land, Dennell's work on the Bulgarian sites also documented the types of multiple-stage cereal processing required for inten-sive cultivation. Dennell studied in great detail different types of seed assemblages from within different buildings, from different parts of building interiors and from rubbish areas. From these assemblages, he was able to recognize several stages in the processing of plants and, perhaps less certainly, was able to propose that people were growing single crops via monocropping.

Overall, Dennell's work suggests that, at some of the larger, longer-lived villages, the cultivation of plants had become an intensified food-producing activity that was a major factor in the location and longevity of villages and that left traces of several stages of plant processing which took place within the buildings of the village. These early villages, which became the foci for long sequences of occupation and activity, may very well represent the elevation in significance and perhaps status of cereals and legumes over other foodstuffs.

Consequences of increased commitments to cultivation

The new post-6500 BC commitments to cultivation had important conse-quences for the amount of labour, time and knowledge needed and in the ability to manage that labour. The number of different sets of activities required is impressive, regardless of the scale of cultivation (although large-scale, field-based agriculture, which developed in all parts of the Balkans perhaps not until after 5500 BC, represents another more significant increase in labour and time requirements).

Each set of cultivation and processing activities had different labour, skill, time and scheduling requirements. Thus, in some cases preparation activities included vegetation clearance and tilling of soil. Planting, one of the most labour- and time-consuming activities in the cultivation year, had to be completed within a relatively short period, perhaps within two or three weeks. Once planted, crops required attendance through the various stages of growth and each stage required different concentrations of labour for different periods of time: germination (shoots appearing above ground within two weeks), tillering (growth of secondary shoots within the following two weeks), stem elongation, shooting, flowering and grain maturation. During the growth of the grain, weeding by hand-pulling and hoeing would have been required at relatively frequent intervals and would have been critical for success. Other methods of weed control may have been practised: grazing livestock or rotating crops to prevent weed communities from developing. The ripening of grain occurred over a 10–14-day period and proceeded through a series of stages, the knowledge and observation of which would have been vital for a successful harvest. Within the two weeks of ripening, grain proceeded through stages: milk-ripe, soft-dough ripe, waxy ripe, full-ripe and dead ripe (Gregg 1988). Special attention would have been required, especially in the critical full- and dead-ripe phases. The former stage came on very rapidly and was the best time for harvest; in the latter stage, ears would have become very brittle and the chance of large-scale loss during harvest would have been high. During all of the ripening stages it would have been important to guard against lodging, when crops lay down and harvest is difficult and more laborious; the chances of lodging increased as the crop ripened.

Along with planting, harvesting required the most concentrated investment of labour over the shortest period of time. Planting, of spring-sown crops at least, needed to be scheduled to take place not before the spring floods had finished and yet not delayed either until the ground hardened. The timing of harvest would have been crucial as well. Too early, and the crop would not have been sufficiently ripe and yield would have been low; too late, and grain may have spilled from brittle ears or been lodged by its own weight or rain.

Potential methods of harvesting varied as regards time consumed and consequences for later grain-processing activities. Most time-consuming would have been ear-by-ear plucking, which would have ensured that few weeds were collected, thus reducing processing times, and would have allowed the remnant standing straw to be harvested for other purposes or be left for grazing. Less time- and labour-consuming would have been to harvest handfuls of plants at a time by grabbing and cutting or pulling plants out whole; greater speed in harvesting by this method would have entailed more laborious stages of grain processing.

Processing harvested plants also consisted of stages through which food was made edible, digestible and storable. Hulled wheats like einkorn and emmer required parching on a hearth or in an oven in order to make threshing more effective. For hulled wheats, threshing separated the straw from the seed and its covering; for naked varieties it freed the kernels and chaff from the rachis. Subsequently, grain was cleaned with a winnowing sieve or basket to separate the kernels from the chaff and rachis. A second stage of parching, roasting or malting was required before pounding took place. Additional stages of sieving or winnowing preceded either storage or further processing for consumption such as milling, cooking, brewing.

Dennell's analysis of the seed samples from the Bulgarian sites documented the various stages of plant processing that had taken place in these villages. At both Chavdar and Kazanluk the evidence that emmer was dehusked, cleaned, stored and consumed came from samples taken from house-floors that contained tail-corn left over from cleaning the staple crops and from samples from refuse areas (Dennell 1978: 116). At Chavdar some buildings contained evidence that sieves were used to clean unwanted weeds such as *Galium* and *Polygonum* from cereal harvests (Dennell 1978: 88).

Other solid evidence for processed plants comes from the Slatina house, where over 200 kg of carbonized wheat, barley and beans were found in half a dozen storage containers (Docheva 1990, 1992; Nikolov 1992a). All of the containers held a mixture of seeds, although two were dominated by a single species (container 8 was 99 per cent barley; container 9 was 67 per cent lathyrus); the other four contained varying amounts of emmer (and other wheats), lentils, vetch and peas, each making up between 42 and less than 1 per cent of the pot's contents.

Cycles of plant cultivation

Although, relative to other species, cereals were high-energy providers, they required highly managed programmes of cultivation that entailed not insubstantial technical expertise and effort if repeated success was sought (Ellen 1994: 215). Strategies to reduce labour input or increase relative yield may have included combining different crops with cereals, such as nitrogen-fixing legumes, and planting crops on their own in order to reduce the amount of weeding required and to make effective harvesting easier; monocropping removes subsequent cleaning and sorting stages of crop processing. Additional management strategies may have included artificially adjusting the moisture and nutrient levels of the soil by leaving areas fallow, rotating crops, draining areas, irrigating drier areas or adding organic fertilizers (Ellen 1994: 217). The choice of plant species also would have affected labour requirements; thus the advantage of naked wheats would have been that they required less effort in the processing stages as kernels are easily released in processing. While there is little recoverable evidence for many of these techniques, there is little doubt that, overall, agriculture involved larger inputs of labour than did other comparable methods of obtaining subsistence.

The efforts to reduce labour or increase yields came with increased risks. The use of naked wheats would have increased the chances of losing kernels that fell to earth naturally if harvesting was mistimed and delayed. In this regard the cultivation of naked cereals would have increased the importance of regulating the mobilization of labour and retaining precise specialist knowledges such as knowing the correct time to plant and harvest.

On the basis of the proposed sequences of cultivating and processing events, it is possible to recreate the following annual calendar for the spring planting of wheats such as emmer or einkorn (see D. Bailey 1999).[4] Almost all of the activities related to the growing, tending, harvesting and initial processing of spring-sown cereals would have taken place between March and August. At the end of winter and the beginning of spring the soil required preparation and tilling. Sowing of seeds had to occur next, with initial tending of seedlings and weeding for the first several weeks of plant growth. The remainder of, less intensive, tending and weeding would have taken place from the end of March to the end of July. Harvest would have been a short period of intensive work in August after crops were completely ripe but before they dropped their seeds or were lost to lodging or disease. Initial processing of harvested seed would have required significant labour over the short-term, in August, followed by very little labour for the rest of winter.

Clearly, a calendar for the sowing of autumn crops would alter the temporal parameters but would entail very similar variations in the amount and types of labour required and the scheduling and duration of that labour. Furthermore, the labour and skill requirements of other scheduled activities, such as the grazing calendars proposed above, would have introduced other requirements for the organization and management of people through time and across space.

Cultivation: Conclusion

Any commitment to the new plant species of the post-6500 BC Balkans would have entailed new schedules of activities based around the adaptation of new technologies. These were significant alterations to long-established lifestyles in which knowledge of environmental resources facilitated the scheduled movements of people to landed and mobile resources with changing seasons. A commitment to cultivation was a commitment to particular places in the landscapes, places where people focused their living activities, to which people directed their own labour and skills and attracted the labour and skills of others. Although mobility was still a significant part of life, in animal grazing among other activities, the commitment to cultivation, in any of its different scales, was a significant component of a fundamental shift in the relationship between people and the natural environment; it was a shift evident in the new ways in which people constructed their physical environment as discussed in Chapter 2.

The question of the actual importance of any of the domesticated plant and animal species to the nutritional requirements of Balkan villagers is difficult to assess. There have been no isotopic analyses to suggest patterns

146

of diet such as land-based versus aquatic or marine; in attempts to argue for the numbers of animals needed to support village populations, some work has calculated meat yield per animal for the frequency of that animal at a site (e.g., Dennell 1978). All of these calculations ignore the problems inherent in not knowing enough about the relevant patterns of consumption, let alone in not having reliably sampled information on patterns of deposition.

Perhaps the early phases of the Danube Gorges provide some initial answers. Large game was the prime animal in the faunal records from the Gorge sites; red deer was especially important as was the aurochs, at least in the upper Gorges sites. Pig was also important in the lower Gorges. Fish was a significant component as well and second in importance to large game (Radovanović 1996a: 56). However, fishing may been more of an ideological than a vital economic resource; Radovanović has suggested that fishing tied the communities to spatially limited areas along the river. The presence of fish and water imagery on boulder sculptures and stone elements in buildings supports this suggestion (Radovanović 1996a: 40–1). Similarly, the roles of both red deer and fish may have gone beyond simple matters of economy as deer antler and skulls and fish teeth were common inclusions in inhumations. Thus, among the main species exploited by people in the Gorges, red deer and fish had other, non-economic, meanings and roles for the people of the Gorges. It is perhaps significant that red deer remained of importance, as did wild pig, in burials at other sites of both contemporary and later communities, as will be seen in the use of antler in Hamangia burials discussed in Chapter 6.

As discussed in Chapter 2, Karen Vitelli has suggested that the earliest uses of pottery in the Balkans are best viewed in the light of technological experimentations linked, in part at least, to the collection of medicinal and homeopathic plants and seeds. Perhaps both early potting and the intensified interest in cultivation share a common philosophy that was to do neither with cooking food (for the pots) nor with producing food for nutritional consumption (for the seeds and bones). In this respect, it is highly significant that a small pot at Chavdar contained hundreds of *Rumex* (*crispus*) seeds (Dennell 1978: 85). Dennell suggested that *Rumex* may have been used for its leaves as a spinach-like plant or for its seeds, which could have been ground into flour (Dennell 1978: 91). However, *Rumex* has also been used traditionally as medicine to loosen the bowels; perhaps this represents another, less acknowledged, consequence of the changes in the post-6500 BC Balkans. If this was the use of the Chavdar *Rumex*, then the role of early plant cultivation and, perhaps more importantly, the use to which early plants were put, may have been much less closely related to purely economic ends.

Vitelli reminds us that with the appearance of domesticated plants and animals after 6500 BC, it was only the species that changed. The Neolithic diet was not very different from that of the previous millennia. Although the means of acquisition and the quantity and quality of foodstuffs had changed due to domestication, the food itself was little changed and required no new forms of processing (Vitelli 1989: 25).

After 6500 BC Balkan people supplemented existing sources of nutrition with new, non-indigenous species of plants and animals and through the application of new technologies to manage the cultivation of particular plants and the breeding of particular animals. The importance of these changes lies less in any nutritional advantages of new species than in their organization requirements and social consequences. As with all of the changes to people's lives that occurred at this time in the Balkans, the rule across the region is one of variation.

While there was variation in practices and preferences for producing and consuming different plants and animals, there is no reason to assume a logical unilinear sequential development from one scale of cultivation to another, from garden horticulture to swiddening to larger field-based culti- vation. Nor can one assume that the practice of type or intensity of cultivation at one village precluded the practice of other types and scales at other contemporaneous and neighbouring villages. The poor resolution of existing data prevents any closer investigation into the degree, stimulus or consequences of such potential variation.

Also unanswered must remain the questions of how much of what we understand as novel in plants and animals after 6500 BC was indeed entirely new. How revolutionary were patterns of behaviour that were common in previous millennia, such as knowledge of the environment? How new was the application of new species to existing strategies such as the grazing of ovicaprids and cattle? How radical was the application of new technolo- gies to traditionally exploited species such as cattle and pig? Much of the novelty of the faunal and floral material may have had more to do with what people did with plants and animals, why they grew, slaughtered (or harvested) and consumed them, where they carried out these activities and with whom. Perhaps the uses of plants and animals, like the contemporary new applications of permanent architecture, were but symptoms of larger changes in how people defined themselves as individuals, as members of groups tethered to particular places. It is especially curious that in the south these new architectural complexes contained what appear to be completely novel sets of plant and animal remains (sheep and goat and wheats) that are dominated by a very high proportion of domestic to wild, with a predom- inance of ovicaprid. What else was going on in the landscape around the more visible (both archaeologically and prehistorically) villages? It is highly likely that people were engaged in other activities involving plants and, especially, animals at less permanent, less conspicuous non-village sites that have drawn little archaeological attention to date. In this respect, it is highly significant that some animals, such as cattle, appear in patterns suggesting that primary butchery, and perhaps consumption, was taking place away from the permanent villages at yet undiscovered activity areas. Dennell's proposal for smaller grazing sites for the Nova Zagora region is another possibility for spatial variation in activity.

The social significances of plant and animal management

The role of these new elements in community life was symptomatic of other developments in post-6500 BC life and had important repercussions for how people interacted, that is, for the social organization and structure of the time. In this respect, the major importance of these new species, of cereals especially, may have had more to do with their inherent require- ments for scheduled labour or varying amounts and skills required at different times of the cultivation cycle than it had to do with any change in nutri- tional benefit.

Cutting across the economic variability evident after 6500 BC were new relationships between people. These new relationships and their core mech- anisms and facilities are what made the post-6500 BC human exploitation of plants and animals distinct from what had come before and, undoubt- edly, from what continued in many places for long periods of time after 6500 BC. In these new relationships, the plants and animals themselves occupied a secondary role and are perhaps best understood as symptoms of deeper changes running through many other aspects of community lifestyles. The changes are most explicit in the requirements for managing animals and cultivating plants and in the ways in which new identities emerged, were required and were created.

Schedules and organizing labour

The timing and labour requirements for successful cereal cultivation presented not insubstantial challenges to post-6500 BC communities, regard- less of whether crops were spring- or autumn-sown. The ability to bring together and motivate the requisite number of appropriately skilled people at the required time to carry out the correct tasks would have been an important skill for an individual or group of individuals to possess; indeed it would have been critical in the larger-scale programmes of cultivation. Different parts of cultivation and processing would have required different abilities; people possessing requisite skills and their reputation in supplying them successfully would have formed an important part of those people's individual identities.

The recognition of the range of abilities required need not mean that every member of a community participated in every aspect of cultivation or even in any part of cultivation. Other elements of village life entailed similar ranges of skills. Similarly, particular individuals had different abilities

149

and experience in practising these skills. Ranges of skills, such as those related to animal grazing, knowledge of the environment, gathering plants, making and decorating pottery vessels, or any of a wide range of other activities, would have been as important as abilities which were linked to cultivation.

The major distinction that separates cultivation from other contemporary activities, however, is that the organizational skills required for successful cultivation entailed the ability to aggregate, motivate and then disperse relatively large groups of people. In this the organization of cereal cultivation, processing and storage required the skills of sociopolitics as much as it required the skills of scheduling sowing and harvesting or timing the parching of grain prior to grinding.

Equally important must have been the new perceptions people held of the land and its living and dead (e.g. mineral) resources. The differential distribution of these resources, particularly of soils with different potential for grazing and especially for cultivation, was a fundamental contributor to the new identities that must have been assigned to particular places.

If one of the symptoms of larger-scale cultivation was the emergence of new types and strengths of identities for individuals (as organizers, as labourers – skilled and unskilled), for places and for expressing the relationships between places and people, then the significance of the contemporary developments in organizing the built environment may become clearer.

As argued in Chapter 2, variation in the forms of architecture distinguished between relatively small, temporary pit-huts with little if any internal division or permanent areas for different activities and, on the other hand, the more substantial surface-level structures with multiple rooms and activity areas. It was aggregations of the latter that formed early villages; the former are best understood as camps. Furthermore, one can distinguish between a northern distribution for pit-huts and a southern distribution of above-ground structures.

In terms of faunal evidence, the pit-huts are associated with higher proportions of cattle and the surface structures with ovicaprids. In this sense, the pit-hut sites represent the built environment of communities that focused their animal management on grazing and herding animals (mainly cattle, with some ovicaprids) while also benefitting from the independence of pigs browsing in local forests. In such a reconstruction, pit-hut groups may have been larger, more flexible and perhaps less exclusive communities living lives in which large herbivore management, slaughtering and consumption was founded on more open relationships between people and across several landscapes. The dominance of cattle in pit-hut sites is not absolute across the regions; Körös sites have a predominance of ovicaprids. Perhaps the correct analogy is with hunter-gatherer and forager groups who managed their existence through the flexibility offered by mobility and periodic group fissioning, through sharing within and between groups, and by engaging in open distributions of slain animals and the requisite feasting and alliance networking. The extra-domestic consumption requirements of cattle would have been especially significant for these communities, requiring large-scale consumption events.

Villages of surface-level structures represent something altogether different: the emergence of smaller, more exclusive social units based on individual buildings. As argued in Chapter 2 and as will be elaborated in Chapter 8, these buildings mark the emergence of the household as a funda-mental unit of social and economic decision-making. Compared to the more open, flexible groups of more mobile grazers or foragers, the occupants of these households lived in more permanent buildings, herded mostly ovicaprids and cultivated and processed cereal grains in a scheduled and relatively intensive fashion.

In such villages, the organization of activities was based on, and took place within, individual buildings. Communities and groups within commu-nities were attached in a very physical fashion not only to particular places in the landscape but also to particular places within the village; thus membership of household or village was fixed to physical structures perhaps as suggested in Chapter 3 through rituals involving representational mate-rial culture such as figurines. Any co-operation of labour or sharing of resources would not have extended, on one level, beyond the physical dimensions of the household and on other levels beyond the physical dimen-sions of the village aggregation. Again, there is variation within this general pattern: for example, the use of inter-building activity areas at some sites such as Achilleion, although these appear to be the exception.

CHAPTER CONCLUSIONS

The trends in formally disposing of the deceased, acquiring and working flint, planting, cultivating and processing plants and tending animals refine our understanding of the components of identities proposed at a general level for the overtly expressive material culture described in Chapter 3.

In almost all of the burials of individuals, a physical link was created between the deceased and the structures of the newly created social envi-ronments. Just as it was suggested that anthropomorphic figurines were used in ceremonies to declare membership within households, so also can one contend that inhumations of bodies in and around buildings were declarations of household membership. The pattern of child and infant burials is important in this respect. The birth of a child would have added to household membership and its core identity. Birth was not prob-lematic to the continued existence of a household or the maintenance of its membership.

Like birth, death was an anticipated component of household reproduction (Pine 1996: 453–4). However, death contained potential threats to
household coherence and continuity. A good death, that is a natural death
of an adult, would have posed little or no threat to household existence.
An untimely death, such as that of an infant or child, was very different
and would have threatened the continuity of the household and may have
required special, perhaps ritual, activities to counteract the danger. Perhaps
the intramural burial of children and the deposition of disarticulated
body parts into house floors and into their surroundings are evidence of
such rituals occasioned by untimely deaths. If intramural burial expresses
relationships between individuals and households, perhaps the large proportion of personal ornaments in the Gorges burials suggests the expression of
identity on the level of the individual within a community. Perhaps the
inclusions of animal and fish bones were part of expressions of individual
knowledges, skills or group affiliation.

In a similar way, though not evident in material culture or burial, the
skills and knowledges required in the different activities of cultivating
and processing plants and in tending animals were parts of the personal
identities which distinguished particular individuals from others and may
have been part of what distinguished one household from its neighbours.

SUMMARY

In this chapter, I have argued that in many elements of post-6500 BC life
in the Balkans one can recognize threads of continuity with earlier millennia.
Thus there are clear links, in some places at least, in lithic production techniques, some aspects of burial and the general range of knowledges about
environment, animals, plants and seasonality employed in animal tending
and management.

In these elements, however, there were important distinctions from
previous traditions. Most important among these were the focus of burial on
the house and the village, the organization of larger-scale cultivation and
processing of some plants, and the adoption of new lithic working strategies
that approached flint tool-making with a longer view to planning for tasks
to be undertaken and in the preparation of blades to perform these tasks.

Most distinctive – and this continues arguments made in the previous
chapter – is that at a general interpretive level most of the activities of
burial, plant and animal management and, even, lithic acquisition can be
seen within new trends in displaying and arranging human relationships
based on personal and group identities. These trends, in combination with
those noted in the previous two chapters continue over the next 1000–1500
years, although there are important developments in their scale and degree.
These developments are the subjects of the next two chapters.

5

CONTINUITIES, EXPANSION AND ACCELERATION OF BUILDING AND ECONOMY (5500–3600 BC)

The ways in which people built their social environments and managed their natural world during the two millennia after 5500 BC were marked with the continuity, expansion and acceleration of the trends that had developed from the previous millennium. As with the previous millennium there is variation between the different regions in how these changes and continuities occurred. Patterns of behaviour and activity that had developed earlier in other areas now appeared for the first time in new places, as in the emergence of tell villages in northern Bulgaria and southern Romania. In other regions some new developments appear infrequently, if at all, for example, the very limited role of tells in the western Balkans. Acceleration of economic patterns follows a pattern of broader similarities across regions.

THE BUILT ENVIRONMENT

From the middle of the sixth millennium BC people continued to construct their social environments in various ways in different regions of the Balkans. In many regions buildings were now larger than in the previous millennium and contained more internal divisions. Houses were made of more durable materials and increasingly became the focus of a wider range of activities practised in the same place over longer periods of time. People continued to mark the boundaries within and between buildings as well as at the limits of settlements. These developments towards durable, continuous, bounded settlements were not absolute. In some regions loose aggregations of pit-huts continued. In others, there occurred important changes such as the first appearance of tell villages. There are seven regions in which variations in development are evident: the lower Danube; south-central Bulgaria; Serbia, north-western Bulgaria and southern Hungary; south-western Bulgaria; eastern Hungary; northern Greece; and north-west Anatolia.

153

The lower Danube

The most dramatic changes in building strategies occurred north of the Stara Planina, or Balkan Mountains, along the lower Danube in northern Bulgaria and southern Romania. The appearance of tell settlements in this region from the beginning of the fifth millennium BC is striking. From a landscape of terraces and hill-slopes dotted with small collections of temporarily occupied, short-lived simple pit-dwellings and surface structures, the river and stream plains were increasingly marked with long-duration villages (see Figure I.1 on p. 4–5).

The north Balkan shift to tell settlement was not complete or immediate. With the early exception of the tell village at Samovodyane, people continued to dig pit-huts into the soil of river plateaux in northern Bulgaria, as at Podgoritsa-platoto (Figure 5.1), Usoe (Figure 5.2) (Todorova 1973b) and Kachitsa. Some of these sites, like the one at Kachitsa, were rebuilt through several architectural phases. Similarities in material culture link some of these pit-huts with the early phases of some of the tell villages in the region. Thus the lithics from the Usoe pit-huts are comparable to those from the early levels of the Golyamo Delchevo tell; indeed the earliest level of Golyamo Delchevo was an aggregation of pit-huts.

In southern Romania the pattern of digging pit-huts in sites of the Boian culture continued methods that had been evident in the Dudeşti sites of the early and middle sixth millennium BC, as discussed in Chapter 3. As to the south of the Danube, some of the material culture from the Boian pit-huts had links with that found at the base of tells as at Căscioavele, Hirşova, Glina and Gumelniţa.

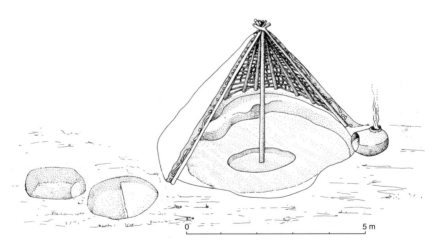

Figure 5.1 Reconstruction of pit-hut and pits at Podgoritsa-platoto (after Todorova and Vajsov 1993)

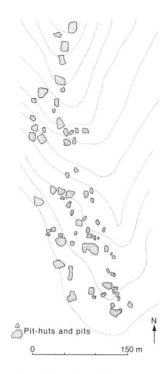

Pit-huts and pits

N

0   150 m

Figure 5.2 Plan of pit-hut aggregation at Usoe in northern Bulgaria (after Vajsov 1990b)

While pit-huts dominated the earlier Boian sites, in the final phases of the sequence, surface-level structures became more frequent. The end of the Boian sequence is marked by an increase in the number of sites, although the total number of Boian sites, from all of its subphases, does not exceed fifty.

Contemporaneously with the Boian pit-huts, similar structures were created to the east, on both sides of the Danube, in Dobrudzha. Here, in the second half of the sixth millennium BC, small pit-huts (up to 2 m in diameter) contain cultural material of the early phases of the Hamangia culture sequence, Hamangia I and II. At Durankulak on the Bulgarian Black Sea coast people built two somewhat larger oval pit-huts; one was 7.8 × 5.4 m (Dimov 1982; Haşotti 1997: 24). The interior of the larger pit-hut was divided into three sections by walls made of well compacted clay. An entrance to the hut was in the northern section, a rectangular hearth was built in the central area and a bench was constructed in the southern part. By the end of the sixth millennium BC, more pit-huts like these were being built in Dobrudzha. Floors were made of beaten earth and walls of clay, mud and wood (Haşotti 1997: 24). Some pit-huts, like those

155

at Durankulak, are distinctive for their larger size. One, at Medgidia Cocoaşa, was 4 m in diameter and contained in its southern part a hearth and a large quantity of pottery, figurines and tools; the northern part contained animal bones, the majority of which were of cattle. In a smaller pit, at Tîrguşor Urs, people had stored a very large number of flint tools. Similar pit-huts have been found at Ceamurlia de Jos (Berciu 1966), Limanu (Galbenu 1970) and at Baia-Goloviţa (Berciu 1966; Lăzurcă 1980).

At some sites, such as Baia-Goloviţa, next to the pit-huts were built rectangular surface-level structures with thin walls made of twigs and reeds (Haşotti 1997: 24). As with many other pit-hut camps from the previous millennium, structures were scattered across living areas; the three huts from Medgidia-Satu Nou were spread over an area of 500 sq m (Haşotti 1987).

Combinations of pit-huts and surface-level structures were being built together more frequently in the first half of the fifth millennium BC, in the third phase of the Hamangia sequence. More buildings overall were constructed. The majority were surface-level structures, as were nine of the ten buildings from this phase at Tîrguşor Urs (Haşotti 1997: 24). Often, the surfaces upon which buildings were created had been specially prepared. One building at Tîrguşor Urs was built over well trampled ground; another was constructed over a ground-layer of burnt earth.

By the middle of the fifth millennium BC all of the buildings were surface-level structures. Buildings were modest in size (12–15 sq m) but the quality of construction had improved. At Ceamurlia de Jos walls were made with the trunks of small trees and saplings and hearths were constructed on thin floors that had been built over levelled ground surfaces (Haşotti 1997: 25). In some of these buildings, grinding-stones were built into the floors. At some distance from the main aggregation of buildings at Ceamurlia de Jos two structures were built over a surface of burnt red earth. These buildings were separated by a path and the excavator has suggested they represent a special place where visitors were received (Berciu 1966: 147–8).

The small aggregations of Hamangia surface-level structures and pit-huts were located on terraces, on the slopes of hills or, in the later phases, along shorelines. Caves were also a focus for activities, although they may have been used only on a seasonal basis. There is little if any evidence that these structures were rebuilt through successive generations (Haşotti 1997: 23).

The emergence of tells

After the middle of the fifth millennium BC, in southern Romania and in northern Bulgaria, people began to rebuild their villages over long periods of time in the same particular place in the landscape. Indeed, there were now many more villages being built. The increase in the numbers of sites and the emergence of tell settlements suggest a filling-in of the lower Danube landscape. Todorova has estimated that in north-eastern Bulgaria alone there were over two hundred settlements in use at some time in the fifth millennium BC (Todorova 1986: 272–9). Almost all of these were new tell villages.

Most frequently tells developed on small hills or peninsulas near the forks of rivers. Less frequently they were established bounded on one side by a river, stream or dry valley, and on the other by the wooded slopes of low mountain foothills (Todorova 1986: 44). Access to a combination of water resources, forested foothills and arable land were priorities.

As with earlier tells in the southern regions, the tell villages of the lower Danube were well organized aggregations of many-roomed buildings of substantial size. They were coherently laid out settlements built to a plan that was repeated over successive generations of house reconstruction through long periods. The best documented of these tells are those that Henrietta Todorova and her colleagues excavated in north-eastern Bulgaria at Ovcharovo, Polyanitsa, Turgovishte, Radingrad and Golyamo Delchevo (Todorova *et al.* 1975; I. Angelova 1982, 1986a, 1986b; T. Ivanov 1982; Todorova *et al.* 1983).

All of these tells are strikingly similar in the ordered layouts of their villages and in the similarly arranged floorplans of individual structures (Figure 5.3). Buildings were rectilinear and large, measuring up to 10×10 m. Narrow paths separated individual houses, which stood alone or abutted other buildings. Almost without variation buildings were oriented with their longer axes running N–S. The structures themselves were robust affairs made of large wooden posts sunk into foundation trenches and joined together with wooden planks or branches covered with mud or clay.

In all building horizons, although less so in the earliest, as in horizon I at Ovcharovo I, buildings were internally divided into separate, mainly rectilinear rooms. Some buildings contained many rooms: up to three or four in the smaller, more short-lived tells of Radingrad and Turgovishte and up to six in the larger and longer-used village at Ovcharovo. Most buildings contained an oven; some contained several ovens in separate rooms. Grinding-stones were increasingly frequent as were low clay platforms and benches built along the insides of room walls. Pits were dug into building floors and, in the later horizons, substantial permanent storage facilities, such as the 2×3 m grain silo at Ovcharovo, appeared. At the same time, concentrations of increasingly large pottery vessels, some with capacities up to 200 litres, appeared in some houses (D. Bailey 1991).

The complexity of the internal architecture of these buildings is impressive. Some of the rooms were located very 'deep' within houses, with access from the outside requiring passage through three, four or more intermediary rooms. At some sites, such as Polyanitsa, access to the innermost areas of some houses required passage through six or seven other rooms. Less durable partitions were erected across room interiors using smaller posts set

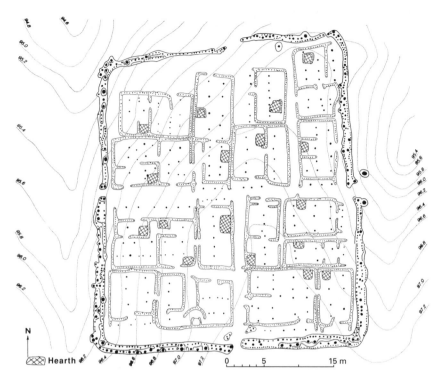

Figure 5.3 Plan of village at Polyanitsa (phase II) (after Todorova 1986)

into floors. Other, perhaps mobile, partitions are represented in the miniature clay 'screens' found at many sites (Figure 5.4) (Marangou 1996: 189;
1992: 180). As in the tell village houses of other regions in previous
millennia, people also demarcated internal building space by dedicating
particular interior space to different activities such as grinding, parching
and storing grain, weaving textiles and storing agricultural tools.

Successive phases of village reconstruction marked community residence
through long periods of time, regardless of any short- or long-term breaks
in occupation. The emphasis on continuity of successive buildings was such
that one can speak of living structures tethered through time by repeated,
perhaps ritual, events of building repair and reconstruction (D. Bailey 1990;
1996c).

Miniature clay house models are frequent finds (Figure 5.5). Many of
these tectomorphs have detailed renderings of exterior wall decoration,
window location, and gable ornament as well as internal arrangements of
furniture, ovens and grain bins. Few of the models have survived unbroken
and their use and fragmentation may have been associated with rituals
of construction, repair or re-occupation. Perhaps the suggestions made in

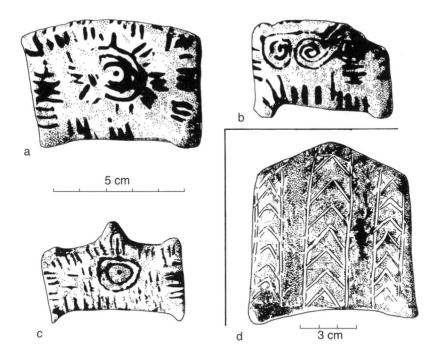

Figure 5.4 Miniature clay models of room partitions from Ovcharovo: a–c) horizon
IX; d) horizon V (after Todorova *et al.* 1983)

Chapter 3 about the role of anthropomorphic figurines in ceremonies of
household membership can be applied to these building representations as
well. Perhaps similar ceremonies were played out to declare the positions
and identities of individual houses and households in relation to other
households within the same village. The precision of building reconstruction may have complemented these rituals by expressing claims of long-term
residence of individual households by ancestors.

In view of the substantial size of individual buildings within each tell
horizon, the extent of the land covered by each village was surprisingly
small. Unlike some of the earlier tells in Greece, these in the north Balkans
appear cramped, with buildings butted up tightly to each other. Chapman
has calculated the proportion of space that was built upon to that which
was kept free of structures. He found that the proportion of built to unbuilt
space was high, reaching 8 : 1 in some phases of the lower Danube tells
(Chapman 1990: 68). This suggests that almost all activities taking place
on these tells occurred within buildings; indeed some activities, such as
grinding grain, were carried out in the deep, inner rooms. Except for
narrow path- and alley-ways, there was little open space available between
individual structures.

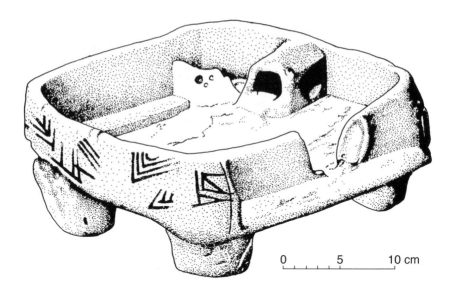

0   5   10 cm

Figure 5.5 Tectomorphic miniature from Ovcharovo (after Todorova *et al.* 1983)

As with the earlier tells to the south, there was something permanent and decidedly fixed about the character of these villages. The fact that they developed in the direction they did, up and not out, owed much to the continuing development, across the Balkans, of people's perceptions of space and boundary constraints. These perceptions focused on what areas were appropriate and necessary for building and what areas were not. In some cases these constraints were environmental. There is evidence from at least one tell from this region, at Podgoritsa, suggesting that changes in the level of the local water-table played an episodic role in confining building and activity areas to the tell itself (Bailey *et al.* 1998).

As with other earlier tells to the south, the boundaries of those of the fifth millennium BC lower Danube were frequently marked out physically, especially during early stages in a village's life; the early phases of the tell villages at Ovcharovo (Horizons I–IX) and Polyanitsa (Horizons I–IV) have perimeter banks made of stone and earth as well as post-and-daub walls. The recent soil augering work at Podgoritsa has revealed part of a ditch and two banks at the site's north-west perimeter (Bailey *et al.* 1998). It is perhaps significant that these boundary banks and ditches, which were also common north of the Danube at tells of the Gumelniţa, and Salcuţa culture (Dumitrescu *et al.* 1983), go out of use as the villages developed into more substantial tells and as the village took on its own visibly monumental presence in the landscape.

South-central Bulgaria

In south-central Bulgaria, changes in the built environment, though not so dramatic as those which occurred to the north, were equally important. As discussed in Chapter 2, in this region people had been building and rebuilding generations of surface-level structures in the same places since the beginning of the sixth millennium BC. After the middle of the sixth millennium BC, however, important alterations are evident in the patterns of building organization at existing settlement tells.

Changes include an increase in the size of individual buildings, an increase in the number of rooms within buildings and in the organizational complexity of the arrangement of rooms and space inside these buildings. As occurred to the north, there was an increase in the number of these more permanent sites in the south where sites, such as Azmak, were also increasingly bounded by perimeter walls and banks. At Yunatsite a complex set of internal demarcations of village space culminated in a deep ditch cutting off a third of the tell. Initial excavation reports suggest that the bank of the ditch had a palisaded fence built along its interior bank (Matsanova 1992; Katincharov and Matsanova 1993, 1995; Katincharov *et al.* 1995). Many of the features of village architecture that had been present in the south in the preceding millennia continued.

Serbia, north-western Bulgaria and southern Hungary

As was clear for the late sixth and even into the fifth millennium BC in the lower Danube, aggregations of buildings need not have developed into vertically repeated tell settlements. Many of the earlier Romanian and Bulgarian sites, such as Usoe, were unenclosed camps and villages of pit-dwellings and surface structures. Indeed a case could be made for rooting the developed tell villages in local late pit-huts and early surface-structures. In the western Balkans it is much clearer that tells such as Vinča and Gomolava and large flat sites, like those which developed at Selevac and Opovo, shared the landscape.

The major variation marking the western Balkans from the lower Danube and south-central Bulgaria was the continued presence (and perhaps dominance) of sites which, though in use over long periods of time, did not develop vertically into multi-level tells. In many places successive generations of buildings expanded horizontally. In their arrangement of buildings and patterns of rebuilding, these villages appear less bounded and enclosed than those in the east and south-east. To the west the proportions of built to unbuilt space are much lower than for the tells of the lower Danube; Chapman's calculations of built-to-unbuilt space for the western unenclosed sites range from 1 : 3 to 1 : 13 and document a significant difference from the ratios for lower Danube sites such as Polyanitsa and Ovcharovo, which ranged from 6 : 1 to 1 : 1 (Chapman 1990: 68).

Selevac

One of the best studied examples of an unenclosed flat site in the western Balkans is Selevac, excavated in the late 1970s and early 1980s by Ruth Tringham and Dušan Krštić (Tringham and Krštić 1990a). Selevac was the largest of many flat unenclosed sites in this part of Serbia; it covered an area of more then 200 m × 300–400 m spreading up the western bank of a stream. The settlement was established on high ground close to the river floodplain and its inhabitants would have been able to take advantage of the well drained fertile soils and rich forests (Tringham and Krštić 1990a: 2).

Selevac was rebuilt through four major architectural phases (I–IV) and was in use over seven hundred years beginning at the end of the sixth millennium BC. The village is of particular interest as these four phases cover an important shift in the ways in which layouts of unenclosed sites were organized and the ways in which buildings were constructed. It is the later phases of the Selevac occupation (the end of phase II and all of phases III and IV) that are of most relevance here.

The later phases of Selevac are characterized by a shift to more permanent architecture and to buildings with more highly organized interiors. In phase II the first new elements of building construction technique appeared; people used dense rows of posts to support deeply embedded walls, which they covered with thin layers of clay plaster (Tringham and Stevanović 1990a: 108). More significant new developments in construction appeared in phases III–IV, when wall-posts were packed more solidly in their foundation holes and walls were covered with a thick layer of clay. Central roof-support posts had become larger and buildings were wider (now 4.5–5.0 m).

When structures were rebuilt at Selevac during the later phases, they were rebuilt adjacent to their predecessors, with continuity between generations of houses represented in similarities of floorplan alignment; the longest axes of houses from successive phases were aligned WSW–ENE. Tringham suggests that this horizontal continuity of settlement was equivalent to the successive vertical rebuildings of the tell settlements (Tringham and Krštić 1990b: 587).

Phase III–IV structures were built to last. Tringham suggests that while phase I and II constructions may have lasted up to thirty years, the buildings from the later phases lasted for at least three times as long. Furthermore, people invested more time in planning and constructing these later houses. Tringham reads this as an increase in people's commitment to the land (Tringham and Stevanović 1990a: 111). In addition to longer-lasting houses, as new land was built upon when the village expanded horizontally, the total area taken in by the site expanded in the later phases. With successive horizontal expansions, the focus of settlement gradually shifted up the slope in an unconstrained manner.

In these later phases of the village the interiors of individual buildings became the principal foci for domestic and production activities such as food-processing, food storage, pottery making, textile production and, perhaps, copper working. Several buildings contained ovens; production activities were located deep within buildings in areas furthest from the doorways (Tringham and Stevanović 1990a: 112). Although initial preparation of lithic raw materials took place away from the site, final stone tool processing now occurred inside individual buildings (Voytek 1990: 483). In earlier phases of Selevac storage of foodstuffs probably occurred outside buildings in shallow clay-lined pits; in the later phases storage occurred in large pots dug into the floors of houses deep inside buildings, perhaps even lodged in second storeys (Tringham and Krštić 1990a: 114). Analysis of non-vessel ceramics also suggests that more activities were now taking place inside buildings and that, overall, a greater significance was now attached to building interiors (Tringham and Krštić 1990a: 350).

Similar patterns are evident at other sites in the western Balkans. In the last quarter of the sixth millennium BC, after a long period of abandonment, people started building again at Divostin (phase II). Buildings had thick, compact floors (8–12 cm thick) with wooden subflooring constructed from split beams. Walls were embedded into foundation trenches. Bases of ovens were set into floors as were clay, rectilinear or curvilinear bins. Most buildings contained one hearth; some had several. In some buildings, people built tables out of daub. Some structures were segmented into two, three or four separate rooms (Figure 5.6). Although the spread of buildings covered 13–14 ha (Bogdanović 1988: 85), buildings were grouped into four mini-aggregations with individual houses separated by 3–4 m and each aggregation by 10–25 m. Areas between mini-aggregations were empty of building material.

In some buildings people were weaving textiles (Rasson 1988: 337–8). Distinct concentrations of lithics, copper and animal remains document clear spatial segregation of other activities as well. Small chipped-stone tools were made and used in the south-western end of building 15 (McPherron and Gunn 1988: 365, figures 13.7–9). Stone axes were manufactured in building 10 and in, or near, building 14 (McPherron and Gunn 1988: 365). A pit was completely filled with thin porcellanite flakes produced from flaking roughouts in preparation for grinding; the number of flakes (1 cu metre in total) represents the production of several hundred axes (McPherron and Christopher 1988: 486). Buildings 10 and 14 each contained concentrations of antler tools. In addition to the dense concentration of debris from axe production, a second major accumulation of debris represents a disposal area for animal bones.

Taking Selevac and Divostin as well documented examples, it is clear that the unenclosed flat sites of the western Balkans, though different in several respects, shared many of the themes that characterize the changes

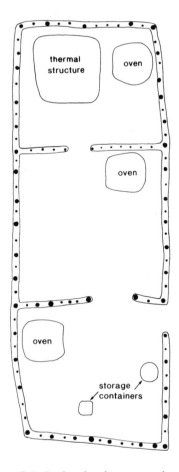

Figure 5.6 Surface-level structure from Divostin II (house 14). Orientation NNE-SSW; width 6.4m; length 16.2m (after Bogdanović 1988)

occurring during the fifth millennium BC to the east and south-east. Chief among these was an increasing focus on individual buildings and on the separation of activities and people by the erection of internal site boundaries and barriers.

House destruction

As in many other parts of the Balkans, the later Selevac buildings were burnt down before episodes of rebuilding and at the end of the village's use. Tringham and Stevanović have suggested that such conflagrations were deliberate and were focused on individual houses and households (Tringham and Krstić 1990a: 115; Tringham 1991, 1994; Stevanović 1997). Stevanović carried out a detailed analysis of the forensics of building burning at Selevac. She documented the multiple locations of high-temperature fires in particular parts of house interiors, traced the paths of these fires and underlined the difficulty of completely burning wattle if additional fuel were not added at the time of firing and if several ignition fires were not started within any single structure (Stevanović 1997). Stevanović concluded that the fires, at Selevac at least, were deliberately set conflagrations intended to destroy the buildings.

This research is important. It focuses attention, once again, on the developing importance of houses and households and emergence of a new ideology of buildings manifest not only in rituals of construction, continued occupation and membership but also of destruction. Just as the breaking of figurines may have played a role in ceremonies of negating household membership, so the intentional burning of houses may have played a similar role in declaring (or precipitating) the end of household units and of the cohesion of co-resident groups. Similar patterns of house burnings are found across the Balkans towards the end of the period considered in this chapter; their occurrence should demand that similar attention is directed at the potential social dynamics of house destruction as is devoted to processes of building.

Overall, Selevac demonstrates that even in villages that did not develop vertically into tells, there are clear indicators of increasing attention devoted to buildings. This is evident in the new importance of durability, in the increased complexity of internal organization and the increase in the number and range of domestic and production activities now included within buildings. Attention to buildings, through construction, reconstruction and deliberate destruction, suggests that a new social ideology based on the house and, probably, the household, was present in both east and west Balkans by the fifth millennium BC.

South-western Bulgaria

Contemporary sites in south-western Bulgaria extend the geographic range of similarities in the developments in building social environments, especially of the expansion of settlement into new areas. From the mid sixth millennium BC, there was a peak in settlement activity in the Struma valley (Pernicheva 1995: 114). Sites were established in both the valley bottoms and at altitude as at Petrovo in the alpine belt of the Slavyanka mountains. In the southern Struma valley there are many newly founded sites, like Damyanitsa, that are large, covering dozens of hectares. Houses were rebuilt through several successive generations: three at both Damyanitsa and the smaller site, Topolnitsa.

In the northern Struma valley, there was continuity with earlier occupations of sites as at Strumsko and Bulgarchevo; the former had three generations of building, the latter four (Pernicheva 1995). A fortification system has been claimed for Strumsko (Pernicheva 1993; 1995: 126), although it may be more accurate to recognize this as a village boundary marker. In the first half of the fifth millennium BC sites of the lower and middle Struma valley had cultural affinities with those in Aegean Thrace and eastern Macedonia (specifically Sitagroi and Paradimi) and not surprisingly some buildings were made with sun-dried mud-blocks (Todorova 1995a: 86).

One of the better studied sites in the lower Struma is the unenclosed settlement at Slatino, which dates from the first quarter of the fifth millennium BC (S. Chokadziev 1986; 1995: 141). The site covered 0.5 ha and had five building horizons. Individual buildings were rectangular and large, ranging from 4.0–5.5 m to 2.5–4.4 in length and width, respectively. Building floors were made of trampled yellow clay and, while there is little preserved evidence of wall construction, the evidence that does survive reveals that some walls had engraved decoration and were painted white.

The best preserved features from most building interiors are ovens constructed on stone bases and covered with thin layers of clay. In the site's earlier horizons ovens were less substantial, being built on bases made of smaller foundation stones; the ovens of the later horizons were made with large stones and suggest an increase in concern for durability of features and perhaps of longer continuity of occupation. All of the ovens were large (1.30–1.46 m in length, 0.85–1.30 m in width) and had vaulted roofs and two openings. Adjacent to some ovens were clay bins for storing grain and in several instances a grinding-stone was embedded into building floors. Clay platforms were also found near the ovens. Slatino's final occupation phases were destroyed by burning (S. Chokadziev personal communication).

The attention given to oven construction and the increasingly substantial oven-bases is magnified by the production and display of miniature clay models of ovens. Oven models were decorated in a variety of ways. Many bore complex incised designs; modelled applications of zoomorphic forms are common. On the base of several models were incised patterns which appear to depict a system of notation, counting or recording (Figure 5.7) (S. Chokadziev 1984; D. Bailey 1993). Again, as in the tectomorphs of tell villages to the west, the oven models suggest that people were using and perceiving particular parts of their built environments in special new ways which may have involved ceremonies and rituals that employed representational material culture to make claims for continuity of residence or reaffirmation of household identity.

With the later part of the fifth millennium BC many more sites were in use in the Struma valley, as at Dyakovo during the early phase and later at Kolarovo. Most sites were new occupations located on terraces and have thin cultural layers (Pernicheva 1995: 130–1). Buildings were rectangular, megaron-shaped structures constructed with mud-blocks (Todorova

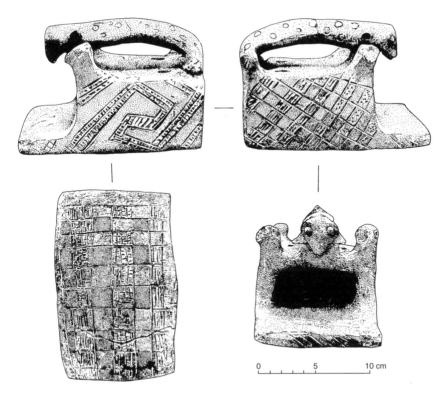

Figure 5.7 Miniature clay model of an oven from Slatino (after Todorova 1986)

1995a: 89). At Kolarovo two dwellings from its earlier occupation phase were destroyed by fire (Pernicheva 1995: 131).

Tells are absent from the Struma valley. Most settlements have cultural layers less than 2 m thick and many have no evidence of multiple episodes of occupation and rebuilding. Sites cover large areas and, if any evidence for successive phases of occupation is present it appears, like the unenclosed settlements further north, as a horizontal distribution (Pernicheva 1995: 101).

In south-western Bulgaria, therefore, many of the key themes in the new perceptions of the landscape and interior space that have been seen in each of the other regions, are present once again. Special attention was focused on building interiors and ovens were accorded special treatment. If the highly decorated oven models were employed in rituals surrounding houses, households and the declaration of occupation or group membership, then further connections can be made with the developing ideology of the house in other regions.

167

Eastern Hungary

In eastern Hungary the semi-sedentary character of the structures of the preceding millennium of Körös culture sites graded into more anchored built environments in the second half of the sixth millennium BC related to the Alföld Linear Pottery complex. People continued to build pit-huts, although there were now more of them and aggregations of 10–15 structures were common (Makkay 1982b). Further north in the Hungarian Plain are new Linearbandkeramic longhouses. At the beginning of the fifth millennium BC, the Szakálhát cultural phase, buildings continued to be clustered in small groups and continuity of occupation or rebuilding occurred horizontally (Kalicz 1957; Kalicz and Makkay 1977). Also at this time, the earliest beginnings of multi-layered tells appear; in some cases Szakálhát structures form the lower levels of tell villages. People built with wood-framed walls dug into foundation trenches and, in some cases, as at Lebő-Felsőhalom and Csanytelek-Újhalastó, dug a ditch around structures (Trogmayer 1957; Galántha 1985). At Csongrád-Bokros a triple row of posts was constructed inside a foundation ditch. Building interiors were segmented by walls and partitions. Some houses were large and longer than they were wide; one structure at Csanytelek-Újhalastó was 19.4 × 9.2 m (Hegedüs 1982–3: 7–8).

In the first half of the fifth millennium BC, the Tisza culture, people built structures with walls made of clay, mud, saplings and branches and formed floors of beaten earth. In some cases, as at Vésztő and at Kökénydomb, people built walls with wooden planks. Many of these buildings form the lower levels of long repetitions of villages which grew into settlement tells. Buildings were arranged in rows of structures. In some cases, as at Vésztő, new structures were built directly over, and with identical floorplans to, buildings from the previous Szákahlhát phase (Hegedüs and Makkay 1987: 92–3). Indeed there is good evidence, as at Szentes-Ilonapart, for the contemporaneity of both pit-dwellings and multi-generation tells (Horváth 1983). Large single-layer aggregations contained several loosely connected concentrations of buildings, in some cases, such as Öcsöd, Kökénydomb, Szegvár-Tűzkoves, separated by natural ditches (Raczky et al. 1985: 267; Raczky 1987: 63; Siklódy 1986; Korek 1987). Many buildings in tell villages contained an oven plastered with mud; most had one or two rooms (inner partitions were few) and their size ranged from 3.5 × 8.0 m to 5 × 19 m. Other interior features included raised platforms (at Lebő).

Increasingly, through the second half of the fifth millennium BC, people dug boundary ditches around tell villages (Horváth 1986; 1989: 90); this can be seen at Herpály and Gorzsa (Kalicz and Raczky 1984: 99–109; Horváth 1987: 32–40). Building interiors were divided with multiple partitions; at Lebő, ceilings were built with thickly plastered planks. Some buildings, as at Herpály, were expanded upwards with the addition of second storeys (Kalicz and Raczky 1984). During this period, the Tiszapolgár cultural phase, there were significant changes in how people perceived and exploited their environments. In some places, people continued to build on tell villages, but this, perhaps, represents a minority of the population, most of whom were living in less permanent structures.

Northern Greece

In northern Greece, as in south-central Bulgaria, continuity and acceleration characterize the ways in which people constructed their physical environments. Pit-huts and surface-level buildings continued to be aggregated into horizontally expanding spreads and vertically growing tells respectively. At the end of the sixth and the beginning of the fifth millennium BC people established camps and villages in many new places in central and eastern Macedonia. At some sites, such as Vasilika, Thermi and Arethousa, hiatuses in occupations interrupted building sequences. In central Macedonia, some sites are huge, flat spreads covering up to 100 ha. Overall, people continued to divide village from non-village space, to separate one area of a village from another and to segment parts of building interiors.

In western Macedonia more sites are evident from the middle of the sixth millennium BC (Andreou et al. 1996: 556). At Makriyalos near the current coastline of the Thermaic Gulf (Gulf of Sabruikà) surface remains cover a large area (50 ha). Pit-huts were arranged into groups separated from each other by large open spaces. While Makriyalos appears as an unenclosed site, the site is surrounded by a system of three concentric ditches, the largest one of which is 4 m deep and 5 m wide (Pappa 1994; Andreou et al. 1996: 572). At the end of the sixth millennium BC a second phase of occupation at Makriyalos reveals a denser concentration of pits each of which had post-and-frame superstructures. During this second phase of the site people also built several rectangular megaron-shaped structures with apsidal ends (Pappa 1994; Andreou et al. 1996: 573). Clearly there is both continuity and change between the two phases of the site: an enclosed phase of settlement was followed by one with a more structured architectural plan characterized by more substantial building techniques and materials and an increased attention to crowding buildings together and to segmenting interior space.

In the middle of the fifth millennium BC, 60 km to the west of Makriyalos, tells such as Megalo Nisi Galanis contained houses built of very solid materials such as a calcereous cement made of lime and sandy stream sediments; some surfaces were covered with layers of fine plaster (Fotiadis 1988: 43–6; Andreou et al. 1996: 570). At about the same time, 40 km to the northeast at the Mandalo tell, people built wooden-framed structures with large posts and walls covered with compacted mud. Floors and hearths were covered with layers of clay and white plaster. Buildings were tightly packed across the site which, towards the end of its use, was bounded by a large field-stone wall 2.5 m wide and 1.4 m high (Andreou *et al.* 1996: 571 n. 250).

In western Macedonia overall, sites from the mid-sixth to the end of the fifth millennium outnumber those from the previous 1200 years by two or three to one (Andreou *et al.* 1996: 575). Increase in site numbers is usually explained in terms of increases in population due to changes in economy or by immigration. Again, as was the case with contemporary increases in site numbers to the north, perhaps it is better to view the appearance of more substantial, durable sites in the light of changing attitudes towards marking out space in a more permanent manner both across the landscape and within individual buildings.

In central Macedonia from the mid-sixth millennium BC a previously, apparently, empty landscape was filled with tells and unenclosed, extended flat sites. At Vasilika a flat site covers 25 ha and, although there is very little evidence of large-scale building projects, buildings were made with mud-blocks on stone socles (Grammenos 1991: 30–1, 36–7). Thermi, another flat site, came into use from the middle of the fifth millennium BC, extended over 12 ha and had two successive paved central 'courts' 60 m square. Evidence for a wide range of activities was found in both phases of the square's use. Remains of a hearth and several pits were recovered from the earlier yard; the later one was covered with post-built walls and clay floors (Grammenos *et al.* 1990; 1992; Andreou *et al.* 1996: 582–3).

In eastern Macedonia, field survey in the Drama plain revealed a significant increase in the numbers of settlements utilizing a greater variety of locations in the landscape from the end of the sixth to the middle of the fifth millennium BC (Blouet 1986: 135). After this followed a phase of aggregation of settlements into fewer, but larger, villages (Blouet 1986: 137). Indeed the large tell villages of Sitagroi and Dikili Tash were established only at 5500 BC. At Dikili Tash evidence for architecture is scanty; walls were post-built with compacted mud and stone socles; people stored parched lentils in a silo and built many hearths and ovens (Treuil 1992: 23, 43–4). In Dikili Tash II people built large buildings (10 × 5 m) in regular rows separated by narrow pathways (Koukouli-Chrysanthaki 1993: 70–4; Andreou *et al.* 1996: 589). Further to the east in Thrace evidence of architecture is sparse.

To the south in Thessaly, as in Macedonia, the numbers of settlements increased after the middle of the sixth millennium BC, especially in the Volos area (Andreou *et al.* 1996: 549). From the end of the sixth millennium BC, at the Dimini tell, people constructed internal boundaries to divide the village into well segmented zones. They built six concentric perimeter walls enclosing four main courtyard areas; at the centre of the village was an open court. Each courtyard area contained a large building, storage

170

facilities and areas for food preparation and other activities (Hourmouziadis 1979a: 110–140; Andreou et al. 1996: 542). Large storage vessels increased in number as found at Sesklo, Tsangli, Tsani and Zerelia (Demoule and Perlès 1993: 390) and large storage pits appear at Argissa, Arapi, Otzaki, Ayia Sophia and Pefkakia (Milojčić et al. 1976; Hourmouziadis 1979b). At other villages at this time people built megaron-shaped buildings in central places; at Sesklo a two-roomed building with a porch was constructed. A rectangular hearth was built in the larger room and the floor was made of red clay and small stones. In the smaller room were two semicircular raised platforms lined with vertical slabs (Tsountas 1908). Other central buildings were constructed at Visviki (Benecke 1942) and at Ayia Sophia where, as a base for the structure, people used a mud-block platform separated from the rest of the building by a large ditch (Milojčić et al. 1976). Perimeter walls, ditches or both formed boundaries of villages, not only at Dimini but also at other sites in Thessaly such as Arapi, Argissa, Ayia Sophia, Soufli, Otzaki, Servia and Nea Nikomedeia (Demoule and Perlès 1993: 390; Andreou et al. 1996: 543: note 36).

At Dimini, food preparation, storage facilities and assemblages of tools were found inside buildings more often than outside and this may distinguish sites like Dimini from earlier communities, such as that at Achilleion, that had established places for activities in the open air between buildings (Halstead 1992b: 30–31). Halstead has suggested that people divided off parts of Dimini for use by elites at the end of this period and afterwards in the early Bronze Age (Halstead 1984; Andreou et al. 1996: 545).

The pattern of the consumption of prestige materials, such at *Spondylus*, at Dimini, suggests that particular areas, and thus perhaps particular groups of people within the village, had differential access to valued materials and, perhaps more provocatively, rights to their consumption. Significantly, although debris from working *Spondylus* is spread evenly across the village, deposition of finished and burnt *Spondylus* objects is restricted to particular areas (Halstead 1989b, 1993: 607). Halstead argues that Dimini was divided into separate courtyard groups made up of a larger and several smaller buildings (Halstead 1995: 14) and that the central megaron structure here, as well as at other sites, represents a 'megaron elite' supported through institutionalized inequality within communities (Halstead 1995: 16).

To the east of Dimini, at Pefkakia, from the middle of the fifth millennium BC three architectural phases contained rectangular buildings with clay floors and walls built on stone foundations. Houses were arranged in parallel rows separated by narrow alleys. Although the area excavated was limited, it is clear that storage facilities such as lined pits and large vessels were abundant. One large rectangular pit was lined with sun-dried mudblocks. Hearths were present and internal boundary walls segmented interior space (Weisshaar 1989; Andreou et al. 1996: 546). Structures continued to be built packed tightly together. As the numbers of new sites declined

171

towards the end of the fifth millennium BC, large surrounding walls were constructed at Pefkakia (Schachermeyr 1976) and Mandalo (Pilali-Papasteriou and Papaefthimiou-Papanthimou 1989). At Otzaki, there was a ditch 6 m deep and 4.5 m wide (Milojčić 1955).

Sixty kilometres to the north-west, at Ayia Sophia, three phases of a mud-block platform in the centre of the low tell date from the mid- to late sixth millennium BC. A megaron-shaped structure was associated with the later of these platforms as were two mud-block walls that have been inter-preted as a gateway. In the earlier part of the fifth millennium BC the platform complex was cut off by a ditch that may have surrounded the central part of the site and bears similarities to Dimini's isolated central court (Milojčić 1976: 1–14; Andreou et al. 1996: 553).

Overall in the eastern Thessalian plain there was a marked increase in settlements at the end of the sixth millennium BC, although the numbers of sites decreases after the middle of the fifth millennium BC, when fewer settlements might represent a concentration of the population (Gallis 1989; Andreou et al. 1996: 554).

While there are significant differences between the architectural records of northern Greece and areas further to the north, significant similarities remain. Taken as a change in attitudes to space and not as an increase in population, the general rise in numbers of sites may reflect similar conti-nuities and expansions in people's desires to mark out particular parts of the landscape in permanent ways.

Certainly the emergence of settlements out of an apparently empty land-scape, as in parts of Macedonia, has close parallels with the appearance of tell villages in the lower Danube. In some parts of Thessaly, the continued use of durable building technologies, such as mud-blocks and stone-socled walls, invested structures and their arrangement with permanence in order to suggest continuity with earlier periods. However, the shift of activity areas into buildings and out of open, shared yards or courts was new and may reflect a further development in the enclosure of activity areas.

North-west Anatolia

The evidence from north-west Anatolia suggests that people were creating and dividing their social and natural environments in ways very similar to those present in south-central Bulgaria. From the middle of the sixth millen-nium BC people established a village that was to develop over the succeeding millennium into one of the largest settlement tells, reaching 12 m in height, in eastern Turkish Thrace. This is the village of Toptepe (Özdoğan et al. 1991; Özdoğan 1991). In earlier phases of the site, before the middle of the sixth millennium BC, people had built a series of clay floors and six oval hearths or ovens (phase 2, layer 1) and numerous thin layers of shell, ash and building debris (phase 2, layer 3). No architectural remains were recovered from the latter layer and the excavators suggested that this phase represents either a dislocation of occupation or a series of seasonal occupations of the site (Özdoğan *et al.* 1991: 76).

In the next major phase of Toptepe (phase 3, layer 5), at the end of the sixth millennium BC, people built structures with posts, mud and mud-block. One building, 7.5 × 3.1 m in size, had wall-posts set into narrow but deep trenches which were then filled with mud. People built an oval, domed oven at the western end of the building; around it was a scatter of animal bones, and immediately to the east was a deep, clay-lined pit full of ash. Charred grain was found along the western and south-western walls. Along the northern wall, a raised platform was built and plastered. To the east of this was a very large storage vessel. A small partition wall separated the eastern part of the building in which coarse-ware pots and ground stone were found. The floor was plastered and burnished with clay; walls bore painted red designs (Özdoğan *et al.* 1991: 78).

At Ilipinar the major change in patterns of spatial organization occurred in the middle of the sixth millennium BC, in the shift to layer VI. While people had built and rebuilt earlier structures with post, plank, mud and clay, in layer VI they started to build in a more stable and permanent manner using sun-dried mud-blocks. Although no complete floorplans were recovered during excavation, layer VI contained eight successive building generations of mud-block structures (Roodenberg 1993b: 252).

The buildings at Ilipinar were small (25–30 sq m), rectangular, single-roomed structures with floors covered by mud-plaster. Mud-block walls supported wooden roofs. Although houses were still arranged with a common orientation of floorplans, the direction of orientation had changed to E–W (Roodenberg *et al.* 1990: 77). Ovens occurred exclusively in external courtyards and outdoor space was increasingly structured (Thissen 1993b: 300). With the end of layer VI comes the end of a long sequence of village rebuildings. Dramatic change marks the subsequent phase of the village (layer V) when large pits containing new pottery wares and forms, which have analogies with complexes in the western Balkans, are accompanied by shifts in economy; emphasis shifts from the exploitation of ovicaprids to that of pig and cattle (Roodenberg 1993b: 258; Buitenhaus in Roodenberg *et al.* 1990: 113–4). These changes in architecture, ceramic production and economy suggest a shift from groups of people anchored to separate buildings of households to smaller groups or perhaps even individuals who lived in more flexible relationships with others (Thissen 1993b).

The built environment after 5500 BC: conclusion

For a 1000–1500-year period from the middle of the sixth millennium BC there were important continuities, expansions and accelerations and, in a few regions at least, novelties in the ways people marked out parts of the landscape by constructing and arranging buildings and villages, and building interiors. Similar events were evident over all of the regions of the Balkans considered here. Although they appear in slightly different forms in different regions (e.g., the dominance of unenclosed flat sites in the west and multi-level tells to the east), common trends link the regions: the increasingly rigid demarcation of intramural building space, the increase in building durability and the increasing focus on building interiors for economic and production activities.

On the larger scale, as in previous millennia, particular areas of activities and residence were marked out from larger portions of the landscape. The bounded tells are a strong and frequent example of macro-scale spatial demarcation. In other cases a sharp marking off of settlement from non-settlement areas is less evident, if it appears at all. Unenclosed sites such as Selevac, which spread horizontally through time apparently without boundary, are a good example. Despite these differences, both the enclosed tell and the unenclosed flat sites share similar trends in the organization of space within buildings. On both types of sites the interiors of houses were increasingly segmented by durable walls and temporary partitions or divisions of activity areas.

The other common trans-regional link in the attitudes towards and manipulations of the built environment was the trend, especially evident in regions where it had not appeared before, towards the use of more permanent technologies and materials in building construction. This includes not only the continuation of mud-blocks and stone in northern Greece but also the shift to more substantial post-and-frame constructions on the unenclosed sites. Repeated short-term repairs to wall, floor and oven plasters were further efforts to extend the lives of structures and make claims on continuity of residence. On a longer time-scale, the extension of building duration was the consequence of reconstructing buildings either in exact vertical replication of preceding floorplans (as on tells) or in the horizontal replication of alignments and orientations of building axes (on unenclosed buildings). In some regions, such as the lower Danube, the building and rebuilding of aggregations of surface-level structures produced, for the first time, the very long-duration tell settlements.

Did tell villages dominate the landscape?

The research attention devoted to tell settlements in the lower Danube and in southern Bulgaria and the absence of intensive field surveys have produced an unbalanced picture of the range of fifth millennium BC settlement types in this region and to the south. While some attention has been directed to sites occupied away from tells, such as the mid-fifth millennium BC unenclosed site at Stara Zagora Bolnitsa, little non-tell settlement has been studied in this region. For most, the assumptions that settlement was limited to the topographic boundaries of tells and that non-tell activity areas were of little significance have remained unchallenged. In this unbalanced picture, tells stand up as the only points within an otherwise empty landscape.

Geophysical survey, augering and sondaging at Podgoritsa in north-eastern Bulgaria located buildings beyond the limits of, though still quite close to, the tell's topographic boundaries (Figure 5.8) (D. Bailey et al. 1998). In other regions, greater attention to non-tell activities has revealed a similarly wide and full picture in northern Greece, as for an earlier period at Sesklo and in the northern Hungarian Plain at Csőszhalom (Raczky et al. 1997). These off-tell research programmes have fleshed out the reality of the fifth millennium BC landscape in these regions.

In many ways the emerging conception generated by the work in northern Bulgaria, Greece and Hungary supplements our understanding of the fifth millennium BC emphasis on spatial boundaries and segmentation that characterizes much of the architecture within tell villages and between village space and non-village space. A clearer picture of what was beyond the topographic limits of the tell has started to emerge (D. Bailey 1999). In this, the emergence of bounded tell settlements out of an empty landscape or as altered continuations of existing settlements become a less dramatic event. Indeed, at least one site (Golyamo Delchevo) the lowest cultural level of the tell consists of pit-huts (Todorova et al. 1975) that are very similar in form, size and contents to the pit-huts of contemporary and earlier unenclosed aggregations. The sequences in southern Romania and eastern Hungary both contain examples not only of contemporaneous pit-huts and surface structures but also of early phases of later tell sequences linked to earlier non-tell architecture and material culture.

A traditional interpretation of these patterns is to read the increase in substantial, durable sites across all of the regions in terms of an infilling of population. In light of the growing body of off-tell work perhaps it is more accurate to see the 'filling' of the landscape not as a direct consequence of population increase but as a rearrangement and a new more archaeologically recognizable anchoring of individuals and groups of people who had lived through these landscapes for many generations. Recent work on off-tell activities and structures has complemented the existing, albeit limited, evidence from the basal layers of sites that became tells. As a result it is clear that tell villages did not spring from empty landscapes. Very probably, tells arose out of a social landscape which, far from being stable and immobile, was full of movement and alive with impermanent activity areas and short-lived structures. In this context, tells may have appeared as symptoms of people's increasing desires, and needs, to make permanent, visible statements of continuities in occupation and residence. Such statements might have developed from a combination of the use of walls and

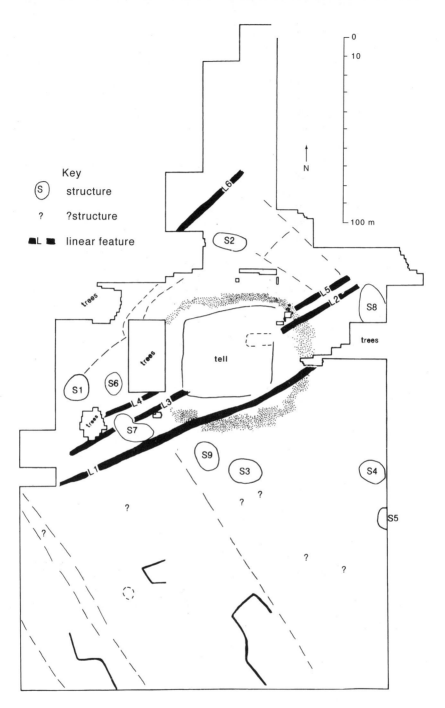

Key

S structure

? ?structure

L linear feature

Figure 5.8 Off-tell structures from Podgoritsa (after Bailey *et al.* 1998)

banks around small villages of surface-level structures and subsequent social restrictions or incentives on where successive generations of building could be grounded. Upon these developed the tell villages of this period as well, perhaps, as did those from the previous millennia in northern Greece and south-central Bulgaria. Thus interpretations that take the relatively swift appearance of tells as the main evidence for infilling and population increases may be missing what was going on in the majority of the landscape.

Furthermore, in many regions, especially those where programmes of intensive fieldwalking have been undertaken, such as Greece, Serbia and Hungary, the evidence is mounting for landscapes filled with activities and structures not physically attached to the big visible sites. The picture that emerges from all of this is not of an infilling of population but of a major rearrangement of people and their physical relationship with their natural and built environments. The increase in marking places in an otherwise mobile landscape was a symptom of these relationships that was new in some places and strengthened through continuity in others. The major mechanism of this rearrangement across the diverse regions was the enclosure of settlement space. Together all of these core trends underline the increasing importance of the built environment and, most particularly, of village aggregations of houses in the perceptions and actions of people during the fifth millennium BC.

MANAGING THE LIVING ENVIRONMENT

Although there were novelties, such as the appearance of long-duration tell settlements north of the Stara Planina, people's perspective on their built environment after 5500 BC continued many of the trends from the previous millennium. In many ways the same is true of people's attitudes and motives in managing plants and animals. There were no novel species of plants or animals after 5500 BC as there had been after 6500 BC, as was discussed in Chapter 3. At least for the animal bones deposited in settlement contexts, domesticated species continued to dominate over wild ones and the significant species remained unchanged. Sheep, goat, wild and domestic cattle, wild and domestic pig and red deer account for the majority of animal remains. Wheat, barley, legumes and pulses continue to dominate palaeobotanical samples.

The changes of significance in the fifth millennium BC were not in the species exploited but in the manner and scale of their exploitation. Two developments in economic activities distinguish the fifth millennium BC: an intensification of plant cropping activities and the gradual emergence of managing animals for secondary, as well as, primary products.

177

Large-scale cereal cultivation

The first of the two significant changes in the ways people manipulated their living surroundings was the spread of the more organized, scheduled, field-based cultivation of cereals and a greater investment in post-harvest processing of plants. While Dennell's analysis (Dennell 1978) suggested that this scale of cultivation was present in central Bulgaria in the sixth millennium BC to the south, large-scale field cultivation was a new development in the lower Danube and in the western Balkans. As discussed in Chapter 3, during the previous millennium and a half in these northern regions and in many other parts of the Balkans cultivation had been based around shorter-term garden horticulture, most probably in plots set close to dwellings. From the beginning of the fifth millennium BC plant cultivation was practised on a larger scale and, perhaps, at increasing distances from the foci of settlement structures and activities.

As in previous millennia to the south, evidence for the introduction of field-based cultivation is indirect, consisting of crop purity and the appearance or increase of cereal processing and storage facilities. Despite Dennell's example, systematic recovery and study of botanical samples from fifth millennium BC sites remain infrequent. For those sites in the lower Danube where detailed work has been carried out the botanical evidence for mono cropping, though not in itself conclusive, at least suggests that people were investing more time and more effort into parts of the agricultural sequence.

High-purity plant samples

As in the earlier material from southern Bulgaria, evidence for increased investment of effort in crop processing, and perhaps monocropping, may be found in palaeobotanical samples containing large concentrations of single species. It is unclear whether or not high purity samples such as one containing 100 per cent barley and another 98 per cent durum wheat found at Golyamo Delchevo (Hopf 1975) are proxies for monocropping or whether they are the results of post-harvesting and depositional processes. Questions also remain about how representative a few individual archaeological samples are for community-wide practices. Of samples analysed from Golyamo Delchevo, those with pure crop compositions are in the minority. The majority of samples are mixtures dominated by emmer, einkorn and barley. Einkorn appears in samples from all horizons but emmer drops out after horizon XII (Hopf 1975). In a third of the samples studied in detail from horizons X and VIII einkorn dominated, accounting for up to 94 per cent of each sample, with emmer and barley making up minority portions. In another quarter of the samples from these levels barley dominated, in one case accounting for 98 per cent of the sample, with einkorn and emmer making up the rest. Spelt wheat is found in samples from a quarter of all

178

levels and is evenly distributed through the life of the site. At Ovcharovo botanical evidence for crop purity is less secure. As at Golyamo Delchevo, emmer, einkorn and barley dominate three-quarters of those samples studied, all of which come from a phase of the site, horizon X. *Vicia, Triticum compactum* and durum wheat make up minority components of many samples (Yanushevich 1983). At Valea Anilor, a Salcuţa culture site in southern Romania, one pot contained mainly *Triticum aestivum* and another mostly barley (Cârciumaru 1996: 197). Jane Renfrew has argued that crop purity was on the increase in Greece at this time (J. Renfrew 1973).

If high-purity samples document highly planned sowing and processing of a single crop in a separate field, then these samples argue for monocropping. It is unclear, however, whether high-purity species do represent monocropping. It is more likely that single-species samples represent stages in the agricultural cycle after harvest and cleaning but before use, consumption or sowing; that is, they represent short- or medium-term storage. Regardless of whether the single-species samples represent growing individual species in separate fields or whether they represent intensive post-harvest processing of mixed-crop yields, it is clear that people were investing more substantial time and effort in cleaning and, perhaps isolating, particular species of plants than they had been in the previous millennium.

Agricultural equipment

Although purity of seed samples is inconclusive evidence for monocropping, it does suggest some increased focus on the post-harvest treatment of plants. More secure evidence that people were engaged in higher-labour agricultural production comes from the agricultural tools and facilities that were widely used in the fifth millennium BC. Foremost among these were permanent grain-storage facilities constructed inside village buildings. Some of these, such as the ones from a three-phase building at Ovcharovo, are impressive in size (2×3 m). Storage pits, dug into building floors at the same site, though less capacious, would have been equally important. At Selevac, storage facilities were found in the site's later phases. In the eastern Hungarian Plain inhabitants of the early fifth millennium BC site Berettyóújfalu-Herpály built clay storage bins (Raczky 1987; Whittle 1996: 109). At the end of the sixth and in the first half of the fifth millennium BC in northern Greece people built large storage pits at Argissa, Arapi, Otzaki, Ayia Sophia and Pefkakia (Milojčić *et al.* 1976; Hourmouziadis 1979b).

The production and use of large, wide-mouthed lidded storage vessels also suggests an increase in high-capacity container facilities. In their size – and the largest ones had capacities of several hundred litres – these pots were comparable to the built grain silos. Secure evidence for the increase in vessel capacity is infrequent. Where capacities have been calculated, as for Ovcharovo (D. Bailey 1991), the frequency of large vessels is clear. In the later phases of the site, pots with very large volumes (up to 200 litres and more) were common (Table 5.1). Some lidded vessels were smaller, had tighter necks and may have been used to store other, perhaps liquid materials (Figure 5.9). In south-central Romania large clay vessels often contained cereal remains, as was the case at Valea Anilor (Cârciumaru 1996: 194). Chokadzhiev has estimated the capacity of one large pot at Slatino in west-central Bulgaria as 65 litres (S. Chokadzhiev personal communication). In Macedonia the increase in the importance of jars at the end of the sixth millennium BC at Sitagroi has been read as an increase in emphasis on food storage; an increase in vessel capacity in the second half of the fifth millennium BC is even more striking and suggestive (Keighley 1986: 351). At the end of the sixth millennium BC at Toptepe in north-west Anatolia one well preserved building contained a storage vessel described as 'huge', although capacity in litres is not available (Özdoğan et al. 1991: 78). In northern Greece at the end of the sixth and in the first half of the fifth millennium BC people were also making large storage vessels at Sesklo, Dimini, Tsangli, Tsani and Zerelia (Demoule and Perlès 1993: 390).

Equally important indirect evidence for the intensity of agricultural production are the frequent finds of grinding-stones. Whether noted for their frequency (as in the tells of north-eastern Bulgaria), their permanent embeddedness in building floors near hearths and silos, or their increase in size in some regions, grinding-stones were an important, regular

Table 5.1 Range of vessel capacities from fifth millennium BC phases at Ovcharovo, showing change through the millennium from the earliest (I) to the final (XIII) building horizon (after Bailey 1991)

| Horizon | Capacity (litres) | | | Sample size | Destruction |
	Mean	Minimum	Maximum	(no. of pots)	by fire
XIII	1.95	0.86	3.66	4	none
XII	23.08	0.19	197.57	55	complete
XI	13.62	0.12	184.14	27	none
X	25.34	0.39	189.97	82	complete
IX	24.64	0.04	200.51	78	complete
VIII	24.32	0.25	285.26	89	complete
VII	10.63	0.15	73.66	15	partial
VI	10.46	1.78	24.96	10	none
V	6.89	0.07	31.84	53	none
IV	7.17	0.35	43.94	40	none
III	9.70	0.15	75.23	33	one house
II	7.02	0.20	41.89	15	none
I	8.25	0.34	12.98	3	none

Figure 5.9 Lidded pot from Sava (no scale) (after Todorova 1986)

component of fifth millennium BC village life. Also suggestive are the common finds of large ovens associated with grinding-stones and grain-storage areas as at Slatino in south-western Bulgaria. Sickles made of flint-blades inserted in pieces of wood, antler or jawbones were in use on Boian sites north of the Danube and may at this time be more frequent overall (Cârciumaru 1996: 194). Antler tools, potentially useful for preparing soil for planting or for tending plants and weeding, are frequent finds at almost every site.

The management and social significance of animals

Fifth millennium BC animal exploitation continued the programmes of seasonal grazing of ovicaprids and cattle that had developed during earlier millennia. The main development was a shift away from ovicaprid, and towards cattle. At Divostin (phase II) wild and domestic cattle predominated (Bökönyi 1988: 421), a preference repeated at Hamangia and Boian sites in southern Romania. At Hamangia sites, cattle accounted for more than 50 per cent of domesticates, as has been documented at Techirghiol (Necrasov and Haimovici 1962). In Hamangia cemeteries, although domesticated animals made up a smaller proportion of all animal bones deposited in burials than they did in camp and village sites, of cemetery domesticates cattle were dominant, accounting for 67.4 per cent (Haşotti 1997). At Boian sites, similar patterns emerge; domesticates dominated faunal assemblages and cattle (47–57 per cent) were more frequent than pig (18–21 per cent) or ovicaprids (13–23 per cent) (Necrasov and Haimovici 1959a; Cârciumaru 1996: 42). At Bogata, a Giuleşti phase Boian site, cattle accounted for 88 per cent of domesticates (Necrasov and Haimovici 1959b); at Graeca, they made up a similarly high proportion (Cârciumaru 1996: 42), while at Vărăşti, although they accounted for less (only 60 per cent), they were still in the majority (Bolomey 1966).

In the subsequent villages of the Gumelniţa culture, cattle continued to dominate faunal assemblages; at Radovanu, in the transitional phase between Boian and Gumelniţa, cattle accounted for 48 per cent of domesticates (Necrasov 1973); at Izvoarele they made up 54 per cent (Necrasov and Gheorghiu 1970); and at Gumelniţa itself 61 per cent (Necrasov and Haimovici 1966). In the three Gumelniţa levels at Tangîru, however, cattle and ovicaprids both ranged between 44 and 30 per cent (Cârciumaru 1996: 46). Vadastra and Salcuţa sites in south-western Romania reveal similar proportions of cattle (Gheţie and Mateesco 1978; Trâncă 1981; Cârciumaru 1996: 42). In north-western Anatolia, the major shift which occurred at 5500 BC in layer VI at Ilipinar and which corresponds with a shift in architectural technique, was a move away from ovicaprids to cattle and pig (Buitenhaus in Roodenberg et al. 1990: 113–4).

Compared with the earlier patterns of animal exploitation, as seen in the first phase of activity at Divostin, sheep and goat were now a third less important, and pig and dog much more significant. The shift from primary reliance on ovicaprids to cattle and pigs was a common pattern in the northern Balkans (Bökönyi 1988: 431). One possibility is that the changes reflect the long-term consequence of local availability of wild cattle and pig stock for maintaining domestic breeding stock and the absence of similar wild reserves for supporting ovicaprid populations. A second possibility is that the shifts in species majorities reveal a shift in people's perceptions and uses of particular animals. One part of these new perceptions was the use of the main domesticates for non-subsistence activities.

The use of animals for secondary products

The shift in animal exploitation to cattle and away from ovicaprid and the contemporary increase in plant cultivation, processing and storage occurred as people were beginning to use some animals, especially cattle but also ovicaprid, for secondary products (Sherratt 1981, 1983c; Chapman 1983b). Cattle were now being used for transportation, traction and dairying, sheep for milk and goat for wool. Where detailed analyses are reliable, the faunal record reveals that people were keeping great numbers of older cattle, sheep and goats; the limited evidence for sexing of faunal remains also suggests some preference for feeding and caring for more female than male cattle, and for doing so to a greater age. The evidence for sheep and goat is not as clear.

At Divostin, most cattle (65 per cent) were adult (Bökönyi 1988: 423). Bökönyi has argued that some bulls were castrated and he suggests that the large numbers of cattle were kept for a variety of reasons other than subsistence (Bökönyi 1988: 431). Villages in which bulls outnumbered cows may represent the use of cattle for traction or status; where cows outnumber bulls milk production may have been the stimulus (Bökönyi 1988: 423). The move away from sheep exploitation and the low proportions of adults suggest that they were exploited for their meat and not for wool; inverse patterns for goats suggests exploitation for milk (Bökönyi 1988: 425).

The material record supplements these patterns. Spindle-whorls and loomweights for textile production and ceramic sieves for dairying are frequent finds. At Sitagroi, although present in early levels, sieve fragments only became frequent forms in the later phases (phase III) (Keighley 1986: 368). At Divostin groups of loomweights were found on building floors (Rasson 1988: 337–8); a single loomweight comes from the Hamangia site at Tîrgusor Urs (Haşotti 1997: 8). Impressions of textiles left on clay surfaces number more than a hundred at Divostin (Adovasio and Maslowski 1988: 12.1). At Ovcharovo, loomweights and spindle-whorls are frequent finds, though more so in the earlier phases of the village.

Patterns of animal exploitation were not constant across the Balkans. Unlike at other sites in northern Yugoslavia, at Selevac the ages established for cattle suggest that dairying was not a priority (Legge 1990: 230, 236) and, though present, the evidence for the use of cattle as draught animals was slight. Patterns of sheep mortality also produced no clear evidence for wool production despite the presence of spindle-whorls and loomweights at the site.

Social consequences of animal management

These changes in animal management were part of important shifts in people's valuations and perceptions of animals. This is especially clear in the case of cattle. The evidence for the changing role of cattle within communities is not limited to age and sex distributions of animals at time of death. Bökönyi has suggested, for Divostin (II) at least, that the maintenance of older cattle reflects not only their use for secondary products but also their position within emerging systems of wealth and status (Bökönyi 1988).

As noted in Chapter 3, Nerissa Russell has addressed similar issues in the western Balkans (Russell 1998). She suggests that we view animal consumption from a social rather than a purely economic perspective. Russell argues that the large body-size of cattle would have meant that the consumption of any single animal would have been an extra-domestic event involving individuals from beyond the boundaries of any one single social or economic unit such as a house or household. Thus, perhaps the apparent increase in the importance of cattle in faunal records should be understood in terms of communal activities. It was proposed in Chapter 3 that the earlier dominance of cattle at north Balkan pit-hut sites implies the aggregation of people to consume cattle; the fifth millennium BC cattle dominance in village sites may have had different consequences. In the tell villages eating beef may have provided a focus for the expression of communal cohesion between households or across the village. Perhaps the rise in the importance of cattle marks a rearrangement of the relations within village communities. Cattle and other large-bodied animals such as red deer may best be understood as inter-household animals, the use, care and eventual consumption of which had village-wide consequences and requirements.

The role of cattle as animals of increasing social significance is amplified by the contemporary production of two- and three-dimensional representations of horned quadrupeds, most of which appear to be cattle. Zoomorphic figurines are commonly found in village sites, although they were not as numerous as anthropomorphic figurines. Marangou has suggested that we should read the recovery of several zoomorphs in close association as at Ovcharovo, Sabac-Jela and Drenovac (Chapman 1981: 73; Todorova 1982: 136) as representations of animal herds (Marangou 1996: 179).

Although other animals, such as dogs or cats, were represented in figurine form, the predominance of horned quadrupeds identifiable as cattle is striking. Cattle zoomorphs from Ovcharovo, Sitagroi and Drama have packs or baskets modelled onto their backs (Figure 5.10). More striking are the flat cattle zoomorphs made of gold and found in the Varna cemetery, discussed in more detail in Chapter 6. One grave at Varna, no. 36, contained not only two pierced gold zoomorphs representing two cattle in profile (Figure 5.11), but also a collection of thirty flat gold representations of horns, presumably of cattle.

Additional evidence for non-economic relationships between animals and people in the fifth millennium BC includes the use of ruminant astragali (knucklebones) as ornaments, or perhaps as gaming-pieces, and the

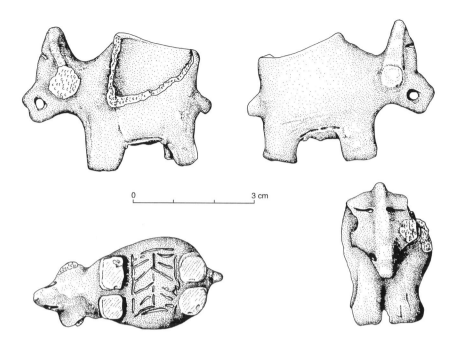

Figure 5.10 Zoomorphic figurine of a pack animal with incised sign on belly, from Drama (after Bertemes and Krustev 1988)

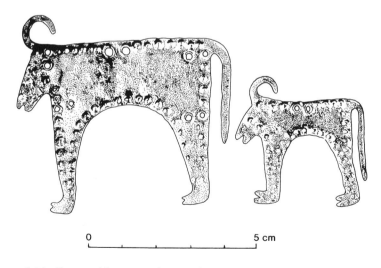

Figure 5.11 Sheet-gold zoomorphic appliqués from grave 36 at Varna (after I. Ivanov 1988a)

fashioning of astragali from prestige materials. Most notable is the solid gold astragalus from the Varna cemetery. Less well known uses of astragali come from other sites where the bone itself has one or two holes drilled through it, perhaps so that it could be used as a pendant, and with one or both lateral sides polished. At Divostin (phase II) nine astragali were found: five from small ungulates were found together, and each had ground lateral and medial faces and drilled perforations. Two were from large ungulates and two other, unspecified ones came from other parts of the site (Lyneis 1988: 313–6). As was seen in the placement of animal bones in early burials at Lepenski Vir, non-economic human-animal relationships, in the north Balkans at least, had a deeper tradition; this continued in the fifth millennium mortuary ritual of Hamangia burials. Indeed the fifth millennium BC manifestations of the social or prestige importance of animals such as cattle may only represent an intensification of this longer tradition.

Running alongside communal interests and events, however, may have been other dimensions of animal use and consumption, of both primary and secondary products, that were limited to smaller social groups (many of which existed within any village community). These were patterns established in the previous millennium. Thus the consumption of smaller animals such as sheep, goat and pig may have continued to represent more routine activities (social as well as nutritional) through which smaller household or activity-related groups reaffirmed both their intramural cohesion and their separation from other small groups of the same larger village community.

Herding patterns

The patterns of seasonal movements of grazing animals that had developed in previous millennia also continued after 5500 BC. If there was a change to the pattern of herd movement during the fifth millennium BC, it may have been the establishment of stronger, more permanent and socially important village bases to which seasonal herding strategies were tethered and which also served as centres for cereal and pulse planting, cropping, processing and storing. In south-central Bulgaria and Thessaly this can be seen in the increase in the numbers of tells across the landscape and in terms of the increase in vertical presence, and thus monumental visibility, of each tell. The same trend in the increasing importance of occupational anchor-points for herding strategies may be reflected in northern Bulgaria and Macedonia and Thrace in the appearance of tells as the record of a new form of village organization. In the western Balkans, areas without tells have evidence for new short-term, upland, sites and in Serbia sites such as Opovo have evidence that significant proportions of animal management probably took place away from the site (Russell 1998).

Expanding land-use

The intensification of cereal and pulse agriculture, the increased social importance of grazing animals for secondary products and the contemporary increase in density of settlement sites all suggest that the landscape was increasingly occupied in new and permanent ways by people, their animals, their fields and their villages. Further evidence of the expansion of land-use by village-based communities comes from detailed work on soil and site distribution around the Selevac village.

Analysis of soil distribution in the immediate vicinity of Selevac and in the site's micro-region suggested to the excavators that, through the life of the village, the villagers expanded the areas that they cultivated (Chapman 1990; Tringham 1990). The potential increase in the amount of land now under cultivation at Selevac, as well as at contemporary sites in other Balkan regions, may have been stimulated by increases in planting technology. Chapman has argued that the use of simple wooden or antler ploughs or ards for breaking up heavier, but richer, soils was an important part of the changes evident in the temperate Balkans from the beginning of the fifth millennium BC. For Selevac, he has argued that the adoption of ard technology brought agriculture to the richer brown forest soils further from the centre of settlement at the site (Chapman 1990: 38). Certainly this would have been a technological development with important repercussions for expanding the range of available, and rich, arable land such as the *smolnitzas* and *chernozems*. Tringham has argued that during the later phases of Selevac's occupation, the area under cultivation became increasingly separated from the built-up area (Tringham 1990). As noted above, fifth millennium BC sites contained large numbers of antler tools that could have been used as ards. Shaft-hole antler tools also were used at many sites, particularly impressive examples coming from Căşcioavele and Piscul Cornişorului in southern Romania (Cârciumaru 1996: figures 8, 10). Together ard and draught animals would have enabled larger areas to be exploited.

Human effects on the environment

An increasing body of palynological data suggests that the changes in the ways, and intensities, in which people were managing their environment were having significant impact upon the landscape. Willis has noted that a major shift in vegetation occurred across the Balkans between 5500 and 3000 BC (Willis 1994). At this time species such as *Carpinus*, *Fagus* and *Abies*, which had existed in small numbers in upland areas during the late and early post-glacial periods, were now growing in a wider range of local environments. While their appearance in the pollen record in new places may have been a consequence of cooler winter temperatures, it may equally have been a factor of human alteration of fifth millennium BC landscapes.

The recognition of significant soil events occurring at this time adds to the proxy evidence for increasing human alteration of the landscape. The first major Holocene erosions were taking place at this time, stimulated probably by an increase in forest clearance (Willis 1994: 783), perhaps for farming. Very few excavation programmes have undertaken detailed studies of local sedimentological processes. At Selevac, one of the exceptions, the site's early occupation occurred in an undisturbed environment, a substantial proportion of which was woodland. A decrease in forest-habitat animals such as deer and wild pig suggests that subsequent alteration of the landscape included programmes of tree-clearance (Legge 1990: 236; Tringham and Krštić 1990b: 594).

Social consequences of accelerations in cultivation

Although the amount and precision of palaeobotanical data in many places are slight, the indirect evidence suggests that during the fifth millennium BC people expanded their practice of plant cultivation. This may have included the increase in the size of areas under cultivation and an increase in the number and capability of crop-processing and storing facilities. These changes were perhaps limited to temperate regions of the Balkans such as the lower Danube and the western Balkans. To the south, long-established strategies of autumn planting of wheat continued during the fifth millennium BC, although even in these regions the evidence for increasing use of storage facilities for cereals suggests an intensification of agricultural activities.

The presence at some fifth millennium BC sites of naked wheats, such as *Triticum durum*, suggests an increase in the requirements of scheduling planting and harvesting as well as in the effort invested. As discussed with respect to wheat cultivation in previous millennia to the south, naked varieties, although advantageous in reduced time- and labour-requirements during processing stages, do require increased attention to the timing of the harvest. Ripened naked crops left too long in the field will be lost through droppage of grains and, potentially, through lodging if rains come.

Naked wheat (i.e., *Triticum durum*) was found in almost half of the samples studied at Ovcharovo, in some samples from Golyamo Delchevo (in one of which it made up 98 per cent), but at few other sites. *Triticum aestivum*, another naked wheat, was found at a larger number of sites in south and north Bulgaria such as Banyata, Devebargan, Kodzhadermen, Karnobat, Sava, Sadovec and Sturmen (Lisitsyna and Filopovich 1980: 70–1).

Regardless of the potential adaptation of more productive, but attention-dependent, varieties such as naked wheats, the range of species exploited during the fifth millennium BC was little changed from those of the preceding 1000–1500 years. The novelty of fifth millennium BC cultivation may have been in the expansion in the size of areas now taken into cultivation and the distancing of them from settled areas. These developments would have had important consequences in the organization of labour needed for planting, tending, harvesting and processing plant resources (D. Bailey 1999).

Organizational requirements included bringing adequate numbers of individuals together at particular places at appropriate times (at some times at short notice and when they were required in other places) to carry out a range of activities: to prepare land before planting, to plant, tend, harvest and process. Some periods of the agricultural cycle had low labour requirements: the majority of crop tending activities between the time when plants had become established and when they were harvested. The amount of labour required for other individual agricultural tasks was greater. Planting and harvesting were the most time-consuming parts of the cycle and would have required large concentrations of people. As detailed in the discussion of early cultivation requirements, the length of time for which different amounts and rates of labour were required also varied. Harvesting had to be completed over a short period of time, especially in the case of naked species. Delay would have increased the risk of crop loss.

While it would have been critical to have been able to attract appropriate numbers of labourers at appropriate times in the cycle, it would have been equally important to be able to disperse or redeploy individuals when they were not needed and when their labour might not have been appreciated, desired or supportable. Dispersal would have been especially critical at the end of the harvest cycles when grain needed to be retained and stored and, perhaps, not distributed to all of those who had carried out the work.

Furthermore, the expansion and acceleration of agricultural production and processing would have magnified the importance of retaining, controlling or recalling particular knowledges and skills, or more particularly individuals with particular knowledge and skills, required for successful cultivation. Essential knowledge included knowing when to plant (too early and seeds became waterlogged) and, even more critically, knowing when to harvest (delay increased the potential for crop-loss due to lodging, grain dropping and diseases). Other types of essential knowledge were required at individual stages of post-harvest processing (from threshing to pounding – for hulled species – to winnowing and sieving) as well as during subsequent activities when errors of judgement would have proved especially costly (e.g., parching and storing). While some of these organizational and many of these knowledge requirements accompany cereal cultivation in general, the fifth millennium BC shift to large-scale agriculture would have heightened their importance.

Management of plants and animals: conclusion

During the fifth millennium BC, therefore, people managed the living environment through a combination of long-standing practices of animal and plant tending and exploitation. From these continuities emerged an increase in the attention, time and effort people devoted to plant cultivation and processing. Part of this entailed increases in the areas taken into cultivation, the amount of plant products processed and stored (and presumably consumed), and an increasing dislocation of village-space from cultivation-space. In other parts of this trend people's perceptions and uses (both economic and social) of particular animal species shifted, or at least were amplified. The rise in the importance of cattle, the increasing exploitation of animals for secondary products and the social consequences of consuming large animals were major components of this trend.

CHAPTER CONCLUSIONS

Across the Balkans the fifth millennium BC is best characterized as a period in which people continued existing practices of building their social environments and actively managing particular plants and animals. Distinctions from the previous millennium were less about novelties than they were about accelerations of particular activities such as the planting and processing of cereals or the herding and management of cattle. In terms of building, architectural methods and materials also reveal less about new procedures than they do about the expansion and adaptation in one region of forms and techniques that had been in place in earlier centuries in other regions. However, that there were many continuities with the previous millennium does not lessen the significance of the expansion of these building techniques and the accelerations of these economic activities.

The continuation and expansion of marking out space across the landscape and of dividing intramural space would have had important social consequences. The increase in villages of greater permanence, the introduction of site boundaries and location of some rooms deep within houses suggest that access to a greater number of particular places across the landscape was increasingly restricted. If animal and planting activities were also expanding, then access to appropriate arable and grazing land may also have required restriction. Differential access to parts of the landscape, parts of villages and areas within houses may have led to increasing conflict within and between communities. Tension between people would have risen. One way of claiming rights of access would have been the marking of residence in particular places by increasingly permanent and visible constructions. Claims to residence would have been extended through time by rebuilding, especially when new structures were superimposed precisely over older buildings or, in the case of horizontally developing sites, when they followed the same orientation of floorplans. The making and display of tectomorphic imagery may also have been employed in ceremonies intended to declare and legitimate residential continuities. If, as suggested

190

above, the actual occupation of these sites was fragmented by seasonal or longer abandonments then these ceremonies and architectural statements of continuity would have been even more important.

The house, the household and aggregations of these into villages as a community institution remained the focus of claims to residence as well as of many other activities; the ideology of the household, which emerged in the previous millennium, continued. If conflict and tensions were increasing, then the roles of individual households, their inhabitants and their identities would have remained, and perhaps increased in significance. At another level aggregations of households would have provided community identities to which claims of access and residence would also have been made. Whether ceremonies involved the consumption of particular animals, the eating of which had particular social consequences, or whether they involved rituals surrounding house rebuilding, such activities would have served to reaffirm and declare identities of individuals, small groups and the larger communities. In these senses, the fifth millennium BC was a period of potential rises in tensions and conflicts over access to resources and places. Further consequences of these tensions are addressed in the following chapter.

SUMMARY

In this chapter I have examined the developments in the built environment and in the exploitation of plants and animals after 5500 BC. Although there is variation in these trends between different regions, important similarities are evident. Buildings were large and made of more durable materials and there developed a greater concern for repeatedly marking particular places with villages. Continuity of occupation was marked by superimposition of structures in tells and by horizontally displaced but commonly oriented buildings at unenclosed flat sites. In some villages particular architectural elements were the main focus for continuity; such may have been the case for ovens at Slatino. In all of these cases there continued the emergence and development of an ideology of the house and of the household; this included the importance of intentionally destroying buildings as well as episodes of building and rebuilding.

Cultivation and animal management also continued, with earlier trends accelerated. The exploitation of some species for secondary products, the increase in the time and effort devoted to crop-processing activities, if not conclusively to monocropping, suggest greater emphasis on plant and animal resources. Consequences ranged from potential erosional effects on the landscape to changes in social practices of meat consumption.

A consequence of all of these trends was an increase in the potential for conflict between and within communities. Some attempts to resolve or prevent tension from becoming conflict were based on patterns of building that declared residence and on communal activities such as tending and consuming extra-domestic animals such as cattle. Other attempts to resolve conflict took advantage of two other major developments of post-5500 BC Balkan life: the emergence of a new suite of prestige materials including gold and copper and the deposition of the deceased in extramural cemeteries. These developments are addressed in the following chapter.

6

BURIAL AND EXPRESSIVE
MATERIAL CULTURE
(5500–3600 BC)

While the changes in constructing and perceiving the built and natural environments were gradual developments linked, in some places, to previous patterns, abrupt changes in the character of material culture and its deposition mark the fifth millennium BC. The most striking of these novelties were the use of new (and existing) materials to make novel visually expressive objects and the deposition of the deceased in extra-mural cemeteries. As with the trans-regional patterns in constructing the built environment, people practised distinct local traditions of material expression and extra-mural inhumation.

MORTUARY PRACTICE

The inhumation of individuals in extramural cemeteries was a striking innovation in mortuary ceremony. Not all regions shared this development. It appears most strongly in the lower Danube and in eastern Bulgaria, with special manifestations along the Black Sea coast, and, to a much more limited extent, further to the west in Serbia and in the Hungarian Plain. It occurred in northern Greece, although cremation was used in place of inhumation; cemeteries were absent in southern and western Bulgaria.

As seen in Chapter 3, people were intentionally burying deceased individuals during the late seventh and sixth millennia BC and Epi-palaeolithic and Mesolithic groups in the Danube Gorges and at Franchthi had done the same in the previous millennia. Almost without exception, these earlier burials were simple affairs in which people placed all or parts of the deceased under the floors of buildings or in refuse pits around them. Where present, grave-goods were few and simple. In the fifth millennium BC dramatic changes mark out some regions, particularly the lower Danube; the, literal, brilliance of these cemeteries stands out not only from previous millennia of simple mortuary ceremony but also from the context of contemporary practices in other parts of the Balkans. Let us look at these other areas first before turning to the more dramatic lower Danubian areas.

Northern Greece, southern and western Bulgaria and Serbia

The evidence for burial from the late sixth millennium BC in northern Greece, southern and western Bulgaria and Serbia suggests, in the main, continuity with previous patterns of behaviour. At Dimini in Thessaly at the end of the sixth millennium BC, eight cremation burials were found under floors or in pots near hearths in some of the buildings (Hourmouziadis 1979b, 1982; Andreou et al. 1996: 544). In the western Thessalian plain at Ayia Sophia two burials were associated with a mud-block mortuary structure (Milojčić 1976: 6–7; Andreou et al. 1996: 553). In the second half of the fifth millennium BC, at Pefkakia near Dimini, people placed a burial, along with two obsidian cores, beneath a building floor (Weisshaar 1989; Andreou et al. 1996: 547).

Further north, at Makriyalos in western Macedonia in the second half of the sixth millennium BC, primary and secondary burials were found in one of the site's three concentric ditches (Pappa 1993; Besios and Pappa 1994; Andreou et al. 1996: 572). During the site's later phase, people placed an infant cremation in a small pot and deposited several inhumations in pits. Sixty kilometres to the south at Mandalo, in the second half of the fifth millennium BC, people placed a child burial in an urn and the remains of an adult in a pit lined with clay and mudbricks (Pilali-Papasteriou and Papaefthimiou-Papanthimou 1989). Perhaps most unexpectedly, at Platia Magoula Zarkou, people deposited cremation burials in a cemetery several hundred metres from the tell. Besides the Zarkou cemetery, little differentiates these northern Greek burials from the similarly limited number of burials from the previous period. The striking distinctions in mortuary behaviour which marks the fifth millennium BC occur further north.

In Serbia, other parts of former Yugoslavia and south-western Romania there appeared increasing evidence of special attention devoted to burial ceremony and placement. At Gomolava, during the first half of the fifth millennium BC, people buried the deceased within the limits of the settlement, although they deposited them in an unused part of the site (Brukner 1975, 1978, 1980, 1988a, 1990; Brukner and Petrović 1977; Petrović 1984, 1990b; Živanović 1977; Clason 1979; Zoffman 1987b; Borić 1996). Indeed some have termed this an intramural necropolis (Borić 1996). In many cases the Gomolava inhumations were deposited with a new range of grave-goods including powdered malachite and copper ornaments as well as polished stone axes, flint and pottery vessels. Nearly thirty individuals were buried at Gomolava. The majority of the deceased were male, very few (perhaps two) were female and the remainder were children (Borić 1996).

An association between adult male burials and stone axes, copper bracelets and flint artefacts is distinct from one which links children with bone and copper pendants and beads; no grave-goods accompanied the female burials. People also deposited inhumations in cemeteries away from settlements, although the numbers of cemeteries are strikingly few. At Botoš, at the end of the sixth millennium BC, people buried more than thirty individuals with differential associations of grave-goods in an area unassociated with a village (Chapman 1981).

In western Romania burial remained within building contexts; at Parţa an adult was placed under the floor of a structure (Miloia 1933). In north-west Anatolia, at the beginning of the fourth millennium BC, people buried the bodies of young children under the floors or next to buildings at Ilipinar (layer IV) (Roodenberg 1993b: 257). Forty burials were found; some contained pottery grave-goods, others metal; a total of seven copper objects – axes, chisels, dagger or knife blades and a pin were found in the burials (Begemann et al. 1994: 204). In one burial two infants were buried together, facing each other, with a copper chisel. In other cases, infants were placed in pithoi.

In the Hungarian Plain at Berettyóújfalu-Herpály, at the start of the fifth millennium BC, several inhumations were placed in disused parts of the site (Kalicz and Raczky 1984, 1987). From the middle of the fifth millennium BC cemeteries appeared as places in their own right. At the end of the fifth millennium BC, at Tiszapolgár-Basatanya in the northern Hungarian Plain, people arranged many dozens of burials into rows (Bognár-Kutzián 1963; Derevenski 1997). Some of these burials had elaborate assemblages of grave-goods including jewellery made of copper (finger-rings, arm-rings and bracelets), limestone (beads) and boar's tusk (pendants) as well as very long flint blades, deer antlers and boar jaws. Tiszapolgár-Basatanya occurs in the phase after tell settlements had been in use in this region.

In the southern and western regions of the Balkans, therefore, continuities from previous millennia of mortuary activities mixed with gradually appearing new practices and materials. The inclusion of particular new types of grave-goods, such as the copper at Tiszapolgár-Basatanya and obsidian at Pefkakia, was an important innovation; so also was the grouping of individual burials in particular parts of village space or, in a few cases, the choice of a place outside of the area of settlement as appropriate for inhumation. While these developments can be seen clearly after the period of tell settlement at Tiszapolgár-Basatanya and in rare instances in the Vinča region, as at Gomolava and Botoš, many more numerous and dramatic examples have been recovered from the lower Danube.

The lower Danube

In some places, mortuary activities in the lower Danube followed patterns described for regions to the west. Thus people placed the body of a child under the floor of a building at Glina dating to the Boian culture (Comşa 1974a: 202–3). At Andolina burials were placed in small areas of settlement; in the burial of one adult, people placed a copper axe and a necklace of copper and shell beads (Comşa 1974a). At another site they buried a child with fifty-nine *Spondylus* beads (Comşa 1974a: 210).

In southern Romania and northern Bulgaria the major development, however, was that people chose extramural areas for the inhumation of individuals. This can be seen in south-eastern Romania, in the last half of the sixth and the first half of the fifth millennium BC (Haşotti 1997: 28–32) at Mangalia (Volschi and Irimia 1968), Limanu (Volschi and Irimia 1968; Galbenu 1970), Cernavoda (Berciu and Morintz 1957) and Corbu de Jos (Haşotti 1984). In many of these burials, grave-goods included animal bones (Cârciumaru 1996: 43). In some burials people placed bracelets made of *Spondylus*; five bracelets were found at Limanu, four at Mangalia, one at Medgidia Satu Nou and many at Ceamurlia de Jos. Also deposited were beads made of *Spondylus*, *Dentalium*, bone, clay, marble and copper; a necklace of 700 *Dentalium* beads was found in a burial at Limanu and others have come from Ceamurlia de Jos and Medgidia Cocoaşe. Pendants made of marble have been uncovered in burials at Ceamurlia de Jos; one pendant made of clay but fashioned and fired to resemble *Spondylus* was included in a burial at Agigea. A small pot (11.7 cm in diameter and 3.0 cm high) was placed in one of the Limanu burials. Copper grave-goods were few but included a bead at Limanu and two bracelets from Agigea.

Cernavoda

Cernavoda is one of the largest of cemeteries of this period in this region and contains over four hundred burials separated into two zones based on differences in grave-good associations. Along with the contemporary cemetery in the Hamangia phase at Durankulak, Cernavoda is the only well documented cemetery of south-eastern Romania and north-eastern Bulgaria from this part of the period (Berciu et al. 1955; Berciu and Morintz 1957, Berciu et al. 1959).

At Cernavoda, as at other contemporary burials in the region, people placed *Spondylus* bracelets, marble pendants and copper and *Dentalium* beads in burials. In many, stone axes, chisels and adzes were placed near the right hand or the head of the deceased; few of these tools bear traces of use. Pottery was a frequent grave-good and, in their forms, vessels were different from those found in settlement contexts. Burials in Hamangia cemeteries, such as Cernavoda, also contained anthropomorphic figurines and in this respect are distinct from all other contemporary patterns of mortuary activities.[1] Beyond traditional morphological and racial classifications of anatomy, very limited biological information, especially about the age or sex of the deceased, is available. In a large majority of burials at Cernavoda, people deposited parts, especially the skulls, of domesticated animals; this practice has similarities with earlier mortuary practices in this and other regions of south-east and central Europe as seen especially clearly in the Danube Gorges sites. People used Cernavoda over a long period of time; the later phases of use appear to have disturbed earlier episodes of inhumation (Haşotti 1997: 29).

Durankulak

At Durankulak 270 burials from the Hamangia phase date to the end of the sixth and the beginning of the fifth millennia BC (Todorova and Vajsov 1993: 224). The earlier burials have very few or no grave-goods; those that do appear include *Spondylus* ornaments or small pottery cups. In later burials people placed in the graves the heads of animals, most frequently of wild ass but also cattle, sheep or goat. During part of the burial ceremony people feasted at the cemetery and used large pots (10–15 litres) and may have consumed meat from the skulls of animals (Todorova and Vajsov 1993: 227). In some of the later burials people placed small pots containing food.

Differentiation in the patterns of deposition of grave-goods between individual burials was limited. Some graves had schematic anthropomorphic figurines in them. A few burials, however, contained a disproportionate number of grave-goods. In grave 751 were placed the skulls of two cattle across the legs of a woman (Todorova and Vajsov 1993: 227). More striking is a small number of other graves that have very high concentrations of grave-goods. In grave 626, a woman's body was buried in a crouched position on her left side. In the burial were placed a large *Spondylus* bracelet, a bone ring, a necklace of hematite, malachite and copper beads and four figurines placed under the head of the deceased. Grave 1036 contained a man's body stretched out on his back. Near his head was a clay anthropomorphic figurine; two others were placed on his chest. Other grave-goods include a sceptre or digging stick made from a deer bone, a small stone axe, a flint blade and a large *Spondylus* bracelet. Perhaps most spectacular is grave 644 (Figure 6.1). It contained a woman's body, seven sets of perforated reindeer teeth (the sets consisted of 8, 9, 5, 12, 9, 9 and 8 teeth respectively), four *Spondylus* beads, a *Spondylus* anthropomorphic figurine, seven flint blades and three *Spondylus* bracelets or armbands (Vajsov 1992b).

North-eastern Bulgaria

In many cases in north-eastern Bulgaria, people buried the deceased in cemeteries close to tell settlements; this was the case at Ovcharovo, Turgovishte, Radingrad and Golyamo Delchevo. In other cases, as in one of the most spectacular instances at Varna on the Black Sea coast, cemeteries had no clearly associated settlement. Most of these cemeteries do not

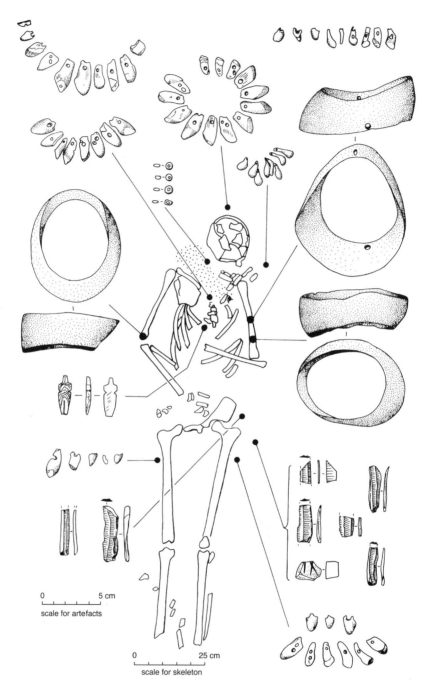

0   5 cm

scale for artefacts

0   25 cm

scale for skeleton

Figure 6.1 Grave 644 from Durankulak (after Vajsov 1992b)

contain very large numbers of graves. Varna, with almost three hundred burials, is an exception, as are burial grounds further north; this later phase of Durankulak has over eight hundred and, as noted above, the cemetery at Cernavoda had over four hundred. The small number of inhumations in the tell-associated cemeteries is especially striking in light of the long periods during which the tells were in use.

Although good dating evidence is infrequent, typological comparison of grave-goods suggests that all these cemeteries were in use during the later part of the fifth millennium BC, as was Tiszapolgár-Basatanya in eastern Hungary, noted above. It is tempting to read the low numbers of burials in the smaller cemeteries as evidence that only restricted members of village communities were being selected for inhumation. It is also possible, and perhaps more likely, that the distinctions in cemetery size may reflect the length of time during which a burial ground was in use. This appears to have been the case at Durankulak, where the extremely large cemetery was in active use over a long period of time (Dimov et al. 1984); Tiszapolgár-Basatanya also had several major phases of use through the end of the fifth and the fourth millennia BC. The tell-associated, inland Bulgarian cemeteries appear to have been in active use during the later phases of tell use. Thus the limited number of inhumations in these cemeteries may represent the brevity of extramural mortuary ceremonies, not any social limitations of selecting eligible individuals for inhumation. The wide diversity in the size and consistency of grave-good assemblages from the small cemeteries offers additional support to the latter interpretation.

Grave assemblages

There are clear patterns among grave assemblages. Varieties of types of grave-good and variations in the number of grave-goods in different burials show distinctions between individual burials and, perhaps, between the individual deceased themselves. In brief, these patterns distinguish between the treatment of males and females on the one hand and between the treatment of children and adults on the other.

While it is tempting to focus on the most dramatic cemeteries at Varna or Durankulak, these are perhaps not the best places to start. Neither has been fully published; preliminary reports have focused on the most spectacular graves (I. Ivanov 1978a, 1978b, 1988a, 1988b; Dimov et al. 1984; Vajsov 1987, 1990a, 1992b; Fol and Lichardus 1988a; Musées Nationaux 1989; Avramova 1991). Also, in the case of Varna, the cemetery may represent extra-ordinary mortuary behaviour unrelated to the reality of everyday life as documented from settlements. Furthermore, the absence of inter-burial dating criteria makes it impossible to distinguish between patterns of body treatment and assemblages that represent diachronic change from those due to contemporary social intentions.

A better approach to the dynamism of the fifth millennium BC mortuary pattern of the lower Danube is to look first at the smaller inland cemeteries associated with settlement tells. There are four published cemeteries to examine: Golyamo Delchevo, Vinitsa, Devniya and Turgovishte (Todorova 1971; Todorova et al. 1975; Raduncheva 1976; I. Angelova 1986b; Todorova 1986: 184–5). (Two other cemeteries, one at Radingrad and the other at Ovcharovo, have been excavated but the former remains unpublished and the latter was only partially investigated – only three burials were examined) (Todorova et al. 1983). Together these four published cemeteries provide a corpus of almost a hundred burials; individual cemetery size ranges from 12 burials at Turgovishte, to 16 at Devniya, to 28 at Golyamo Delchevo and 41 at Vinitsa.

With some minor exceptions, each cemetery displays similar patterns in grave assemblages and ages and sexes of those buried. Although men, women and children are included in each cemetery, they are not present in equal numbers: overall male burials are the most frequent, accounting for 43 per cent of all graves. In relatively even proportions women, children, and cenotaph (burials without skeletal material) make up the rest (22, 19 and 16 per cent respectively). For those cases in which the age of the deceased has been determined (seventy burials overall), just over half (51 per cent) were between 16 and 40 years old. Of the remainder, 26 per cent were over 40, and 23 per cent were children (identified as under 16 years of age). These proportions varied between the different cemeteries, ranging from no individual over 40 years old at Devniya to 11 per cent of this age at Golyamo Delchevo and 37 per cent at Vinitsa.

Grave-goods include ceramic vessels, bone and metal utensils and bone, shell and metal ornaments and tools. Across all four cemeteries, pottery was clearly the most common grave-good, representing 66 per cent of all grave-goods and appearing in 82 per cent of graves. Flint and bone utensils were much less frequent (18 per cent of all goods found in 29 per cent of graves) as were ornaments (9 per cent of goods, in 18 per cent of graves) and copper objects (7 per cent of goods, in 19 per cent of graves). In some graves (14 per cent) ochre had been placed on or under the bodies; where ochre has been preserved it has been found in all types of burials except for those of children.

Grave-goods were disproportionately distributed over four distinct types of burials: male, female, body-less (or 'cenotaph') and children's. In crude terms of numbers of goods per burial and numbers of metal goods in burials, several patterns are clear. First, cenotaphs and male burials contain, on average, more goods than female burials, while children's burials have few goods at all (Figure 6.2). With respect to the inclusion of metal objects, a similar pattern is evident: cenotaphs and male burials dominate; female burials have very few metal grave-goods and children even fewer (Figure 6.3). Not all burials contained grave-goods: 13 per cent had none.

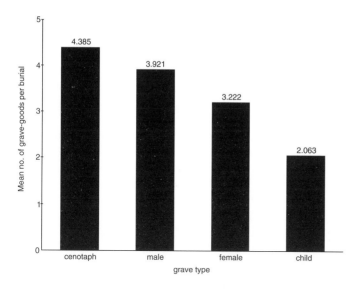

Figure 6.2 Mean number of grave-goods for different types of graves at Devniya, Golyamo Delchevo, Turgovishte and Vinitsa (data from Todorova 1986; Raduncheva 1976; Todorova *et al.* 1983)

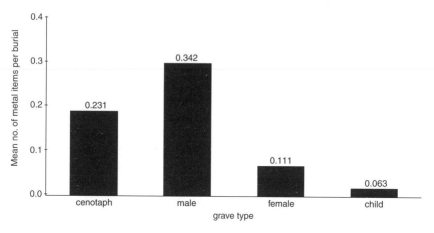

Figure 6.3 Mean number of metal grave-goods for different types of graves at Devniya, Golyamo Delchevo, Turgovishte and Vinitsa (data from Todorova 1986; Raduncheva 1976; Todorova *et al.* 1983)

The pattern of grave types without grave-goods mirrors the pattern that linked male and cenotaph burials with larger assemblages of goods. Thirty-eight per cent of children's burials and 17 per cent of women's burials had no grave-goods. Among men's burials only 6 per cent were without goods; none of the cenotaphs was empty.

Burial interpretation

These patterns are suggestive. While in the fifth millennium BC it was appropriate to include individuals of all age and sex categories in cemeteries, it was not appropriate for all categories to receive similar burial treatment. Burial appears to have been a context in which intra-group differences were expressed. There were particular patterns in the numbers and types of grave-goods that were included in a particular person's burial. There is a clear association between male and cenotaph burials and larger quantities of grave-goods and metal objects; a second clear association exists between children (and to a lesser extent women) and few, if any, grave-goods. Regardless of the significance one attaches to the meaning of individual artefacts deposited in burials, the patterns of differentiation between individual people's burials are clear.

The repeated patterns in the positioning of bodies within each inhumation and the orientation of bodies across the cemetery are as striking as are the disproportionate patterns in grave-goods. There are two separate patterns of body positioning, one for the cemeteries located near settlement tells, such as Golyamo Delchevo, Vinitsa and Turgovishte, and one for the Devniya cemetery, which was not associated with a tell. For the tell cemeteries, the majority of bodies (69 per cent) were placed on their left sides in a crouched position; all but one of the rest were placed in a crouched position on their backs. Almost all bodies are placed so that they faced the east and, as most cemeteries were located west of their respective settlements, almost all bodies face the nearest settlement. At Devniya, on the other hand, most of the bodies (75 per cent) were placed extended on their backs and the rest were placed in a crouched position on their right hand side (Todorova 1986: 184–5).

Thus, while there are clear patterns of distinction between individual inhumations as displayed by grave-good association, there are also larger patterns of similarity across individual cemeteries as displayed by the positioning of bodies, regardless of their sex or age. While the first pattern of distinction may reflect the expression of alternative personal identities within the community, the latter patterns of similarity may reflect the inclusion of differently identified individuals within a larger group buried within the cemetery and attached to the nearby tell settlement. Furthermore the fact that both sorts of patterns are repeated with little variation in each separate inland cemetery across the region suggests that similar ideas of appropriate ways of expressing both interpersonal distinctions and community cohesion were shared by the separate communities.

The possibility that burials in these communities were the means for making statements on several different levels, referring to both the individual and the communal, suggests that one of the main, if not the main, significances of fifth millennium BC burial may have been the event of burial itself, regardless of the individual inhumed. If this was the case, then perhaps it is easier to understand the presence of the body-less (cenotaph) burials in these cemeteries. Though similar to other burials in concentrations of grave-goods and orientation, cenotaphs were burials which did not contain human remains. Cenotaphs appeared in almost all lower Danubian cemeteries. For the corpus of inland cemeteries in north-eastern Bulgaria, they account for 16 per cent of burials: five were found at Devniya, six at Vinitsa and three at Golyamo Delchevo. Of all graves in the corpus, they have the highest average of goods per grave (4.385 per grave versus 3.921, 3.222, 2.063 for male, female and child burials respectively) and, after male burials, they have the highest average of metal goods per grave (0.231 per grave versus 0.342, 0.111, 0.063 for male, female and children) (see Figure 6.2).

Most interpretations have read cenotaphs as symbolic burials made to mark the deaths of important community members who died while far away from home (Chapman 1990; see Todorova 1978, 1986). It may be more accurate to understand cenotaphs in terms of the community importance of the event of burial. In this sense, cenotaphs may have been mechanisms for expressing both community cohesion and reaffirming distinctions between different groups within a community. Thus cenotaphs may be the remains of ritual events employed to express, and perhaps reinforce, community structure. Furthermore, the inclusion of the high proportions of goods and metal objects in cenotaphs suggests that their accompanying burial rite may have been extended, and especially dramatic, occasions. Perhaps cenotaph burials marked times when it was necessary to make a loud public statement about social structure regardless of whether or not a member of the community needed burying. These statements may have been made with special reference to community ancestors.

Varna and Durankulak

Following the suggestion that fifth millennium BC burial was as much about community cohesion as it was about the display of distinctions among individual identities, it is perhaps easier to understand the extraordinary concentrations of burials on the Black Sea coast at Varna and Durankulak. These cemeteries are extraordinary for two reasons. Compared to the inland cemeteries, they are very large: with over eight hundred burials, Durankulak is larger than anything else in the Balkans at this time or before; Varna's close to three hundred burials makes it less extraordinary, although only marginally so. The coastal cemeteries are also distinct in the large concentrations of exotic grave-goods found in some inhumations.

The Varna cemetery was found by chance in 1972 and the local museum carried out extensive excavations of the site under the direction of Ivan Ivanov (I. Ivanov 1978a, 1978b 1983, 1988a, 1988b). The large concentrations of gold and copper in several of the burials immediately attracted international scientific attention; exhibitions of the finds from the most sensational burials have visited many European cities as well as museums in East Asia and the Americas. In their catalogues, these exhibitions provide the fullest reports on the cemetery (Fol and Lichardus 1988a; Musées Nationaux 1989); complete publication has yet to appear. The site has also attracted the attentions of international interpretation (Renfrew 1986c; Chapman 1990; Whittle 1996: 96–101).

As at Devniya, the Varna cemetery is unaccompanied by a tell settlement; attempts have been made to link it with poorly understood pile-dwellings found nearby at Ezerovo on land which is now submerged under Varna Lakes but which would have been an estuary in the fifth millennium BC (Todorova and Toncheva 1975; Margos 1978). The Varna cemetery, as excavated up to 1986, covered a large area (1200 × 600 m). Doubtless more burials exist on all sides of the investigated area except perhaps to the south (see Fol and Lichardus 1988a: figure 222). The amount of detailed information available does not match that for the inland cemeteries; there is no complete published inventory of all burials with sex, age and lists of grave-goods. What information is available reveals that a quarter (70) of the Varna graves have been badly disturbed by modern construction projects and that the remaining 211 burials include a full range of male, female, cenotaph and child burials. Of all burials at Varna, 23 had no grave-goods and 170 had between one and ten grave-goods. The remaining 18 graves (8.5 per cent of the total) have attracted the most attention. They contained extraordinarily large grave assemblages consisting of up to hundreds of individual objects (I. Ivanov 1988a: 58). The contents of these large-assemblage graves are almost overwhelming. Two examples will suffice.

Grave 43 contained the skeleton of a male aged between 40 and 50 years. The body was laid out on its back and ochre was found to one side near a pot. Both the quantity and the appearance of the grave-goods are striking. The grave contained over a thousand objects, including 890 gold beads, 42 round gold appliqués, 16 gold rings; 11 gold lip- or ear-plugs, 10 other gold appliqués, six sheet-gold rings for covering an axe handle, five sheet-gold rings for covering a bow, a *Spondylus* bracelet with two pieces of sheet-gold covering, two convex gold discs positioned over the deceased's knees, a stone axe-sceptre with four sheet-gold shaft-coverings, two flat gold plates at the deceased's waist, a gold penis-sheath, four gold arm-rings, three copper axes, a copper chisel, a copper awl, a copper point, a flint point, three flint blades (one of which was 39 cm long), two stone axes, four pots, a vessel lid and two bone points (I. Ivanov 1988b: 200–3). Grave 43 contained 990 gold objects which, together, weigh 1.5 kg.

Such extravagant grave-good deposition was not limited to male burials but was also found in cenotaphs. Fifty-six of the Varna burials (27 per cent) were cenotaphs and many were extravagantly supplied. Grave 4 is a good example. As with grave 43, grave 4 contained a sensationally impressive assemblage of goods: 242 gold beads, 49 round perforated gold appliqués, 19 gold rolled spirals, seven sheet-gold coverings for a handle, seven gold rings, four gold arm-rings, a sheet-gold pectoral, a gold plate, eight other gold objects, a copper awl with a bone handle, two copper chisels, two hammer-axes, a copper axe, four flint blades between 12 and 31 cm long, two stone axes, 53 red quartz beads, 30 kaolin beads, 1400 *Dentalium* shells, two open shallow ceramic dishes, one of which was decorated with gold leaf (or powdered gold), two ceramic pots with lids, one of which was decorated with gold and one of which was decorated with red paint, and a shaft-hole deer antler axe (I. Ivanov 1988b: 189–91). As with grave 43, the total weight of gold in grave 4 amounted to 1.5 kg. Although there was no body in the burial, the finds were placed as if on and around a body and traces of black organic material and ochre were found on the floor of the grave and on grave-goods.

The spectacular nature of the large-assemblage burials at Varna, such as graves 43 and 4, has often masked the overall patterns of grave-good distribution. While it is impossible to investigate trends in grave-good variety, quantity and association with grave-type until the cemetery is fully published, several comments may put these extraordinary graves into context. Twenty-three (8 per cent) of the Varna graves contained no grave-goods at all. Although more than 100 (36 per cent) had more than ten goods, a significant proportion (170 burials, 61 per cent) had between one and ten goods. These rough calculations illustrate a significant amount of variation within the total population of burials at Varna. In fact, this variation is close to that found in the inland cemeteries. Furthermore, as in the inland burials, ceramic vessels predominated as grave-goods at Varna: over six hundred pots were found distributed over 80 per cent of the burials. Gold objects were found in only 22 per cent of the Varna burials and 60 per cent of all gold was found in cenotaphs (I. Ivanov 1988a: 58, 63). Thus, while more secure conclusions are impossible before complete publication of the cemetery, similar broad patterns of distinctions between individual burials link the inland and the Varna coastal cemeteries.

If there is a significant distinction between the Varna and inland cemeteries perhaps it is manifest in the positioning of bodies in graves. Where most of the inland bodies were positioned crouched on their sides with very few laid out flat on their backs, almost a third of the Varna bodies (32 per cent) were fully extended; only 23 per cent of Varna burials were buried in a crouched position. Thus, while similar ranges of intra-group distinction may have been played out in both areas, the attendance to different fashions of arranging individual bodies suggests that different rules applied. The distinction in body positioning is reinforced by the patterns at the inland cemetery closest to the coast (Devniya), where a very large proportion of the burials (75 per cent) were laid out on their backs. If, as suggested above, body positioning in inland burials was a reference to cemeteries accompanying settlement tells, the difference in body positioning at Varna and Devniya may be nothing more than a reflection of the absence of permanent settlement associated with these cemeteries. Regardless of whether or not bodies were positioned facing towards settlements, two patterns in body arrangement emerge: bodies in coastal cemeteries were laid out extended on their backs; bodies in inland cemeteries were crouched on their right sides.

Thus, some patterns which emerged from the study of inland cemeteries also appear at Varna. On the coast as well as further inland, the main purpose of burial may have been the simultaneous expression of group and intra-group identities. At first, the large concentrations of objects made of exotic materials found in the burials on the coast is striking. However, the distinction in the quantity of exotic grave-goods at the coast is less abrupt than it appears. The proportion of metal grave-goods increases directly with the proximity of the cemetery to the coast. The nearer the coast, the greater the frequency: none at Turgovishte; 10 per cent at Vinitsa; 14 per cent at Golyamo Delchevo; 50 per cent at Devniya.

The picture from Durankulak is less clear. The cemetery and associated settlement tell have been investigated since 1975 by Henrietta Todorova but publication of cemetery details has been limited (Dimov 1982; Dimov *et al.* 1984; Vajsov 1987, 1990a, 1992a; Todorova 1986; Avramova 1991). From the limited information available, it is clear that some (an unquantified minority it would appear) of the Durankulak burials are as extravagantly equipped as were the more dramatic Varna graves. Thus, in grave 447 at Durankulak the body of a female accompanied five bracelets (three of *Spondylus* and two of copper), two copper rings, three copper plaques (covering the deceased's lips or teeth) and a string of beads made of various materials; 20 beads were of green schist, 15 of *Spondylus*, 13 of malachite, 5 of gold, 3 of copper and 1 of chalcedony. Also made of *Spondylus* were a nine-piece diadem and 28 appliqués. Male and children's burials (graves 732 and 223 respectively) were also supplied with similar disproportionately high numbers and diverse ranges of grave-goods.

Most of the limited information available focuses on the Durankulak burials containing the disproportionate numbers or types of grave-goods. Of the 99 burials with copper objects (i.e., copper was placed in less than 10 per cent of burials), more female burials included copper objects (43 per cent) than did male burials (27 per cent). Adolescent, children's and cenotaph burials make up the rest (Avramova 1991: 44–5). Among different grave types, there is little difference in the average numbers of individual copper objects included: male 1.96 per grave, female 1.79, cenotaph 1.71 and children 2.10. Gold is much less frequent, although when it is included it appears in similar proportions in different burial types: male 5.71 per burial, female 5.14, and for children in the one burial in which it appears it was the only grave-good. Notably none of the Durankulak cenotaphs contain gold objects.

In addition to gold and copper, people also deposited a wide range of other grave-goods: ceramic vessels, flint blades, *Spondylus*, green schist, lignite, bone, chalcedony and malachite. Most of these materials were used to make body and clothing ornaments; 235 of the Durankulak burials contained body- or clothes ornament grave-goods (Avramova 1991: 44).

Thus in many ways Varna and Durankulak are similar. They are both large cemeteries containing some significantly high concentrations of exotic grave-goods. Both sites contain marked differences between individual burials in terms of the numbers and types of grave-goods. It appears that the range of intra-group differentiation among burials (and so perhaps individuals) that was clear to the south and south-west, at Varna, Devniya, Golyamo Delchevo and Vinitsa, is also evident at Durankulak.

There are, however, potentially important differences between Varna and Durankulak. First, there is a significant difference between the type of copper goods deposited at Durankulak and at the other cemeteries: the large, extravagant axe-hammer-adzes found at Varna and many of the inland cemeteries do not appear to be present at Durankulak, where copper was used exclusively for body and clothing ornament. In addition to bracelets and rings, copper was also used to make flat plaques to cover lips and teeth. Perhaps, in the place of the large copper tools found at other contemporary cemeteries, people at Durankulak used objects made of bone. Twenty-five of the Durankulak shaft-hole objects were made of bone; they were placed in male and cenotaph burials. Avramova describes them as similar in form to the sceptre found at Varna II in grave 3 (Avramova 1991: 46–7).

The second significant difference between the two sites is the placement of clay anthropomorphic figurines in some of the cenotaphs. Grave 453 at Durankulak is one of four cenotaphs containing a figurine. The grave also contained a figurine with a copper bracelet on one of its arms, five green schist beads and four pots, one of which contained a bone awl and needle, a flint knife and a river shell. Anthropomorphic figurines are conspicuous by their absence from other Balkan burials. Perhaps, as Avramova suggests, the use of figurines at Durankulak recalls the use of clay face-masks in several of the Varna cenotaphs (Avramova 1991: 47). Perhaps another factor is local continuity with earlier, Hamangia burial traditions, in which figurines were a frequent grave-good.

Third, Durankulak differs from Varna in that at the former people used gold for fewer grave-goods, especially with respect to body and clothing ornamentation. Avramova's study lists less than a hundred individual pieces, 81 of which are beads (Avramova 1991: 45–6). Gold appears not to have been used to make clothing or body appliqués at Durankulak; in addition to the copper plaques noted above, *Spondylus* appears to have been the main material from which appliqués were made. A final difference between Varna and Durankulak is that the latter site is associated with a contemporary settlement and the former is not.

Overall, although there are clear differences between Varna and Durankulak, the over-riding pattern is one of similarity in inter-burial contents; the symbols of differentiation were the same (axe-hammer-adzes; body ornament) although the material medium through which these symbols were expressed were different (copper and gold at Varna, bone and *Spondylus* at Durankulak).

Burials: conclusion

There are clear internal distinctions in fifth millennium BC grave assemblages in the lower Danube cemeteries. Where detailed information has been published, clear patterns emerge. In the north-east Bulgarian graves there are repeated trends in the frequencies and types of objects that were deemed appropriate to be included in the inhumations of some men's and in all cenotaph burials; the inverse is the case for the burials of most women and all children. These distinctions suggest that differences between particular individuals were expressed during burial ceremonies. The presence of these inter-individual distinctions does not negate the equally probable function of these cemeteries in expressions of community unity, as can be recognized through trends in body position.

The fact that these expressions of interpersonal distinction and community cohesion were made in extramural cemeteries is also significant. Burial in cemeteries away from, but in sight (and perhaps sound) of, the tell villages or, in the case of Varna, not associated with any settlement, was burial in the open and on the public stage. This is very different both from previous millennia of burial associated in and near village buildings and from contemporary fifth millennium BC burial trends in other regions of the Balkans. In the lower Danube, the separation of burials from buildings (but not from the vicinity of villages) adds further weight to the suggestion, made in Chapter 5, that the built environment held new meanings for people in the fifth millennium BC, meanings of which burial was not an appropriate constituent. Equally, the need to create and repeatedly use an open, public ceremony to express individual and group identity marks a significant change in people's perceptions of death and its appropriate treatment.

In other parts of the Balkans longer-term changes in mortuary treatment were less dramatic than in the lower Danube. While the differences from the northern Greek scene are clear, it is surprising that to the south, in south-central Bulgaria, where tells dominated landscapes and where a major source for the majority of early copper raw materials was located (as discussed below), there were no cemeteries. This absence appears not to be a factor of lack of research; areas around Stara Zagora have long histories of field-work. Only further to the west do similar things occur, although the Vinča and Tiszapolgár cemeteries offer less dynamic and less frequent images of the new ideas which appear so markedly along the lower Danube. Thus, in the burial record, as with the record of the built environment, although variation across the regions is characteristic, there is a common link in an increase in the attention given to the deceased and in the ways in which that attention was deemed to be appropriate. Although the particulars of mortuary treatment varied across the region more than did variations in built environment, there were trans-regional similarities on a more general level.

EXPRESSIVE MATERIAL CULTURE

As seen in most of the burial records, and especially in those from the lower Danube, an important part of the new perception of death was the attention given to objects made from a range of new raw materials, mainly minerals and molluscs. For the most part, people used these new materials to make objects which they placed in graves. Five new raw materials are noteworthy: copper, gold, graphite and the shells *Spondylus* and *Dentalium*. Other materials, such as red quartz and kaolin, though important, appeared less frequently.

Copper

The mining and processing of copper ore and the deposition of objects made of copper were major developments of southern and central Europe from the late sixth millennium BC. In the fifth millennium BC, the Balkans (especially Bulgaria) played a major role in large-scale extraction and far-ranging distribution of copper. Copper was mined extensively at Aibunar in south-central Bulgaria and at Rudna Glava in Serbia as well as at other places. Where detailed sourcing analyses have been undertaken objects made from copper ores extracted at Aibunar appear across and beyond the Balkans (Chernykh 1978a; 1978b; 1992).

The earliest copper objects were simple, cold-hammered trinkets which appeared in the late sixth millennium BC; malachite and azurite beads come from a Starčevo IIIa context at Lepenski Vir (Srejović 1969: 173) and a fragment of malachite was found in association with Starčevo pottery at Zmajevac in Sumadja. In its early forms, copper was made into simple hooks, as at Gornea in an early Vinča context (Lazarovici 1970: 477), and rolled beads, as at Vinča, Selevac, Čoka in the western Balkans, at Cernica in southern Romania and at Ovcharovo I and Usoe II in north-eastern Bulgaria (Berciu and Morintz 1957; Slobozianu 1959; Cantacuzino and Morintz 1963; Todorova 1975; Todorova 1981; Comşa 1991a: 78). There is strong evidence from Divostin (phase II) for the manufacture of copper or malachite beads in two sizes, the larger of which had a mean diameter of 7 mm, the smaller 4 mm (Glumac 1985, 1988: 457). To make these beads, people ground down malachite nuggets into parallel-sided pieces through which they drilled holes with flint micro-borers. Individual beads were then snapped off and their edges finished (Glumac 1988: 458). People at Divostin also used malachite to make lunate and tear-shaped pendants. A small copper bracelet, similar to the one from the Gomolava burial and another from a hoard at Pločnik (Stalio 1964), was also found at the site. Small copper beads and undistinguished copper or malachite pieces have been found at a number of contemporary sites in the western Balkans: at Ratina (Valović 1985), Stapari (Jurišić 1960), Grivac (Gavela 1956–7), Vinča-Belo Brdo, Gornja Tuzla (Čović 1961) and Obre I (Sterud and Sterud 1974: 258). At Selevac, over 200, albeit small, fragments of copper objects date from the second quarter and the middle of the fifth millennium BC (Glumac 1983; Glumac and Tringham 1990: 555–7). At some sites, people were engaged in processes more complex than cold hammering; finds of crucibles and slags from Vinča-Pločnik sites suggest that people were smelting copper (Glumac 1983; Glumac and Todd 1991).

At Usoe II, in north-eastern Bulgaria pieces of oxidized copper sheet containing 10 per cent iron were found. Gale has interpreted this as early evidence for copper smelting (Gale *et al.* 1991; Todorova 1981: 4). To the north in Romania, a double-pointed awl was recovered at Balomir and a lump of copper at Iernut: both sites are in Transylvania and both date from late Criş contexts, that is to the start of the sixth millennium BC (Comşa 1991a: 51; Vlassa; 1967: 407; 1969: 504). Two thin flakes of copper were found with late Körös pottery at Szarvas 23 in county Békés in Hungary (Makkay 1982a).

The production of trinket-ornaments continued into the first half of the fifth millennium BC. As mentioned above, beads were placed in Hamangia burials at Cernavoda and Agigea in Romanian Dobrudzha (Berciu and Morintz 1957; Slobozianu 1959). The finds at Agigea also include two copper bracelets (Slobozianu 1959). At the same time, in south-central Romania, a similar range of objects were in use: a small awl-chisel from a Boian-Giuleşti context at Giulesti-Sîrbi (Leahu 1963); 28 beads from a Boian-Vidra phase burial at Andolina (Comşa 1961); two awls, a ring and copper wire from Boian-Vidra phase burials at Vărăşti (Christescu 1925); beads and an awl from burials at Glina (Nestor 1928: 123; Comşa 1991a: 79); and copper wire from a late Boian context at Radovanu (Comşa 1991a: 79). At Hirşova in the Danube delta, small copper ornaments were made in what has been identified as a workshop. Exceptionally, terracotta moulds for making copper axes come from a Gumelniţa context at Caşcioarele (V. Dumitrescu *et al.* 1983: 105). Much of the copper from Gumelniţa contexts was made into small ornaments, such as double-spiral headed pins, although larger tools, such as various forms of axes were also produced (Vulpe 1975). Further west in southern Romania at Vădastra and at Fărcaşul de Sus the patterns of form and technology are similar in contemporary levels which have produced awls, beads and small indistinguishable fragments of copper (Christescu 1933: 203; Mateescu 1959, 1965; Nica 1976: 77). Though present, copper objects remained much rarer further west in Vinča contexts: a ring comes from a Vinča B2 phase at Liubcova (Comşa 1991a: 80) and an awl from a later Vinča context at Verbicioara (Berciu 1961: 39).

Todorova suggests that this early ornamental use of copper represents a first phase of development in Balkan metallurgy when the majority of copper was made into small objects such as awls, beads, rings and armbands (Todorova 1981: 4). However, larger objects were being produced at this time as well. Stefan Chokadzhiev's excavations at Slatino in south-western Bulgaria recovered large copper objects from levels dated to this period (S. Chokadzhiev 1995). The Slatino finds, however, appear as exceptions to the production of decorative objects in copper's early exploitation.

In addition to the production of ornamental trinkets, people may have used copper ores in other ways to decorate human bodies. Todorova has suggested that the lumps of azurite found in small pots from settlements in south-central Bulgaria were used for body painting (Todorova 1981). Gale has argued that some of the pieces of copper ore found at sites in the Aibunar region were used as a cosmetic or pigment to paint the body (Gale *et al.* 1991). Support for both of these suggestions comes from Chernykh who confirmed that small, thick-walled ceramic pots found at these sites were not, as originally assumed, crucibles, but had served as pigment containers (Chernykh 1978a: 75).

In Todorova's second phase in the development of Balkan copper production, large copper tools appeared. The first flat copper axes come from middle of the fifth millennium BC contexts and the earliest shaft-hole hammer-axes appeared slightly later (Figure 6.4). Also at this time began the production of the large, heavy, copper objects, such as axe-adzes as well as hammer-axes and large chisels, that appear so striking in the lower Danubian burials. As noted above, copper was deposited in significant concentrations in the cemeteries of the lower Danubian and Black Sea coast. At Varna, 82 of the 281 graves contained copper artefacts as did 91 of the burials at Durankulak. Chisels, awls and shaft-hole tools were also deposited in the burials at Golyamo Delchevo, Vinitsa and Devniya. On the other hand, pieces of copper ore have been found at settlements in Bulgaria, at Stara Zagora Bolnitsa, Bereket, Azmak, and Chatalka as well as in former Yugoslavia, at Divostin, Gornja Tuzla, Fafos I and Grivac (Gale *et al.* 1991: 59, table 6).

The frequency of heavy tools and weapons increased at the end of the fifth and the beginning of the fourth millennia BC. Todorova has argued that production of increasingly slim-profiled hammer-axes at the beginning

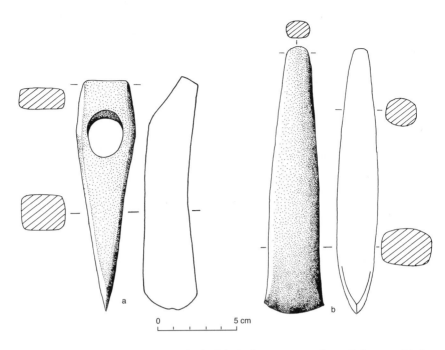

Figure 6.4 Copper implements: a) shaft-hole hammer-axe from Cabarevo; b) flat copper axe from Devebargan (after Todorova 1981)

of the fourth millennium BC reflects a more efficient use of copper raw materials. From the first half of the fourth millennium BC (Todorova terms this the Transitional Period between her Eneolithic and early Bronze Ages) the copper-working and copper-consumption which had dominated Thrace and north-eastern and eastern Bulgaria tailed-off and the centres of extraction and production appear to have shifted to the north-west. The remarkable axe-adzes and thin, flat-axes produced at this time may represent a major shift in the organization of copper production and distribution. Finished copper-goods were now being traded into former areas of extraction and production, like Bulgaria, from other regions, probably in the Carpathians. At the same time, the variety in the forms of objects made of copper diminished. The emergence of objects made with arsenic and eventually tin (and lead and zinc) accompanies the beginning of a very different set of cultural and social perceptions which mark the beginning of the early Bronze Age which are discussed in Chapter 7.

Although the centre of fifth millennium BC copper production and deposition was central and eastern Bulgaria, copper was found throughout the Balkans regions at this time. However, the concentrations of large copper objects common in north-eastern and eastern Bulgaria are not frequently found in other regions. To the west, large copper tools are limited, for the most part to late Vinča phase hoards. In the eastern Hungarian plain at Berettyóújfalu-Herpály at the start of the fifth millennium BC, copper rings, pendents and beads come from Tisza-Herpály contexts. As was noted for the late fifth millennium BC burials at Tiszpolgár-Basatanya, the amounts of copper deposited were small.

In northern Greece, a copper flat-axe and an earring are the only metal finds from Dimini in Thessaly (McGeehan-Liritzis and Gale 1988; Andreou *et al.* 1996: 544 n. 46). A single, small, copper bead comes from early contexts at Dikili Tash (Séfériadès 1992). At Pefkakia two copper axes date from the end of the fifth millennium BC (Weisshaar 1989: 48, pl. 19; Andreou *et al.* 1996: 547, n. 66). At Mandalo an awl, chisel, axe and pieces of copper sheet were found in late fifth millennium BC contexts (Pilali-Papasteriou and Papaefthimiou-Papanthimou 1989: 24; Andreou *et al.* 1996: 571). A series of small copper objects come from Sitagroi III contexts at the eponymous site (Renfrew 1986a: 482). The frequency of copper objects in northern Greece, even during the period when sources such as Aibunar were producing large amounts of metal, was low. Copper pins dating to this period have been recovered from Dikili Tash II (nine examples), Paradeisos (three), Dimini and Sesklo. There is no evidence for local metal production (Demoule and Perlès 1993: 395). The infrequency of copper finds sets apart northern Greece from contemporary depositional and expressive events occurring to the north.

Contexts of copper deposition

Overall, objects made of copper appear in two contexts during the fifth millennium BC. On the one hand most of the large copper axes, adzes, hammer-axes and chisels have been found in burials (although note the corresponding deposition of hoards and the infrequency of cemetery burials in Vinča contexts). Smaller objects, such as beads and awls, and pieces of copper ore have been found both in burials and in village buildings. These patterns reflect contemporary perceptions of appropriate places of deposition. The appropriateness of the context and event of deposition was probably linked to copper's capacity as an expressive material used to produce objects employed during occasions of conspicuous display, in the main in the events surrounding burial. Copper objects found in village contexts are mostly small (such as awls), fragmentary and related to body decoration.

The large axes, hammers and chisels found in the burials are extravagant items. Even taking account of Todorova's identification of the 'slimming' of shaft-hole axes late in the sequence of copper tool production, the amount of copper dedicated to the large objects is outrageously disproportionate to the use of copper to make other things. The formal variety of the large objects is limited to two types of cutting tools: axe-adze-hammers and chisel-flat axes. They document an inefficient over-use of copper ore in the production of tools which seldom bear any traces of use.

It is surely significant that many of the large copper objects bear little evidence of heavy use. Of the 200 chisel-flat-axes and shaft-hole axe-hammer-adzes which Todorova illustrates in her inventory (Todorova 1981: 23–51, plates 1–18) less than 10 per cent show any sign of significant use-wear; each formal category of large copper cutting objects contains a similarly low proportion of used examples (between 8.1 per cent to 9.1 per cent). Of the small objects made of copper (for Bulgaria, Todorova lists 31 awls, hooks, 'harpoon-points' and wire) over half have traces of significant use (Todorova 1981: 52–5, plate 19). The absence of evidence of significant wear on the extravagant copper objects further supports the suggestion that they were intended for display and deposition and not for other more functional uses.

Based on the Bulgarian material, therefore, three patterns emerge. First, large tools dominate the inventory of copper objects (86.6 per cent); second, very few (9.5 per cent) of the large tools (but over half of the small objects) have significant traces of use-wear; and third, the vast majority of large copper tools were deposited during burial ceremonies. As discussed above, the distribution of copper objects among burials was not even; it was disproportionately distributed across cenotaph and male burials. These patterns suggest that most copper objects played an expressive role in events during which fifth millennium BC communities declared, claimed and confirmed individual and group identities within their society.

The production of copper tools and ornaments and the possible use of copper ore to decorate skin or clothing fit together in a suite of expressive objects and activities. The early uses of copper were limited to fashioning body ornaments; the large objects made of copper in the more developed phases (extravagant tools and weapons) were expressive more than functional; and painting the body with copper ore would have had similar, though perhaps less permanent, significance and purpose in expression. It is little surprise then that some anthropomorphic figurines had bands of copper around their legs and probably rings of copper through ear-holes and lip perforations.

Copper working and mining

The evidence for copper working and copper mining is not insubstantial. Intensive analytical work on sourcing copper ores has been carried out by Evgen Chernykh (1992) and by Noel Gale in collaboration with Bulgarian specialists (Gale et al. 1991), although the latter work awaits full publication. The major conclusions of Chernykh's work document the important central role which the Balkans, particularly sources in the Sredna Gora in south-central Bulgaria, played as the major source of raw material found in objects recovered from sites in eastern Europe, western Russia, the Ukraine and Moldova in the fifth millennium BC. In addition to the links thus established between finished products and ore sources, substantial evidence for copper mining has come from two mines in use during the fifth millennium BC: Rudna Glava in Serbia and Aibunar in south-central Bulgaria.

The Aibunar mines are located in low hills (330–400 masl.) near the modern town of Nova Zagora and consist of several areas of ore extraction (Chernykh 1978a, 1978b). The mines were narrow open trenches, between 10 and 80 m long, 3–10 m wide and 2–20 m deep. In the trenches were found characteristic fifth millennium BC ceramics (i.e. Karanovo VI wares). Copper objects and ore, sourced to Aibunar, have been found in Karanovo V levels at several sites in south-central Bulgaria. Thus Gale and his colleagues have argued that mining at Aibunar was under way from the first half of the fifth millennium BC, and perhaps from as early as 5100 BC (Gale et al. 1991: 64–5).

In addition to diagnostic ceramics, the Aibunar mines contained mining tools, as well as the remains of three individuals. The tools include over twenty fragments of antler picks, two shaft-hole copper tools (one a hammer-axe and the other an axe-adze) and very large hammer stones (Chernykh 1978a; Musées Nationaux 1989: 185–7) (Figure 6.5). Unlike the hammer-axes deposited in burials, the copper one found in the mine trench had been heavily used. At some distance from the mining area (i.e., up to a dozen kilometres away) people had built seven habitations which contained over a hundred pieces of copper oxide; spectographic analysis has confirmed that these came from the Aibunar trenches. While most of the habitations date from after the middle of the fifth millennium BC (e.g. Kodzhaderman-Gumelniţa-Karanovo VI contexts, hereafter K-G-K VI), some were in use several centuries earlier (i.e. during the Karanovo V-Maritsa phase). There was no evidence to suggest that these habitations were places in which copper ore processing took place. It is most probable that once the copper ore had been extracted and broken up, it was taken out of the immediate vicinity of the mines.

Aibunar was not the only source of the copper in the objects found at settlements in south-central Bulgaria. Gale's lead isotope analysis of thirteen objects from Aprilovo, Azmak, Mudrets, Stara Zagora Bolnitsa and Stara Zagora Mineralni Bani determined that there were at least four other, as yet unidentified, copper ore sources being exploited at this time (Gale et al. 1991: 65). Furthermore, these non-Aibunar sources account for the majority of this, albeit small, corpus of artefacts. Chernykh identified other mines in northern Thrace at Christene, Rakinitsa, Tymnjanka and Prochorovo. The latter site contained pottery distinctive for Karanovo V and K-G-K VI phases of the fifth millennium BC (Chernykh 1978b: 216). On a larger scale, natural copper sources in Bulgaria are widespread with

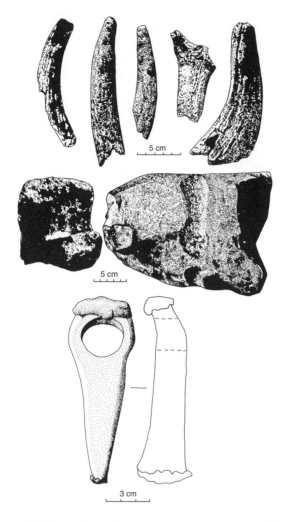

Figure 6.5 Tools from the copper mines at Aibunar (after Chernykh 1978b)

special concentrations in north-west and central Bulgaria and in south-east Bulgaria in the Stranzha mountains (Gale *et al.* 1991: 54)

Gale suggests that the non-Aibunar ores at sites in the Aibunar vicinity strengthen Chernykh's conclusions that copper smelting was not taking place at these sites (Gale *et al.* 1991: 65). While the work at Aibunar, at the other Thracian sources and at the slightly later Rudna Glava mines in Serbia (Jovanović 1982) provide details about ore extraction, the evidence for copper working is much more limited, being almost exclusively limited to infrequent finds of copper slag. The absence of sites specifically dedicated to ore processing and manufacture (or even parts of villages given over to these activities – excepting the axe moulds from Caşcioarele in southern Romanian) is all the more perplexing in light of the size of many of the tools. The production of both the simple flat chisel-axes and the more complex large, shaft-hole axe-adze-hammers would have required significant pyrotechnical work involving the consumption of large amounts of fuel and special equipment. Production of the large forms would have been difficult without two- and three-piece clay moulds. Large crucibles and moulds remain absent from almost all of the settlement and mining sites.

Todorova has suggested that charcoal found at Golyamo Delchevo marks a potential location for copper working, although there is little else in the site's inventory to support this conclusion (Todorova *et al.* 1975). In light of the number of tell settlements which have been investigated in the key areas, that is north-eastern, eastern and south-cental Bulgaria, the absence of a copper-working record suggests that ore processing and copper tool moulding took place away from the tell villages.

Away from the core area of copper production in central Bulgaria, finds of copper slag have been made at Slatino in south-western Bulgaria (S. Chokadzhiev personal communication) although the copper ore for this came from the western Balkans from the Rudna Glava sources (Musées Nationaux 1989: 181). In south-central Romania, two pieces of slag were found in Vădastra levels at the eponymous site (Christescu 1933: 203). In Yugoslavia, copper slag was found at Anza IV and suggests that copper smelting took place here at 5000 BC (Chapman and Tylecote 1983). At Sitagroi a concentration of solidified copper and sherds with copper slag adhering to them came from a Sitagroi III context (Renfrew 1986b: 215). At Mandalo a clay crucible suggests that copper-working took place here by the end of the fifth millennium BC (Papanthimou and Papasteriou 1993: 209; Andreou *et al.* 1996: 571). In the western Balkans, the final phase at Selevac produced a single piece of copper slag and Tringham has suggested that a collapsed hearth or oven from House 2 in the preceding phase was associated with copper processing (Glumac and Tringham 1990: 557). Glumac and Tringham argue that the presence of parent material and other minerals (such as quartz) at Selevac shows that processing of copper took place on the site (Glumac and Tringham 1990: 560).

Copper: conclusion

Success in acquiring and processing copper ores and in producing the large copper tools found in fifth millennium BC burials was grounded on specialist knowledge, skills and alliances. Trading links, or at least exchange partnerships, on a wide range of levels must have played an important part in the acquisition of raw material ores, especially as the Aibunar evidence suggests raw material ore being moved out of the immediate vicinity of the mines. In addition, the almost complete absence of copper-working facilities within settlements suggests that the establishment and maintenance of exchange links also must have played an important role in moving finished goods to their places of use or deposition. If the pattern of copper deposition is any guide, then access to raw material ore and finished objects was probably equally differentially distributed within and between communities. Perhaps the possession of the abilities to acquire and control acquisition alliances formed the basis of copper's intrinsic potential to be an appropriate medium for expressing intra-group distinctions. Like acquisition of ores and finished objects, perhaps the abilities and craft-knowledge required to work copper were another source over which control of access was required.

In one respect there was nothing new in the presence of long-ranging acquisition networks; as noted in Chapter 1, the acquisition of sourcable materials (most notably flint) over large distances had been a component of life since before even the arrival of anatomically modern humans in the Balkans *c.* 45,000 years ago. Over a shorter-range, acquisition of clays for potting (and even animals from hunting) had developed as important components since the seventh and sixth millennium BC and from much earlier periods respectively. The fifth millennium BC trends in acquisition were the same but the materials and its production were new. A material such as copper was radically novel: it had new expressive qualities, such as its colour and reflectability, and its acquisition entailed new technologies and, perhaps, a more refined understanding of source location.

Perhaps the message conveyed in the extravagantly produced large copper tools was written in the extraction and processing activities required for copper tool acquisition and production. The particular range of tools made of copper suggests additional links between the processes of copper acquisition and production and the messages of the mortuary assemblages: tools which would have been used in the extraction of ore, such as the shaft-hole axe found in the Aibunar mines, in the processing of ore (e.g. hammering) and in the cutting of trees required as fuel for copper pyrotechnology (e.g. chisels and axes-adzes). These links are connections of form and not of actual utility: most of the large copper tools were never used for their intended function. As with the early use of ceramic technology for making vessels and other objects, creation was a process of transformation producing an end-product which was much more than its parts.

Gold

A very different set of objects was fashioned out of gold, the second major new material which appeared in the fifth millennium BC Balkans. In a few exceptional cases gold was used in the creation of large objects such as the coverings of the copper shaft-hole tools found in several of the Varna graves. Most gold objects, however, were small and were attached as ornamentation to body-parts, especially around the face and hands, or to clothing. Although less frequently found than copper, and certainly found in much less weight, the majority of gold objects have come from the extraordinary burials of the Bulgarian Black Sea coast.

The Varna finds stand out in their volume and in the variety of their forms. Over 3000 objects, weighing over 6 kg in total, were recovered in more than thirty shapes: hammered sheet plates or pectorals; thin strips of beaten gold rolled into tight spirals; beads made of small single loops of beaten sheet; diadems, earrings, lip-covers and lip-plugs; convex circular appliqués; convex-profiled hammered bracelets; horn-shaped appliqués; and sheet gold coverings for sceptre-heads and axe-shafts. More extraordinary finds include a solid gold perforated astragalus and a penis sheath.

Most frequently at Varna, gold appears in the form of cinched beads; more than 1,000 have been found. Convex appliqués are also numerous (almost 300). The remainder of gold objects includes more than 100 beads and many fewer circular perforated appliqués or pendents (22), coverings for axe, hammer and sceptre shafts (21) and bracelets (12) (Eleure 1989). Most of these objects are ornaments and would have been sewn onto clothes, attached to head or facial hair, pushed through holes in ears or lips or worn around wrists and upper arms. Even the inclusion of gold in the making of the sceptre-, axe- and hammer-shafts has a decorative quality to it: in almost all cases gold was used to enhance the expressiveness of something else (a sceptre, a body, a face). The fashioning of the gold-sheet penis sheath from grave 43 is the same: it was a covering or extension. Similar was the use of gold to decorate the pottery vessels in graves 4 and 43. The form of the pots and motifs of their decoration are the same as non-funerary ceramics; the gold is a supplementary addition.

As is the case with all exotic grave-goods at Varna, the large concentrations of gold objects were limited to a small number of the burials (most especially graves 1, 4, 36 and 43). Indeed, only 22 per cent of graves at Varna contained any gold at all. The four mentioned here contained almost 5 kg of gold in almost 2000 individual pieces.

The extravagant copper objects were clear copies of tools and weapons which were made from other, more mundane materials; chisels, axes, hammers and adzes made of stone, antler and bone are frequent finds from settlement and burial contexts. Most of the gold objects (e.g. the numerous beads and circular appliqués) were different; they do not have such clear formal referents. Exceptions are the gold objects made in the shape of animals or animal parts. In Grave 36, two sheet-gold appliqués were fashioned in the form of horned quadrupeds and in Grave 36, 30 sheet-gold appliqués were made in the form of horned animal heads. In grave 36, a perforated astragalus (anklebone) of solid-gold was found. The fashioning of gold into objects which refer to specific categories of animals, such as horned grazers may be at the core of the horn-appliqués from grave 36. Perhaps, as Poplin has suggested for the astragalus, they refer to a general concept of grazing animals such as cattle or ovicaprids (Poplin 1991: 32).

In addition to the Varna grave-goods, gold objects have been found at contemporary sites across the Balkans in settlement as well as mortuary contexts. As noted above gold objects were also deposited in burials at Durankulak. At the Gumelniţa tell in southern Romania, a horned appliqué, not dissimilar to those from Varna, was found as were a ring, an ingot of gold and another, circular, appliqué (V. Dumitrescu 1925: 34, 99, figure 73; H. Dumitrescu 1961: 91, 79, figure 7). From contemporary, and later, Gumelniţa levels at Vidra other appliqués were found (Rosetti 1934: 23; 1939: 38, 43). Gumelniţa contexts at the Vărăşti cemetery contained beads, an appliqué, a lip-plug and a perforated cylindrical tube of sheet-gold, the latter two objects, again, have similarities with objects from Varna (Comşa 1991b: 86). A suite of similarly Varna-like objects were deposited in a burial at Sultana: appliqués, rings and a bracelet (Halescu 1986). From slightly later levels at Vladiceasca were found a collection of appliqués, a tubular object, a bead and pin (Comşa 1991b: 87). Eugen Comşa has referred in print to other, unpublished, gold objects, including over 110 beads, from Sultana and Vladiceasca (Comşa 1991b: 89). Similar finds, though fewer in number, have been recovered in Transylvania at Tîrgu Mures, Ariusd and Traian (Comşa 1991b). Perhaps the most extraordinary gold object is a circular gold appliqué which was part of a group of gold artefacts from the Moigrad region (in Transylvania) which was acquired by a local museum in the early part of the twentieth century. The peculiarity of this appliqué is its size; while almost all other circular appliqués are less than 5 cm in diameter, the Moigrad specimen is over 24 cm in height and, at its widest point, over 31 cm in breadth. At 750 g it is the heaviest of any of the Romanian gold (Comşa 1991b: 87).

In Bulgaria, in addition to the coastal burial assemblages, the pattern of shapes and contexts of gold finds is very much the same as in Romania. Individual circular gold appliqués have been found at Debar and Sofronievo in north-west Bulgaria, at Pazardzhik in west south-central Bulgaria, at Ruse and Radingrad in north-eastern Bulgaria, at Sava in eastern Bulgaria, and at Kosarita and Daneva Mogila (Musées Nationaux 1989: 60). A burial at Reka Devniya contained 34 gold rings. At Polianovo a gold circular appliqué and two earrings were found. The only clearly anthropomorphic object made of gold comes from the Kosharic in south-eastern Bulgaria.

The most dramatic of the inland Bulgarian gold finds is the collection found at the Hotnitsa settlement in north-central Bulgaria. Weighing 310 g, it consists of four amulettes, 39 spiral rings and a spiral bracelet and was found in a pit and perhaps represents a cache or hoard (Angelov 1959). Evidence for the use of gold for decorating ceramic vessels, as most well known from Varna, also exists further west at Bubanj Hum and Krivodol (Eleure and Raub 1991: 20).

Work on the sourcing of gold and on gold processing technologies and sites has not proceeded apace with the corresponding research on copper (but see Eleure 1989; Eleure and Raub 1991; Hartmann 1978). Gale has drawn our attention to the presence of gold deposits in Bulgaria, such as the alluvial deposits in western Bulgaria near Kyustendil in the south and near Montana in the north-west as well as east of Sofia and in south-east Bulgaria (Krustev 1987; Gale *et al.* 1991: 54, figure 3). The Varna area, however, is without known gold sources (Eleure 1989: 68); the closest sources were in south-central Bulgaria, in the hills of Bakadjik near Jambol and in Pangurishte in central Bulgaria (Eleure 1989: 68). Eleure and Raub suggest that, for the large gold-decorated dish from grave 4 at Varna, the raw material was obtained from river or stream deposits (Eleure and Raub 1991: 20).

Few gold objects come from contemporary contexts in northern Greece, central-southern Bulgaria or the Vinča area (Eleure 1989). In the middle of the fifth millennium BC in western Macedonia, sheet gold and gold wire was used at Megalo Nisi Galanis (Andreou *et al.* 1996: 569). At Dimitra gold beads came from mid to late fifth millennium BC contexts (Grammenos in press; Andreou *et al.* 1996: 590). An uncontexted 'small hoard' of gold objects was found at Aravissos in Macedonia; the objects have formal similarities with the Varna finds (Grammenos 1991: 109, plates 30.1–6; Makkay 1993: 821–3).

Gold: conclusion

Thus, although gold appears in many of the same contexts as copper objects (i.e. burials), it does so in quite different forms and is limited, almost exclusively, to additive decoration either of bodies, clothes or tools. There are, however, important similarities between copper and gold and perhaps these explain the similarities in the patterns of their deposition. Both are visually expressive materials and, thus, would have been ideally equipped to participate in the public ceremonies of burial and the associated expressions of individual identities and inter-group distinctions. As with copper, part of the message in the use of gold may have been as much in the medium as in the identifiable forms of objects made. Furthermore, as with copper, gold (in raw or finished form) was a fifth millennium novelty in both the inherent expressiveness of its medium and in the restricted location of its natural occurrence as an ore.

Thus, just as copper objects may have spoken of control over knowledge and skills of acquisition, processing and craftsmanship of copper technology, so also would gold have spoken of control over the same processes and knowledges for gold acquisition and craftsmanship. Furthermore, when gold and copper appear in burials (i.e. in a minority of burials) objects made of both materials are often found in large quantities: extravagant copper tools, thousands of gold beads, hundreds of gold appliqués. For both materials, their significance may have rested more in the form of the objects they represented (axes, necklaces, cattle, sexual organs) and in more deeply rooted meanings of the material and what gold and copper meant in terms of control, knowledge and skill than in any functional sense.

Shell

In addition to the appearance of objects made of copper and gold, the fifth millennium BC also witnessed the novel use of *Spondylus* and *Dentilium* as raw materials of social significance. As with the new minerals, objects made out of *Spondylus* and *Dentalium* are found most abundantly in mortuary contexts. The Varna and Durankulak cemeteries dominate in gross abundance of *Spondylus*. One grave at Durankulak (grave 466) contained a sixteen-piece diadem, five pierced appliqués and forty-five beads, all made of *Spondylus*. At Varna II, grave 3 contained an enormous number of *Spondylus* objects: four bracelets, 150 little tubes, and 128 'buttons' or appliqués (I. Ivanov 1978a; Musées Nationaux 1989: 105–9). In smaller quantities *Spondylus* has also been found at Radingrad (three bracelets and a bead from grave 4; V. Nikolov 1988: 226) and at Turgovishte where grave 9 contained forty-eight beads and a bracelet (Angelova 1986b; V. Nikolov 1988: 226). In addition to the burial finds a cache of *Spondylus* ring fragments has been found at Hirşova in Romanian Dobrudzha (Comşa 1973).

As *Spondylus* was an Aegean mollusc (though it now appears in the Black Sea), it is not surprising to find the shell in northern Greek sites, especially at Sitagroi and Dikili Tash, and also further south at Dimini. The north Greek finds of *Spondylus* all come from building contexts and the distribution from Dimini has attracted most recent attention (Tsuneki 1987, 1989; Halstead 1993). Two hundred and twelve finished rings, beads and buttons and sixty-three pieces of waste from *Spondylus* working (or unfinished objects) were recovered from the Dimini village.

The recovery of several separate concentrations of debris from *Spondylus* working at Dimini and the spatially differential distribution of finished *Spondylus* rings, buttons and cylindrical beads in different building complexes suggests that the site may have occupied an important position in long-distance exchange networks (Tsuneki 1987, 1989). Halstead has underlined the markedly uneven distribution of *Spondylus* pieces across the site. There are two main concentrations: one in domestic area A in the eastern part of the site; the other in domestic area C to the west (Halstead 1993: 604, figure 2). These two areas account for 92.5 per cent of *Spondylus* from all domestic areas at the site. Halstead argues that this is a symptom of marked inequality between domestic groups in the ability to accumulate or dispose of shell ornaments through exchange (Halstead 1993: 607).

The marine mollusc *Dentalium* was also a frequent find in fifth millennium BC burials. At Varna, grave 4 contained 1400 *Dentalium* beads. Grave 5 had 2200 beads and grave 36 had another 2100. As with the gold and most of the copper objects, shell was used exclusively in the production of ornaments: bracelets, beads, pendants predominate.

Like gold and copper, *Spondylus* and *Dentalium* fitted into the new set of fifth millennium BC materials: they are all bright, visually expressive materials the acquisition of which required access to specialist knowledge and networks reaching over long distances.

Other expressive raw materials

In addition to gold, copper, *Spondylus* and *Dentalium*, a range of other materials come into use. Although they appear less frequently during the fifth millennium BC, taken together, objects made of these materials further illuminate the emerging picture: the appearance of expressive materials fashioned (mainly) into the same decorative forms as were metal and shell and deposited, almost exclusively, in burial contexts.

Closely linked to copper, malachite was another mineral from which people made beads. One hundred and thirty-nine malachite beads were found in grave 3 at Varna II. Beads made of quartz are another, infrequent, find. Grave 4 at Varna I contained 53 red quartz beads, grave 41 had 31 and grave 97, 13. People also made beads of talcite, as found in grave 466 at Durankulak; the same burial contained beads made of cornelian chalcedony. Kaoline (hydrated aluminium silicate) was also used to make beads, as found in grave 4 in Varna I (30 beads), in grave 41 (90) and in grave 36 (20). Finds of marble were infrequent but noteworthy: anthropomorphic figurines made of marble come from the Sadievo and Sulicha tells in southern Bulgaria and nine marble beads made a necklace in grave 466 at Durankulak. Small marble bowls have been found in graves 3, 36 and 41 at Varna and from Limanu in southern Romania. Marble was also used to make a wrist-guard from grave 3 at Varna and grave 41 contained a perforated, round marble weight (perhaps a spindle-whorl?) and a conical 'rhyton'-shaped vessel. An axe made of white calcite was deposited in grave 3 at Varna II.

As noted above, red ochre was used in some Varna burials. At Selevac, red hematite paint-stones were found in the site's later phases and a few figurines (fifteen) bore traces of hematite. Occasionally, animal bone was used to make ornaments deposited in burials. In addition to the deer antler shaft-hole axe noted above, grave 3 at Varna II contained eighty pierced deer teeth. Grave 644 at Durankulak contained seven separate sets of red-deer teeth. Burials at Tiszapolgár-Basatanya contained antler, deer and boar jaws; animal bones (especially skulls) were frequent inclusions in Hamangia culture cemeteries. As with the metal and shell objects, those made from malachite, quartz, talcite, cornelian chalcedony, kaoline, marble, calcite and animal bone and teeth are almost exclusively used in the production of body ornaments.

There is one other raw material to consider with respect to grave-goods: flint. While there was nothing new in the use of flint, the size of some blades included in several of the cemetery burials was novel. In cenotaph grave 1 in Varna I, among the extraordinary numbers of gold ornaments and copper tools was also deposited a number of flint blades. While five of these blades were less than 15 cm in length, one was quite large (44 cm). A number of the other graves had blades of impressive length: grave 3 contained a 17 cm blade; grave 4 had blades of 13, 14, 27 and 31 cm; grave 5 had a 20 cm blade; grave 97 had blades 11, 12, and 27 cm long; grave 36 had a 30 cm blade, and grave 43 had several blades the longest of which was 40 cm.

As with all of these exotic raw materials, the significance of the large flint blades may have rested in the skills and knowledge required for acquisition and craftsmanship. Especially relevant may have been the ability to produce these very large blades, an ability that comprised strength as well as experience. All of these raw materials were appropriate media for producing objects to be positioned in burials for similar reasons: they were all bright, visually expressive media; and they all represent access to, and probably control over, special systems of acquisition, processing and production.

Graphite decorated pottery

Graphite is another novel expressive material that appeared in the fifth millennium BC Balkans. Throughout almost all of the area under consideration (with important exceptions to the west and south) fine-ware pottery was increasingly decorated in a new dramatic style through the application of paint and graphite (Figure 6.6). Motifs included single and multiple parallel lines, often forming spirals and meanders, and geometric shapes, such as circles, rhomboids and triangles, and were executed in 'positive' and 'negative' fashions. In the few cases where close analytical attention has been directed at trends in popularity of motifs (i.e. at Sitagroi) it appears that wide variety was the rule, with individual pots having 'unique' designs.

Graphite decoration was applied on vessel interiors, especially on flat, open dishes, as well as on vessel exteriors. Although it often appears on exteriors alone, it seldom appears only on interiors. At Sitagroi, at least, bowls appear to have been the shapes most frequently decorated with graphite ornamentation although graphite decoration is found on a wide range of vessel forms including lids and jars (Evans 1986: 397–400, 411).

Figure 6.6 Decorated pottery vessels from Polyanitsa phase III (no scale) (after Todorova 1986)

In addition to pottery vessels, graphite decoration was also applied to non-vessel ceramics such as the 'stands' at Sitagroi and 'altars' at Slatino.

Elaborate surface decoration of pottery was nothing new in Balkan pre-history: visually stimulating red and white traditions of painted decoration characterize the north Greek and west Bulgarian sixth millennium BC; the production and use of wares with intricate incised, impressed and excised surface treatment were widespread across the Balkans from the similarly

225

early times. The emergence of graphite-decorated pottery in the fifth millennium BC is striking because of its aesthetic qualities, which were much in line with other contemporary novelties of expressive material culture, and because of its wide distribution across the region.

As part of his work on the fifth millennium BC ceramics from Sitagroi (phase III), Robert Evans made a study of the material from Sitagroi comparing it with that from other parts of the Balkans. In eastern and central Macedonia and Greek Thrace graphite-decorated and black-on-red painted wares were distinctive from the middle of the fifth millennium BC. At Sitagroi itself graphite decoration was among the most frequent of the decorated wares (Evans 1986: 393, table 12.2). Evans found that the single most characteristic feature across almost all of the regions at this time was the presence of graphite-decorated pottery (Evans 1986: 407). He found close parallels between Sitagroi and local sites (e.g. Dikili Tash), as well as with sites to the west in eastern Macedonia (Akropotamos, Dimitra), in west Macedonia (Servia, Vardina and Stivos A and B) and sites to the east in Greek Thrace (Paradimi). To the south, only general similarities (e.g., in black-on-red painted wares) could be found with sites in Thessaly (Sesklo, Dimini, Rhakhmani) (Evans 1986: 406–7).

Close parallels with the Sitagroi and east Macedonian material are found to the north, not only in southern Bulgaria, as in Thrace at sites of the Maritsa and Karanovo VI cultures, but also in western Bulgaria in the Krivodol-Salcuţa-Bubanj culture, in northern Bulgaria in the Kodjadermen culture, in southern Romania in the Boian, Salcuţa and Gumelniţa cultures and in Serbia in the Bubanj Hum culture. In Thrace, by the beginning of the fifth millennium BC, graphite-painted as well as white-filled incised wares were common (Todorova 1995a: 86). To the east, in the Varna region, at the beginning of the fifth millennium BC graphite decoration was in use, though rarely, along with the more common inlaid linear decorated wares (Todorova 1995a: 87); graphite decoration was still rare in the middle of the fifth millennium BC on the Bulgarian Black Sea coast. Deep black-surfaced wares painted with manganese oxide (i.e. pyrolusite) pre-dominated and inlaid white and red-paste ornamentation were common (Todorova 1995a: 88).

In south-west Bulgaria, from the end of the sixth millennium BC, graphite-decorated pottery appears along with black or black-and-red, black-topped wares with graphite, fine cannalures, brown-painted or polychome decoration (Todorova 1995a: 86). In south-west Bulgaria during the first half of the fifth millennium BC, as seen at Slatino, black-topped pottery continued to be frequent but was supplemented by graphite-decorated wares as well as by black-and-red painted, incised and impressed wares. By the middle of the fifth millennium BC rich linear graphite decoration had become characteristic (Todorova 1995a: 86). Pottery of the Krivodol-Salcuţa-Bubanj complex also included graphite decoration (Todorova 1995a: 89).

The common ceramic link for all of these regions was the presence of graphite-decorated pottery, although there are other similarities such as with excised decoration (Evans 1986: 407–8). For most of the region, but most particularly its eastern part, the common ceramic features, especially the use of graphite for surface decoration, have been subsumed under one broad culture designation (Kodjaderman-Gumelniţa-Karanovo VI) (Todorova 1995a: 88).

The contexts of graphite decoration

Graphite-decorated pottery is visually striking. In the context of the contemporary developments in expressive material culture its appearance in the fifth millennium BC is not surprising. Indeed there are a number of important connections between the appearances of graphite decoration and metal-working. Some connections are obvious: like copper and gold, graphite-decorated pottery surfaces have highly light-reflective qualities. Other connections are perhaps less familiar. At the level of a raw material, graphite has links with the acquisition, processing and use of metals. As with copper and gold and almost all of the other new expressive materials, the acquisition of raw graphite would have required participation in specialist acquisition networks. It has been suggested that the graphite used in decorating fifth millennium BC pottery, for eastern Bulgaria at least, came from metamorphic sources in the Rhodope and Stara Planina ranges (Musées Nationaux 1989: 190).

Renfrew was one of the first to suggest a technological link between the temperature required for copper metallurgy (over 1,000°C) and that required to produce graphite-decorated pottery. Regardless of the temperature required, the successful processing of graphite and its application to pottery surfaces also would have required specialist craft knowledge. In his discussion of the Sitagroi ceramics, Evans notes that although in many cases it is clear that graphite was applied to pottery surfaces by painting (i.e. brush strokes can be seen in the decoration), it is also apparent that graphite was applied by drawing using a lump of natural material (Evans 1986: 397).

Similarities in production and acquisition aside, the appearance of graphite decoration adds a twist to our understanding of expressive material culture in the fifth millennium BC. Clearly, like the metals, shells and other materials found in mortuary contexts, graphite decoration was a visually powerful medium for investing objects with expressive potential. However, graphite-decorated pottery is significantly different in its context of use and deposition: graphite-painted pots are almost exclusively found from building contexts. While in some cases lumps of raw material graphite were deposited in burials, they have also been found within settlements as at Yanka, Kodjaderman and Metchkur (R. Popov 1912; Mikov 1966; Evans 1986: 397; Musées Nationaux 1989: 190). Thus, in the same way that distributions of metals and shells provide information about intra-group differentiation in the mortuary contexts, distributions of graphite-decorated pottery may provide information about intra-village differentiation among buildings.

Variations in research methodologies make such information difficult to extract. In those numerous meticulous excavations of settlements that note, precisely, the location of concentrations of graphite-wares, the total area of settlement space investigated prevents comparison among more than a few buildings across any one site. At the other extreme, excavations that open very large surface areas and thus reveal total settlement, have paid less attention to precise recording of ceramic concentrations, frequently ignoring all but chronologically informative diagnostic forms and decorations, and seldom quantifying counts of wares in terms that make comparison feasible (e.g. of sherds per kilogram). What can be extracted from re-investigation of site archives and inventories, however, does provide some insight into the distribution of graphite-decorated pottery within settlements. In the later horizons at Ovcharovo, high concentrations of pots decorated with graphite were found in particular houses (D. Bailey 1991). The concentrations of such pots in particular buildings mark them out, and perhaps what occurred within them, as distinctive.

Just as graphite-decorated pottery fits into contemporary patterns of expressive material culture and patterns of differential access to resources and materials, so also the increase in productive investment that graphite decoration represents fits into contemporary trends in surface decoration in parts of the Balkans in which graphite wares do not predominate. The appearance of graphite-decorated pottery coincides with a wider trend of increase in the frequency of elaborate surface decoration. Despite the amount of material published on Balkan ceramic sequences, in many regions very little work has been carried out on detailed fabric analysis. The attention which has been directed at reconstructing ceramic production techniques has revealed a shift towards an increase in the effort devoted to new labour-intensive methods of surface treatment (Kaiser 1990). At Selevac during the later phases of the site the frequency of extensive surface decoration increases (Tringham and Krstić 1990b: 597), as does the overall production of pottery vessels. In the second quarter of the fifth millennium BC at Opovo in Serbia pottery was decorated only with highly polished channelled lines or with incised bands filled with impressed dots (Tringham et al. 1992). It is perhaps significant that the evidence for increases in effort invested in pottery production and surface treatment has been found in the west Balkans, an area where graphite-decorated pottery was never a significant element.

It is thus not surprising that the practice of decorating pots with graphite is contemporaneous and present with the extraction and processing of copper ore and the production and deposition of copper artefacts. Their contemporaneity was not fortuitous; graphite surface decoration was another symptom of the wider trend in producing and using visually expressive objects. Graphite-decorated pottery is distinct from other symptoms of that trend, however, its primary depositional context was in buildings and, as such, it provides information about inter-household differentials that are less obvious (if visible at all) in the mortuary-dominated corpus of expressive material culture.

Figurines

In addition to the graphite pottery, another category of visually expressive material culture which focuses our attention on building contexts is anthropomorphic figurines (Figure 6.7). As discussed in Chapter 3, anthropomorphic figurines appeared in Balkan prehistory in the seventh and sixth millennia BC. Their appearance was not a fifth millennium novelty, but important changes in their frequency and decoration occurred at this time: more anthropomorphic figurines were made and used and surface decoration became more elaborate.

Figurine frequency

The claim that there was an increase in the production and use of anthropomorphic figurines is difficult to assess. Trends through time in the numbers of anthropomorphs during the later fifth millennium BC in north-eastern Bulgaria suggest that the frequency of figurines did increase with time (Bailey 1991: 172). Gimbutas argued for a similar diachronic increase in figurine frequency and has documented it at Sitagroi. Of all figurines from the site, 57.4 per cent came from phase III, 39.2 per cent from phase II and the remainder from phases I, IV and V (Gimbutas 1986: 225). To the west at Selevac more than three hundred figurines were recovered and one is struck again by the frequencies of finds from sites where regular sieving has been built into research designs. The majority of figurines come from the later phases of the site. Tringham has suggested that the increase in the production of figurines of high formal variability is part of a larger scheme through which building-based groups expressed their autonomy (Tringham and Krštić 1990b: 609). At Slatino, although exact numbers are unavailable, it appears that figurines are most frequent in the later phases of the site (S. Chokadziev personal communication).

North of the Danube, the number of Boian figurines, like those from the earlier Dudeşti contexts, are few, although this may be more a factor of the correspondingly low number of Dudeşti sites excavated than it is of the frequency of figurines in use. Recent field-walking and sondage excavations at Lăceni in south-central Romania have produced more (Andreescu 1998). Form and amount of decoration vary among Boian figurines. Some are quite

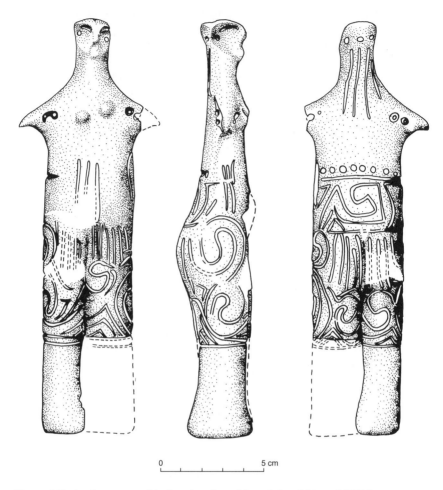

Figure 6.7 Anthropomorphic figurine from Usoe (after Vajsov 1990b)

simple with little surface decoration other than modelled breasts and simple featureless faces (Andreescu 1998: plate 53: 1, 6, 7, 13). Others have intricate patterns of lines incised in spirals or angles. Some of these also have breasts modelled and much of the incised decoration focuses on the hips, buttocks and thighs. On some, incised decoration covers almost all of the body and on a few, holes were perforated through the arms.

The trend of variation in the amount of surface decoration increases with Gumelniţa figurines (Andreescu 1998: plates 2–52). Many figurines from Gumelniţa contexts have perforations through their arms and the sides of their heads. Also frequent are figurines with small holes impressed into the lips. However, many Gumelniţa figurines have very little decoration, usually limited to incised lines over the pubis, on the chest and upper back, and on the insides of legs. The pattern of Gumelniţa clay figurine form and decoration is of variation with no two anthropomorphs modelled or decorated in exactly the same way. The same attention to facial detail is also found in a series of hollow-backed facial figurines or 'masks' (Andreescu 1998: plate 52). On these, features are depicted with incision and perforations.

In addition to figurines of clay, a significant number were made of bone. Two types were made. The first, made from metapodials, is very simple in form and only recognizably human by the drilled holes that represent ears and eyes and the grinding of bone to form the nose. The second type is made of flat bone, is more obviously human and has more surface decoration. The majority of decorations are shallow drilled points that mark out body parts, especially facial features such as eyes, mouths and lips, as well as pubic triangles and knees. Also, perforations were made through the sides of heads, arms and waists. Ground incisions mark pubic regions and, in some cases, knees. One of these flat bone figurines from Căscioarele has bands of copper round its neck and waist (Andreescu 1998: plate 57: 5) though others have no surface decoration at all. In addition to bone other materials were used to make figurines; stone anthropomorphs, including some made of marble, appear infrequently. Figurines made of sheet-gold come from Ruse and Koşariţa (Andreescu 1998: plate 72: 11–2).

There are also anthropomorphic and anthropographic vessels from this period in the lower Danube region. Some are simple in form with a small area hollowed out inside; others are very large (the one from Vidra is 35 cm tall) and have considerable capacities and intricate patterns of incised and painted decoration on the exterior. The tops of some figures' heads form the mouths of these pots; matching anthropomorphic lids were made in the shape of heads with ears, eyes and hair. Other clay vessel lids have handles modelled very simply as human heads. Some figurines are hollow and their closed interiors contain stones or balls of clay suggesting their use as rattles (Andreescu 1998: plates 78, 79). On some anthropomorphic vessels, miniature pots were modelled resting on top of heads and supported by the figures' hands. Anthropomorphic figures are also applied as relief decoration onto the sides of pots. At Dolnoslav in Bulgaria, a simple figure was applied to the inside of an open bowl; at Sultana in Romania, two figures were placed arm-in-arm inside a wide dish (Andreescu 1998: plate 51). Another couple, apparently male and female, came from the village at Gumelniţa (Andreescu 1998: plate 50: 3).

If there is a pattern to Boian and Gumelniţa figurines it is one that distinguishes heavily decorated figurines from those with little ornamentation. Similarities can be found in the distinctions in contemporary extramural burials, where some inhumations contained very large numbers of grave-goods while others contained few if any.

Clearly, it is possible that the increase in figurine frequency is nothing more than a symptom of the contemporary increase in durable buildings, in the aggregation of buildings into village settlements and in settlement continuity. Each of these factors alone could be held accountable for increases in figurine deposition. Furthermore, the increase in frequency may be nothing more than a single component of the larger increase in the production of all material culture, as Tringham has argued (Tringham and Krštić 1990). There may also be taphonomic factors linked to the increase in the destruction by fire of many buildings throughout the fifth millennium BC; these fired contexts are preservational godsends.

Figurine elaboration

The increase in elaboration of figurine surface decoration and form is less difficult to document (but see D. Bailey 1991). People decorated figurines with a range of techniques including incision, impression and painting (although never with a graphite solution). The range of decorative symbols is vast, the most frequent being combinations of parallel lines, V-shapes, spirals, circles and dots (Biehl 1996: figure 6). Some decoration is clearly intended to represent items of clothing or ornamentation, such as skirts or necklaces, others to represent body parts such as eyes, mouth, hair, breasts, vulva and others which have no clear formal correlation (Figure 6.8). Although some scholars, such as Gimbutas, have argued for standard sets of motifs, the reality is that among fifth millennium BC figurines variation is the rule for surface decoration.

Gimbutas has argued for the Sitagroi figurines that the 'style and ornamentation' are particularly rich in the later part of phase III (Gimbutas 1986: 237). My own study of figurines from north-eastern Bulgaria concluded that the majority of figurines had increasingly complex patterns of formal variation, although this included both surface treatment and body shaping, such as facial features, pregnancy and breasts (D. Bailey 1991). In a very few cases figurines have been preserved with copper bands wrapped around parts of their bodies: a bone figurine from Karanovo has a copper band around its waist and copper ring through a hole at the side of its head (Fol and Lichardus 1988b: figure 5). In many more cases the ears and lips of figurines were perforated and undoubtedly would have contained rings or bands made of metal or other materials.

Again, although attention to quantifying trends in the range of decorative motifs or the frequency of their appearance are not a primary focus of existing research (but see Biehl 1996), the overall pattern is for an increase in attention to decorating anthropomorphic figurines. It is interesting to note that the one significant exception to this pattern of increasing figurine decoration occurs in Hamangia contexts; Hamangia figurines are almost devoid of any individual characteristics that could be used to distinguish

0   5 cm

Figure 6.8 Anthropomorphic figurine from Golyamo Delchevo (after Todorova *et al.* 1975)

them one from another. Significantly, perhaps, Hamangia figurines are also an exception in terms of deposition: they are frequent inclusions in burials.

As discussed in Chapter 3, it is perhaps most accurate to understand the making and use of miniature representations of the human form as attempts to define and manipulate the identities and positions of particular people in the natural and socially constructed world (D. Bailey 1996a). Particular connections were suggested between figurine use in ceremonies and rituals linked to declarations and legitimizations of membership within households. The emergence in the fifth millennium BC of extravagant burial rituals in which an individual's identity was displayed (or claimed) can be seen as a parallel to the expression of identities through figurines, though made in a separate spatial, social and ceremonial context. The presence of lip-plugs and ear-rings both on figurines and in burials, however, suggests that a connection may be made between the two.

While it is clear, as Peter Ucko pointed out long ago (Ucko 1968), that not all anthropomorphic figurines could have served the same purpose, the increasingly complex representation of the human image in three dimensions suggests a widespread desire to understand and manipulate the relationships of people to people and people to places. Similar contemporary trends have already been discussed with respect to using increasingly complex arrangements of the built environment and the equally complex (and more novel) attention to the proper treatment of some members of society after death and their positions within the landscape and in relationship to other members of their communities. It is this increase in the attention to defining and expressing (by depicting) human form and identity that is the important message of the study of figurines and not the particularist attribution of figurine type to gender or even to social, economic or religious class.

Incised symbols

Another component of the material culture of the fifth millennium BC is the incision, on the bottom of vessels, of particular rectilinear and curvilinear motifs. In addition to pot bases, these motifs also appear on spindle-whorls, models of ovens, flat clay plaques and other undefined non-vessel ceramics. While people used clay sealing-stamps in the previous millennium, the marking of ceramics with incised symbols increased in frequency from the end of the sixth and into the middle of the fifth millennium BC.

Todorova has identified a series of basic motifs that appear repeatedly on sealing-stamps: spirals; spiral-meanders; angled meanders; hatching or interlinking triangles; points in the centre of ornamental composition; cross-shapes (in reality swastikas); concentric circles; rhomboids and ellipses (Todorova 1986: 207–10, figures 113–4). While incised signs appear across the Balkans at this time, they appear most frequently in western contexts, especially in western Bulgaria as at Gradeshnitsa and at Brenitsa (B. Nikolov 1986). Marks on vessel bases were also found at Selevac during the later phases of the site; Tringham has interpreted these as expressions of differentiation between households within the village (Tringham and Krstić 1990: 609).

Some of the basic motifs are very similar to the ones employed in other methods of pottery decoration. The distinction is that the incised motifs appear on vessel bases; thus they appear to have been intended not to have been seen during the normal use of the pot. The relegation of particular motifs to hidden fields of pottery surfaces suggests that they had a purpose different from the motifs applied to the visible parts of pot interiors and exteriors. Perhaps the incised base motifs were intended to be seen in only a limited range of contexts when the pot was made, moved, stored, sold, bought, or transported and not when it was being used. A second distinction between the base motifs and the visible surface decorations is that while the marks were incised the majority of fine-ware pottery decoration was painted or excised and filled. Perhaps the use of incision on the base reflects the intention to make a durable mark that could last through the life of the vessel.

It is less easy to understand the patterns of incised marks found on clay oven models from Slatino and on other less easily definable objects such as the plaques from Gradeshnitsa and the rectangles and pyramids. In its most evocative manifestation on the base of one of the Slatino oven models (see Figure 5.8), a grid of incised lines forms a series of boxes similar in appearance to a game-board or a calendar. The site's excavator has emphasized the differential fillings of the boxes in the grid to argue that it was used as a calendar (S. Chokadziev 1984). As mentioned above, the wall of one of the Slatino houses was 'engraved' and had painted surfaces. The walls of many other contemporary houses, like some at Ovcharovo, had painted layers of coloured plaster and some, such as Dolnoslav, had engraved decoration, although the evidence is slight. The discovery, at Drama in south-central Bulgaria, of a zoomorphic figurine with an incised mark on its belly extends the range of objects bearing symbols of this type (Bertemes and Krustev 1988: 351, figure 195).

It is difficult to read a single function or meaning from any of the marks that people made on objects or structures. Attempts such as Chokadzhiev's calendar interpretation appear anecdotal at best. Perhaps the position of marks on pot bases was part of the vessel's production, and not of its use; thus perhaps these marks were one means of identifying whose pots were whose during the collective firing of vessels made by several potters. Perhaps, at a general level, it is better still to take the marking of pots, non-vessel ceramics and houses as evidence for attaching symbolic identities to particular places and things, be they buildings, pots or the contents of the pots themselves. It is striking that in many cases the more frequent use of incised marks occurs at the flat unenclosed sites to the west, such as Gradeshnitsa and Slatino. Perhaps in such social and physical environments the need to mark objects with group or individual identities was greater than it was in villages such as the tells where the duration of occupation and the boundaries of personal and group space were expressed through different, more physically imposing and durable mechanisms.

Expressive material culture: conclusion

The impression that emerges is of a wide range of new, visually exciting, exotic materials used to make objects, either of personal ornament or of extravagant inutility. With the exception of graphite-decorated pottery and the figurines, almost all of these objects ended up in burials. I have suggested that burials were one of the major contexts in which people expressed differentiations of personal identity as well as expressing overall group cohesion. While it would be foolhardy to attempt to weigh different materials in terms of wealth or status and then to try to calculate indices of prestige between individual burials or different cemeteries, it is reasonable to read a range of personal identities whose differences from or similarities with others were played out through a particular set of materials such as metal or shell, in specific contexts, such as burials, and ceremonies, such as rituals of household or village membership.

With the exception of the flint super-blades, all of the fifth millennium BC's special materials shared a common aesthetic that made them extremely powerful media for producing expressive objects: all of the materials were in some way reflective and brilliant. Whittle has made the point that gold and copper objects were made to be used, displayed and consumed but not to be personally accumulated (Whittle 1996: 120). There is some truth in this as the significant concentrations of large metal objects occur as remains of public activities of deposition, such as burials or hoards, or of consumption, such as the burning of *Spondylus* at Dimini.

There is also the probability that the appropriateness of places in which expressive (non-functional) objects such as large copper tools and figurines could be used and deposited was tightly controlled. Does this perhaps explain the lack of metal (except for individual and fragmentary pieces accidently lost or discarded) in house and settlement contexts and their, corresponding, frequency in public places such as burials? Such objects were intended to function in those open public places. Other expressive objects such as graphite-decorated pottery and figurines may have had very different areas in which it was appropriate for them to serve their functions successfully.

The role of much of fifth millennium BC material culture in visually expressive acts such as burial (but also perhaps extraction/acquisition, processing, exchange) directed a great deal of attention to open and public spaces and events. However, the concentrations of graphite-decorated serving bowls and dishes and large storage jars in settlement buildings (and the deeper, more durable, impermeable nature of these buildings) turns our attention back to the enclosed parts of fifth millennium daily life.

CHAPTER CONCLUSIONS

The fifth millennium BC Balkans is distinctive in the rise of visually expressive materials used and deposited in both new and existing contexts. The inclusion of metal and shell ornaments and tools in burials introduced a new component of ceremonial life; the display of anthropomorphic imagery in buildings continued trends from previous millennia. Together both of these phenomena make it possible to flesh out details of individual and group identities in ways that were not feasible for the previous period.

In some senses, the foundations of individual identities in the fifth millennium BC reveal continuities with earlier trends. Thus the skills and knowledges required for finding, acquiring, processing, preparing and working metals and shells resemble, in kind, the types of skills and knowledges which surrounded initial potting and earlier patterns of lithic acquisition and working. The emphasis that Vitelli placed on the identity of early potters as distinct members of communities who were held in special esteem can also be proposed for people involved in the new fifth millennium BC materials. Similarly, one can suggest that the special meanings attached to early pots, the process of their creation, as transformative and mystical, the pots themselves and their contents, also applied to metal, shell and the other newly exploited materials.

The continuation of making and displaying anthropomorphic figurines and their physical links to houses and households suggest a continuation of ceremonies through which the identities of households, and their inhabitants, were made visible and legitimate. The difference in anthropomorphic figurines of fifth millennium BC was the increase in their number and in the variation in their decoration and form. The increase in variation in figurine decoration may correlate with an increase in the ranges and types of components of individuals' identities that it was deemed appropriate to represent. Certainly, the ideology of the household continued; if anything it intensified, as suggested in the discussion of architecture in Chapter 5. The collections of special pots with graphite decoration and the, more occasional, finds of shell and metal within buildings supplement the description of fifth millennium BC houses characterized by increasingly restricted interior places and rooms.

The striking fifth millennium BC innovations in burial and patterns of grave-good deposition widen our perspective on people and their interrelationships. In the types and numbers of grave-goods and in the associations of grave-goods with men, women and children, there are clear differentials. Male burials are distinct from those of women and children. If differences of individuals' identities were being expressed in figurine decoration and display (as well as in their breakage) then they also appear to have been expressed in treatment of the deceased; the similarities between certain types of ornamental grave-goods, such as ear- and lip-plugs, and particular perforations of figurine heads and mouths, strengthen this link.

While figurines and burials can be seen as declarations of individual identities, the position of cemeteries as contexts for cohesive rituals and the role of villages as places for figurine use and consumption, suggest another level of communal or corporate identity. The similarity in body position within cemeteries and the restriction of figurines to the built space of the village suggest that underneath the more particular patterns of social differentiation between individuals there ran expressions of communal village identity. In some regions of the Balkans these patterns are barely traceable, if indeed they were present at all: the very limited number of cemeteries in the western Balkans is an example. In others they appear in different combinations; thus the burials of pit-dwelling inhabitants of Hamangia communities, exceptionally, contain featureless figurines. In all other regions the patterns of identities are very clear.

Major consequences of the novelties of the fifth millennium BC in the Balkans were new ways for expressing the human condition and, more particularly, one's relationship both to a particular place, be it household or village, and to other people. Expressions and declarations were made in new ways that took advantage, sought out, or created materials and cere- monies which were visually striking. The use of gold, copper, *Spondylus*, *Dentalium*, graphite- and gold-painted pottery and other less frequently found but equally brilliant materials in ceremonies and rituals that took place in the open space of extramural cemeteries make the fifth millennium BC Balkans an aesthetically striking period of expressive material culture. All of the key new materials were highly light-reflective and suggest potential for use in display ceremonies. Furthermore, the effort made to emphasize eyes, ears and mouth in both burials and on figurines suggests that the rituals and ceremonies in which these objects and processes took part were visually and aurally centred. While figurines may have been employed in the more closed contexts of the interiors of individual buildings and village space, burial and burial imagery suggest that there was also a more open, perhaps public, context of ceremony and expression.

Increases in the acts and props of expressing identity and the accelera- tion of economic and settlement activities discussed in Chapter 5 illustrate a changing social environment characterized by competition for, or at least an increase in differentiated access to, places, resources, people and their abilities. Increases in differentials among households, their contents and their inhabitants (living or ancestral) within a village and similar differ- entials between villages reveal the basis for an increase in sociopolitical tension and the potential for conflict. The repeated rituals and ceremonies of individual and group identities, many of which were based around the household and its inhabitants, may have been part of the resolution of conflict or the lowering of its potential.

The new phenomenon of extramural burial with its distinctive types and concentrations of grave-goods may have been another way of reducing potential conflict by repeatedly restating the differentials within commu- nities. Cemeteries, like patterns of household and village rebuilding, were one of the ways in which existing differentials within society could have been publicly legitimated and, undoubtedly, disputed. The types of objects placed in graves and the materials of which they were made amplify this possibility. Metals may have had special mystical connotations that inflated the expressive value of their use within rituals; the same can be argued for shell, graphite and the other special materials. Furthermore, the form of some objects, such as the copper axes, adzes and chisels, and the extrava- gant use of raw materials mark the emergence of new symbols of power and status. These may have been linked purely with connotations of activities and may not have been intended to have been used in the activ- ities themselves. Thus axes, adzes and chisels may have referred not only

238

to abilities to cut or dig, chop or work wood; their importance may have been as symbols of the control over these activities and over the people who could carry them out. Similar arguments could be made about the use of gold, especially in its representations of horned animals and the control over herding and the new secondary animal products. The fifth millennium BC was an expressive period of Balkan prehistory full of declarations attempting to create, maintain, legitimate as well as negate claims to identity within several levels of individual and group interrelationships.

SUMMARY

In this chapter I have described the major novelties of the fifth millennium BC Balkans. The use of new materials and the appearance of cemeteries were associated with new ceremonies of expressing identities both individual and communal. In many ways these new elements of life had correlates within other fifth millennium BC phenomena, such as the types and densities of architecture within village environments and the accelerations of plant cultivation and animal tending, which had links with earlier millennia. The dramatic expressions of identities through objects and ceremonies that occurred at the end of the fifth and in the beginning of the fourth millennium BC were followed by a strikingly different set of material and social phenomena at the end of the fourth and in the third millennia BC. This change is addressed in the following chapter.

7

TRANSITIONS TO NEW
WAYS OF LIVING
The Balkans after 4000 BC

Starting from 4000 BC fundamental changes in Balkan life are evident. Settlement, burial and material culture all were very different from the preceding two and a half millennia. In this chapter, the main changes are outlined and the principal explanations for these changes are discussed.[1] In brief, major changes are evident in the ways people marked out places in the landscape for settlement, in the shift in the forms and decorations of ceramics and the tasks for which these vessels were employed. There was, however, some continuity from the previous period, expressed particularly in lithics, but also in the nature of the economy.

SETTLEMENT

Across large parts of the Balkans, most if not all of the long-lived tell villages were abandoned after 4000 BC. This is clearest in the lower Danube, where almost no tell was reoccupied after final abandonment; in many cases the final periods of occupation were closed by fire. Although there are a few exceptions, as at Salcuţa in south-western Romania, where early Bronze Age occupations overlay the fifth millennium BC remains, almost all of the key sites in north-central and north-eastern Bulgaria and southern Romania have no evidence of use after the fifth millennium BC. New sites of the Cernavoda complexes have thick occupational layers representing several successive phases but do not accumulate into tells.

In other regions the shift away from monumental villages was less complete. Thus in south-central Bulgaria early Bronze Age horizons overlay the latest fifth millennium BC phases. At Ezero there are eight separate new phases of rebuilding (Georgiev et al. 1979). The tells at Yunatsite, Dyadovo and Karanovo also were reoccupied after significant periods of abandonment (Tokai University 1990; Katincharov and Matsanova 1993, 1995; Katincharov et al. 1995). Some tells, such as Sozopol, on the Black Sea coast were also reoccupied after a hiatus (Draganov 1994, 1995).

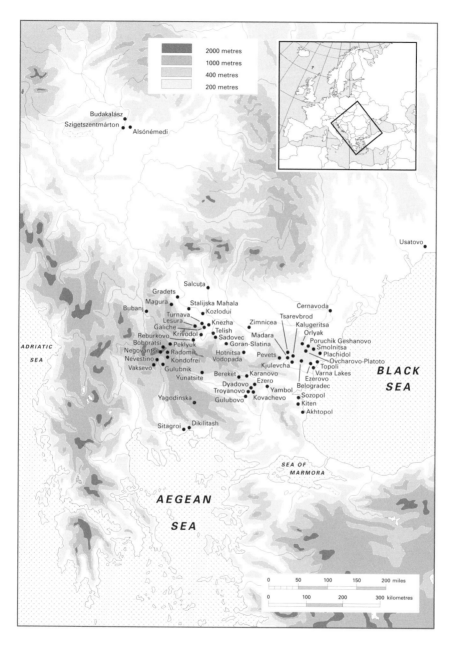

Figure 7.1 Map of key sites discussed in Chapter 7

In northern Greece, there is greater continuity at many of the well established tells, although fewer sites over all were in use. At Sitagroi there is
reoccupation at 3500 BC, after a break between phases III and IV. Buildings
in the later phase are larger and some are more complex, combining rectilinear and curvilinear floorplans. One well preserved building consisted of
a main room, rectangular in shape and bounded by plaster-faced timber-
framed walls, as well as a more open, outer room, rounded on one side,
which was bounded by a thin ditch (Figure 7.2). Further south, in the
Aegean, the islands took on a more prominent role with substantial evidence
for increased trading activities and craft specialization, more settlements
and, perhaps, fortified sites.

The case for continuity can also be made for north-western Bulgaria,
south-western Romania and Serbia. Here, settlement took a variety of forms
and occurred in a range of different places, including caves. There were
many sites located high in the hills and mountains: at Bubanj and Hum,
Krivodol, Telish-Redutite, Reburkovo, Lesura and Mezdra (Mikov 1948;
Gergov 1992a, 1992b; Gergov *et al.* 1985). Some buildings were made of
sun-dried mud-block architecture (Todorova 1995a: 90), some, such as
Telish-Redutite had two storeys. The final phases of many were destroyed
by burning. Other sites were located on low river terraces. In some micro-
regions, collections of smaller settlements were arranged around one, larger
village (Alexandrov 1995: 256). Buildings were small and rectangular and
included both surface-level structures and pit-huts with walls made of posts,

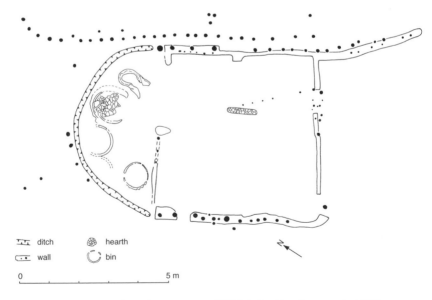

Figure 7.2 Burnt building from Sitagroi IV/V (after Renfrew *et al.* 1986)

242

clay and mud. In south-western Bulgaria, as at Negovantsi, Boboratsi, Cherven and Gulubnik, more sites were established along rivers than at higher altitudes.

In no region was there complete depopulation. Even in the northern regions where the shift away from tell villages is clearest, there is good evidence that people were now living in different ways in different places. At Ovcharovo-platoto II in north-eastern Bulgaria, for example, people built five small pit-huts (5 × 3 m in area and 0.7 m deep) in which were built hearths and ovens (Todorova *et al.* 1983). Sites such as these were short-lived and are striking in their resemblance to the much earlier architecture of the seventh and sixth millennia BC. In north-central and north-eastern Bulgaria, small settlements similar to the one at Ovcharovo-platoto II were established at rivers' edges with buildings, containing hearths and grinding-stones, constructed on platforms above marshy, frequently flooded terrain. Other settlements, such as those at Hotnitsa-vodopada, Shemshevo, Kachitsa, Borovo and Krasen, have recently been discovered and help to fill in what had traditionally been considered to be a region empty of people after 4000 BC. These sites are small collections of less than a dozen pit-huts, located on foothills near streams; they exemplify the new pattern of less permanent habitation. To the east, by the Varna Lakes, the site of Ezerovo was another platform village (Toncheva 1981); further south at Urdoviza and Sozopol (Draganov 1995) similar platform structures were built in wet marshy areas between rivers and the Black Sea.

Urdoviza and Sozopol provide well preserved evidence of methods of construction. Pointed timber-posts were driven into the ground and then connected by ropes with a series of jointed wooden beams that formed level platforms 1 m above ground level. Onto these platforms mud was compacted to make floors. Wattle-and-daub walls were erected to form houses. At Sozopol, at least, numerous replacements and shoring up of the supporting piles and repairs to floors and walls were made. In form, a house model from a later phase of the site (Sozopol II, 3000 BC) closely resembles buildings from inland settlements such as Yunatsite. A rising local water-table made the area inhabitable and the end of the occupation is marked by burning.

In south-central Bulgaria, the reoccupation of tells came with new forms of architecture. In the reoccupation of the tell at Ezero in the last quarter of the fourth millennium BC, new buildings had stone footings, a technique not used previously in this region, and floorplans reveal rounded, apsidal ends. A stone wall surrounded the village, although within the site buildings were not tightly packed.

At Yunatsite, the reoccupation of the tell at the end of the fourth and the beginning of the third millennium BC (horizons XVII–XIV) was marked by the construction of rectangular, usually single-roomed buildings containing ovens, grain storage bins, platforms and millstones as well as a variety of tools and pots (Katincharov and Matsanova 1993, 1995). There was also a larger central structure in the final phase of this first extended episode of reoccupation (horizon XIV); the end of this phase is marked by the digging of a curving palisaded ditch which cut off the northern quarter the village space (D. Bailey 1996d: 208, figure 4). In the next phase of site occupation (horizons XIII–IX), buildings were larger and more permanent in their construction. Some buildings had rounded, apsidal ends and one (house 13 from horizon XII) had four rooms and a floor-area of 230 sq m. Some buildings now contained special areas for processing clay (Katincharov et al. 1995: figure 5; D. Bailey 1996d: 209).

Although a better understanding of these phases of reoccupation of Yunatsite will come with fuller publication of the excavations, the first episodes of rebuilding on the tell suggest a much more open arrangement of settlement space than had been evident in fifth millennium BC tell villages, when buildings were tightly packed and activities were separated from the open village space. The open arrangement of village space at sites such as Yunatsite is reminiscent of the similar, but much earlier, villages in northern Greece, such as Achilleion, and even of the unstructured collections of pit-huts and surface-level buildings in the northern Balkans.

While boundaries within individual buildings were few, the digging of a palisaded ditch cutting off the northern part of the tell surface marks a very substantial segmentation of site space. The creation of the stone site-boundary wall at Ezero suggests a similar function. The second phase of post-4000 BC re-use of Yunatsite is more similar to the organization of village space characteristic of the fifth millennium BC tells. Buildings were deeper, had more private, interior rooms with restricted access and more elaborate decoration of interior walls; some buildings contained special activity areas which the excavators have suggested were reserved for ritual and ceremony.

At Yunatsite at least, the initial reoccupation of tell villages shows that the fifth millennium BC places were re-used, but for non-fifth millennium purposes and, perhaps, for different reasons. Can these reoccupied tells be termed villages or were they parts of much larger, looser, more flexible networks of activities and less permanent patterns of residence that stretched across landscapes? The simplicity and arrangement of buildings in the early reoccupation of Yunatsite suggest that the latter characterization of these late fourth and third millennium BC tells is the more accurate. Indeed, further south in the Rhodope mountains post-built houses containing ovens and hearths were built inside caves, as at Yagodina (Avramova 1993) and Haramijska Dupka (Todorova 1995a).

Thus, the places built upon and forms of buildings constructed in the post-4000 BC Balkans show substantial changes in architectural strategies and in people's perceptions of the types of arrangements of space appropriate for activity and residence. Fewer sites, the use of a variety of different locations, and a variety in building forms and materials suggest that the relatively ordered, and widely repeated, manner of marking the landscape with permanent villages that had dominated the previous two-and-a-half millennia had disintegrated. In its place emerged a more open landscape in which the ideology of the house, the household and the aggregated village held less, if any, sway.

BURIAL

While there was a significant shift in the perception of settlement space and architecture in the Balkans after 4000 BC, equally striking was a new set of funerary ceremonies and associated monuments, although even in these variety was the key across the regions. From the middle of the fourth until the end of the third millennium BC, three methods of burials were practised. To varying degrees, each was different from the mortuary practices of the fifth millennium BC (Nikolova 1995).

Intra-village inhumation

In some regions individuals were interred within the limits of settlements. This was the practice in south-central Bulgaria, where burials were placed beneath house floors, between houses and on the periphery of settlements. Thus, at Ezero, sixteen burials were excavated within the settlement limits. Ten of these were infants or babies and were buried separately in shallow graves with their knees drawn up towards their chests. Stone was used to build some burial pits and babies were buried in ceramic urns. There was no shared orientation of body position and only two of the Ezero burials contained grave-goods. One contained a necklace made of a marble pendant and *Dentalium* beads; another a pan-shaped vessel (Georgiev *et al.* 1979). Burials were also made within settlements in northern Bulgaria and in south-western Romania and in mainland Greece. The practice of settlement and house-associated burial recall earlier traditions of linking the dead, especially infants and children, to the household.

Extramural inhumations

Fourth and third millennium BC burials were also made in flat necropolises and in single flat-graves beyond the limits of villages and houses. This is especially clear in northern Bulgaria and in the upper Thracian Valley. Crouched inhumations were typical for north-eastern and south-central Bulgaria, cremations for north-western Bulgaria. A flat cemetery at Bereket in the upper Thracian Valley contained a number of crouched inhumations (Katincharov 1980). Here, inhumations included one, two or more individuals. Often, ochre was sprinkled on the head of the deceased and grave-goods were more common than in other cemeteries and included ceramic jugs and askoi, jewellery and bronze daggers. At Yambol a single flat-grave contained a bronze dagger. Flat cemeteries were also in use in north-eastern Bulgaria at Devniya (I. Ivanov 1972), Topoli (Toncheva 1981), Batin (Stanchev 1989) and Durankulak.

The five burials at Devniya date to the end of the fourth millennium BC. As was the case for graves in south-central Bulgaria, the Devniya burials were positioned without concern for a common orientation. One of the burial pits had a stone covering and in others grave-goods included ceramic bowls, cups and a flint knife. At Batin, the eleven burials were arranged in two rows with all but one oriented north–south. Four burials contained ceramic pots and one a piece of ochre. Similar burials were found at Zimnicea in southern Romania.

Mound burials

While both the settlement-associated burials and the flat cemeteries have similarities with earlier traditions, the third variation of post-4000 BC burial was new: inhumation in a pit which was then covered with an earth and stone mound. Mound cemeteries appear in northern and south-central Bulgaria, eastern Hungary and western Romania (Ecsedy 1979; Panayotov 1989; Panayotov and Dergachov 1984). In north-western Bulgaria, at Ostrov, Galiche and Selanovtsi, bodies were cremated and buried with ceramic cups, spouted pouring and other vessels. To the east and in south-central Bulgaria bodies were placed in crouched positions in rectangular pits; sometimes the body lay on top of a woven mat. In many cases ochre was sprinkled on the bodies. The pits were covered with timber beams and the whole unit was covered with a large mound of earth and stones. In some cases stone anthropomorphic stele were placed on top of the barrows. In many cases, the mound that covered the original became the new 'ground-level' into which subsequent burials were inhumed and which in turn were covered with new mounds. Secondary burials were often placed off-centre from the position of the original burial at the base of the mound.

Most mound cemeteries were located on elevated areas of plains and in watersheds between dry valleys (Panayotov 1989: 169). Some were collections of many mounds; the largest ones, such as those at Turnava (B. Nikolov 1976), Plachidol and Poruchik Geshanovo, contained up to twenty separate mounds (Panayotov 1989). Others consisted of fewer; concentrations of 5–10 mounds were found at Goran-slatina (Kitov et al. 1991), Kalugeritsa, Belogradec and Madara (Panayotov 1989). Some were smaller still, such as those at Zheglarci-Orljak, Trojanovo, Kjulevcha and Tsarevbrod (Panayotov 1989: 169).

Variation is also evident in the heights of individual mounds. At Plachidol and Tsarevbord some are almost 8 m high. Ten other mounds are smaller,

3–5 m in height, more are between 1.5 and 3.0 m and many more are between 0.5 and 1.0 m. There is also variation in the arrangement of mounds within cemeteries. In some cases, as at Plachidol I and II and at Kavarna, the smaller tumuli surrounded a larger one, and were probably built after and in relation to the central one. In others, such as Kalugeritsa, Goran-slatina and Poruchik Geshanovo, mounds were aligned, respectively, in one, two or three parallel rows. At Goran-slatina, mounds were separated into groups. The barrows of the first were arranged about 250 m from each other; those of the second were spaced between 80 and 250 m apart (Panayotov 1989). Similar spacing is evident at the other cemeteries in this region.

Mound II at Plachidol I is a good example of the contents of a mound burial and the sequential growth of tumuli with successive inhumations. Located 110 m to the south-east of mound I, mound II reached 42 m in diameter, more than 3.0 m in height and contained ten individual inhumations and one body-less pit. The earliest burial (grave 8) was dug into the humus of the ground level and formed the centre of the mound's circumference. Grave 8 was very poorly preserved and it was only possible to record that the body was oriented NE–SW.

More information is available about the contents of the eight secondary burials. Of these half were inhumations of children or infants; two were babies, one was 4–6 months old and the other 6 years. These burials, like all of the rest, were oriented NE–SW and in every case the bodies were placed so that their heads were to the north. Red ochre was sprinkled in three of the children's and infant burials as well as in three of the adults. Three of the four adults were male, aged 30, 35 and 35–40; the woman was aged between 20 and 30. In two of the male burials the ochre was sprinkled on the deceased's head and around his feet. With the exception of three pieces of red ochre placed by the head of the infant in grave 1 and the six astragali included with the infant in grave 3, the only grave-goods were found with the 35–40-year-old man in grave 6 (a copper spiral and two silver beads, all of which were found below the deceased's head) and in the 4–6-month-old child in grave 7 (a copper spiral, a piece of ochre and a handled pot). The body-less pit (grave 2) contained burnt wood and may best be understood as the focus for activities surrounding the ceremonies and practicalities of inhumation. As each successive burial was inhumed a new layer was added to the mound so that it grew in height and diameter.

As seen in the contents of mound II, the number and type of grave-goods placed in mound burials were restricted and grave-goods occur almost exclusively in the largest barrows; this was also the case at Goran-slatina and Turnava. The grave-goods that do appear include twisted spiral pendants made of metal, rings of silver, copper and, less frequently, gold, and necklaces of metal beads and animal and human teeth and bone. Pieces of ochre, crystal and single ceramic vessels were also deposited. At Goran-slatina a limestone hammer-axe was placed on its own in the burial of a child in mound III, but is exceptional; a bronze burin or blade with an arched edge was placed in the burial of an adult in grave 8 of the same mound. Also exceptional was the placement, in grave 1 of mound I at Plachidol I, of four wooden wheels at the four corners of a burial pit containing the remains of a 25-year-old women (Figure 7.3). The grave-pit was covered with wooden planks.

For many mound burials, detailed evidence on the age and sex of the deceased is limited. It is clear, however, that men, women and children were all interred. For the burials at Plachidol I, Zheglarci-Orljak and Poruchik Geshanovo, where reliable information is available, the ratio of men to women to children was 14 : 3 : 4 with the oldest men reaching 40–45 and women 25–30 years of age.

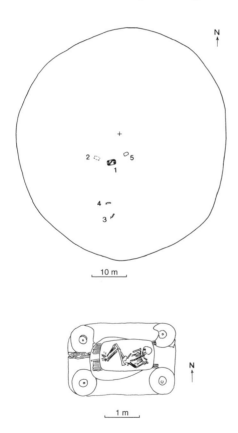

Figure 7.3 Above: Plan of mound I at Plachidol I showing distribution and numbering of burials and centre of mound. *Below:* Detail of central burial 1 (after Panayotov 1989)

Further to the west in the eastern Hungarian Plain, flat cemeteries continued in use after 4000 BC, as in the Bodrogkeresztúr phase of the Tiszapolgár-Basatanya burial ground (Bognár-Kutzián 1963, 1972); Bodrogkeresztúr contains many elements of continuity from the previous fifth millennium construct, the Tiszapolgár culture. The big changes appear after 3500 BC with the Baden cultural phenomenon. Some Baden flat-graves have extraordinary contents; two in the cemetery at Alsónémedi contain pairs of individuals accompanied by pairs of cattle (Bökönyi 1951; Korek 1951; Nemeskéri 1951; Whittle 1996: 122). Mound burials like those to the south and east were also being used (Sherratt 1984; Whittle 1996: 130–1).

Considering post-4000 BC Balkan burial on the whole, the changes in the funerary architecture, quantities and types of grave-goods and, in the north at least, the dislocation of burial from settlement space, and the inclusion of entire animal bodies, all are strikingly different from the mortuary record of the previous millennium. Most dramatically different is the appearance of collections of monumental burial tumuli. In many ways they appear as the new markers of place in the landscape, perhaps filling a role that tell settlements had played in the previous periods; perhaps it is not a coincidence that burial mounds appeared in those regions where the fifth millennium BC tells were most completely abandoned.

The second significant change in post-4000 BC burial is the absence of the extravagant grave-goods which distinguished some of the burials in the fifth millennium BC cemeteries of the lower Danube. Statements of inter-personal and intra-group identities were made in new and different ways after 4000 BC. If the contexts of such declarations involved burial they now did so with other methods and materials; the grave-goods, and thus perhaps the actual event of burial, were a less significant component than was the creation, in the raising of a substantial, visible mound, of a living memory of the deceased. While, in its creation and first use, the mound may have served as a monument to one particular individual who was buried in the central pit, the successive inhumations of other bodies, especially those of young people and babies, may represent the inclusions of related members within one kin- or activity-group. The connection between the secondary burials and the original one is both direct and tangible yet dislocated enough to suggest a potentially subservient position. Thus, although successive inhumations were made within the same mound and their bodies were oriented in the same direction, they were placed off-centre within the circle of the mound, dislocated from the central space held by the primary burial. If these mounds represent small descent groups, with separate mounds representing different descent groups, then a very different use of death had emerged in at least part of the Balkans after 4000 BC. Where fifth millennium BC burial had been engaged in the expression of both individual and village-based group identities through extravagant events of burial that appear to have been relatively short-term ceremonies, the post-4000 BC burials involved the expression of the coherence of small groups, over time and based on lasting expressions of the group existence.

The position of death, its meaning and the appropriate relationship between the dead and the living had changed fundamentally. If the fifth millennium BC had been about the routine visibility, control and occupation of the living space of the house and the village, with burial playing a partial, if dramatic part, then the post-4000 BC Balkans was about the enforced daily visibility of the dead concentrated in particular places in the landscape. The subsequent internments of the dead, especially of infants and children, in the mound burials remind us of the connections that people had drawn in earlier millennia between the household and dead children and infants. Perhaps the fundamental mechanism of expressing and maintaining group membership had shifted from the space of the living and doing to the space of the dead. The analogies between marking out particular places with lasting monumental structures by the rebuilding of villages during the fifth millennium BC and by burial tumuli after 4000 BC are striking. It is not surprising, in this sense, that the only post-4000 BC anthropomorphic, representational objects are the stone stele placed on top of some of the burial mounds; they may have served a similar function, though in different ways requiring different numbers and forms, as served by anthropomorphic figurines within the contexts of houses and households during the sixth and fifth millennia BC. Thus, while there are substantial differences in the forms of expressions of group membership and individual identity within groups, there are significant similarities of intention; people used materials and special places to make legitimate displays of identities.

MATERIAL CULTURE

The scale of change that is evident in burial and settlement after 4000 BC is also apparent in material culture. Most striking is the disappearance of almost all categories of representational and brilliantly reflective expressive objects and materials; occasional finds of gold (as well as the appearance of silver) and the continuation of some graphite-decorated pottery suggest some continuity in a few regions such as north-western Bulgaria. On the whole, however, the number and range of objects made of special materials such as gold, copper, and *Spondylus* were very small. With the exception of anthropomorphic grave stele, human representation as well as animal representation disappeared. Pottery decoration reveals a similar dramatic reduction of stylistic variation and aesthetic brilliance. Against these dramatic changes, there were some elements of continuity, especially in lithic technology and, though to a lesser extent, in the exploitation and management of animals. Let us look at the novelties in ceramics before considering continuities in lithics and animals.

Pottery

One of the clearest changes of the post-4000 BC Balkans is in ceramic form and decoration. New shapes include one- and two-handled cups and handled bowls, jugs and other spouted pouring vessels and mark the appearance of sets of vessels used for serving and drinking liquids (Figure 7.4). Change is also evident in surface treatment. The visually stimulating use of graphite,

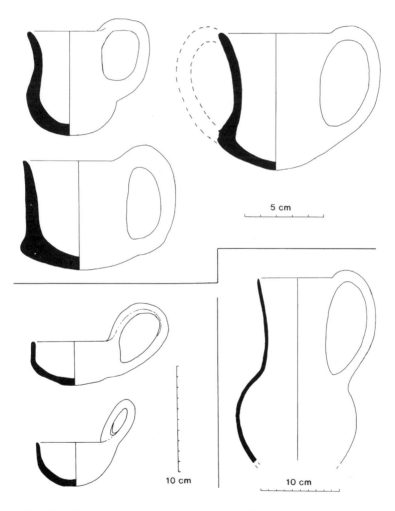

Figure 7.4 Vessel forms of the fourth and third millennia BC from Sitagroi phases IV and V (after Sherratt 1986a)

paint and gold to decorate vessel surfaces was almost completely abandoned and channelled ornamentation on a lustrous grey surface became
common.

Not all of the changes in ceramics were absolute or immediate. Thus, at
the beginning of the fourth millennium BC, in the Rhodope Mountains in
southern Bulgaria, Yagodina culture sites have black pottery with graphite
or whitish pseudo-graphite; these traditional decorative techniques were,
however, used on the new handled forms (Avramova 1993; Todorova 1995a:
90). Similar combinations are evident on the Black Sea coast in the earliest
occupation of Sozopol and in north-west Bulgaria at Telish-Redutite III
(Gergov 1992a, 1992b). In western Bulgaria cups appear with two, or more,
handles and surface treatment includes impressed or inlaid decoration with
graphite, barbotine and polychrome motifs. By the end of this initial post-
fifth millennium BC phase, however, these transitional elements had tailed
off and pottery, as seen in the final phases of the Krivodol-Salcuţa-Bubanj
culture complex, had lost its high quality and varied decoration. In the
following Coţofeni phases pottery forms included semi-spherical bowls and
plates, small cups with tall, looped handles, askoi and large storage jars. In
north-central and north-eastern Bulgaria pottery of the Pevets culture
includes many handled forms and is thin-walled, though there is almost no
decoration. Where present, surface treatment most commonly consisted of
incisions, which were often filled with white paste, although impression
and indentation were also evident.

Sitagroi pottery

One of the more detailed investigations of fourth and early third millennium pottery is Sherratt's study of the material from phases IV and V at
Sitagroi (Sherratt 1986a). The pottery from these phases was made with a
relatively homogeneous set of fabrics. Most wares are dark with channelling
or white-filled incisions. In the early part of these sequences at the site
(phase IV), many of the most finely produced vessels are small vessels for
drinking and eating (Sherratt 1986a: 435). Some bowl forms have a high
strap-handle and have been proposed as dippers or cups; Sherratt suggests
that these shapes are the result of adding handles to the traditional flat,
shallow bowl form. Jars and handled jugs also appear in the phase IV inventory, as do flat-based urns and larger-capacity storage vessels.

In the subsequent phase at Sitagroi (Va) bowls, cups, jugs and urns
continued to dominate the pottery inventory (Sherratt 1986a: 437). In
surface treatment burnishing continued, as did white-filled impressions.
Again the finer vessels are the small cups and bowls ideal for hand-held
drinking and which were decorated on their bases. Sherratt sees in these
forms, as in the earlier addition of strap handles to bowls, the potential of
a metal prototype.

In the final phase of relevance at Sitagroi (phase Vb) vessel forms were simpler, fabrics were coarser and surface treatment attracted less attention and effort (Sherratt 1986a: 438–40). Small, handled cups with pointed bases are characteristic. In distinction to the earlier phases, there were few large bowls; urns, vessels with cylindrical necks and lidded forms were popular. The high handles so distinctive of phases IV and Va were not present.

Overall, the material from these three phases at Sitagroi documents that pottery of the second half of the fourth millennium BC was distinct in character from that of the previous millennium and a half. The painting of surfaces had given way to channelling of surfaces, which in turn degenerated into simple grooving before being replaced by new systems of incised white-filled designs (Sherratt 1986a: 440). The dramatic distinction in ornamentation marks out these vessels from ones of the previous millennia. Pottery had become less of a medium for expression. It is not surprising, therefore, that there was a coincident decline in the overall quality of pottery (Sherratt 1986a: 441). With respect to vessel form, cups, jugs and the application of looped handles were important novelties. The new pottery shapes suggest an increase in the importance of activities involving the preparation, manipulation and consumption of liquids. Sherratt suggests milk and wine but also soup made of barley, vetch and lentil as candidate liquids.

Metal

After the large-scale mining, production and conspicuous deposition of copper and gold in the fifth millennium BC, the fourth millennium was a metallurgic anticlimax. During the earlier period the Balkans had been at the centre of a large Carpatho-Balkan mining and metallurgic region in which copper metallurgy was limited to the use of unalloyed copper ores (Chernykh 1992: 15). By late in the fourth millennium BC the Balkans had become a peripheral component in a larger group of communities that made up a circumpontic metallurgic zone covering a wide area stretching from the Adriatic in the west to the southern Urals and the Volga in the east, and from the upper Volga in the north to the Aegean and Asia Minor in the south.

The metals made and used in this larger, later, group ranged in composition from unalloyed copper ores that continued to be exploited, as in the Carpathians and the upper Volga region, to the arsenic bronzes that appeared in other areas. At this time in the north Balkan region, both of these variations were evident; tin-bronzes, however, did not appear in quantity until the second millennium BC and thus remain beyond the scope of the present discussion.

The shift to the fourth millennium BC pattern of metallurgy represents a massive discontinuity, with fundamental changes in the forms of copper tools and weapons. The processes and scale of metal-working also changed; metal-working was now of a more primitive nature, mining activities were greatly reduced and the number of copper objects produced and deposited decreased (Chernykh 1992: 51).

As noted above in the discussion of the new mortuary rituals and monuments, the extravagant axe-adze-hammers and chisels of the fifth millennium BC were no longer deposited in burials. Instead objects made of metal were limited almost exclusively to ornaments and jewellery. These were, however, new forms, including objects, such as spear-heads, daggers and knives, whose function was to cut, but to cut in very different ways, and perhaps cut very different materials, than represented in the larger chisels and axe-adzes of the fifth millennium BC.

As in the previous millennium, much of the post-4000 BC metal was deposited during burial ceremonies, although the differentials in the scale of deposition during the two periods are very great. Metal objects have also been found outside of burial contexts; a copper dagger comes from the Haramijska cave and two small daggers and awls were found in mid-fourth millennium BC contexts at Hotnitsa-vodopada in northern Bulgaria (Ilcheva 1986).

In north-western regions especially, copper was alloyed with arsenic from the middle of the fourth millennium BC. From Coţofeni contexts come needles and daggers with triangular blades made from a mixture of copper and 2–3 per cent arsenic. At the end of the fourth millennium BC, arsenic bronzes were in use on the Black Sea coast at Urdoviza where a dagger and an adze have been found.

The new forms of ceramic vessels, especially the jugs, cups and askoi, and the high looping handles used, resemble very closely forms made of metal at this time and in previous centuries in the Aegean and Anatolia. If the ceramic forms from the Balkans were imitations of the southern metal shapes, then it is highly likely that the significance of the ceramic vessels, like the metal vessels, rested not necessarily in their material of manufacture but rather in their use in pouring and drinking liquids.

It is significant that after 4000 BC the importance of objects such as vessels used for handling liquids rested more in the activities in which they were held, such as drinking, and less in the material of their manufacture, as had been the case in the graphite-decorated fine-wares or copper, gold or *Spondylus* objects of the fifth millennium BC. The increase in the importance of the practice of activities, and not in any inherent qualities of raw materials employed, marks an important change in people's perceptions of their material world. If a large part of the fifth millennium BC expressions and negotiations of social relationships was about loud, visible, open events such as extramural burials, then the declarations and negotiations of similar relationships after 4000 BC appear to have been focused on much more closed activities and ceremonies the significance of which were not immediately recognizable from the appearance or material of the objects involved.

The exception to the infrequent appearance of metal objects in the fourth millennium BC is a metal 'boom' that occurred in north-west Bulgaria, south-western Romania and Serbia in the first half of the fourth millennium BC as seen in the end of the Krivodol-Salcuţa-Bubanj-Hum complex. This increase in metal-working may have been linked to western sources of metal such as Bor in Serbia and Majdnpek in northern Transylvania. In these regions large numbers of copper objects were produced, including cruciform axe-adzes, flat copper spear-heads, knives and jewellery. But this region appears distinct from others after 4000 BC in many aspects of life and perhaps its exceptional metal record should not be compared with trends to the east and south.

CONTINUITY IN LITHICS AND ECONOMY

With the exception of parts of the western Balkans where continuity is evident in metallurgy, the fourth millennium BC patterns of pottery, metals, burial and settlement were distinct from the patterns of the previous millennia. There is evidence, however, for continuity in two other elements of life, in flint-working and in the species and patterns of animal tending.

Flint

Detailed studies of flaked stone industries are infrequent for later periods of Balkan prehistory and in most cases we have little if any idea whether or not the dramatic changes seen in ceramics, settlement and burial were also present in the more mundane, but perhaps potentially more informative inventories of flint tools. One exception is Sirakov and Tsonev's study of the flint assemblages from the two-phase settlement at Hotnitsa-vodopada in north-central Bulgaria, a site that was in use during the first half of the fourth millennium BC (Ilcheva 1982, 1986, 1987, 1989a, 1989b, 1990; Sirakov and Tsonev 1995). Hotnitsa-vodopada is an important site as its first two horizons were formed during the period transitional from the local Copper Age to the early Bronze Age; it is one of several sites in the region that have been assigned to the Pevets culture (Todorova 1995a: 91).

Sirakov and Tsonev's study of the Hotnitsa-vodopada lithics reached several important conclusions. The most important of these was the high degree of local continuity in lithic typology and technology that they found between the fourth millennium BC occupation at Hotnitsa-vodopada and the typology and technology of lithic assemblages from earlier, fifth millennium BC sites in the region. Elements of continuity included the use of carefully prepared elongated conical and pyramidal single-platform cores; the predominance of end-scrapers and retouched blades and a rarity of burins; the location of raw material sources; knapping techniques employing a moderator; and blade-oriented production which is typical of the super-blades. Sirakov and Tsonev concluded that the fourth millennium BC Hotnitsa-vodopada flint assemblage was deeply rooted in the local fifth millennium BC tradition and contained no evidence for any external influences (Sirakov and Tsonev 1995: 252).

Animals

If the lithic evidence suggests that, at least for one region, an underlying current of continuity ran beneath the more obvious changes that occurred after 4000 BC in the Balkans, then the evidence for continuity in animal exploitation provides a greater sense of continuity. After 4000 BC cattle, sheep, goat and pig were still the main species of tended animals, although variation is evident between individual sites. Vasilev suggested that for Bulgaria, cattle decreased in frequency while sheep and goat increased as did pig, although to a lesser extent (Vasilev 1982: 308–9). Haskell Greenfield has made a similar suggestion for Serbia (Greenfield 1988).

In north-eastern Bulgaria, Pevets culture settlements reveal faunal records dominated by goat and sheep with little limited evidence for agricultural activities (Todorova 1995a: 91). The fauna from Urdoviza on the Black Sea coast contains a high proportion of wild animals, such as waterfowl, deer, wild boar and wolf, which would have been at home in rich forest and coastal vegetation (Boev and Ribarov 1990). While the new, less permanent settlements such as the coastal ones at Urdoviza have large proportions of locally available aquatic species, at Ezero it also appears that wild animals accounted for a larger component in post-4000 BC sites (Dennell 1978: 151).

Another factor in post-4000 BC economies was an increase in the role of grazing species within the more mobile communities of the period. The seminal, and still unique, work of Dennell and Webley (Dennell and Webley 1975; Dennell 1978: 131–68) documented important changes in the composition and potential for cultivation and grazing of soils in south-central Bulgaria. In brief, Dennell and Webley showed that the villages, such as Karanovo, dating to the fifth millennium BC and earlier had been established and had thrived relatively close together in parts of the landscape that contained high proportions of arable land. Indeed, as suggested in Chapter 2, the selection of appropriate places in which to establish the early village sites in south-central and west-central Bulgaria such as Chavdar and Kazanluk was based, in part at least, on the presence of arable land.

After studying the patterns of change in soil composition around the Azmak River, Dennell and Webley concluded that the amount of arable land had been drastically reduced after 4000 BC due to relatively rapid changes in soil formation in the river valley. The change was from a region with extensive land made up of light soils suitable for cultivation to land with heavy, river- and flood-deposited soils that, though very fertile, could only be used for pasturage. Dennell and Webley suggested that the erosion that led to the deposition of these heavy soils was caused by overgrazing of relatively unstable uplands in the foothills of the Sredna Gora or by increases in the felling of trees to provide fuel for smelting copper ores. Dennell suggests that these erosional events were rapid and occurred over two or three centuries (Dennell 1978: 141).

One response to the change in soil potential would have been to increase community reliance on animal products (both wild and domestic) and to decrease reliance on cereals. If, as suggested in Chapters 2 and 5, a significant part of the function of tell settlements was to serve as a focus for agricultural activities, then these changes may have played a part in the end of their use-lives. If similar erosional events occurred in other regions at this time, then the shift to animal grazing and the dislocation of field-based agriculture may have been a widespread phenomenon across the Balkans.

After 4000 BC, certain animals appear to have taken on new positions within the ceremonial space of some Balkan communities. Thus, in eastern Hungary cattle were placed in human burials, especially in those of the Baden culture. Whittle has suggested that these human–animal burials represent the definition of people in terms of animals as well as the definition of the latter in terms of the former (Whittle 1996: 124). Similar definitions, which however took place in different contexts, had been widespread across the Balkans during the previous millennia. Not only had zoomorphic and animal bone grave-goods been placed in lower Danube burials but zoomorphic figurines were also used inside village contexts probably in ceremonies defining household membership. The new element in the post-4000 BC use of animals, animal parts and animal imagery was that deposition now involved the inclusion of entire animal skeletons in burials.

The burials of pairs of cattle in some human inhumations may suggest that animal traction was one of the intended implications of their inclusion (Whittle 1996: 123; also see Sherratt 1986b, 1987). Traction may have referred to transportation by cart or wagon as well as to pulling ploughs during farming. The burial, noted above, of the four-wheeled wagon in one of the Plachidol mounds in north-eastern Bulgaria is another example of the changing role of animals in society, at least terms of human mobility. Other evidence takes the form of the ceramic cups fashioned in the forms of wheeled vehicles that have been found in Baden contexts in eastern Hungary at Szigetszentmárton and Budakalász. All of these examples strengthen the connection between animal transportation, if not necessarily ploughing, and the burial of particular individuals (Kalicz 1976; Sherratt 1981; Bondár 1990; Whittle 1996: 124). While an emphasis on animal-aided mobility and transportation was present in the previous millennium, as represented in the zoomorphs of pack animals from southern and northern

Bulgaria, the importance of vehicular mobility, or perhaps mobility in general, in people's conceptions of individual-based identities had taken up a new position; the shared human–animal burials were one symptom of the elevation of mobility.

Another symptom of animal-aided mobility in the post-4000 BC Balkans was the appearance of horse bones in the archaeological record for the first time since the disappearance of equids in the upper Palaeolithic. To the north-east of the Balkans proper, in the forest-steppe north-west of the Black Sea in the lower Dniepr and Don valleys, there is evidence for the hunting of horse in Sredny-Stog culture contexts. Sredny Stog was a fifth millennium BC phenomenon very different from those described in the previous chapters for the Balkans proper (Telegin 1973). Sredny Stog communities lived more mobile lives with temporary settlement based in simple rectilinear structures containing hearths. Activity areas were in areas outside of buildings and boundary fences marked the limits of sites. Burial was often collective and subsistence based on a mixture of fishing, hunting and animal-keeping (Anthony 1986; Mallory 1989; Chernykh 1992; Whittle 1996: 132–3).

At one Sredny Stog site, Dereivka, the most frequent faunal remain was horse bone, although it is not conclusively clear whether these assemblages represent the managed culling of wild animals or the maintenance of a domestic herd (Telegin 1986; Anthony et al. 1991; Anthony and Brown 1991; and see Whittle 1996: 133–4 for a balanced discussion). Whether or not horses were used for riding or pulling or whether they were used purely for meat is also not clear. Worked pieces of antler that may have func- tioned as bridles and the wear patterns on some horse teeth suggest that some form of reining was being used. Besides Dereivka, horse bone has been found at other Sredny Stog sites, although it appears as a minority component of faunal assemblages. Further to the south, on the Bulgarian Black Sea coast, the faunal record from the platform site at Urdoviza also contained wild and domestic horse bones (Ribarov 1991).

If horses were being used for traction or transportation, then they would fit into the larger model of an increase in the use of animals for their secondary products proposed by Sherratt some time ago (Sherratt 1981). However, the use of animals for purposes other than nutrition had been a part of people's lives in the fifth millennium BC; the frequent finds of loomweights and spindle-whorls suggest the use of goat (if not necessarily sheep) for wool; the finds of perforated clay sieves suggest the use of goat and cow for milk, and the pack-animal figurines provide clear evidence of cattle used for transportation. Certainly the emphasis placed on horned animals, probably cattle, in the representational material culture of the fifth millennium BC Balkans documents the shifting perceptions of animals well before the fourth and third millennia BC. As Whittle has emphasized, the suggestion of a secondary products revolution occurring in the fourth and third millennia BC may be more accurately understood in terms of the acceleration of activities already in progress (Whittle 1996: 142).

CHAPTER CONCLUSIONS

In many senses, therefore, people lived their lives in very different ways after 4000 BC. Compared to the anchored, repeatedly reaffirmed community cohesion of large villages and extramural cemeteries of the fifth millennium BC, the more temporary pit-huts and riverside platform dwellings of the following millennia appear ephemeral. Even in those instances where tells were reoccupied, architecture reveals a difference in intention of site use. In many regions, especially to the north, the ideologies of the house, the household and the village as individual and community institutions were no longer relevant.

In the place of these older ideas, a new philosophy emerged that placed emphasis not on investing areas of living with continuity but on creating monuments of death used by a more restricted group of individuals who were linked over large areas by common groupings of artefacts such as sets of drinking and pouring vessels and wheeled vehicles. In some regions, such as south-central Bulgaria, the burial of children and infants within settlement space reminds us of seventh and sixth millennium BC practices; perhaps here the ideology of the household retained some of its former power. Indeed, the use of stone foundations for house walls suggests a strengthening of the durability of some buildings.

After 4000 BC, there emerged new logistics and mechanisms for expressing group and individual identities. If there is spatial order imposed on activities, it appears most clearly in the arrangement of mound cemeteries, in the placing of one mound in relation to others, in the arrangement of groups and rows of mounds, and in the placement of successive individuals within particular mounds.

The whole atmosphere of the Balkans had changed. Even taking account of the threads of continuity such as the similarities in some lithic working techniques and forms, in the re-use of some tells, and continuities in the key animal species exploited, there were fundamental differences in almost every part of people's lives. From a higher interpretive level, one can see a shift in the orientation of the Balkans in relation to other regions. It appears most clearly in the pattern of copper acquisition, with Carpathian mines replacing Balkan ones as the main sources of raw material (Chernykh 1992). As a unit, the Balkans appears to have changed from being at the centre of a very dynamic fifth millennium BC to being on the border of a less sensational fourth and third millennia BC; new, dramatic developments in material culture, settlement, burial and exchange were starting to happen to the south, in the Aegean, and to the east in Mesopotamia (Harding 1983; Sherratt 1994).

Explanations of change

The scale of the changes that distinguish the post-4000 BC Balkans from the previous two-and-a-half thousand years has stimulated equally grand explanations. For a long time, the most influential interpretation was phrased in terms of population replacement caused by an invasion of horse-mounted warriors pouring from the steppelands of the east (Gimbutas 1973, 1977, 1991). According to this school, the invaders were a mobile male-dominated, patriarchal, aggressive group which swept all before them, destroying the villages and lifestyles of the late fifth and early fourth millennium BC communities. Accordingly, the bodies inhumed in the mound burials along the Danube were proposed to be the invader's remains. As we expand and refine our understanding of fifth millennium BC Balkan communities, as well as of those who lived in the steppes to the east and those who lived along the Danube after 4000 BC, the invasion explanation finds increasingly little support.

The many separate phases of fire destructions of fifth millennium BC houses and villages occurred over a long period and, as argued in Chapter 5, probably had more to do with severing local relationships of people and households or negating household identities than they had to do with thundering troops of testosterone-exuding arsonists. Furthermore, as Whittle has noted, if the geo-chronology of the changes in the Balkans suggests anything, it is that some of the earliest changes took place to the west and not closer to the steppes as the invasion hypothesis would suggest (Whittle 1996: 138–40). In many versions of the population replacement explanation, it is proposed that the new inhabitants of the Balkans were speakers of a common, imported language, Proto-Indo-European, the appearance of which in the Balkans can be dated, through a not uncontroversial connection of linguistic and archaeological evidence, to the fourth millennium BC (see Mallory 1989 and discussion in Whittle 1996: 137–8).

There are inconsistencies in all of these explanations and Whittle has reviewed them in detail (Whittle 1996: 136–43); at their core is the mistaken assumption that dramatic change in material culture, settlement and burial such as are evident in the Balkans between 4000 and 3000 BC demands an explanation in terms of population replacement. Considering the time-span over which these changes took place, the regional diversity, especially in settlement and burial, and the threads of continuity noted above, it seems a much wiser approach to look for local patterns and rates of change. Clearly, when it comes, the comparison of DNA taken from pre- and post-4000 burials will provide some more refined evidence, although even this will only offer information about limited portions of communities.

A more accurate reading of the post-4000 BC changes may be to consider them in terms of new patterns of living. Perhaps these lifestyles developed independently of any potentially causal events occurring outside of the region. Perhaps people in the Balkans took advantage of non-local developments in technologies. Perhaps perceptions shifted with respect to what was an appropriate or desirable level of settlement permanence or visibility or with respect to the ways in which communities established and maintained links to particular parts of landscapes.

In the light of the, at times, reductive explanatory mechanisms involved in traditional European prehistoric archaeology, perhaps it is not surprising that big-event causation is sought. As argued throughout this book, the archaeological record of the previous 50,000 years of Balkan prehistory is one of long-term gradual change, with important developments in settlement, burial, economy and material culture marking accelerated spurts of adaptation, innovation, adoption and exaptation. Even the 1000–1500-year period over which the changes considered in this chapter occurred is, on the human scale of daily life, still long enough for significant changes to take place without the interference of any single event.

Regardless of the preferred explanation for the changes that mark the post-4000 BC Balkans, the new and varied forms of settlement, burial and material culture reveal that people were living their lives in very different ways. The scale of the changes was similar to that which distinguished the early Holocene mobile hunter-fisher-foragers from the early villagers of the mid-seventh millennium BC Balkans. However, where the mid-seventh millennium BC shift had been from flexibility and mobility to the physical demarcation and anchored residence of increasingly divided communities, the post-4000 BC shift was from stable, but perhaps inflexible, village communities, in which the ideology of the household held sway, to mobile communities in which the principal visible links or expressions of relationships were grounded in death. The post-4000 BC shift was from the visible and explicitly symbolic, in which significance was proclaimed in a lasting and visually available fashion, to the implicit and invisible, in which meanings and identities were contained either within drab, apparently blank, sets of material culture or drew their power and significance from the impermanent elements of unrecorded events and ceremonies.

SUMMARY

In this chapter I have described the character of the changes that distinguish the post-4000 BC Balkans from the preceding two and half millennia. Significant were changes concerning where people chose to live, the ways they organized those places and the lengths of time over which they repaired, rebuilt or returned to those places. In this sense the period was marked by a relative disappearance of monumental settlement; even at those fifth millennium BC tells that were reoccupied after 4000 BC, there is a suggestion of a reorientation of the relationship between people and landscape.

Equally significant were changes in the ways people treated the deceased. As with the settlement record, so with burial method, variety was the rule. The fifth millennium BC tradition of marking the events of certain individuals' inhumations with extravagant amounts of metal or shell objects was replaced by rather unimpressive collections of grave-goods. As with almost all categories of material culture, it appears that the event of burial or of serving and drinking was more important than any extravagance invested in the production or consumption of the objects involved or in their decoration. If anything stood out as monumental and visually striking in the post-4000 BC landscape, it was the mound burials and not the long-term rebuildings of villages.

The changes in settlement and burial and, perhaps, the increase in importance of grazing animals, suggest that living was less tied down to particular places than it had been previously. The physical links between individuals and places of living and doing and the links between groups of people and such places were no longer significant in expressing relationships between individuals and groups. The strongest ties among people and places were made through new events and ceremonies of death; this is especially clear in the successive interments of children and infant burials in the lower Danube mound burials.

The question of why these changes occurred when they did and where they did may only be answered in terms of small-scale local changes in people's perceptions of what it was appropriate to do, and where and when it was appropriate to do it. While new technologies and fashions from neighbouring regions may have been borrowed and adapted in the Balkans, there were important, though often overlooked continuities; there is no reason to invoke huge migrations or invasions to explain the changes neatly. Perhaps the explanation rests in a larger consideration of the longer-term trends that run through the changes in life in Balkans discussed in this and the preceding chapters. Such a consideration is the topic of the next and final chapter.

8

THE BALKANS (6500–2500 BC)

Exclusion, incorporation and projection

In the Balkans from about 6500 BC people started living their lives in new ways. This included very substantial changes in people's relationships to each other, both within and between groups, and especially in the ways individuals thought it appropriate to identify themselves and their places of residence and activity. The changes included important alterations in people's conceptions of the landscapes they lived in and the appropriate ways of inhabiting these landscapes. Significant changes also occurred in the particular components of the natural world that people chose to exploit, the way they exploited them and the things they did with the resources exploited. Equally importantly, daily life came to be increasingly full of a widening variety of new objects. The post-6500 BC Balkans was very much about the combination of this new materiality and the new ways in which people built social environments. Any attempt at understanding the significance of the long-term changes in the region from 6500 through 2500 BC must take account of these two developments.

THE BUILT ENVIRONMENT

Across the Balkans after 6500 BC people constructed their social and living spaces in new ways that were physical and dramatic. They employed a limited number of techniques and materials. Wood was used in most, if not all, of these constructions, especially in combination with mud and clay, straw, twigs and dung; stone was used across a more restricted area. Regardless of the materials with which they were made, most of the earlier buildings were single-roomed structures; many later buildings had more complex interiors.

Despite the potential for variety in building form, two designs dominated: circular or oval pit-huts and rectangular surface-level structures.[1] As seen in the examples described in Chapter 2, the distinction between pit-huts and surface dwellings was not grounded in a unilinear development of technique or builders' ability through time. Not only did both pit-huts and surface structures occur in many places at the same time, but in some instances, as in northern Bulgaria, some pit-huts followed surface-level structures.

It is commonly assumed that oval pit-dwellings reflect episodes of temporary occupation and rectangular surface structures document longer periods of residence. In a much cited article, Kent Flannery suggested that circular buildings were more portable than other forms because they were easier to construct (Flannery 1972). For Flannery, round-floored pit-huts either were the structures of nomadic or semi-nomadic groups or marked the places of more transient activities, such as hunting or grazing, carried out by members of more permanent communities (Flannery 1972: 29–30). In his report on the pit-huts at late seventh millennium BC Divostin, Bogdanović followed many of these ideas, arguing that the pit-huts at the site were built for temporary use. He even suggested that they should be taken as architectural descendents of late Pleistocene pit-structures from other parts of Eurasia such as have been found at Gagarin and Andijevo, Olten, Barka, Vestonice, Pavlow, Kostienki and Timakova (Bogdanović 1988: 87). Again, the emphasis is on pit-huts as part of more mobile existences.

The association between floorplan shape and degree of sedentism, however, is neither secure nor proved. In other parts of Europe, such as Britain and central Europe, rectangular buildings were part of more mobile existences. The correlation between the single variable of structure-form and the degree of sedentism or residential continuity of its occupants may be an oversimplification and certainly cannot lend itself to a generalized application across regions or through the millennia.

It may be more useful to compare the two dominant architectural forms of Balkan prehistory in terms of the numbers, arrangements and types of activities and the number of people each could have accommodated. As described in Chapters 2 and 5, there are important distinctions between circular pit-huts and rectangular surface structures in terms of their size and shape and the types, numbers and arrangements of activities and people associated with or contained within each architectural form. A closer inspection of these differences suggests more general trends in community organization during the millennia considered in this book.

Oval semi-subterranean pit-huts

Balkan pit-huts were generally small, although there are exceptions such as some of the larger Starčevo examples. Limited floor-space implies that the numbers of people and activities that could have been accommodated were low. Flannery suggested that pit-huts could have provided space for no more than one, or at most two, people (Flannery 1972: 30). Limitations of interior space also would have restricted the range of activities which could have been carried out in any one pit-hut, a range that may not have extended beyond the manufacturing and maintenance of clothing and hunting gear (Hunter-Anderson 1977: 313). Certainly there are few interior features in pit-huts; other than small hearths, pit-huts seldom contained more than one distinct activity area, piece of furniture or specific internal fixture.

There is no single activity that took place in all Balkan pit-huts; in many cases different individual activities, such as storage or pottery firing, were anchored in separate pit-structures. In this sense, within a pit-hut camp different activities were spread across the area of occupation. If there was any linkage between different activities, then that linkage was extramural. Most activities took place outside of pit-huts, and many were carried out away from the camp. If there was any linkage between individual pit-huts within a camp it was not co-ordinated. Most often, pit-huts were not laid out in any organized fashion across a camp; seldom were the floorplans of different pit-huts arranged in common orientation. There was, therefore, little evidence for any co-ordinated initial spatial planning of pit-hut camps.

Hunter-Anderson has suggested that few of the activities that took place within pit-huts were ones (such as herding or hunting animals, working flint, or distributing meat from a kill or cull) that brought a person into a shared group activity, and few were activities participation in which would have been part of a person's recognized identity or character within a group. The absence, or at least the very limited number, of these role-related activities within any one pit-hut suggests that in such communities there was a low level of social- or task-role differentiation. Perhaps, as with many mobile and foraging communities, people carried out the majority of role-related activities away from the camp (Hunter-Anderson 1977: 313).

Almost without exception, people built pit-huts that were oval or round in plan. In using this shape their builders created the most efficient form in which things could be sheltered and contained; in three-dimension, pit-hut ovals and circles closely resemble spheres and, as Hunter-Anderson has noted, spheres have very high ratios of volume-to-surface area. Pit-huts with round floorplans were, therefore, very efficient forms for exploiting internal space even if that space was small (Hunter-Anderson 1977).

Overall, the oval pit-huts of Balkan prehistory were small, simple structures which, though lacking the capacity for many different activities or individuals and, though probably only used for limited periods of time, were very efficient structures for using space to contain people and things. While the simple correlation of floorplan shape with degrees of sedentism may be, on its own, over-ambitious, consideration of the limited range of activities and people who could be accommodated at one time suggests that much social and economic activity took place outside of and probably away from pit-hut interiors and, indeed, probably away from pit-hut camps. Although this does not confirm community mobility, it does make it clear that pit-huts were not the dominant focus of activities after 6500 BC.

Rectilinear surface structures

Rectilinear surface-level structures were distinct from pit-huts in many ways. Most obviously, they were larger and thus could have accommodated a number of individuals and activities at any one time. Indeed, there was sufficient space for people to carry out many different activities at the same time and for particular places within the structure to have been permanently dedicated to particular tasks; thus, different areas within a building were given over to grinding, weaving, cooking and baking, tool-working and repair, and a range of other activities.

This difference is significant. In pit-hut camps activities were spread outside of pit-huts and no two activities could take place within a pit-hut at the same time. In villages of rectilinear surface structures several different activities were focused within buildings and could be carried out contemporaneously. People in pit-hut camp communities dwelt in an open, relatively unbounded environment in which they lived in the presence of others without restriction; people in rectilinear village communities dwelt in bounded and closed built environments in which they lived in the presence of a limited and, perhaps, particular group of people.

Rectilinear surface structures also provided greater potential for subdividing internal space in increasingly complex fashions. Interior space could be subdivided by building partition walls and thus creating more, but smaller rooms. The potential for the internal division of circular pit-huts was limited to single walls or fences cutting structures in two; subsequent subdivision would have been increasingly problematic not only because of useless acutely angled corners created but also because of the very small rooms that would have been produced. It is not surprising, then, that in pit-hut camps different activities were separated into different huts, were placed outside of huts or, if they were to take place within the same hut, had to take place sequentially. In most rectilinear structures distinct activities and facilities, such as storage areas and silos, were constructed as internal features; distinct activities were either arranged within a single room or placed in separate rooms. As noted for sites such as Achilleion in northern Greece, there were exceptions to the internal containment of activities in rectilinear surface structures. However, the distinction between activities based inside rectilinear surface structures and activities spread around and between pit-huts holds as a general pattern.

Within the larger, rectilinear structures a greater number of separate activities could take place at the same time. Significantly many of these activities, such as textile production, grain processing, storing and cooking, were role-related tasks. That these buildings could accommodate several people carrying out different tasks, especially role-related ones, at the same time suggests that the rectilinear surface structures provided the contexts in which small group relationships were forged and maintained.

These structures represent the physical contexts of building-based co-resident groups. Individuals brought to, and displayed within, these buildings different skills and knowledges related to the activities carried out there; differences in skills and abilities suggest that co-residence groups contained people of different skills and, perhaps, identities. Furthermore, if the different buildings within a village contained different sets and ranges of activities and individuals able to carry them out, then perhaps further differentials existed between co-residence groups.

The architectural differentiation of internal space within buildings may have been a way of coping with the spatial and social problems inherent when multiple contemporary activities needed to be carried out within a single building. The segmentation of internal space and the making of rooms prevented interference and disturbances between contemporary activities (Hunter-Anderson 1977: 305). This not only suggests further differentials within co-residence groups but reinforces the distinctions between the structure of pit-hut camps and villages of rectilinear surface structures.

Rectilinear structures were distinct. While the round floor-plans of the pit-huts were an efficient way of maximizing interior building space, rectilinear structures were more efficient users of external community space. In their cubic, cellular form, rectilinear structures could be 'packed' into limited amounts of settlement space. If the village space in which it was deemed appropriate or desirable for building was increasingly valued and bounded, and thus restricted, for social, ideological, economic or other reasons, efficient use of internal village space would have been a priority. Building rectilinear structures would have been one way of addressing this priority.

Overall, the rectilinear surface structures of Balkan prehistory were complex architectural forms. They enabled multiple, contemporary, activities to occur within, although perhaps in segregated parts of, a single building and their form lent itself to efficient use of settlement space available or appropriate for building. The differences between rectilinear structures and round pit-huts may have important social, political and economic correlates but it is unlikely that these are as simple as a distinction between degrees of sedentism.

Division, cohesion, households and villages

The distinction between the pit-huts and the rectilinear surface structures brings our attention to the particular social significance that buildings came to acquire after 6500 BC in a few parts of the Balkans and after 5500 BC across the whole region. In the development of these rectilinear structures lie the origins of the house and the household.

The house, the household and the village were the key social institutions that emerged in the Balkans after 6500 BC.[2] As noted above, in architectural terms rectilinear buildings were better equipped to accommodate groups of people. Flannery suggested that these groups were families (Flannery 1972: 39), although there is no reason to assume any connections through marriage or birth of the people who used these spaces. The important factor is that in these houses there was room for several people to live or work together on different tasks at the same time and that the group could be expanded, relatively easily, with the subdivision of interior space or the construction of additional cellular rooms easily attached to the main structure.

The emergence of houses was a significant development. It represented the creation of tangible, physical, impermeable and relatively permanent boundaries around a group of people and their activities, be they mundane activities of biological existence, such as eating and sleeping, or more social role-related activities noted above. Regardless of the daily, or longer-term, movements of people in and out of the bounded space of the house, the physical presence of a structure containing people's objects, food, activity areas and tools served to lock that particular group into a fixed place within a village community.

The physical presence of houses would have heightened and reinforced in tangible terms the sense of cohesion within the co-resident group. The structure would have pulled together the group members and, at the same time, introduced a sense of separation dividing the household and its members from other people and groups within the larger village community. Issues of group membership were addressed in Chapter 3 in the context of ceremonies in which anthropomorphic figurines very likely played a part; there is every reason to assume that there were other ceremonies in which declarations of membership in building-based groups were made; some of these may have involved the house-shaped tectomorphic models that are found within and around houses. The inhumation of newborns and infants into house-floors, noted in Chapter 4, suggests other ways in which house-hold membership may have been declared and confirmed. The intentional destruction of houses by burning, discussed in Chapter 5, suggests that houses (and households) were social entities important enough to require deliberate acts of closure and negation as well as of creation and maintenance.

Village houses, therefore, became the physical foci for small groups of people; unquestionably they were instrumental in tangibly defining membership within these groups and in the distinction between intra-village groups. In a visible fashion, houses established and declared a set of social relationships that otherwise were either invisible or present only in the ephemera of the spoken word of verbal declaration. The potential for creating and repeatedly declaring the cohesive character of a group and the distinction between different groups present in household villages was not present in the looser aggregations of pit-hut camps.

Just as there was a division between individual co-resident units, each anchored to particular buildings, so also was there a higher level of cohesion among these groups across the village communities. The ordered layout of buildings within village plans, the adherence to a common orientation of floorplans and the great similarity in the size and shapes of surface-level structures lend an atmosphere of shared values to these sites. Again it is in the aggregations of surface-level rectilinear structures and not in the more haphazard collections of pit-huts that this community cohesion is felt.

The contemporary divisions between household groups and the cohesion across village space were all the more powerful and legitimate for the depth of their occupational presence. If the surface-level structures represent the visible, spatial, tangible definition of households, then the repair and reconstruction of houses through successive generations of both people and buildings represent the continuity and extension of the life of that group and its position within the village. Some sequences of building regenerations lasted a long time. The most dramatic manifestations of this were the tell settlements, which remain, even today, striking monuments to the continuity of settlement at a particular location. In other places, less dramatic but equally effective generations of settlement continuity developed outwards into less constrained horizontal expansions of building through time. In some places, such as Sesklo, both constrained and unconstrained building programmes were carried out at the same time. In still other places people chose not to rebuild at all, moving on after a single generation of site-use.

Fictional kinships

The distinction between the architectural creation of household groups and village communities and the looser camp-based groups represented by pit-hut sites is perhaps best understood in terms of the development, maintenance and, perhaps, imposition of fictive social relationships.[3] In the case of pit-hut communities, social organization and structure were based on shifting, relatively invisible, ties of marriage, alliance, co-operation, communality and birth. Descent through human generations was important, but it was not dependent on place. With pit-hut communities, relationships between people and groups were regulated, negotiated, reaffirmed and altered on a constant basis, through series of ceremonies and more mundane activities and materials on a daily basis. Relationships flexed and morphed through the twists and turns, pressures and comforts of the ongoing reality of daily life.

In the case of household villages relationships between groups and among people within groups were founded on fixed, visible, tangible and relatively inflexible constructions. While there was some room for alteration, especially in the composition of household membership, on the whole relationships between people and groups were relatively static. The anchoring of people to place had assumed a powerful role in the form and development of social structure and organization. The inflexibility of social relationships within households and villages was hardened by the repetition of spatial relationships through time in the rebuilding of houses and, consequently, through the regenerations of households. Within this physical, tangible, repeated inflexibility and fixicity, I suggest, rests the fictional character of the social relationships of these communities. Regardless of the realities of daily existence that unquestionably will have required mobility of groups, fissioning of communities and abandonment of houses and villages, the imposed reality of the built environment and all of its accompanying physical strictures and tangible dimensions of social relationships are best understood as an unreal, or fictional construct.

Thus, in the emergence of permanent buildings and in their aggregation into villages, we see two of the essential social institutions to emerge from Balkan prehistory: the household and the village. With the contemporary increase in the quantity and the changes in the quality of material culture, the emergence of houses and villages after 6500 BC suggests that the Balkans was a region across which the principles that directed the arrangement of people, things and places became factors of paramount importance.

THE NEW MATERIALITY

In quantitative terms, things come to dominate daily life in the Balkans after 6500 BC. Whether it is pottery (both vessels and non-vessel ceramics), animals, plants, objects made of bone, horn and stone and even people themselves, life was cluttered with an extraordinary range and number of new things. This new materiality had a qualitative dimension as well; it was grounded in a significantly new way in which things were created.

In a radical addition to previous philosophies of creation, the new objects were produced by transformative and additive processes. The production of objects of fired clay is the most obvious example of this. In making ceramics, objects were created by adding individual elements such as the raw clay matrix, temper and, eventually, solutions or pastes for surface treatment. Together, these components were fashioned into forms that were then transformed by processes, such as firing, that altered their physical state, durability, appearance and touch.

In a similar sense the construction of buildings involved the combination of a range of raw materials such as branches, posts, stones, twigs, clay, mud, dung, plaster, paint and reeds in order to produce a new and distinct entity, a hut or a house. The aggregation of buildings into camps or villages followed the same philosophy; the collection of individual structures created a built community. The, later, working of gold and copper were similar processes combining raw materials of one physical condition and transforming them by hammering or heating into objects very different in appearance, feel and use.

One of the significances of the post-6500 BC additive, transformative processes of making was that the finished products were greater than the sum of their parts; indeed the finished products were of a different physical dimension from that of any of their component parts. While composite tools had been a part of pre-6500 BC Balkan world, their physical condition never became anything more than the condition of any one of their assembled parts.

After 6500 BC ceramics and buildings were things that existed beyond the physical and chemical properties of their constituent elements and materials. A fired pot bore little resemblance to a riverbed of clay in either its visual appearance or its capabilities as a container. Similarly a simple hut was an extension of saplings, reeds and mud in terms of appearance and capabilities. In this sense a camp or a village can be understood as a collection of separate buildings which, taken together, stand for more than any of the individual structures or their contents.

In addition to its generative character, the process of working clay was significant for another reason; it allowed for an extremely wide range in the variability of the form of the objects created. For ceramics, this was critical both for the number of different objects produced with the same technological knowledge and equipment and, perhaps more importantly, for the potential of expression they delivered.

Clay provided an especially malleable medium for expression. The potential range in form and, more importantly, additions and modifications of surfaces, was wide. From simple monochrome dishes to intricately decorated figurines, ceramic working was a fundamental element within what was distinctive about material life in the post-6500 BC Balkans. The record of the development of surface decoration reveals similarities in style and technique that connect people, houses and villages across broad regions. Furthermore, the broadening range of vessel forms may reflect the development of a series of distinct social contexts of use, display and deposition. Forms ranged from simple bowls in the experimental stages of the adoption of ceramic working and use, through intricate and complicated, multi-carinated forms many of which were richly decorated, to the comparatively plain handled cups and jugs of the fourth millennium BC.

The potential power, expressive or otherwise, of ceramic objects was exponentially multiplied by the durability and permanence provided by the proper preparation, tempering and firing processes. Making objects out of various components was one thing, making them in an almost endless variety of forms and decorating them in an equally great range of ways was another, but making these combinations last beyond the short or medium term was a significant achievement.

The ability to invest expressive creations with an almost unlimited durability fundamentally redefined the role of material culture in Balkan prehistory and had significant consequences for community flexibility and for the strength of restrictions on the possibilities for negotiating inter-personal relationships. Similarly fundamental alterations to the ways rela-tionships varied through mobility, spatial aggregation and dispersal were discussed above in terms of the built environment.

While it is their potential for formal variation, for supporting wide-ranging patterns of surface decoration and their durability and permanence that lie at the heart of the expressive potential of ceramic objects, intrinsic sensory characteristics were the significant novelties of other materials. The most obvious of these new materials were copper and gold, which began to appear, mainly in burials, in the fifth millennium BC. As discussed in Chapter 6, the important characteristics of copper and gold, and of other materials such as marine molluscs and graphite for decorating pots or people, may have rested as much on the visual impression caused, of highly reflec-tive brilliance, as on any calculations of distances between raw material source and finished product deposition. Additional, important factors such as the skills, craft knowledge and strength required to acquire and work any of these post-6500 BC materials, were developments of abilities that had very long histories in the Balkans, running back to the bifacially flaked leaf-points of the transition from the late middle Palaeolithic to the early upper Palaeolithic.

Thus, as with developments in the ways people built their social envi-ronments after 6500 BC, so also with developments of new technologies of material culture, some of the most significant consequences were the new arrangements of things and places within which people lived and through which social relationships were defined.

THE ARRANGEMENT OF PEOPLE AND THINGS

The increase in the quantity and the changes in the qualities of material objects, together with the new commitments to building social environ-ments in particular places after 6500 BC, focus our attention on recurrent patterns and devices with which objects and people were distributed across the landscapes and within camps, villages, houses and huts. As much as the variability of form and potential for expression, it is the specific phys-ical and increasingly permanent arrangement of people and things that sets post-6500 BC lives apart from those of earlier millennia.

The accepted explanation for the post-6500 BC changes in Balkan lifestyles has vacillated between arguments for colonization from the Near East to indigenous development of technologies and economies (see the discussion in Whittle 1996: 39–44). I suggest that a more accurate way to understand the period is to examine the patterns in the spatial and temporal arrangement of people and things. At an interpretive level, three processes of arrangement are evident: exclusion, incorporation and projection. These processes are important because they clarify our understanding of the diverse relationships between people and between people, places and things in the post-6500 BC Balkans.

Exclusion

Exclusion is a physical or symbolic process that imposes an explicit order on daily life and the people and things in that world. To exclude is to arrange people and things in a preferred manner. Exclusion is about the control of both physical things and of information about those things. Often it is manifest in the restriction of physical access to people and places; thus it can create privacy and can define private space. Exclusion also can prevent sensory access to people, things or activities. By preventing contact, familiarity and knowledge, exclusion can reduce the amount of information available about a person, place or activity. Paradoxically, exclusion is indispensable from the development of an individual's sense of personhood and self-directed thought; it is critical to the emergence of individual identities. Exclusion can be directed against other individuals or against groups of people. Because it makes explicit the relationships among people and things, exclusion is a critical process of social life.

Despite the fundamental distinctions noted above between pit-huts and surface-level structures, the two architectural forms were linked by a common principle in the wider social significance of the new built environments of the post-6500 BC Balkans: they both were facilities of exclusion. As such both were the manifestations, symptoms and active components of new arrangements of people, things and activities.

The potential to exclude was everywhere in the architectural record of the Balkans during the first thousand years after 6500 BC. Exclusion was present at its most precise where people used semi-permanent and permanent materials to build structures with impermeable walls that closed off particular places in the landscape or divided off sections within camps and villages. The use of mud, timber and sometimes stone or sun-dried mud-blocks as building materials made walls impermeable barriers preventing physical access of people (and animals?) to enclosed places. The physical characteristics of the same materials also created walls impermeable to sound, vision and smell. In this sense, restriction in physical access to a place was supplemented by the prevention of the acquisition of information about what was happening and who was involved in any internal activities.

Elements of spatial and sensory exclusion were also manifest in the interiors of individual structures. People divided interior space into separate rooms. In some houses, such as the one at Slatina, post-framed partitions and screens were erected to separate one activity area from another or to prevent visual access to activities and people; similar internal post-structures are seen in buildings at many other sites.

273

Also evident are other, less physically tangible, patterns of segregating activities within buildings and across aggregations of buildings. At many sites in the Danube Gorges, for example, there are clear patterns in the ways in which the appropriateness of places for different activities and acts of deposition pivoted on the location of hearths within buildings; substantial stone thresholds marked the boundaries between building interiors and exteriors. Similar distinctions between different parts of sites can be seen in the separation of up- or downstream concentrations of buildings or burials in several of the Gorges sites.

Exclusion can also be seen on a larger spatial and, undoubtedly, social scale. In many cases, as at Karanovo *Bauhorizont* 3 and at Divostin in phase Ic, people used walls and ditches to separate parts of village interiors. At other sites, such as Souphli, Achilleion and Nea Nikomedeia, people used ditches and banks to segregate all or part of a built-up area from the surrounding landscape. At the Chavdar tell and at many terrace-edge aggregations, like the one at Kovachevo, people took advantage of, and supplemented, natural features of the landscape to create boundaries to the built environments they had created.

In the fifth millennium BC these trends in dividing and marking out places in space continued. The shift from garden-plot horticulture to field-based agriculture was part of a longer-term pattern in which a once open landscape was increasingly parcelled off into camps and villages, cemeteries and fields. The increasing, social or economic, emphasis on large grazing animals such as cattle would have increased the importance of gaining and maintaining access to sufficient areas of good grazing lands. The allocation of parts of the extramural landscape to particular activities and resources, spatially separate from but linked to villages, was an important trend manifest in other spheres of domestic and ritual life, such as burial. By the middle of the fifth millennium BC, then, the general pattern of exclusion had expanded and accelerated; access was controlled and restricted on several significant levels.

At one level, access was restricted to special places in the landscape that continued to be marked with camps or villages. The rise of tells in the lower Danube, central and eastern Macedonia and in eastern Hungary (during the Tisza phase) is the most obvious extension of exclusion at this time. Tell villages were places in which settlement space was especially valued as distinct from other parts of the landscape. People separated aggregations of buildings from their surroundings with settlement walls, ditches and banks; this was the case not only at tell sites but also at flat village sites such as Strumsko in south-western Bulgaria. On the other hand the interior space of villages was also valued in physical ways. In many cases buildings occupied as much village space as was available; in other cases, such as at Selevac in Serbia, the distinctive value of village space is reflected in increasing commitments of time and labour in the choice of architectural design and materials.

At a second level, exclusion continued in the fifth millennium BC within camps and villages where restricted access to particular places is evident in the placement of buildings, the digging of ditches or the erection of isolated walls. At Divostin II, for example, buildings were grouped into separate mini-aggregations and there were clearly separate areas dedicated to lithic- and copper-working and to animal butchery. North of the Danube people were dividing the interiors of pit-hut structures in similar ways. At Tîrguşor Urs areas with burnt ground that were suitable for building were distinguished from other areas of the village; at Ceamurlia de Jos special structures may have been intended for entertaining visitors. People were also dividing off parts of villages by digging ditches, as at Yunatsite in southern Bulgaria, at Lebő-Felsőhalom and Csanytelek-Újhalastó in eastern Hungary and at Ayia Sophia in northern Greece. Other examples of intra-village exclusion can be found in the central courts at Thermi and the division of village space at Dimini.

At a third level, exclusion continued and expanded in the fifth millennium BC through the restriction of access to internal parts of individual buildings. Not only were there increasingly deep rooms at many of the north-east Bulgarian tells, but there were also multi-roomed buildings both to the west, as at Selevac, and to the east, as seen in the separation of internal parts of pit-huts at Durankulak and Medgidia Cocoaşe. In the clay platforms at Slatino and Lebő, and the associations of storage bins, grinding-stones and ovens at many sites, the creation and use of spatially distinct activity areas distinguished particular areas within buildings. At other sites such as the north-east Bulgarian tells and the villages in eastern Hungary and northern Greece, temporary, moveable room-partitions or screens separated portions of rooms at many sites.

At another level, the potential to exclude can be seen in the adoption and, perhaps more especially, in the development of ceramic vessel production. While many ceramic vessel forms were open shapes such as bowls, plates and saucers, a significant proportion of inventories consisted of closed shapes including S-shaped jugs and, especially, the large lidded forms of the late fifth millennium BC. The emergence of increasingly large, closed and lidded pots may have as much to do with restricting physical access to, and sensory knowledge of, pot contents as it does with any functional correlates between the use of open and closed shapes within contemporary economic activities. Similar inferences could be drawn from the creation of large, permanent silo fixtures in house interiors as at Ovcharovo or of grain bins by hearths or storage pits dug into building floors.

In terms of the built environment and at least some of the material culture, a significant element in the routine of daily life after 6500 BC was the potential for the exclusion both of physical access to spaces and of sensory knowledge of activities, objects and people within the new enclosed environments. While exclusion was a major component in new ways in which people and things arranged, the apparently paradoxical process of incorporation was present in many of the same structures and objects.

Incorporation

Like exclusion, incorporation makes explicit the relationships between people, places and things. Most simply incorporation is a way of taking possession. Through the process of incorporation things are physically brought into a place or a body. In this sense both body and place can stand for an institution; thus a house may stand for a household, a village for a community, or a burial for an individual or a group. While the physical containment of an object or person is the clearest manifestation of incorporation, in the majority of cases the incorporated object or person remains outside of the physical boundaries of the body. In this sense, much of incorporation requires the establishment of indirect, or symbolic, links to connect things, people and places.

Just as the creation of built social environments excluded (intentionally or not) people and things from particular places, so also the emergence and development of huts, houses, camps and villages became a fundamental facility of incorporation. In creating enclosed places, to which physical and sensory access was denied to some, people created places into which other people, things and activities could be incorporated.

In the same way that processes of exclusion worked at different levels of specificity, ranging from the scale of the landscape to that of the individual pottery container, processes of incorporation can be detected at different levels. Whether people realized it or not, in their daily existence, the routine of living took place within and around very efficient facilities for incorporation. At the most basic level, with the construction of built environments, people created enclosed places that contained people and things. Whether in the form of ditches, banks, walls or partitions, the physical boundaries to camps or villages, huts or houses, rooms or activity areas created institutional spaces in which were based particular people, activities and objects. The facilities for incorporation are evident from 6500 BC in both the emergence of permanent architecture and the adoption and development of ceramics as a new container technology.

The distinction between pit-huts and pit-hut camps on the one hand and surface-level structures and villages on the other can be refined in terms of the increasing importance of creating closed corporate or household groups. The enclosure of activity areas, tools, stored goods and large numbers of other objects within individual village houses was distinct from what was possible in pit-huts, where activities seemed to have spilled out of these smaller structures in an unconstrained and unordered fashion. In villages sets of people, tasks, resources, tools and goods were gathered within the

276

walls of individual houses. The early practice of burying the dead within the floors of village houses can be understood in this light as a process through which individuals were incorporated into household groups. The fact that most in-house burials were of infants and children suggests that their intramural burial was part of a larger series of ceremonies by which the cohesion of household membership was declared and maintained. As suggested in Chapters 3 and 6, the house- and pit-bound use of anthropo-morphic, zoomorphic and tectomorphic figurines was probably another component of ceremonies that accompanied the creation and maintenance of corporate groups such as households.

On another level the village, as an institutional unit, can be seen as a facility of social incorporation. While individual houses may have focused people, activities and objects, the aggregation of houses into a village was a process of incorporation on a grander scale. The digging of boundary ditches, the erection of banks and walls were common ways of marking the limits of the corporate space. The adherence to common techniques of construction, the replication of a common orientation in floor-plans and the strikingly similar appearance of individual houses within villages suggest that a broader cohesion ran alongside any intra-village distinctions between houses and households.

Burial and sub-corporate groups

A similar, apparently paradoxical, coexistence of distinctions between households and cohesions across village communities can be seen in the extramural cemeteries that emerged after 5500 BC. While there are clear discrepancies in the quantity and quality of grave-goods deposited in indi-vidual burials, an equally distinct degree of cohesion ran through corporate cemetery populations. This is seen in the common orientation of bodies and the relationship of the cemetery with the associated village. On the one hand, repetition of a common body orientation across a cemetery would have suggested that all individuals inhumed were part of one corpo-rate unit.

At a more particular level, it is highly likely that the deposition of specific quantities of particular grave-goods had the effect of incorporating a limited number of individuals into subgroups within the burial communities of each cemetery. Furthermore, at the trans-regional scale of different villages and their cemeteries, the shared practices of depositing particular objects, such as extravagant versions of cutting and chopping tools and ornaments made from the shells of exotic marine molluscs, suggest that a larger group of people were connected, not in any direct physical proximity but by the formal and material homogeneity of the grave-goods. The adherence to common depositional rituals incorporated these individuals into a group that was spread across long distances.

The appearance of mound-burials in the fourth and third millennia BC also can be understood in terms of social incorporation. Burials in pits under mounds may have played a similar role to that fulfilled by household villages during the preceding millennia; in this respect mounds resemble houses and households while mound-cemeteries resemble the village. Sequences of inhumations in a burial mound and the consequent additions of successive layers were as much processes of incorporation as constructions and re-buildings of houses and burials of children and infants in house floors had been during the fifth millennium BC. Furthermore, the sequential positionings of new mounds relative to earlier ones in mound-cemeteries were as much acts of incorporation as were the aggregations of houses into villages. Secondary, tertiary and successive episodes of inhumation and their attendant ceremonies can be seen as acts of declaring the incorporation of individuals into longer lineages.

Economic acceleration and the incorporation of labour

In the acceleration and expansion of agricultural and grazing activities after 5500 BC the potential need or desire to bring things and people into individual household and village spaces also increased. Not only would the intensification of field-based agriculture have created more harvested products, it would also have necessitated the making and storage of more agricultural equipment and the construction of more facilities related to the agricultural cycle. It is hardly surprising that a very high proportion of buildings in use at this time contained grinding-stones, storage bins, silos and large pots and ovens for parching grain.

A more significant consequence of accelerated agricultural activities would have been a heightened importance attached to the ability to gather sufficient and appropriate labour for particular episodes of agricultural work. This would have been especially important when it was necessary to prepare ground for planting, to plant seeds and to harvest crops. Individual houses and, more certainly, villages of houses would have served as important foci for the aggregation of the requisite skilled and unskilled labour. Physical foci for cohesion and aggregation would have been especially important within social landscapes that for most of the year were fluid and mobile. In this sense, therefore, buildings and villages were the physical mechanisms for ensuring re-aggregation, or the re-incorporation, of households and village communities.

Somatic incorporation

While many of the processes of incorporation that ran through daily life in the Balkans after 6500 BC can be seen at the extra-somatic level of village, building and room interiors or cemetery inventories, a more corporal level is evident as well. In this sense, rather than assuming a nutritional

278

value for new plant and animal foods, such as sheep, goat and wheat from 6500 BC and the later emergence of secondary products such as milk and cheese, it may be more accurate to view the significance of these food novelties in terms of their consumption. As suggested in Chapter 3, there was nothing new in the types of post-6500 BC foodstuffs; meat and plants had been the basic components of human nutrition for hundreds of thousands of years. Perhaps the significance of goat and sheep, wheat and barley as well as their secondary and other products was realized where they were eaten and entered the body. In this sense, eating would have been a series of perhaps daily declarations of individual or group rights to incorporate special, exotic and perhaps fashionable foodstuffs. A similar perspective has most frequently been taken for interpreting the changes in economy and ceramics after 4000 BC, changes commonly interpreted in terms of a rise in social importance of the act of drinking. Perhaps a similar perspective can refine our understanding of earlier millennia as well.

There is other evidence for processes of incorporation at the level of the human body in the prehistoric Balkans. Most obviously, people pierced, adorned and wore objects and materials with the consequence, if not necessarily the intention, of injecting the social, technologic and economic essences of specific materials into their personal identity. Thus gold was used for lip-plugs and ear-rings that were stuck through skin, for appliqués sown into hair and clothing, for bracelets, rings and penis coverings. In all of these forms, gold and its social connotations were incorporated into a person's identity. Similar connections can be made with objects made of copper, *Spondylus* or any of the other special materials discussed in Chapters 3 and 6 which emerged in the post-6500 BC Balkans.

Like its apparently paradoxical companion exclusion, therefore, incorporation ran through the long-term trends of the post-6500 BC Balkans. More than with exclusion however, in considering incorporation, this discussion has turned repeatedly to non-tangible manifestations of attempts to connect places, people, objects, social institutions and, especially, ceremonies and activities such as burial, eating and wearing material culture. This growing recognition of the expressive aspect of incorporation is perhaps best understood in terms of the third process of spacial and temporal arrangement of things, projection.

Projection

Like exclusion and incorporation, projection is a powerful way in which people, objects and places were arranged in time and space. While the most obvious and frequent evidence for the processes of exclusion and incorporation are found in the physical and tangible realms of the new built environments and materiality of post-6500 BC life, the processes of projection are to be found in less explicit activities and actions.

Through projection, the essence of a person, group, material or activity is injected into a physical place or object. Projection is about creating a symbolic link between an actual subject, such as a person, animal, house or community, and a representational object, such as a figurine, house model or a pattern of ceramic decoration. Thus the majority of projection works through acts of symbolling in which the essence of a person, place or thing is made manifest either in homologous similarities of form or in more abstract connections.

The manifestations of projection in the post-6500 BC Balkans proceed from several key conclusions drawn above about the developments in architecture and material culture. The two most relevant of these are, first, that buildings and villages physically anchored households and larger communities to particular places and, second, that an important element of the new materiality was the expressive potential of new dimensions of formal variability and of the character of novel materials.

Architecture as projection

In addition to their key role in the daily routines of exclusion and incorporation, the new built environments also provided the potential for the physical, visual expression of household and community ideals and identities. Buildings were clear, physical, visual expressions of communal linkages between individual members of a household. Thus, aggregations of houses built in similar forms, with the same range of materials, with common orientations of floorplans and of comparable sizes were unavoidable projections of the essences of household and village organization. In this sense houses and villages were both the active physical structure of social interaction, division and cohesion and the means of declaring that structure.

Processes of projection can also be seen in the creations of permanent built environments that linked households and village communities to particular places. The use of durable building materials meant that statements of occupation were relatively lasting. Long sequences of building repair and reconstruction provided additional depth and strength to these expressions of community continuity and occupation. Similar arguments for the expression of the diachronic succession of social groups can also be applied to the mound-cemeteries of the fourth and third millennia BC. The materials and construction processes of both the earlier houses and villages and the later mound-burials projected visual claims intended to legitimate continuity.

In the fifth millennium BC, houses and village aggregations occupied an elevated position within daily life; it is even possible to suggest that there emerged an ideology of the built environment. Part of this can be seen in the repairs, rebuildings and vertical repetition of house floorplans in tell villages and in the common orientations of horizontally rebuilt structures on flat sites. More significant however, are new fifth millennium BC artefacts, such as miniature clay models of buildings, furniture and ovens (Figure 8.1). These representational objects suggest a different level at which the essence of villages, houses and particular fixtures and furniture were participating in the projection of the ideology of the new built environments.

Other developments in expressive projection

The use of miniature representations of buildings and the varied treatment of life-size structures themselves, such as new ceremonies of constructing and destroying houses, were only two elements in a suite of new expressive materials and practices marking out the fifth millennium BC Balkans that were fully discussed in Chapter 6. All of these new media for expression were parts of processes of projection. While individual elements of material expression and projection are found throughout Balkan prehistory, from the use of pendants, beads and painted body decoration in the upper Palaeolithic to the simple copper spirals and anthropomorphic stelae of fourth and third millennium burial mounds, it is their dominance in the fifth millennium BC that sets that period apart from the others.

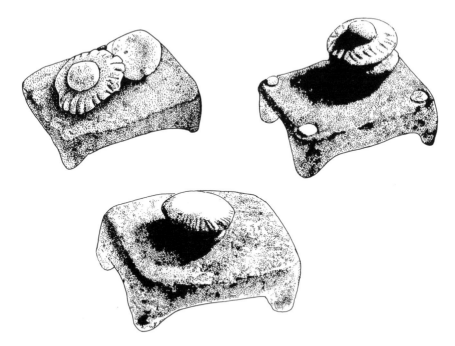

Figure 8.1 Miniature clay furniture and vessels from Ovcharovo (after Todorova 1986)

Among the most significant elements of expression were representational and non-representational projections. Of the former, the most obvious were: anthropomorphic, zoomorphic and tectomorphic figurines; anthropographic representations on pots; copper axe-adzes; the inclusion in some burials of particular bones, such as skulls or horns, from particular animals, such as cattle and deer; and the production of zoomorphic images, such as horned animals, horns, and astragali, made of gold. Non-representational projections included the early late Pleistocene and early Holocene uses of body ornamentation and colouring of tools and boulders; the later marking of symbols on sealing-stamps and the bottoms of pottery vessels; the painting of house walls; and, perhaps most ubiquitous, the region-wide similarities in surface decoration of pottery vessels.

Details of the significance of the specific materials used were discussed in Chapter 6. Important was the increasing use in the fifth millennium BC of raw materials, such as gold, copper, *Spondylus*, graphite, as well as the (less frequent) appearance of quartzite and other materials, all of which were highly reflective and all of which, with the exception of graphite-decorated pottery, were used in loud ceremonies and rituals, mostly related to the bodies of dead individuals.

The projection of identities

One of the most remarkable aspects of daily life after 6500 BC was an explosion in physical expression of individual and group identities. Much of this is manifest in new suites of material culture – the focus of Chapter 3. A large component of the power of these new material elements of identity was founded on spatial organization of deposition, use, production and other activities. The segmentation of the landscape, the enclosure of space, the exclusion of people, things and activities from, and their incorporation into, places were social facilities that lent themselves to very powerful creation of identities.

Through the facilities of exclusion and incorporation, the new built environment of the Balkans after 6500 BC served as a radically new way in which identities were created, expressed and maintained. In the creation of their own built environment relationships were imposed between people, on the levels of both person to person and group to group. In anchoring people and what they were doing to a particular part of the natural environment, parts of that environment were also invested with new identities.

It was not merely the creation of identities through representation and the built environment that was revolutionary about post-6500 BC life in the Balkans; it was the manner of their creation. These new identities were generated on a physical, tangible and direct level. Exclusion was effected by physically preventing access to a place; incorporation by physically containing things, people and activities within an enclosed space. Identities were created by physical associations between different individuals and groups and between different people and particular places. It was the increasingly durable, and in many cases permanent, character of the identities and relationships that was significant. The new durabilities and permanences of these relationships and identities invested them with an implicit legitimacy.

Exclusion, incorporation and projection: conclusion

The ways in which people arranged themselves, the places and activities of their daily lives (and of their deaths) and the material culture and activities that formed routine parts of their existence are significant in distinguishing what was happening in the Balkans after 6500 BC from what had happened before. The distinction is less one of the processes that have been identified here – processes of exclusion, incorporation and projection were unquestionably part of more mobile existences of the late Pleistocene and early Holocene. The distinction has more to do with the ways in which these processes were manifest.

Where the arrangement of people, things and places in forager or gather-hunter communities was based on mobility, many post-6500 BC groups were increasingly anchored through the physical attachment to places and through the developing culture of durable material. Perhaps even more distinctive, the expressions of arrangement among mobile communities were made in the ephemera of spoken word or passing event. In the increasingly anchored communities of the post-6500 BC Balkans expressions of arrangement were made in more durable and permanent manners. In this sense, the critical distinction is between the flexible adaptability of the more mobile communities and the anchored inflexibility of the new settled lifestyles. It is within the inflexibility and the new permanence of exclusion, incorporation and projection that can be found the sources of most dynamic and dramatic components of material and ceremonial life of the post-6500 BC Balkans.

ILLUSION WITHIN THE POST-6500 BC BALKANS

A world in which inflexibility defines social and material relationships is a world in which the potential for illusion and fictitious recreations of reality is high (see Bailey 1996a). The arrangements of people and things that were now being made, and the processes through which they were created and maintained, imposed a false and inflexible structure onto a social landscape that for many millennia had functioned on a different level. The negotiation of daily reality took place through the permanences of places and things; social and material arrangement required permanence in their statements and claims for the appropriate organization of people and things. It is in this more permanent pretension of what is appropriate that rests the sense of illusion that underlies the new materiality of the post-6500 BC Balkans and is especially clear in the dynamic apogee in the late fifth and early fourth millennia BC.

Much of what appeared in the new fifth-millennium display of indirect symbolic expressions of identity can be seen as illusion; the imposition and advertisement of one version of a preferred reality in the place of the actual daily existence. This is best seen in the three phenomena: mortuary ritual, village living and anthropomorphic representation.

Mortuary ritual

At one level, burial had become focused on the public display and legitimation of differences between individuals within a community. Represented by the distributions of grave-goods, differences between inhumed individuals were projections of a preferred reality. In this sense, the extramural area dedicated to burial would have served as a blank canvas upon which one particular, preferred picture of society was painted. The foreground of the preferred picture was dominated by objects made of highly reflective materials such as copper, gold and *Spondylus* that were primarily associated with male inhumations. At the same time as the image of distinctions between parts of the community was being projected, in the background, apparently paradoxical expressions of community cohesion could be seen. Hence the adherence to similar size and shape of graves, the common positioning of bodies within them and, indeed, the inclusion of separate burials within a single area of the landscape dedicated to formal disposal for one community. In the fifth millennium BC burial had become a stage for performance upon which was developed a double-exposure combining community cohesion and intra-group distinction.[4]

Village living

At another level, the actual record of life within the villages associated with the fifth millennium BC cemeteries was most accurately expressed inside buildings where, for the majority of the population, explicit projections of individual distinction of the kind found in the mortuary sphere were absent; hence the clear distinctions between village and burial space in the deposition of objects made of exotic materials. Indeed the image of community life projected from the building materials, longevity, contents, sizes, internal complexities and arrangement of houses within these villages is very different from that projected by the mortuary materials and ceremonies.

The exclusion and incorporation of particular people, things and activities within households projects an image of small, co-resident groups co-operating in tasks and living together. The structure and organization of the membership of a particular household were conditioned by ceremonies and rituals that may have focused on the initiation of new members, the maintenance of household continuity or the changing statuses of existing household members. These ceremonies employed particular objects, such as anthropomorphic, zoomorphic and tectomorphic representations and particular acts of deposition, such as the under-floor inhumations of deceased infants and young children.

As these objects, ceremonies and the daily routines of activity and living projected particular images of the consistency of households, so too did individual households develop identities. The constructions and destructions of houses thus take on new significances as projections of significant episodes in the existence of particular households, in this case their birth and death. Again, as has been argued to have been the case with burial, there was an apparent paradox between distinct identities for individual households and the coherent identity of the village community as a whole. If in all of this there was an ideology of the household, then, as with the burial record, it must be phrased in terms of the performances of preferred arrangements of reality. Where burial employed special artefacts, villages employed the rooms and walls of the built environment.

Anthropomorphic imagery

A third image of the reality of fifth millennium BC life was projected by the decoration of anthropomorphic figurines. I have argued elsewhere that to create a figurine was to have transformed someone into something that he or she was not (Bailey 1996a: 292–3). Part of that argument needs repeating here.

Figurines were representations of people that comprised only a selection of human attributes. In most examples, the selection includes modelling of the torso, shoulders and upper parts of the arms and legs. Some concentrate exclusively on the head and include details of ear-rigs, lip- and nose-plugs and hair-styles. As a transformation of one thing into another, somewhat dissimilar thing, figurines represent a defamiliarization of object from subject (of figurine from human). In doing so they had the capacity to make the familiar appear mysterious and the exotic seem familiar. As a defamiliarized object, figurines had the power to transform not only the physical appearance of their subjects but also the social and political relationships that existed among the people being represented. The making of figurines constituted a potential to delude.

In making figurines, unequal things (people) were made equal and similar; they were placed together within a delimited, visible, understandable category. Physical differences among the living could be altered or removed from their representations as made in fired clay. Potentially, disparate individuals could be included within one common set of values and beliefs. They were levelled within the boundaries of the application of plastic and pyrotechnical abilities and in the perception and use of figurines. In this way a reality marked by a dissimilarity between people could be replaced by a delusion defined by similarity.

In these senses figurines loosened and rearranged the fabric of the actual. It is as if they were unravelling the cloth of reality as it had been woven and then, selecting some threads and discarding others, weaving a new material of different warp and weft bearing an altered design and pattern. In producing their visible, tangible, durable version of a new reality, figurines allowed alternative non-real (or counterfeit) versions of reality to be suggested and accepted. In the power of their durability figurines fixed in time their fictional perceptions of the world. They were both memorative and monumental. In their position as visual representations they held a privileged position over reality. In truth, figurines appropriated reality and created illusion.

Thus mortuary ritual, village life, and anthropomorphic imagery project three different and complex versions of reality in the fifth millennium BC Balkans. Is any one of the competing images of individuality or cohesion more correct than any other? No. All three are equally valid as all three were part of people's perceptions of themselves and their places within their communities. Perhaps, however, the reality projected through the household represents a better image of the actual routine of village life, the reality projected by the burial record represents a better image of what some people wanted to be seen as an accurate picture on a grand community-wide scale and the reality projected by figurines represents a better image of what people wanted to be seen in a more private, intra-household context.

CONCLUSION: WHY WERE THINGS DIFFERENT AFTER 6500 BC?

The traditional dichotomous explanations for the distinction between the pre- and post-6500 BC Balkans seek understanding in diaspora, migration and invasion or in climatically conditioned economic revolutions; they attempt simple answers to patterns that are too internally complex and varied on a local level to fit any single overarching explanation. If change was revolutionary, then it was gradual and not instantaneous; certainly there is little hard evidence for the influxes of population. If there were important climatic changes, then they cannot be married neatly to shifts in economy.

If there was a revolution it was not one that developed in any single component of life but one that permeated the multiple routines of daily life across a broad spectrum of activities, materials and people. Almost all of the most striking post-6500 BC changes can be linked by a common, new, set of processes with which people, places and things were arranged.

Lilka spat into the dirt, 'The bastards! Those bloody bastards.'

She looked out over the plain towards the horizon. The sky was lightening although the sun wouldn't make it over the hills for an hour or so. She shivered as a sharp breeze whipped down the stream and confirmed how late in the season it had become. Lilka pulled the blanket tighter round her shoulders, turned back into the house, and tripped over the wicker basket and the leather satchels they had prepared the night before.

'Mihai, Sveti, get up, they've gone.' She fed some wood into the oven and blew on the embers until first they glowed, then threw up thin flames that licked around the broken branches. The room slowly started to warm.

As the others grumbled under their blankets and shifted closer to the oven, Lilka cursed her brother. Lilka had always followed him through the valleys to the winter camps; could she remember the way, on her own with Mihai and Sveti? Lilka glanced back out of the door towards the horizon; even if she could get the three of them and the animals together quickly, they would never catch the other group; they were out of sight already. Her brother didn't want them with him anyway. He would have let them know he was going if he had. A smile crept onto Lilka's face.

'Maybe,' she thought, 'maybe we should stay the winter here. We could start building where Bogdan's old house had been. The three of us could do most of it ourselves; the charred walls were mostly rubble anyway; we could rip some of the larger timbers out and use them again; the base of the oven was still there, it could be raised; Bogdan's big grinding-stones were still there. Sveti could move in; Mihai would have to stay here but we could shift some of our grainstore into the new house; we could set up a new loom.' When her brother returned in the spring, the new house would be up, a new household in place; and it would be a better house than her brother's, bigger too. 'If Sveti had a baby . . . ,' Lilka smiled to herself. 'Let the bastard go.'

'Here, take this blanket,' and putting it round Sveti's shoulders, Lilka moved back towards the warmth.

NOTES

INTRODUCTION

1 For details of the archaeology of Ovcharovo see the original excavation publications (Todorova et al. 1983; Vasilev 1985). For the interpretation of that record see various publications by D. Bailey (1990, 1991, 1997, 1999). For the interpretation of houses and their destruction see Tringham (1991, 1994) and Stevanović (1997).

2 This conception of the Balkans does not include the, no less interesting, phenomena occurring to the north-east in eastern Romanian, in Moldova and in the western Ukraine. This region really deserves a monograph of its own.

3 The arguments over the role and validity of the culture-historical approach in European archaeology require a volume of its own. As an introduction to the debate see Trigger (1989). For debate over the consequences of the approach see D. Bailey (1998) and Renfrew (1994).

1 SETTING THE SCENE

1 For more detailed coverage of the Balkan upper Palaeolithic see G. Bailey 1992, 1995a, 1995b; G. Bailey et al. 1983a, b; Benac 1957; Bonsall 1989; Boroneanţ 1982; Cărciumaru 1985; Chirica 1986, 1989; Dzhambazov 1964; Gatsov et al. 1990; Hahn 1987; Honea 1984a, b, 1989; Ivanova 1987; Ivanova and Gatsov 1985; Ivanova and Sirakova 1995; Kozłowksi 1979, 1982a, 1984, 1988, 1992; Kozłowski and Kozłowski 1979; Kozłowski et al. 1992, 1994; Mogoşanu 1983; Montet-White 1994; Păunescu 1981, 1984, 1989, 1990, 1993; Sirakov et al. 1993; Soffer 1987; Srejović 1989; Svoboda 1995; Svoboda and Simán 1989; Valoch 1989.

2 For details on middle Palaeolithic sites in the Balkans see the following: Yarimburgaz in Turkey (Howell 1989; Darlas 1995), Petralona (G. Bailey 1992: 9; Stringer 1983; Henning et al. 1981, 1982; Poulianos 1971, 1977) and Theopetra (Kyparissi-Apostolika 1995) in Greece, Gajtan in Albania (Fistani 1993a, 1993b; Darlas 1995), Sandalja in Croatia and Vértesszöllos in Hungary (Kretzoi and Dobosi 1990; Valoch 1995: 78); and see on other individual finds in Greece at Kokkinopilos (Runnels and van Andel 1993; Pope et al. 1984; Runnels 1995; G. Bailey et al. 1992); Aliakmon, Piros and Vrahneïka (Darlas 1995: 54) and Korrissia (Jamet 1982); Korolevo in the Ukraine (Gladilin and Demidenko 1989; Gladilin and Sitivyj 1990); suggestions of very early finds at Dealul Mijlociu and Dealil Viilor in southern Romania with possible dates of 1.7 and 1.2 MYA respectively (Radulescu and Samson 1991; Mertens 1996).

For Bulgarian sites see Beloslav, Devniya (Kozłowski and Sirakov 1974), Devetaki, Dikilitash, Muselievo (Sirakova 1991; Sirakova and Ivanova 1988), Razgrad, Samuilitsa (Sirakov 1979, 1983), Shiroka Polyana, Svinskata, Uglen (Sirakova and Ivanova 1995).

3   For a detailed discussion of the significance of the appearance of Anatomically Modern Humans see Mithen (1994a, 1995, 1996), Mellars (1990).

4   Bacho Kiro was first excavated by Dorothy Garrod in 1938 under the auspices of the American School of Prehistoric Research (Garrod 1939a and b); the cave was the focus of detailed work by a Polish-Bulgarian collaboration from 1971 to 1975. A final report was published in the early 1980s (Kozłowski 1982a).

5   Similar activities are known from the Aurignacian in the Near East (Minzoni-Déroche et al. 1995).

6   There is a growing body of literature on the chronology and scale of post-Pleistocene sea-level rise for the Aegean (Lambeck 1995, 1996; Flemming 1978; Kraft et al. 1977; Kraft and Rapp 1975; Morrison 1968; van Andel 1989; van Andel and Shackleton 1982), the Black Sea (Ryan et al. 1997a, 1997b; Degens and Ross 1972, 1973; Panin 1983) and the Danube (Popp 1969; Panin 1972).

2 BUILDING SOCIAL ENVIRONMENTS

1   In terms of local culture-history, this chapter considers the early and middle Neolithic of northern Greece, the pre-pottery Neolithic to the Fikirtepe culture in north-western Anatolia, the Criş phases in southern Romania, the Monochrome Early Neolithic through the early Neolithic C in Bulgaria (in the Karanovo sequence, thus encompassing Karanovo I II, and II/III), the pre-Starčevo and Starčevo sequence in Serbia, and the Körös sequence in eastern Hungary. It also takes in the so-called late Mesolithic of the Danube Gorges. (For more detailed discussions of these sequences see Demoule and Perlès 1993; Todorova and Vajsov 1993; Hiller and Nikolov 1997; Dumitrescu et al. 1983; Whittle 1996; Özdoğan 1989a, 1995; Özdoğan and Gatsov 1998; Radovanović 1996a.)

2   This is Achilleion Ia, with radiocarbon dates ranging from 7471 ± 77 BP, 7460 ± 175 BP, 7540 ± 140 BP (Gimbutas 1989b).

3   The recent Austrian-Bulgarian excavations at Karanovo suggest the following correlation of traditional Karanovo cultural sequence, calendar years and new building phases: traditional Karanovo I = 6000–5750 BC = *Bauhorizont* 1, 2 and 3; traditional Karanovo II = 5730–5500 BC = *Bauhorizont* 4, 5, 6, 7; traditional Karanovo II/III = no dates = *Bauhorizont* 8 and 9 (V. Nikolov 1997a).

4   The record of early building activity in southern Romania is incomplete. Chronologically, there are no sites for south-central and south-eastern Romania which correspond to those now known in northern Bulgaria, such as Koprivets. The common explanation for the absence of early sites to the north of the Danube is based on post-6500 BC rises in river levels and water-tables. In the discussion contained here, and in that in later chapters, I have used sites from the succeeding Dudeşti culture complex to provide some idea of what might have come before.

5   There is a large literature on the Danube Gorges: further details of sites themselves are best drawn together in Radovanović's *The Iron Gates Mesolithic* (1996a); other reports of note include: Srejović (1969, 1972), Prinz (1988) and Boroneanţ (1989). The extraordinary character of the sites, especially in terms of burials and representational material culture, has generated equal attention; the more accessible of these include: Hodder 1990; Whittle 1996: 24–9; Handsman 1991; Chapman 1989b; Voytek and Tringham 1989.

6   I am following Ivana Radovanović's composite chronology for Danube Gorges sites (Radovanović 1996a: 285–90).

7   Recent publications have realigned the culturo-chronological position of this early tradition, replacing previous arguments (Bittel 1960; 1969–70) which correlated it with Karanovo III (that is, the Balkan middle Neolithic or middle to late sixth millennium BC) with a new correlation which aligns it with Karanovo I or proto-Sesklo, that is, early Neolithic or the late seventh millennium BC (Özdoğan 1989a: 204).

3 NEW DIMENSIONS OF MATERIAL CULTURE

1   FCP1 (Franchthi Ceramic Phase 1) is Vitelli's identification of the early ceramic phase at Franchthi. It correlates to the second half of the seventh millennium BC (Vitelli 1993a: table 13).

4 BURIAL, LITHICS, PLANTS AND ANIMALS

1   This analysis is based on Radovanović's (1996a) reworking of the Gorges sites and focuses on Lepenski Vir, Vlasac, Padina, Hajdučka Vodenica and Schela Cladovei.

2   There is, however, evidence of tool production in the vicinity of Slatina (Gatsov 1992, 1993).

3   Obviously patterns of research vary across modern national boundaries: in some countries, such as Greece, Serbia and Hungary, greater attention to recovery and meaning of 'economic' materials is granted; in others, treatment of plants and seeds borders on scientific negligence.

4   For details on timing and sequencing of particular activities, see also Dennell 1974; Barker 1985; Gregg 1988; de Garine 1994; and Ellen 1994.

6 BURIAL AND EXPRESSIVE MATERIAL CULTURE

1   The very 'schematic' form of Hamangia figurines also distinguishes them from other contemporary anthropomorphic representations.

7 TRANSITIONS TO NEW WAYS OF LIVING

1   A full treatment of the Balkan early Bronze Age deserves lengthier coverage, even a book of its own, as the issues and archaeology involved stretch well beyond the limits of the present volume; see Mallory 1989; Whittle 1996: 122–43; Harding 1983; Dumitrescu et al. 1983; Alexandrov 1995; Nikolova 1995; Coles and Harding 1979; Sherratt 1993, 1994.

8 THE BALKANS (6500–2000 BC): EXCLUSION, INCORPORATION AND PROJECTION

1   The trapezoidal buildings of the Gorges represent another category, perhaps intermediary between the form of the round huts made of less durable materials and the rectangular structures made of more permanent ones.

2   On the emergence of houses and the household in the Balkans see Tringham and Krstić 1990, D. Bailey 1990, Chapman 1990. On the archaeology of houses see Samson 1990.

3   See Pine (1996) for discussion of this concept in the context of houses and households.

4   For more on the use of burial as context for expressing social illusion see the seminal work of the archaeologist Mike Parker Pearson (1982) and more recent writings of the performance artist and scholar Mike Pearson (1998).

BIBLIOGRAPHY

Adovasio, J.M. and Maslowski, R.F. (1988) 'Textile impressions in ceramic vessels at Divostin', in A. McPherron and Srejović D. (eds), *Divostin and the Neolithic of Central Serbia*, pp. 345–58, Pittsburgh, Penn.: Department of Anthropology, University of Pittsburgh.

Alexandrescu, A.D. (1961) 'Les fouilles de Sultana', *Dacia* 1: 51–107.

Alexandrov, S. (1994) 'Po vuprosa za pogrebalnite obredi na kultura Coţofeni', in B. Borisov and Alexandrov, S. (eds) *Maritza-Istok*, pp. 85–90, Sofia: Gutoraov.

—— (1995) 'The early Bronze Age in western Bulgaria: periodisation and cultural definition', in D.W. Bailey and Panayotov, I. (eds) *Prehistoric Bulgaria*, pp. 253–70, Madison, Wisc.: Prehistory Press.

Allsworth-Jones, P. (1986) *The Szeletian and the Transition from Middle to Upper Palaeolithic in Central Europe*, Oxford: Clarendon.

—— (1990) 'The Szeletian and the strategraphic succession in central Europe and adjacent areas: main trends, recent results and problems for resolution', in P. Mellars (ed.) *The Emergence of Modern Humans: An Archaeological Perspective*, pp. 160–242, Edinburgh: Edinburgh University Press.

Andreescu, R.R. (1998) 'Statuteke şi vasele antropomorfe ale Culturii Gumelniţa în lumina cecetărilor de la Căscoarele', unpublished PhD dissertation, Academia Romăna, Institutul de Arheologie Vasile Parvan, Bucureşti.

Andreou, S., Fotiadis, M. and Kotsakis, K. (1996) 'Review of Aegean prehistory V: the Neolithic and Bronze Age of northern Greece', *American Journal of Archaeology* 100: 537–97.

Angelov, N. (1958) 'Selishtnata mogila pri s. Hotniza', *Izsledvaniya v Chest na Akad. D. Dechev* (no editor), pp. 389–403. Sofia: Bulgarskata Akademiya na Naukite.

—— (1959) 'Zlatnoto sukrovishte na Hotnitsa', *Arkheologiya* 1, 1–2: 38–46.

Angelova, H. and Draganov, V. (1995) 'Underwater archaeological investigations along the western Black Sea coast and the evidence provided for determining the shoreline in historical times', *Thracia Pontica* 5: 123–45.

Angelova, I. (1982) 'Tell Tărgovište', in H. Todorova (ed.) *Die kupferzeitliche Siedlungen in Nordostbulgarien*, pp. 175–80, Munich: C.H. Beck.

—— (1986a) 'Eneolitna selishtna mogila Turgovishte', *Interdistsiplinarni Izsledvaniya* 14, A: 33–44.

—— (1986b) 'Praehistoricheski nekropol pri grad Turgovishte', *Interdistsiplinarni Izsledvaniya* 14, A: 49–66.

—— (1988) 'Predvaritelni rezultati ot razkopkite na neolitnoto selishte "Ovcharovo-gorata"', *Terra Antiqua Balcanica* 3: 31–6.

—— (1992) 'Predvaritelnye rezultaty raskopok neoliticeskogo poseleniya Ovcharovo-gorata', *Studia Praehistorica* 11–12: 41–50.

Angelova, I. and Bin, N.V. (1988) 'Kremnevye artefacty iz neoliticheskogo poseleniya Ovcharovo-gorata', *Studia Praehistorica* 9: 16–33.

Anthony, D. (1986) 'The "Kurgan culture", Indo-European origins, and the domestication of the horse: a reconsideration', *Current Anthropology* 27: 291–313.

Anthony, D. and Brown, D. (1991) 'The origins of horseback riding', *Antiquity* 65: 22–38.

Anthony, D., Telegin, D.Y. and Brown, D. (1991) 'The origin of horseback riding', *Scientific American* 265: 44–8A.

Arandjelović-Garašanin, D. (1954) *Starčevačka Kultura*, Ljubljana: Univerza v Ljubljani.

Armit, I. and Finlayson, B. (1992) 'Hunter-gatherers transformed: the transition to agriculture in northern and western Europe', *Antiquity* 66: 664–76.

—— (1995) 'Social strategies and economic change', in W. Barnett and Hoopes, J. (eds) *The Emergence of Pottery*, pp. 267–75, Washington: Smithsonian Institution.

Avilova, L.I. (1984) 'O pogrebal'nom obryade kultur Gumelnitsa', *Studia Praehistorica* 7: 153–63.

Avramova, M. (1991) 'Gold and copper jewellery from the chalcolithic cemeteries near the village of Durankulak, Varna district', in J.-P. Mohen (ed.) *Découverte du Métal*, pp. 43–8, Paris: Picard.

—— (1993) 'Yagodinskaya pestera v Tsentralnkh Rodopakh', *Studia Praehistorica* 11–12: 240–7.

Bailey, D.W. (1990), 'The living house: signifying continuity', in R. Samson (ed.) *The Social Archaeology of Houses*, pp. 19–48, Edinburgh: Edinburgh University Press.

—— (1991) 'The social reality of figurines from the chalcolithic of northestern Bulgaria: the example of Ovcharovo', unpublished PhD dissertation, Cambridge University.

—— (1993) 'Chronotypic tension in Bulgarian prehistory: 6500–3500 BC', *World Archaeology* 25: 204–22.

—— (1994a) 'Reading prehistoric figurines as individuals', *World Archaeology* 25: 321–31.

—— (1994b) 'Representing gender: homology or propaganda', *Journal of European Archaeology* 2, 2: 193–202.

—— (1996a) 'Interpreting figurines: the emergence of illusion and new ways of seeing', *Cambridge Archaeological Journal* 6, 2: 291–5.

—— (1996b) 'The analysis of tells in northeastern Bulgaria: settlement behaviour in the context of time, space and place', *Reports of Prehistoric Research Projects (Sofia)* 1, 2–4: 289–308.

—— (1996c) 'The life, times and works of House 59 from the Ovcharovo tell, Bulgaria', in T. Darvill and Thomas, J. (eds) *Neolithic Houses in Northwest Europe and Beyond*, pp. 143–56, Oxford: Oxbow.

—— (1996d) 'The interpretation of settlement: an exercise from Bronze Age Thrace', *Reports of Prehistoric Research Projects (Sofia)* 1, 2–4: 201–13.

—— (1997) 'Impermanence and flux in the landscape of early agricultural south-eastern Europe', in J. Chapman and Dolukhanov, P. (eds) *Landscapes in Flux*, pp. 39–56, (Colloquenda Pontica) Oxford: Oxbow.

—— (1998) 'Bulgarian archeology: ideology, socio-politics and the exotic', in L. Meskell (ed.) *Archaeology Under Fire*, pp. 87–110, London: Routledge.

—— (1999) 'What is a tell? Settlement in fifth millennium BC Bulgaria', in J. Brück and Goodman, M. (eds) *Making Places in the Prehistoric World: Themes in Settlement Archaeology*, pp. 94–111, London: UCL Press.

Bailey, D.W. and Panayotov, I. (eds) (1995) *Prehistoric Bulgaria*, Madison, Wisc.: Prehistory Press.

Bailey, D.W., Tringham, R.E., Bass, J., Stevanović, M., Hamilton, M., Neumann, H., Angelova, I. and Raduncheva, A. (1998) 'Expanding the dimensions of early agricultural tells: the Podgoritsa Archaeological Project, Bulgaria', *Journal of Field Archaeology* 25, 4: 375–96.

Bailey, G.N (1992) 'The Palaeolithic of Klithi in its wider context', *The Annual of the British School of Athens* 87: 1–28.

—— (1995a) 'Palaeolithic archaeology in Greece and the Balkans', *Current Anthropology* 36: 518–20.

—— (1995b) 'The Balkans in prehistory: the Palaeolithic archaeology of Greece and adjacent areas', *Antiquity* 69: 19–24.

Bailey, G.N., Carter, P.L., Gamble, C.S. and Higgs, H.P. (1983a) 'Epirus revisited: seasonality and inter-site variability in the Upper Palaeolithic of north-west Greece', in G.N. Bailey (ed.) *Hunter-gatherer Economy in Prehistory: A European Perspective*, pp. 64–78, Cambridge: Cambridge University Press.

—— (1983b) 'Asprochaliko and Kastritsa: further investigations of Palaeolithic settlement and economy in Epirus (north-west Greece)', *Proceedings of the Prehistoric Society* 49: 15–42.

Bailey, G.N., Lewin, J., Macklin, M. and Woodward, J. (1990) 'The "Older Fill" of Epirus, north-west Greece and its relationship to the Palaeolithic archaeology and glacial history of the region', *Journal of Archaeological Science* 17: 145–50.

Bailey, G.N., Papaconstantinou, V. and Sturdy, D. (1992) 'Asprochaliko and Kokkinipilos: TL dating and reinterpretation of middle Pleistocene sites in Epirus, north-west Greece', *Cambridge Archaeological Journal* 2, 1: 136–44.

Bankoff, H. and Winter, F. (1979) 'A house burning in Serbia: what do burned remains tell an archaeologist?', *Archaeology* 32: 8–15.

Banner, J. (1931) 'A kökénydombi neolthkori telep (Die neolithische Ansiedlung von Kökénydomb)', *Szbornik ABK* 9: 123–45.

—— (1935) 'Ausgrabungen in Kotacpart bei Hódmezővásárhely', *Dolgozatok-Szeged* 11: 121–5.

—— (1937) 'Die Ethnologie der Körös-Kultur', *Dolgozatok-Szeged* 13: 32–49.

—— (1942) *Das Tisza-, Maros-, Körös Gebeit bis zur Entwicklung der Bronzezeit*, Leipzig: Archaeological Institute.

—— (1943) 'Az újabbkökori lakóházkutatás mai állása Magyarországon (L'État actuel de la recherches des habitations néolithiques en Hongrie)', *Archaeologiai Értesitó* 70: 1–28.

Banner, J. and Korek, J. (1949) 'Negyedik és ötödik ásatás a hódmező'vásárhelyi Kökénydombon (Les Campagnes IV et V fouilles pratiquées au Kökénydomb de Hódmezövásárhely)', *Archaeologiai Értesitó* 76: 9–25.

Barker, G. (1985) *Prehistoric Farming in Europe*, Cambridge: Cambridge University Press.

Basler, D. (1975) 'Stariji litički periodi u Crvenoj Stijeni', in D. Basler (ed.) *Crvena Stijena*, pp. 11–103, Nikšić: Zajednica Kulturnih Ustanova.

Basler, D. (ed.) (1975) *Praistorija Jugoslavenkih Zemalja*, vol. 1, *Paleolit i Mezolit*, Sarajevo: Akademija Nauka i Umjetnosti Bosne i Hercegovine.

Begemann, F., Pernicka, E. and Schmitt-Strecker, S. (1994) 'Metal finds from Ilipinar and the advent of arsenical copper', *Anatolica* 20: 203–19.

Belfer-Cohen, A. (1988) The appearance of symblic expression in the Upper Pleistocene of the Levant as compared to western Europe, in *L'Homme de Néanderthal*, vol. 5, *La Pensée* (no editor), pp. 25–29, Liège: Université de Liège.

Benac, A. (1957) 'Crvena Stijena', *Glasnik Zemaljskog Muzeja u Sarajevu* 12: 19–50.

—— (1971) *Obre II*, Sarajevo: Zemaljski Muzej.

—— (ed.) (1973) *Obre I-II, a Neolithic Settlement of the Butmir Group at Gornje Polje*, Sarajevo: Wissenschaftliche Mitteilungen des Bosnisch-Herzegowinischen Landesmuseums.

—— (1972–3) 'Obre I: neolitsko naselje starčevačko-impresso i kakanjske kulture na Radkršću', *Glasnik (Sarajevo)* 28: 123–45.

Benecke, J. (1942) 'Steinzeitdörfer in den Ebenen am Olymp. Ester Bericht über die Ausgrabungen des Reischsamtes für Vorgeschichte in Griechenland', *Völkischer Beobachter* 18 February 1942: 6.

Berciu, D. (1961) *Contributii la Problemele Neoliticului din România: In Lumina Noilor Cercetari*, Bucureşti: Editura Academiei Republicii Populare Romine.

—— (1966) *Cultura Hamangia*, Bucureşti: Editura Academiei Republicii Populare Romine.

Berciu, D. and Morintz, S. (1957) 'Santierul arheologic Cernavoda', *Materiale şi Cercetări Archeologice* 3: 19–92.

—— (1959) 'Săpăturile de la Cernavoda', *Materiale şi Cercetări Archeologice* 5: 99–106.

Berciu, D., Boeşteanu, D., Comşa, E., Mateescu, C., Morintz, S., Nicolăescu-Plopşor, C.S., Popescu-Ialomiţa, A. and Preda, C. (1952) 'Şantierul Verbicioara', *Studii şi Cercetări de Istorie Veche* 3: 123–45.

Berciu, D., Morintz, S. and Diaconu, P. (1955) 'Şantierul arheologic Cernavoda', *Studii şi Cercetări de Istorie Veche* 6, 1–2: 151–60.

Berciu, D., Morintz, S. and Roman, P. (1959) 'Săpăturile de la Cernavoda', *Materiale şi Cercetări Archeologice* 6: 95–105.

Bertemes, F. and Krustev, I. (1988) 'Die bulgarisch-deutsche Ausgrabung in Drama bez. Burgas – Katalog', in A. Fol and Lichardus, J. (eds) *Macht, Herrschaft und Gold: Das Gräberfeld von Varna und die Anfänge einer neuen europäischen Zivilisation*, pp. 300–61, Saarbrücken: Moderne Galerie des Saarland-Museums.

Besios, M. and Pappa, M. (1993) 'Neolithikos oikismos Makrugialou', *To Arxaiologiko Ergo sti Makedonia kai Thraki* 7: 215–22.

—— (1994) 'Neolithikos oikismos Makrugialou', *To Arxaiologiko Ergo sti Makedonia kai Thraki* 8: 123–45.

Biehl, P. (1996) 'Symbolic communication systems: symbols on anthropomorphic figurines of the Neolithic and Chalcolithic from south-eastern Europe', *Journal of European Archaeology* 4: 153–76.

Bilgi, O. (1984) 'Metal objects from I.kitepe – Turkey', *Beiträge zur allgemeinen und vergleichenden Archäologie* 6: 31–96.

—— (1990) 'Metal objects from I.kitepe – Turkey', *Beiträge zur allgemeinen und vergleichenden Archäologie* 9–10: 119–219.

Binford, L. (1980) 'Willow smoke and dogs' tails: hunter-gatherer settlement systems and archaeological site formation', *American Antiquity* 45: 4–20.

Bittel, K. (1960) 'Fikirtepe kazisi', *V Türk Tarih Kongresi, Ankara*, p. 35, Ankara.

—— (1969–70) 'Bermerkungen über die prähistorische Ansiedlung auf dem Fikirtepe bei Kadiköy', *Istanbuler Mitteilungen* 19–20: 1–19.

Bloedow, E.F. (1991) 'The "Aceramic" Neolithic phase in Greece reconsidered', *Mediterranean Archaeology* 4: 2–35.

—— (1992–3) 'The date of the earliest phase at Argissa Magoula in Thessaly and other Neolithic sites in Greece', *Mediterranean Archaeology* 5–6: 49–57.

Blouet, B. (1986) 'Development of the settlement pattern', in A.C. Renfrew, Gimbutas, M., and Elster, E. (eds) *Excavations at Sitagroi: A Prehistoric Village in Northeast Greece*, vol. 1, pp. 133–43, Los Angeles: UCLA.

Boessneck, J. (1955) 'Zu den Tierknochen aus neolithischen Siedlungen Thessaliens', *Bericht der Römisch-Germanischen Kommission* 36: 1–51.

—— (1962) 'Die Tierreste aus der Argissa Magoula vom präkeramischen Neolithikum bis zur mittleren Bronzezeit', in Milojčić, V., Boessneck, J. and Hopf, M. (eds) *Die deutschen Ausgrabungen auf der Argissa-Magula in Thessalien, I: Das präkeramische Neolithikum sowie die Tier- und Pflanzenreste*, pp. 27–99, Bonn: Rudolf Habelt.

Boessneck, J. and von den Driesch, A. (1979) *Die Tierknochenfunde aus der Neolithischen Siedlung auf dem Fikirtepe bei Kadiköy am Marmarameer*, Munich: C.H. Beck.

Boev, P. (1963) 'Neolitichni antropologicheski materiali ot Karanovo', *Izvestiya na Ethnographskiya Institut i Muzej* 6: 61–9.

—— (1986) 'Anthropologische Untersuchung des neolithischen Skeletts von Chavdar, Bez. Sofia', *Studia Praehistorica* 8: 217–24.

Boev, P. and Kavgazova, L. (1983) 'Neolitni skeleti ot Kurdzhali', *Rodopski Sbornik* 5: 187–92.

Boev, Z. (1994) 'The Upper Pleistocene birds', in Kozłowski, J.K., Laville, H. and Ginter, B. (eds), *Temnata Cave: Excavations in Karlukovo Karst Area, Bulgaria*, vol. 1(2), pp. 55–86, Kraków, Jagellonian University Press.

Boev, Z. and Ribarov, G. (1990) 'Ornitofaunata na potunaloto selishte pri Urdoviza (dn. Kiten)', *Arkheologiya* 32, 2: 53–7.

Bogdanović, M. (1988) 'Architecture and structural features at Divostin', in A. McPherron and D. Srejović (eds), *Divostin and the Neolithic of Central Serbia*, pp. 35–141, Pittsburgh, Penn.: Department of Anthropology, University of Pittsburgh.

Bognár-Kutzián, I. (1963) *The Copper Age Cemetery of Tiszapolgár-Basatanya*, Budapest: Akadémiai Kiadó.

—— (1972) *The Early Copper Age Tiszapolgár Culture in the Carpathian Basin*, Budapest: Akadémiai Kiadó.

Bogucki, P. (1984) 'Ceramic sieves of the Linear Pottery culture and their economic implications', *Oxford Journal of Archaeology* 3, 1: 15–30.

—— (1986) 'The antiquity of dairying in temperate Europe', *Expedition* 28, 2: 51–8.

—— (1993) 'Animal traction and household economies in Neolithic Europe', *Antiquity* 67: 492–503.

Bökönyi, S. (1951) 'Undersuchung der Haustierfunde aus dem Gräberfeld von Alsónémedi', *Acta Archaeologica Academiae Scientiarum Hungaricae* 1: 35–51.

—— (1957) 'A lebői 1956-os ásatás gerinces faunája', *A Móra Ferenc Múzeum Évkönyve (Szeged)* 1957: 61–78.

—— (1959) 'Die frühalluvilae Wirbeltierfauna Ungarn' *Acta Archaeologica Academiae Scientiarum Hungaricae* 14: 175–214.

—— (1970) 'Animal remains from Lepenski Vir', *Science* 167: 1702–4.

—— (1971) 'The development and history of domestic animals in Hungary: the Neolithic through the Middle Ages', *American Anthropologist* 73: 640–74.

—— (1974) *History of Domestic Mammals of Central and Eastern Europe*, Budapest: Akadémiai Kiadó.

—— (1986) 'Faunal remains', in A.C. Renfrew, Gimbutas, M., and Elster, E. (eds) *Excavations at Sitagroi: A Prehistoric Village in Northeast Greece. Volume 1*, pp. 63–96, Los Angeles: UCLA.

—— (1988) 'The neolithic fauna at Divostin and Grivac', in A. McPherron and Srejović, D. (eds) *Divostin and the Neolithic of Central Serbia*, pp. 419–46, Pittsburgh, Penn.: Department of Anthropology, University of Pittsburgh.

—— (1989a) 'Animal husbandry of the Körös-Starčevo complex: its origin and development', in S. Bökönyi (ed.) *Neolithic of Southeastern Europe and its Near Eastern Connections*, pp. 13–16, Budapest: Instituti Archaeologici Academiae Scientiarum Hungaricae Budapestini.

—— (1989b) 'Animal remains', in M. Gimbutas, Winn, S. and Shimabuku, D. (eds) *Achilleion: A Neolithic Settlement in Thessaly, Greece*, pp. 315–32, Los Angeles: UCLA.

Bökönyi, S. and Bartosiewicz, L. (1997) 'Tierknochenfunde', in S. Hiller and Nikolov, V. (eds) *Karanovo: Die Ausgrabungen im Südsektor 1984–1992*, pp. 385–423, Horn: Ferdinand Berger and Söhne.

Bolomey, A. (1966) 'Fauna neolitică din aşezarea Boian A de la Vărăşti', *Studii şi Cercetari de Antroprologiei* 3, 1: 27–34.

—— (1973) 'An outline of the late Epipalaeolithic economy at the Iron Gates: the evidence on bones', *Dacia* 17: 41–52.

—— (1976) 'Pe marginea analisei arheo-osteologice a materialului de la Cârcea-Dolj', *Studii şi Cercetări de Istorie Veche şi Arheologie* 27: 465–75.

—— (1979) 'Gospodărirea animalelor în aşezarea neolitică de la Fărcaşu de Sus', *Studii şi Cercetări de Istorie Veche şi Arheologie* 30, 1: 3–10.

—— (1980) 'Analiza resturilor de animale din locuirea Starčevo-Criş de la Cârcea-Viaduct', *Anuarul Muzeului Olteniei* 1: 9–25.

—— (1983) 'L'homme et son environnement au Pléistocène', in V. Dumitrescu, Bolomey, A. and Mogoşanu, F. (eds) *Ésquisse d'une préhistoire de la Roumanie*, pp. 12–28, Bucureşti: Editura Ştiinţifică şi Enciclopedică.

—— (1986) 'Resturile de animale dintr-o groapă neolitică timpurie din Oltenia', *Cercetări Arheologice* 8: 143–53.

Bondár, M. (1990) 'Das frühbronzezeitliche Wagenmodell von Börzönce', *Communicationes Archaeologicae Hungaricae* 1990: 77–91.

Bonsall, C. (ed.) (1989) *The Mesolithic in Europe*, Edinburgh: John Donald.

Borić, D. (1996) 'Social dimensions of mortuary practices in the Neolithic: a case study', *Starinar* 47: 67–83

Boroneanţ, V. (1970) 'La période épipaléolithique sur la rive roumanie des Portes de Fer du Danube', *Praehistorische Zeitschrift* 45, 1: 1–25.

—— (1973) 'Recherches archéologiques sur la culture Schela Cladovei de la zone des "Portes de Fer"', *Dacia* 17: 5–39.

—— (1982) 'General survey of Epipalaeolithic (Mesolithic) research in Romania (1978–1981)', *Mesolithic Miscellany* 3, 1: 11–12.

—— (1989) 'Thoughts on the chronological relations between the Epi-palaeolithic and the Neolithic of the Low Danube', in C. Bonsall (ed.) *The Mesolithic in Europe*, pp. 475–80, Edinburgh: John Donald.

Bottema, S. (1982) 'Palynological investigations in Greece with special reference to pollen as an indicator of human activity', *Palaeohistoria* 24: 257–89.

—— (1991) 'Développement de la végétation et du climat dans le bassin méditerranéen oriental à fin du Pléistocene et pendent l'Holocène', *L'Anthropologie* 95: 123–45.

Boyadzhiev, Ya. (1995) 'Chronology of prehistoric cultures in Bulgaria', in D.W. Bailey and Panayotov, I. (eds) *Prehistoric Bulgaria*, pp. 149–92, Madison, Wisc.: Prehistory Press.

Braun, D.P. (1983) 'Pots as tools', in A. Keene and Moore, J. (eds) *Archaeological Hammers and Theories*, pp. 107–34, New York: Academic Press.

Brochier, J.L. (1994) 'Étude de la sédimentation anthropique. La stratégie des ethnofaciès sédimentaires en milieu de constructions en terre', *Bulletin correspondance hellénique* 118: 619–45.

Brown, J.A. (1989) 'The beginnings of pottery as an economic process', in S. van der Leeuw and Torrence, R. (eds) *What's New? A Closer Look at the Process of Innovation*, pp. 203–24, London: Unwin Hyman.

Brukner, B. (1974a) 'Rani neolit (the early Neolithic period)', in B. Brukner, Jovanović, B. and Tasić, N. (eds) *Praistorije Vojvodine*, pp. 29–68, 425–33, Novi Sad: Institut za Izučavanje Istorije Vojvodine i Savez Arheoloških Društava Jugoslavije.

—— (1974b) 'Pozni neolit (the late Neolithic period)', in B. Brukner, Jovanović, B. and Tasić, N. (eds) *Praistorije Vojvodine*, pp. 69–112, 434–40, Novi Sad: Institut za Izučavanje Istorije Vojvodine i Savez Arheoloških Društava Jugoslavije.

—— (1975) 'Gomolava, Hrtkovci – višeslojno nalzište', *Arheološski Pregled* 17: 11–13.

—— (1977) 'Beitrag zur Festellung des Beginns der Metallurgie und der Äneolithisierung', *Archaeologia Iugoslavica* 18: 9–12.

—— (1978) 'Novi prilozi proučavanju formiranja neolitskih i eneolitskih naselja u jugoslovenskom Podunavlju', *Materijali* 14: 47–51.

—— (1980) 'Naselje vinčanske grupe na Gomolavi (neolitski i ranoneolitski sloj): Izveštaj sa iskopavanja 1967–1976 g.', *Rad Vojvodanskih Muzeja* 26: 5–55.

—— (1988a) 'Die Siedlung der Vinča-Gruppe auf Gomolava (die Wohnschicht des spätneolithikums und frühäneolithikums – Gomolava Ia, Gomolava Ia-b und Gomolava Ib) und der Wohnhorizont des äneolithischen Humus (Gomolava II)', in N. Tasić, and Petrović, J. (eds) *Gomolava – Chronologie und Stratigraphie der vorgeschichtlichen und antiken Kulturen der Donauniederung und Südosteuropas*, pp. 19–38, Novi Sad: Institut za Izučavanje Istorije Vojvodine i Savez Arheoloških Društava Jugoslavije.

—— (1988b) 'Pečinci/Budimlja bara Alicia', Keramička zanatska zona', *Arheološki Pregled* 29: 147–8.

—— (1990) 'Vinča-Kultur und der Zivilisationskomplex der neolithischen Kulturen des westlichen Teils des Schwarzen Meeres', *Rad Vojvodanskih Muzeja* 32: 123–45.

Brukner, B. and Petrović, J. (1977) 'Gomolava, Hrtkovci – višeslojno nalazište', *Arheološki Pregled* 19: 24–7.

Brukner, B., Jovanović, B. and Tasić, N. (1974) *Praistorija Vojvodine*, Novi Sad: Institut za Izučavanje Istorije Vojvodine i Savez Arheoloških Društava Jugoslavije.

Buchvarov, K. (1994) 'Khronologichni aspekti na neolitnite pogrebalni obredi v Trakiya', *Godishnik na Departament Arkheologiya NBU* 1: 263–8.

—— (in press) 'Rannoneolitno vtorichno pogrebenie ot selishtnata mogila v Karanovo', in *Sbornik na V. Mikov*, Sofia.

Buitenhuis, H. (1995) 'Appendix', in J. Roodenberg (ed.) *The Ilipinar Excavations I: Five Seasons of Fieldwork in Northwestern Anatolia, 1987–1991*, Istanbul: Dutch Archaeological Institute.

Cantacuzino, G. (1967) 'Necropola preistorică de la Cernica şi locul ei în neoliticul românesc şi european', *Studii şi Cercetări de Istorie Veche* 18, 3: 379–97.

—— (1969) 'The prehistoric necropoles of Cernica and its place in the Neolithic cultures of Romania and of Europe in the light of recent discoveries', *Dacia* 13: 45–59.

Cantacuzino, G and Morintz, S. (1963) 'Die jungsteinzeitlichen Funde in Cernica (Bucureşti). *Dacia* 7: 27–89.

Cârciumaru, M. (1985) 'La relation homme = environment élément important de la dynamique de la société humaine au cours de Paléolithique et de l'Épi-paléolithique sur le territoire de la Roumanie', *Dacia* 29, 1–2: 7–34.

—— (1996) *Paleoetnobotanica: Studii în Preistoria şi Protoistoria României (Istoria Agriculturii din România)*. Iaşi: Glasul Bucovinei Helios.

Chapman, J. (1981) *The Vinča Culture of South-east Europe*, Oxford: British Archaeological Reports.

—— (1983a) 'Meaning and illusion in the study of burial in Balkan prehistory', in A. Poulter (ed.) *Ancient Bulgaria*, pp. 1–42, Nottingham: Department of Archaeology, University of Nottingham.

—— (1983b) 'The "Secondary Products Revolution" and the limitations of the Neolithic', *Bulletin of the Institute of Archaeology* 19: 107–22.

—— (1989a) 'The early Balkan village', in S. Bökönyi (ed.) *Neolithic of Southeastern Europe and its Near Eastern Connections*, pp. 33–53, Budapest: Instituti Archaeologici Academiae Scientiarum Hungaricae Budapestini.

—— (1989b) 'Demographic trends in neothermal southeast Europe', in C. Bonsall (ed.) *The Mesolithic in Europe*, pp. 500–15, Edinburgh: John Donald.

—— (1990) 'Social inequality on Bulgarian tells and the Varna problem', in R. Samson (ed.) *The Social Archaeology of Houses*, pp. 49–92, Edinburgh: Edinburgh University Press.

—— (1990) 'The Neolithic in the Morava-Danube confluence area: a regional assessment of settlement pattern, in R.E. Tringham and Krštić, D. (eds) *Selevac: A Neolithic Village in Yugoslavia*, pp. 13–44, Los Angeles: UCLA.

—— (1992) 'Arenas of social power: the case of Serbian prehistory', *Zbornik Narodnog Muzeja* 14, 1: 405–17.

Chapman, J. and Müller, J. (1990) 'Early farmers in the Mediterranean basin: the Dalmatian evidence', *Antiquity* 64: 127–34.

Chapman, J. and Tylecote, R.F. (1983) 'Early copper in the Balkans', *Proceedings of the Prehistoric Society* 49: 40–5.

Charles, J.A. (1969) 'Metallurgical examinations of south-east European copper axes', *Proceedings of the Prehistoric Society* 35: 40–2.

Chase, P. and Dibble, H. (1987) 'Middle Palaeolithic symbolism: a review of current evidence and interpretations', *Journal of Anthropological Archaeology* 6: 263–92.

Chavaillon, J., Chavaillon, N. and Hours, F. (1964) 'Une industrie paléolithique du Péloponnèse: le Moustérien de Vasilaki', *Bulletin correspondance hellénique* 88: 616–22.

—— (1967) 'Industries paléolithiques de l'Elide: I – region d' Amalias', *Bulletin correspondance hellénique* 91: 151–201.

—— (1969) 'Industries paléolithique de l'Elide: II – région du Kastron', *Bulletin correspondance hellénique* 93: 97–151.

Chernykh, E.N. (1978a) *Gornoe Delo i Metallurgiya v Drevneishei Bolgarii*. Sofia: Bulgarsjata Akademiya na Vaukite.

—— (1978b) 'Ai Bunar, a Balkan copper mine of the IVth millennium BC', *Proceedings of the Prehistoric Society* 44: 203–18.

—— (1992) *Ancient Metallurgy in the USSR: The Early Metal Age*, Cambridge: Cambridge University Press.

Chernykh, E. and Raduncheva, A. (1972) 'Starite medni rudnitsi okolo gr. Stara Zagora', *Arkheologiya* 14, 1: 67–75.

Childe, V.G. (1936) *Man Makes Himself*, London: Watts.

Chirica, V. (1986) 'La chronologie relative et absolue des habitats Aurignaciens et Gravettiens de la Roumanie', in O. Soffer (ed.) *Pleistocene Perspective*, pp. 123–45, London: Unwin Allen.

—— (1989) *The Gravettian in the East of the Romanian Carpathians*, Iaşi: University of Iaşi.

Chokadziev, M. (1981) 'Neolitni antropomophni figurki ot dolinata na Gorna Struma', *Izkustvo* 9–10: 73–6.

—— (1983) 'Die Ausgrabung der neolithischen Siedlung in Pernik', *Nachrichten aus Niedersachsens Urgeschichte* 52: 29–68.

Chokadziev, S. (1984) 'Arkheologicheski danni za kalendar v nachaloto na kamenno-mednata epokha', *Arkheologiya* 26, 2–3: 1–7.

—— (1986) 'Frühäneolitische Keramik aus der prähistorischen Siedlung bei Slatino, Bezierk Kyustendil', *Studia Praehistorica* 8: 185–202.

—— (1995) 'On early social differentiation in the Struma River Basin: the evidence from the Slatino settlement', in D.W. Bailey and Panayotov, I. (eds), *Prehistoric Bulgaria*, pp. 141–48, Madison, Wisc.: Prehistory Press.

Chokadziev, S. and Bakamska, A. (1990) 'Étude du site néolithique ancien de Kraïnitsi dans le département de Kustendil', *Studia Praehistorica* 10: 51–90.

Christescu, V. (1925) 'Les stations préhistoriques du lac de Boian', *Dacia* 2: 249–303.

—— (1933) 'Les stations préhistoriques de Vadastra', *Dacia* 3–4: 167–225.

Chrysostomou, P. (1989) 'O neolithikos oikismos ton Giannitson B', *To Arxaiologiko Ergo sti Makedonia kai Thraki* 3: 119–34.

—— (1991) 'Ot neolithikes ereunes stin poli kai eparhia Giannitson kata to 1991', *To Arxaiologiko Ergo sti Makedonia kai Thraki* 5: 111–25.

—— (1993) 'O neolithikos oikismos Giannitson B: nea anaskafika dedomena (1992–1993)', *To Arxaiologiko Ergo sti Makedonia kai Thraki* 7: 135–46.

Chrysostomou, P. and Chrysostomou, P. (1990) 'Neolithikes ereunes sta Giannitsa kai stin periohi tous', *To Arxaiologiko Ergo sti Makedonia kai Thraki* 4: 169–77.

Clason, A.T. (1979) 'The farmers of Gomolava in the Vinča and La Tène period', *Rad Vojvodanskih Muzeja* 25: 60–114.

—— (1980) 'Padina and Starcevo: game, fish and cattle', *Palaeohistoria* 22: 141–73.

Coles, J. and Harding, A. (1979) *Europe in the Bronze Age*, London: Methuen.

Comşa, E. (1961) 'Mormîntul neolitic descoperit lî satul Andolina', *Studii şi Cercetări de Istorie Veche* 12, 2: 359–62.

—— (1971) 'Données sur la civilisation de Dudeşti', *Praehistorische Zeitschrift* 46, 2: 195–249.

—— (1973) 'Parures néolithiques en coquillages marins découvertes en territoire roumain', *Dacia* 17: 61–76.

—— (1974a) *Istoria Comunităţilor Culturii Boian*, Bucureşti: Editura Academiei.

—— (1974b) 'Figurinele de aur din aria de raspîndire a culturii Gumelniţa', *Studii şi Cercetări de Istorie Veche şi Arheologie* 25, 2: 181–90.

—— (1974c) 'Date despre folosirea aurului în cursul epocii neolitice pe teritoriul României', *Apulum* 12: 13–23.

—— (1978) 'L'utilisation du cuivre par les communautés de la culture Gumelniţa du territoire Roumain', *Studia Praehistorica* 1–2: 109–20.

—— (1991a) 'L'utilisation du cuivre en Roumanie pendent le néolithique moyen', in J.-P. Mohen (ed.) *Découverte du métal*, pp. 77–84, Paris: Picard.

—— (1991b) 'L'utilisation de l'or pendent le néolithique dans le territoire de la Roumanie', in J.-P. Mohen (ed.) *Découverte du métal*, pp. 85–92, Paris: Picard.

—— (1995) *Figurinele Antropomorfe din Epoca Neolitică*, Bucureşti: Editura Academiei.

Corvin Singeorzan, I. (1976) 'L'orientation des tombes de la nécropole néolithique de Cernica', *Actes de VIIe Congrès de Union Internationale de Sciences Préhistoriques et Protohistoriques*, pp. 123–45, Nice.

Čović, B. (1961) 'Rezultati sondiranja na preistoriskom naselju u Gornjoj Tuzli', *Glasnik Zemaljskog Muzeja* 15–6: 79–139.

Csalog, J. (1958a) 'Szegvár-Tüzköves', *Régészeti Füzetek* 10: 12–3.

—— (1958b) 'Das Wohnhaus "E" von Szegvár-Tüzköveś und seine Funde', *Acta Archaeologica Hungarica* 9: 95–114.

Cullen, T. (1984) 'Social implications of ceramic style in the Neolithic Peloponnese', *Ancient Technology to Modern Science* 1: 77–100.

—— (1995) 'Mesolithic mortuary ritual at Franchthi cave, Greece', *Antiquity* 69: 270–89.

Darlas, A. (1995) 'The earliest occupation of Europe: the Balkans', in W. Roebroeks and van Kolfschoten, T. (eds) *The Earliest Occupation of Europe*, pp. 51–9, Leiden: University of Leiden.

Degens, E.T. and Ross, D.A. (1972) 'Chronology of the Black Sea over the last 25,000 years', *Chemical Geology* 10: 1–16.

—— (eds) (1973) *The Black Sea: Its Geology, Chemistry and Biology*, Tulsa, Okla.: American Association of Petroleum Geologists.

Delpeche, F. and Guadelli, J.-L. (1992) 'Les grandes mammifères Gravettiens et Aurignaciens de la Grotte de Temnata', in J.K. Kozłowski, Laville, H. and Ginter, B., *Temnata Cave: Excavations in Karlukovo Karst Area Bulgaria* vol. 1(1), pp. 141–216, Kraków: Jagellonian University Press.

Delporte, H. and Djindjian, F. (1979) 'Note à propos de l'outillage aurignacian de la couche 11 de Bacho Kiro', *Prace Archeologiczne* 28: 101–3.

Demitrack, A. (1986) 'The late Quaternary geologic history of the Larissa Plain, Thessaly, Greece: tectonic, climatic and human impact on the landscape', unpublished PhD dissertation, Stanford University.

—— (1994) 'A dated stratigraphy for the late Quaternary in eastern Thessaly and what it implies about landscape changes', in J.C. Decourt, Helly, B. and Gallis, K. (eds) *La Thessalie, Colloque international d'archéologie: 15 années de recherches (1975–1990), bilans et perspectives*, pp. 123–45, Athens: Tameion Archaeologikon Poron.

Demoule, J.-P. and Lichardus-Itten, M. (1994) 'Kovačevo. Rapport préliminaire (Campagnes 1986–1993)', *Bulletin correspondance hellénique* 118: 561–618.

Demoule, J.-P. and Perlès C. (1993) 'The Greek Neolithic: a new review', *Journal of World Prehistory* 7, 4: 355–416.

Demoule, J.-P., Gallis, K. and Manolakakis, L. (1988) 'Transition entre les cultures néolithiques de Sesklo et de Dimini: les catégories céramiques', *Bulletin correspondence hellénique* 112: 1–58.

Demoule, J.-P., Grembska-Kulova, M., Katicharov, R., Kulov, J. and Lichardus-Itten, M. (1989) 'Kovachevo: fouille franco-bulgare de l'un des plus anciens villages Néolithiques de l'Europe', in *Le Premier Or de l'humanité en Bulgaria 5e millénaire*, pp. 33–7, Paris: Musées Nationaux.

Dennell, R. (1974) 'Botanical evidence for prehistoric crop processing activities', *Journal of Archaeological Science* 1: 275–84.

—— (1978) *Early Farming in South Bulgaria from the VIth to the IIrd Millennia* BC, Oxford: British Archaeological Reports.

—— (1979) 'A. Zemedelski kulturi', in G.I. Georgiev, Merpert, N.Ya., Katincharov, R.V. and Dimitrov, D.G. (eds) *Ezero: Rannobronzovoto Selishte*, pp. 415–25, Sofia: Bulgarskata Akademiya na Naukite.

—— (1983) *European Economic Prehistory: A New Approach*, London: Academic.

Dennell, R and Webley, D. (1975) 'Prehistoric settlement and land use in southern Bulgaria', in E.S. Higgs (ed.) *Palaeoeconomy*, pp. 97–110, Cambridge: Cambridge Univeristy Press.

Derevenski, J.S. (1997) 'Age and gender at the site of Tiszapolgár-Basatanya, Hungary', *Antiquity* 71: 875–90.

Dergachev, V., Sherratt, A. and Larina, O. (1991) 'Recent results of Neolithic research in Moldavia (USSR)', *Oxford Journal of Archaeology* 10: 1–16.

Detev, P. (1959) 'Materiali za praistoriyata na Plovdiv', *Godishnik na Narodniya Arkheologicheski Muzej v Plovdiv* 3: 3–80.

—— (1965) 'Modeli za ykrasa ot kammeno-mednata epokha', *Arkheologiya* 7, 4: 65–73.

Dimitrijević, S. (1974a) 'Problem stupnjevanja Starčevačke kulture s posebnim obzirom na doprinos Južnopanonskih nalazišta rješavanju ovog problema', in N. Tasić (ed.) *Počeci Ranih Zemljoradničkih Kultura u Vojvodini i Srpskom Podunavlju*, pp. 59–93, Belgrade: Srpsko Arheološko Društvo.

—— (1974b) 'Sjeverna zona', in M. Garašanin (ed.) *Praistorija Jugoslavenskih Zemalja*, vol. 2, pp. 229–360, Sarajevo: Akademija Nauka i Umjetnosti Bosne i Hercegovine.

Dimov, T. (1982) 'Zemlyanka ot neolitnoto selishte pri s. Durankulak, Tolbukhinski okrug', *Arkheologiya* 24, 1: 33–48.

—— (1992) 'Kulturata Hamangia v Dobrudja', *Dobrudzha* 9: 20–34.

Dimov, T., Boyadzhiev, Ya. and Todorova, H. (1984) 'Praistoricheski nekropol kraj s. Durankulak, Tolbukhinski okrug', *Dobrudzha* 1: 2–18.

Docheva, E. (1990) 'Plant macrorest research of early neolithic dwelling in Slatina', *Studia Praehistorica* 10: 86–90.

—— (1992) 'Rastitelni ostanki ot zhilishteto', in V. Nikolov (ed.) *Rannoneolithno Zhilishte v Slatina (Sofiya)*, pp. 144–52, Sofia: Bulgarskata Akademiya na Naukite.

Dolinescu-Ferche, S. (1964) 'Cîteva date referitoare la cultura Dudeşti', *Studii şi Cercetări de Istorie Veche* 15: 113–9.

Draganov, V. (1994) 'Podvodni arkheologicheski razkopki na potunali selishta ot finala na eneolita i rannata bronzeova epokha v akvatoriyata na pristanishte Sozopol', *Arkheologyiya* 32: 123–45.

—— (1995) 'Submerged coastal settlements from the final Eneolithic and the early Bronze Age in the sea around Sozopol and Urdoviza Bay near Kiten', in D.W. Bailey and I. Panayotov (eds) *Prehistoric Bulgaria*, pp. 225–41, Madison, Wisc.: Prehistory Press.

Drobniewicz, B., Ginter, B., Ivanova, S. and Sirakov, N. (1982) 'Middle Palaeolithic finds', in J.K. Kozłowski (ed.) *Excavation in the Bacho Kiro Cave (Bulgaria): Final Report*, pp. 81–116, Warsaw: Państwowe Wydawnictwo Naukowe.

Drobniewicz, B., Ginter, B. and Kozłowski, J.K. (1992) 'The Gravettian sequence', in Kozłowski, J.K., Laville, H. and Ginter, B. *Temnata Cave: Excavations in Karlukovo Karst Area Bulgaria*, vol. 1(1), pp. 295–501, Kraków: Jagellonian University Press.

Dumitrescu, H. (1961) 'Connections between Cucteni-Tripolue cultural complex and the neighboring eneolithic cultures in the light of the utilization of golden pendants', *Dacia* 5: 60–94.

Dumitrescu, V. (1925) 'Fouilles de Gumelniţa', *Dacia* 2: 29–103.

—— (1972) *L'Arte Preistorica in Romania fino all'inizo dell'età Ferro*, Firenza: Sansoni Editore.

Dumitrescu, V., Bolomey, A. and Mogoşanu, F. (1983) *Esquisse d'une préhistoire de la Roumanie jusqu'à la fin de l'âge du bronze*, Bucureşti: Editura Ştiinţifică şi Enciclopedică.

Dzhambazov, N. (1959) 'Razkopki v peshterata Samuilitsa II', *Arhkeologiya* 1, 1–2: 47–53.

—— (1960) 'Novo Paleolitno nakhodishte po dolinata na Vit', *Arkheologiya* 2, 1: 36–42.

—— (1963) 'Loveshkite Peshteri', *Izvestiya na Arkheologicheski Institut* 26: 195–239.

—— (1964) 'Prouchvaniya na paleolithnata i mezolitnata kultura v Bulgariya', *Arkheologiya* 6, 3: 67–76.

—— (1967a) 'Les pointes bifaciales dans les grottes Samuilitza I et II et les autres stations de Paléolithique récent en Bulgarie', *Quaternär* 18: 195–200.

—— (1967b) 'Rannopaleolitni nakhodki pri gr. Svishtov', *Arkheologiya* 9, 1: 60–70.

—— (1969) 'Rannopaleolitni nakhodki praj gr. Nikopol', *Arkheologiya* 11, 2: 67.

—— (1971) 'Nachalo na kusniya Paleolit v Bulgariya', *Arkheologiya* 13, 4: 1–17.

—— (1981) 'La grotte Samuilica II', *Izvestiya na Arkheologicheski Institut* 36: 5–62.

Dzhambazov, N. and Margos, A. (1960) 'Kum vuprosa za prouchvaneto na Paleolitnata kultura v rajona na Pobitite Kamuni Dikilitash', *Izvestiya na Arkheologicheski Institut* 23: 269–95.

Ecsedy, I. (1979) *The People of the Pit-grave Kurgans in Eastern Hungary*, Budapest: Akadémiai Kiado.

Edwards, K.J., Halstead. P. and Zvelebil, M. (1996) 'The Neolithic transition in the Balkans – archaeologcial perspectives and palaeoecological evidence: a comment on Willis and Bennett', *The Holocene* 6: 120–2.

Eleure, C. (1989) 'L'or de Varna', in *Le Premier Or de l'humanité en Bulgaria 5e millénaire*, pp. 61–71, Paris: Musées Nationaux.

Eleure, C. and Raub, C.R. (1991) 'Investigations on the gold coating technology of the great dish from Varna', in J.-P. Mohen (ed.) *Découverte du métal*, pp. 13–30, Paris: Picard.

Elia, R. (1982) 'A study of the Neolithic architecture of Thessaly, Greece', unpublished PhD dissertation, Boston University.

Ellen, R. (1994) 'Modes of subsistence: hunting and gathering to agriculture and pastoralism', in T. Ingold (ed.) *Companion Encyclopedia of Anthropology*, pp. 197–225, London: Routledge.

Ellis, L. (1989) 'Petrographic analysis of the ceramics', in M. Gimbutas, Winn, S. and Shimabuku, D. (eds) *Achilleion: A Neolithic Settlement in Thessaly, Greece*, pp. 165–70, Los Angeles: UCLA.

Elster, E. (1989) 'The chipped stone industry', in M. Gimbutas, Winn, S. and Shimabuku, D. (eds) *Achilleion: A Neolithic Settlement in Thessaly, Greece*, pp. 273–306, Los Angeles: UCLA.

Elsusi, G. (1985–6) 'Analiza materialeor faunistice provenite din aşezările Starčevo-Criş de la Gornea-Locurile Lungi şi Moldova Veche-Rât (judeţul Caraş-Severin)', *Acta Musei Napocensis* 22–23: 181–290.

Evans, R.K. (1986) 'The pottery of phase III', in A.C. Renfrew, Gimbutas, M., and Elster, E. (eds) *Excavations at Sitagroi: A Prehistoric Village in Northeast Greece*, vol. 1, pp. 393–428, Los Angeles: UCLA.

Fewkes, V.J., Goldman, H. and Ehrich, R. (1933) 'Excavation at Starčevo, Yugoslavia, seasons 1931 and 1932', *Bulletin of the American School of Prehistoric Research* 9: 17–32.

Fistani, A.B. (1993a) 'Human evolution in Albania for the Quaternary Period', in B.A. Signon (ed.) *Before the Wall Fell: The Science of Man in Socialist Europe*, pp. 141–78, Toronto: Canadian Scholars Press.

—— (1993b) 'Découverte d'un humerus d'ursidé à l'oléocrâne perforé dans le site de Gajtan I (Shkodër) en Albanie du Nord', *L'Anthropologie* 97, 2–3: 223–38.

Flannery, K.V. (1972) 'The origins of the village as a settlement type in Mesoamerica and the Near East', in P. Ucko, Tringham, R and Dimbleby, D.W.. (eds) *Man, Settlement and Urbanism*, pp. 23–53, London: Duckworth.

Flemming, N.C. (1978) 'Holocene eustatic changes and coastal tectonics in the northeast Mediterranean: implications for models of crustal consumption', *Philosophical Transactions of the Royal Society of London* A289: 405–58.

Fol, A. and Lichardus, J. (eds) (1988a) *Macht, Herrschaft und Gold: Das Gräberfeld von Varna und die Anfänge einer neuen europäischen Zivilisation*, Saarbrücken: Moderne Galerie des Saarland-Museums.

—— (1988b) 'Archäologie und Geschichte', in A. Fol and Lichardus, J. (eds) *Macht, Herrschaft und Gold: Das Gräberfeld von Varna und die Anfänge einer neuen europäischen Zivilisation*, pp. 19–24, Saarbrücken: Moderne Galerie des Saarland-Museums.

Forsten, A. (1982) 'Equidae', in J.K. Kozłowski (ed.) *Excavation in the Bacho Kiro Cave (Bulgaria): Final Report*, pp. 56–60, Warsaw: Państwowe Wydawnictwo Naukowe.

Fortier, A.C. (1981) *Chronological and Regional Variation with the early Neolithic Karanovo I – Kremikovci Complex of Bulgaria*, Ann Arbor, Mich.: University Microfilms.

Fotiadis, M. (1988) 'Proistroiki hereuna stin Kitrini Limni, Nomou Kozanis: Mia sivtomi hekthesi', *To Arxaiologiko Ergo sti Makedonia kai Thraki* 2: 41–54.

Fridrich, J. (1976) 'The first industries from eastern and south-eastern central Europe', in K. Valoch (ed.) *Les Premiers Industries de l'Europe*, pp. 8–23, Nice: Union Internationale de Sciences Préhistoriques et Protohistoriques.

Galántha, M. (1985) 'Csanytelek-Újhalastő, *Régészeti Füzetek* 38: 8.

Galbenu, D. (1962) 'Aşezarea neolitică de la Hirşová, *Studii şi Cercetări de Istorie Veche* 13: 285–306.

—— (1970) 'Aşezarea şi cimitirul de la Limanu', *Materiale* 9: 77–86.

Galdikas, B. (1988) 'Milling stones', in A. McPherron, and Srejović, D. (eds) *Divostin and the Neolithic of Central Serbia*, pp. 338–45, Pittsburgh, Penn.: Department of Anthropology, University of Pittsburgh.

Gale, N.H., Stos-Gale, Z.A., Lilov, F., Dimitrov, M. and Todorov, T. (1991) 'Recent studies of eneolithic copper ores and artefacts in Bulgaria', in J.-P. Mohen (ed.) *Découverte du métal*, pp. 49–76, Paris: Picard.

Gallis, K.I. (1975) 'Kafseis necron apo tin archaioteran neolithikin epohin eis tin Thessalian', *Athens Annals of Archaeology* 8, 2: 241–58.

—— (1982) (ed.) *Kauseis Nekron apo ti Neolthiki Epochi sti Thessalia*, Athens: Tameion Archeologikon Poron.

—— (1985) 'A late Neolithic foundation offering from Thessaly', *Antiquity* 59: 20–24.

—— (1989) 'Atlas proistorikon oikismon tis anatolikis thessalikis pediadas', *Thessaliko Imerologio* 16: 6–144.

—— (1994) 'Results of recent excavations and topographical work in neolithic Thessaly', in J.C. Decourt, Helly, B. and Gallis, K. (eds) *La Thessalie, Colloque international d'archéologie: 15 années de recherches (1975–1990), bilans et perspectives*, pp. 57–60, Athens: Tameion Archaeologikon Poron.

—— (1996) 'The Neolithic world', in G. Papathanassopoulos (ed.) *The Neolithic Culture in Greece*, pp. 23–37, Athens: Goulandris Museum.

Gallis, K.I. and Orphanidis, D.L. (1991) 'Portreta apo ti Neolithiki Thessalia', *Arhaiologia* 38: 44–9.

—— (1995) 'Twenty new faces from the Neolithic society of Thessaly', in J.C. Decourt, B. Helly and K. Gallis (eds) *La Thessalie, Colloque international d'archéologie: 15 années de recherches (1975–1990), bilans et perspectives*, pp. 155–62. Athens: Tameion Archeologikon Poron.

Gambier, D. (1992) 'Les vestiges humains des nivaux gravettiens', in J.K. Kozłowski, Laville, H. and Ginter, B. (eds) *Temnata Cave: Excavations in Karlukovo Karst Area Bulgaria*, vol. 1(1), pp. 217–22, Kraków: Jagellonian University Press.

Gamble, C. (1982) 'Interaction and alliance in Palaeolithic society', *Man* 17: 92–107.

—— (1986) *The Palaeolithic Settlement of Europe*, Cambridge: Cambridge University Press.

—— (1991) 'The social context for European Palaeolithic art', *Proceedings of the Prehistoric Society* 51, 1: 3–15.

—— (1993) 'People on the move: interpetations of regional variation in Palaeolithic Europe', in J. Chapman and Dolukhanov, P. (eds) *Cultural Transformations and Interactions in Eastern Europe*, pp. 37–55, Aldershot: Avebury.

Garašanin, D. (1958) 'Die Siedlung der Starčevokultur in Nosa bei Subotica und das Problem der neolitischen Lehmscheuneń, *Bericht über den V Internationalen Kongress, Hamburg*, Hamburg.

—— (1959) 'Nosa, Biserna Obala', *Areološki Pregled* 1: 9–12.

—— (1960) 'Biserna Obala kod Nose', *Starinar* 11: 228.

Garašanin, M. (1979) 'Centralnobalkanska zona', in A. Benac (ed.) *Praistorija Jugoslavenskih Zemalja* vol. 2, pp. 79–212, Sarajevo: Akademija Nauka i Umjetnosti Bosne i Hercegovine.

Garašanin, M. and Garašanin, D. (1961) 'Neolitska naselba Vršnik, kaj selo Tarinci', *Zbornik na Štipskot Naroden Muzej* 2: 123–45.

Gardner, E. (1976) 'The technology of ceramics', in M. Gimbutas (ed.) *Neolithic Macedonia as Reflected by Excavations at Anza*, pp. 159–76, Los Angeles: UCLA.

—— (1979) 'Graphite painted ceramics', *Archaeology* 32, 4: 18–23.

—— (1980) *The Pottery of the Neolithic Period in Southeastern Europe*, Ann Arbor, Mich.: University Microfilms.

de Garine, I. (1994) 'The diet and nutrition of human populations', in T. Ingold (ed.) *Companion Encyclopedia of Anthropology*, pp. 226–64, London: Routledge.

Garrod, D. (1939a) 'The Upper Palaeolithic in the light of recent discovery', *Proceedings of the Prehistoric Society* 4: 1–26.

—— (1939b) 'Excavations in the cave of Bacho Kiro. Northeastern Bulgaria', *American School of Prehistoric Research Bulletin* 15: 46–126.

Gatsov, I. (1982) 'The archaeological cultures of the late Pleistocene and early Holocene in the western Black Sea region and their significance for the formation of the Neolithic flint industries', in J.K. Kozłowski (ed.) *Origin of the Chipped Stone Industries of the Early Farming Cultures in the Balkans*, pp. 111–30. Warsaw: Państwowe Wydawnictwo Naukowe.

—— (1984a) 'Technology and typology of cores from the collection "Pobiti Kameni", Dikilitaş, Bulgaria', in J.K. Kozłowski and Kozłowski, S.K. (eds) *Advances in Paleolithic and Mesolithic Archaeology*, pp. 135–51, Warsaw: Archaeologia Interregionalis.

—— (1984b) 'Mestonakhozhdeniya kremnevykh orudij rannegolotsenovogo vremeni v mestnosti Pobite kamuni (Dikilitash)', *Studia Praehistorica* 7: 3–16.

—— (1985) 'Kremuchni ansambli ot neolitnoto selishte Usoeto. Teknikotipologicheska karakteristika', *Sbornik Dobrudzha* 2: 105–16.

—— (1989) 'Early Holocene flint assemblages from the Bulgarian Black Sea coast', in C. Bonsall (ed.) *The Mesolithic in Europe*, pp. 471–4, Edinburgh: John Donald.

—— (1990) 'Le site néolithique d'Oussoe, dépt. de Varna: répartition du matériel en silex par tranchées de fondation: caractéristiques et comparisons des artefacts', *Studia Praehistorica* 10: 91–102.

—— (1992) 'Kremuchen ansambul ot rabotilnitsata', in V. Nikolov (ed.) *Rannoneolitno Zhilishte ot Slatina (Sofiya)*, pp. 99–101, Sofia: Bulgarskata Akademiya na Vaukite.

—— (1993) *Neolithic Chipped Stone Industries in Western Bulgaria*, Kraków: Jagellonian University Press.

—— (1995) 'Flint production from the ninth to the sixth millennium BC', in D.W. Bailey and Panayotov, I. (eds) *Prehistoric Bulgaria*, pp. 73–8, Madison, Wisc.: Prehistory Press.

Gatsov, I. and Kurchatov, V. (1997) 'Neolithische Feuersteinartefakte', in S. Hiller and Nikolov, V. (eds), *Karanovo: Die Ausgrabungen im Südsektor 1984–1992*, pp. 213–38, Horn: Ferdinand Berger and Söhne.

Gatsov, I. and Özdoğan, M. (1994) 'Some epi-paleolithic sites from NW Turkey: Ağaçli, Domali and Gümüşdere', *Anatolica* 20: 97–120.

Gatsov, I, Ginter, B., Kozłowski, J.K., Laville, H., Pawlikowski, M., Sirakov, N., Sirakova, S. and Ferrier, C. (1990) 'Temnata Cave near Karlukovo (Bulgaria) – an important ecological and archaeological sequence in the Northern Balkans (excavations 1984–1985)', *Studia Praehistorica* 10: 7–43.

Gavela, B. (1956–7) 'Eneolitska naselja u Grivcu', *Starinar* 7–8: 227–68.

—— (1960) 'Grivac, eneolitsko naselje', *Starinar* 11: 233.

Georgiev, G.I. (1957) 'Iz zhivota i kulturata na purvite zemedelsko-skotovudni plemena v Bulgariya', *Arkheologicheski Otkritiya v Bulgariya* 1956: 56.

—— (1960) 'Glavni periodi v razvitieto na kulturara prez neolita i mednata epokha v Bulgarija', *Swiatowit* 23: 309–39.

—— (1962) 'Azmashkata mogila kraj Stara Zagora', *Arkheologiya* 4, 1: 59–65.

—— (1963) 'Glavni rezultati ot razkopkite na Azmashkata selishna mogila prez 1961 g.', *Izvestiya na Arkheologicheski Institut* 26: 157–76.

—— (1965) 'The Azmak mound in southern Bulgaria', *Antiquity* 39: 6–8.

—— (1966) 'Mnogoslojnoe poselenie Azmashka mogila bliz Staroj Zagor'i (Bolgariya)', *Kratkie Soobshteniya Instituta Arkheologii, Moskva* 106: 1–10.

—— (1973) 'Die neolitische Kultur in Čavdar und ihre Stellung im Balkan-Neolithikum', in *Actes du VIIIe congrès international des sciences préhistoriques et protohistoriques, Beograd*, vol. 2, pp. 263–72, Belgrade: Union Internationale de Sciences Préhistoriques et Protohistoriques.

—— (1979) 'Choveshkoto obshtestvo prez starokamennata epokha', in V. Velkov, Georgiev, G.I., Danov, Kh., Ivanov, T. and Fol, A. (eds) *Istoriya na Bulgariya. Tom Purvi. Purvobitnoobshtinen i Robovladelski Stroj Traki*, pp. 41–50, Sofia: Bulgarskata Akademiya na Naukite.

—— (1981) 'Das neolithische Siedlung bei Čavdar, bez. Sofia', in G.I. Georgiev and Chichikova, M. (eds) *Culture préhistorique en Bulgarie*, pp. 63–109, Sofia: Bulgarskata Akademiya na Naukite.

Georgiev, G.I., Merpert, N.Ya. and Katincharov, R. (eds) (1979) *Ezero: Rannobronzovoto Selishte*, Sofia: Bulgarskata Akademiya na Naukite.

Georgiev, G.I., Nikolov, V., Nikolova, V. and Chokhadzhiev, S. (1986) Die neolithische Siedlung Kremenik bei Sapareva Banja, Bezirk Kjustendil', *Studia Praehistorica* 8: 108–52.

Gergov, V. (1992a) 'Doistoricheskoe poselenie Telish-Redutite', *Studia Praehistorica* 11–12: 347–57.

—— (1992b) 'Myastoto na selishteto Telish-Redutite v Prekhodniya period kum PBE', *Arkheologiya* 34, 2: 49.

Gergov, V., Gatsov, I. and Sirakov, S. (1985) 'Kremuchni orudiya ot praistoricheskoto selishte v m. Redutite pri s. Telish, Plevenski okrug', *Izvestiya na Muzeite v Severozapadna Bulgariya* 10: 9–25.

307

Gheție, B. and Mateesco, C.N. (1978) 'L'élevage et l'utilisation des animaux pendant le Néolithique moyen à Vădastra (Roumania)', *Zephyrus* 28–9: 135–45.

Gimbutas, M. (1973) 'Old Europe *c*. 7,000–3500 BC: the earliest civilization before the invasion of the Indo-European peoples', *Journal of Indo-European Studies* 1, 1: 1–21.

——— (1974) *The Gods and Goddesses of Old Europe: 7000 to 3500 BC, Myths, Legends and Cult Images*, Berkeley: University of California Press.

——— (ed.) (1976) *Neolithic Macedonia as Reflected by Excavations at Anza*, Los Angeles: UCLA.

——— (1977) 'The first wave of Eurasian steppe pastoralists into Copper Age Europe', *Journal of Indo-European Studies* 5: 277–331.

——— (1982) *The Goddesses and Gods of Old Europe, 6500–3500 BC, Myths and Cult Images*, Berkeley: University of California Press.

——— (1986) 'Mythical imagery of Sitagroi society', in A.C. Renfrew, Gimbutas, M., and Elster, E. (eds) *Excavations at Sitagroi: A Prehistoric Village in Northeast Greece*, vol. 1, pp. 225–89, Los Angeles: UCLA.

——— (1989a) 'Introduction', in M. Gimbutas, Winn, S. and Shimabuku, D. (eds) *Achilleion: A Neolithic Settlement in Thessaly, Greece*, pp. 1–6, Los Angeles: UCLA.

——— (1989b) 'Chronology', in M. Gimbutas, Winn, S. and Shimabuku, D. (eds) *Achilleion: A Neolithic Settlement in Thessaly, Greece*, pp. 23–32, Los Angeles: UCLA.

——— (1989c) 'Figurines and cult equipment: their role in the reconstruction of Neolithic religion', in M. Gimbutas, Winn, S. and Shimabuku, D. (eds) *Achilleion: A Neolithic Settlement in Thessaly, Greece*, pp. 171–250, Los Angeles: UCLA.

——— (1989d) 'Ornaments and miscellaneous objects', in M. Gimbutas, Winn, S. and Shimabuku, D. (eds) *Achilleion: A Neolithic Settlement in Thessaly, Greece*, pp. 251–8, Los Angeles: UCLA.

——— (1991) *The Civilization of the Goddess: The World of Old Europe*, San Francisco, Cal.: Harper Collins.

Gimbutas, M., Winn, S. and Shimabuku, D. (eds) (1989) *Achilleion: A Neolithic Settlement in Thessaly, Greece*, Los Angeles: UCLA.

Ginter, B. and Kozłowski, J.K. (1982) 'Excavation and the stratigraphy of the cave', in J.K. Kozłowski (ed.) *Excavation in the Bacho Kiro Cave (Bulgaria): Final Report*, pp.7–12, Warsaw: Państwowe Wydawnictwo Naukowe.

——— (1992) 'The archaeological sequence', in J.K. Kozłowski, Laville, L. and Ginter, B. (1992) *Temnata Cave: Excavations in Karlukovo Karst Area Bulgaria*, vol. 1(1), pp. 289–94, Kraków: Jagellonian University Press.

Ginter, B., Kozłowski, J.K., Laville, H. and Sirakov, N. (1992) 'Les occupations et les activités humaines dans la séquence gravettienne et épigravettienne', in J.K. Kozłowski, Laville, L. and Ginter, B. (1992) *Temnata Cave: Excavations in Karlukovo Karst Area Bulgaria*, vol. 1(1), pp. 317–35, Kraków: Jagellonian University Press.

Gladilin, V.N. and Demidenko, Yu. E. (1989) 'Korolevo Palaeolithic site: research methods, stratigraphy', *Anthropologie (Brno)* 27, 2–3: 93–103.

Gladilin, V.N. and Sitivyj, V.N. (1990) *Ašel Centralnoj Evropy*, Kiev: Naukova Dumka.

Gleń, E. and Kaczanowski, K. (1982) 'Human remains', in J.K. Kozłowski (ed.) *Excavation in the Bacho Kiro Cave (Bulgaria): Final Report*, pp. 75–80, Warsaw: Państwowe Wydawnictwo Naukowe.

Glumac, P. (1983) 'An archaeometallurgical study of the material from Selevac', *Zbornik Narodnog Muzeja* 11: 135–41.

—— (1985) 'The earliest known copper ornaments from prehistoric Europe', *Ornament* 8: 15–7.

—— (1988) 'Copper mineral finds from Divostin', in McPherron, A. and Srejović, D. (eds) *Divostin and the Neolithic of Central Serbia*, pp. 457–62, Pittsburgh, Penn.: Department of Anthropology, University of Pittsburgh.

Glumac, P. and Todd, J. (1987) 'New evidence for the use of lead in prehistoric south-east Europe', *Archaeomaterials* 2, 1: 123–45.

—— (1991) 'Eneolithic copper smelting slags from the middle Danube basin', in E. Pernicka and G.A. Wagner (eds) *Archaeometry 90*, pp. 155–64, Basel: Birkhäuser.

Glumac, P. and Tringham, R. (1990) 'The exploitation of copper minerals', in R.E. Tringham and Krstić, D. (eds) *Selevac: A Neolithic Village in Yugoslavia*, pp. 549–66, Los Angeles: UCLA.

Grammenos, D.V. (1991) *Neolithikes Hereunes stin Kentiki kai anatoliki Makedonia*, Athens: Athens Archaeological Society.

—— (in press) *Neolithika Themata apo ti Makedonia kai tin Euruteri Periokhi*, Athens: Tameion Archeologikon Poron.

Grammenos, D.V, Pappa, M., Ourem-Kotsos, K., Skourtopoulu, E., Giannouli, E. and Tsigarida, B. (1990) 'Anaskaphi neolithhikou oikismou Thermis, 1987', *Makedonika* 27: 223–87.

—— (1992) 'Anaskaphi neolithhikou oikismou Thermis B kai buzantinis enkatastasis para ton proistoriko oikismo Thermi A', *Makedonika* 28: 381–501.

Grbić, M., Mačkić, S., Nadj, B., Simoska, D. and Stalio, D. (1960) *Porodin, Kasnoneolitsko Naseleje na Tumbi kod Bitolja*, Bitolj.

Greenfield, H.J. (1988) 'The origins of milk and wool production in the Old World: a zooarchaeological perspective from the central Balkans', *Current Anthropology* 29: 573–93.

Gregg, S.A. (1988) *Foragers and Farmers: Population Interaction and Agricultural Expansion in Prehistoric Europe*, Chicago, Ill.: University of Chicago Press.

Haaland, G. and Haaland, R. (1996) 'Levels of meaning in symbolic objects', *Cambridge Archaeological Journal* 6, 2: 295–300.

Hahn, J. (1972) 'Aurignacian signs, pendents and art objects in central and eastern Europe', *World Archaeology* 3: 252–66.

—— (1987) 'Aurignacian and Gravettian settlement patterns in central Europe', in O. Soffer (ed.) *The Pleistocene Old World: Regional Perspectives*, pp. 251–61, New York: Plenum.

Haesaerts, P. and Sirakova, S. (1979) 'Le Paléolithique moyen à pointes foliacées de Mousselievo (Bulgarie)', *Prace Archeologiczne* 28: 3–65.

Haimovici, S. and Dardan, G. (1970) 'Studiul resturilor de faună orivenite din aşezarea neolitică de la Luncaviţa (jud. Tulcea)', *Materiale* 9: 107–11.

Haimovici, S. and Gheorghiu, G. (1969) 'Sur quelques traits de la faune subfossile découverte par les fouilles executées dans la station de Luncaviţa', *Agigea* 3: 337–43.

Halescu, C. (1986) 'Tezaurul de aur descoperit la Sultana, jud. Calarasi', unpublished paper delivered at the 15th Colloque de l'Institut d'Archéologie, Bucureşti, 2 December, 1986.

Halstead, P. (1981) 'Counting sheep in Neolithic and Bronze Age Greece', in I. Hodder, Isaac, G. and Hammond, N. (eds) *Pattern of the Past: Studies in Honour of David Clarke*, pp. 307–39, Cambridge: Cambridge University Press.

—— (1984) 'Strategies for survival: an ecological approach to social and economic change in the early farming communities of Thessaly, N. Greece', unpublished PhD dissertation, University of Cambridge.

—— (1987) 'Traditional and ancient rural economy in Mediterranean Europe: plus ça change?', *Journal of Hellenic Studies* 107: 77–87.

—— (1989a) 'Like rising damp? An ecological approach to the spread of farming in southeast and central Europe', in A. Milles, Williams, D. and Gardner, N. (eds) *The Beginnings of Agriculture*, pp. 23–53. Oxford: British Archaeological Reports.

—— (1989b) 'The economy has a normal surplus: economic stability and social change among early farming communities of Thessaly, Greece', in P. Halstead and O'Shea, J. (eds) *Bad Year Economics: Cultural Responses to Risk and Uncertainty*, pp. 68–80, Cambridge: Cambridge University Press.

—— (1992a) 'Dimini and the "DMP": faunal remains and animal exploitation in late Neolithic Thessaly', *Annual of the British School at Athens* 87: 44–55.

—— (1992b) 'From reciprocity to redistribution: modelling the exchange of livestock in neolithic Greece', *Anthropologica* 16: 19–31.

—— (1993) '*Spondylus* shell ornaments from late Neolithic Dimini, Greece: specialised manufacture or unequal accumulation?', *Antiquity* 67: 603–9.

—— (1994) 'The north-south divide: regional paths to complexity in prehistoric Greece', in C. Mathers and Stoddart, S. (eds) *Development and Decline in the Mediterranean Bronze Age*, pp. 195–219, Sheffield: J.R. Collis.

—— (1995) 'From sharing to hoarding: the Neolithic foundations of Aegean Bronze Age Society?', in R. Laffineur and Niemeier, W.-D. (eds) *Politeia: Society and State in the Aegean Bronze Age*, pp. 11–22, Liège: University of Liège.

Hamilton, N. (1996) 'The personal is political', *Cambridge Archaeological Journal* 6, 2: 282–5.

Handsman, R.G. (1991) 'Whose art was found at Lepenski Vir? Gender relations and power in archeology', in J.M. Gero and Conkey, M.W. (eds) *Engendering Archaeology: Women and Prehistory*, pp. 329–65, Oxford: Blackwell.

Hansen, J.M. (1991) *The Palaeoethnobotany of Franchthi Cave*, Bloomington, Ind.: Indiana University Press.

Harding, A. (1983) 'The regional context of the Bulgarian Bronze Age', in A. Poulter (ed.) *Ancient Bulgaria*, pp. 164–80, Nottingham: Department of Archaeology, University of Nottingham.

Hartmann, A. (1978) 'Ergebnisse der spektralanalytischen Untersuchung äneolithishcher Goldfunde aus Bulgarien', *Studia Praehistorische* 1–2: 27–45.

Harţuche, N. (1979) 'Necropola de la Brăiliţa. Contribuţii la problemele Eneoliticului final şi Trecerea la epoca bronzului tracic la Dunărea de Jos', unpublished PhD dissertation, Bucureşti.

Haşotti, P. (1984) 'Noi date privind difuziunea comunităţilor Hamangia', *Pontica* 17: 25–36.

—— (1986) 'Observaţii asupra ceramicii dintr-un complex al culturii Hamangia de la Medgidia-Cocoaşă', *Studii şi Cercetări de Istorie Veche şi Arheologie* 37: 119–31.

—— (1987) 'Sondajele din aşezarea culturii Hamangia de la Medgidia – Satu Nou', *Pontica* 20: 19–42.

—— (1997) *Epoca Neolitică în Dobrogea*, Constanţă Muzeul de Istorie Naţională şi Arheologie.

Hayden, B. (1995) 'The emergence of prestige technologies and pottery', in W. Barnett and Hoopes, J. (eds) *The Emergence of Pottery*, pp. 257–65, Washington: Smithsonian Institution.

Hegedüs, K. (1982–3) 'The settlement of the Neolithic Szakálhát-group at Csanytelek Újhalastő, A *Móra Ferenc Múzeum Évkönyve* 1982–3, 1: 7–54.

Hegedüs, K. and Makkay, J. (1987) 'Vésztő-Mágor: a settlement of the Tisza culture', in P. Raczky and Tálas, L. (eds) *The Late Neolithic of the Tisza Region*, pp. 85–103, Budapest: Akaémiai Kiadó.

Hellström, P. (1987) *Paradeisos: A Late Neolithic Settlement in Aegean Thrace*, Stockholm: Medelhavsmuseet.

Henning, G.J., Herr, W., Weber, E. and Xirotiris, N.I. (1981) 'ESR-dating of the fossil hominid cranium from Petralona Cave, Greece', *Nature* 292: 533–6.

—— (1982) 'Petralona Cave dating controversy', *Nature* 299: 281–2.

Higgs, E. (1962) 'The fauna of the early Neolithic site at Nea Nikomedeia, Greek Macedonia', *Proceedings of the Prehistoric Society* 28: 271–74.

Hiller, S. (1997a) 'Forschungszeile. Grabungsverlauf. Stratigraphie', in S. Hiller and Nikolov, V. (eds) *Karanovo: Die Ausgrabungen im Südsektor 1984–1992*, pp. 19–48, Horn: Ferdinand Berger and Söhne.

—— (1997b) 'Architektur', in S. Hiller and Nikolov, V. (eds) *Karanovo. Die Ausgrabungen im Südsektor 1984–1992*, pp. 55–92, Horn: Ferdinand Berger and Söhne.

Hiller, S. and Nikolov, V. (eds) (1997) *Karanovo: Die Ausgrabungen im Südsektor 1984–1992*, Horn: Ferdinand Berger and Söhne.

Hodder, I. (1990) *The Domestication of Europe*, Oxford: Blackwell.

Honea, K. (1975) Prehistoric remains on the island of Kynthnos', *American Journal of Archaeology* 79: 277–9.

—— (1984a) 'Chronometry of the Romanian Middle and Upper Palaeolithic: implications of current radiocarbon dating results,' *Dacia* 28, 1–2: 23–39.

—— (1984b) 'Cronologia paleoliticului mijlociu şi superior in România. Implicaţiile rezultatelor actuale ale datării cu carbon radioactiv', *Revista Muzeelor şi Monumentelor, Bucureşti* 3: 59–68.

—— (1989) 'Dating and periodization strategies of the Romanian middle and upper Palaeolithic: a retrospective overview and assessment', in O. Soffer (ed.) *Pleistocene Perspective*, pp. 36–41, London: Unwin Allen.

Hopf, M. (1975) 'Rastitelni nakhodki ot selishtnata mogila pri Golyamo Delchevo', in H. Todorova, Ivanov, S., Vasilev, V., Hopf, M., Quitta, H. and Kohl, G. *Selishtnata Mogila pri Golyamo Delchevo*, pp. 303–24, Sofia: Bulgarskata Akademiya na Naukite.

—— (1988) 'Früneolithische Kulturpflanzen aus Poljanica-plateau bei Targovište (Bulgarien)', *Studia Praehistorica* 9: 34–7.

Horedt, K. (1977) 'Der Goldfund von Moigrad', *Germania* 55: 1, 2: 7.

Horváth, F. (1983) 'A fejlődés megtorpanása', *Szeged Története* 1, pp. 62–6.

—— (1986) 'Late Neolithic ditches, fortifications and tells in the Hungarian Tisza-region', in Tasić, N. and Petrović, J. (eds) *Gomolava – Chronologie und Stratigraphie der vorgeschichtlichen und antiken Kulturen der Donauniederung und Südosteuropas*, pp. 123–45, Novi Sad: Institut za Izučavanje Istorije Vojvodine i Savez Arheoloških Društava Jugoslavije.

—— (1987) 'Hódmezővásárhely-Gorzsa. A settlement of the Tisza culture', in P. Raczky and Tálas, L. (eds) *The Late Neolithic of the Tisza Region*, pp. 31–46, Budapest: Akadémiai Kiadó.

—— (1989) 'A survey on the development of Neolithic settlement pattern and house types in the Tisza region', in S. Bökönyi (ed.) *Neolithic of Southeastern Europe and its Near Eastern Connections*, pp. 85–101, Budapest: Instituti Archaeologici Academiae Scientiarum Hungaricae Budapestini.

Hourmouziadis, G.H. (1971) 'Dio neai egkatastaseis tis archaioteras Neolithikis eis tin dytikin Thessalian', *Athens Annals of Archaeology* 4, 2: 164–75.

—— (1973) 'Burial customs', in D. Theocharis (ed.) *Neolithic Greece*, pp. 210–12, Athens: National Bank of Greece.

—— (1974) *I Anthropomorphi Eidoloplastiki tis Neolithikis Thessalias*, Athens: Etaireia Thessalikon Erevnon.

—— (1979a) *To Neolithiko Dimini*, Athens: Etaireia Thessalikon Erevnon.

—— (1979b) 'Eisagogi stis ideologies tis ellinikis proistorias', *Politis* 17: 33.

—— (1982) *Arxaia Magnisia: Apo tis Palaiolothikes spilies sto Anaktoro tis Dimitriadas*, Athens: Tameion Archeologikon Poron.

Howell, F.C. (1989) 'Yarimburgaz un nouveau site du Pléistocène moyen à occupation humaine dans l'Ouest de la Turquie (Résumé)', in E. Bonifay and Vandermeersch, B. (eds) *Les Premiers Européens*, pp. 233–4, Paris: CTHS.

Hunter-Anderson, R.L. (1977) 'A theoretical approach to the study of house form', in L.R. Binford (ed.) *For Theory Building in Archaeology*, pp. 287–315, London: Academic Press.

Huttunen, A., Huttunen, R., Vasari, R., Panovska, H. and Bozilova, E. (1992) 'Late-glacial and Holocene history of flora and vegetation in the western Rhodopes mountains, Bulgaria', *Acta Botanica Fennica* 144: 63–80.

Ilcheva, V. (1982) 'Archeologicheski razkopki na praistoricheskoto selishte v m. Vodopada, krai s. Hotnitsa, Velikotarnovski okr.', *Arkheologicheski Otkritiya i Razkopki za 1981, Mikhailovgrad.*

—— (1986) 'Neue Metallfunde aus der prähistorischen Siedlung Hotnitsa-Wasserfall (Hotniza-Vodopada)', *Studia Praehistorica* 8: 212–16.

—— (1987) 'Razkopki na praistoricheskoto selishte Hotnitsa-Vodopada, Velikotarnovski okr.', *Arkheologicheski Otkritiya i Razkopki za 1986, Razgrad.*

—— (1989a) 'Vkopani peshti-tandiri ot praistoricheskoto selishte Hotnitsa-Vodopada', *Arkheologiya* 30, 3: 20–7.

—— (1989b) 'Arkheologicheski razkopki na praistoricheskoto selishte Hotnitsa-Vodopada, Velikotarnovska obshtina, prez 1988 g.', *Arkheologicheski Otkritiya i Razkopki za 1988, Kurdzhali.*

—— (1990) 'Razkopki na praistoricheskoto selishte Hotnitsa-Vodopada prez 1989 g.', *Arkheologicheski Otkritiya i Razkopki za 1981, Kyustendil.*

Ingold, T. (1980) *Hunters, Pastoralists and Ranchers*, Cambridge: Cambridge University Press.

Iskra-Janošić, I. (1977) 'Cibala – Vinkovci. Zaštitni radovi. Nama', *Arheološki Pregled* 19: 12.

—— (1984) 'Arheološka istraživanja na prostoru općine Vinkovci', in Majnarić-Pandžić, N. (ed.) *Arheološka Istraživanja u Istočnoj Slavoniji i Baranji, Znanstveni Skup*, pp. 143–52, Zagreb: Hrvatsko Arheološko Društvo.

Ivanov, I. (1972) 'Grobove ot bronzovata epokha', *Izvestiya na Narodniya Muzej Varna* 8: 250–3.

—— (1978a) 'Les fouilles archéologiques de la nécropole chalcolithique à Varna', *Studia Praehistorica* 1–2: 1–26.

—— (1978b) 'Rannokhalkolitni grobove do grad Varna', *Izvestiya na Narodniya Muzej Varna* 14: 81–93.

—— (1983) 'Le chalcolithique en Bulgarie et dans la nécropole de Varna', in A.G. Poulter (ed.) *Ancient Bulgaria* vol. 1, pp. 154–63, Nottingham: University of Nottingham, Department of Archaeology.

—— (1988a) 'Die Ausgrabungen des Gräberfeldes von Varna', in A. Fol and Lichardus, J. (eds) *Macht, Herrschaft und Gold: Das Gräberfeld von Varna und die Anfänge einer neuen europäischen Zivilisation*, pp. 49–66, Saarbrücken: Moderne Galerie des Saarland-Museums.

—— (1988b) 'Das Gräberfeldes von Varna – Katalog', in Fol, A. and Lichardus, J. (eds) (1988) *Macht, Herrschaft und Gold: Das Gräberfeld von Varna und die Anfänge einer neuen europäischen Zivilisation*, pp. 183–208, Saarbrücken: Moderne Galerie des Saarland-Museums.

Ivanov, S. and Vasilev, V. (1975) 'Prouchvaniya na zhivotinskya kosten material ot praistoricheskata selishtna mogila pri Golyamo Delchevo', in H. Todorova, Ivanov, S., Vasilev, V., Hopf, M., Quitta, H. and Kohl, G. (eds) *Selishtnata Mogila pri Golyamo Delchevo*, pp. 245–302, Sofia: Bulgarskata Akademiya na Naukite.

Ivanov, T.G. (1978) 'O nekotor'kh storonakh pogrebal'nogo obryada i pred-stavleniyakh o zagrobnom mire vo vremya neolita i khalkolita v Bolgarii', *Studia Praehistorica* 1–2: 157–162.

—— (1982) 'Tell Radingrad', in H. Todorova (ed.) *Die kupferzeitliche Siedlungen in Nordostbulgarien*, pp. 166–74, Munich: C.H. Beck.

—— (1984) 'Mnogoslojnoe poselenie u s. Radingrad, Razgradskogo rajona', *Studia Praehistorica* 7: 81–98.

Ivanova, S. (1979) 'Cultural differentiation in the Middle Palaeolithic on the Balkan peninsula', *Prace Archeologiczne* 28: 13–33

—— (1987) 'Le Paléolithique supérieur de Tchoutchoura dans les Monts Rhodopes (Bulgarie)', *L'Anthropologie* 91, 1: 241–54.

Ivanova, S. and Gatsov, I. (1985) 'Kusnopaleolitno nakhdishte ot kraya na plejs-totsena v okolnostite na khizha "Orpheij" – sredni Rhodopi', *Izvestiya na Muzeite v Yuzhna Bulgariya* 11: 65–76.

Ivanova, S. and Sirakova, S. (1995) 'Chronology and cultures of the Bulgarian Palaeolithic', in D.W. Bailey and Panayotov, I. (eds) *Prehistoric Bulgaria*, pp. 9–54, Madison, Wisc.: Prehistory Press.

Jacobsen, T. (1969) 'Excavations at Porto Cheli and vicinity, preliminary report, II: the Franchthi Cave 1967–1968', *Hesperia* 38: 343–81.

—— (1973) 'Excavation in the Franchthi Cave, 1969–1971. Part I', *Hesperia* 42: 45–88.

—— (1981) 'The Franchthi Cave and the beginnings of settled life in Greece', *Hesperia* 50: 303–19.

Jacobsen, T. and Cullen, T. (1981) 'A consideration of mortuary practices in Neolithic Greece: burials from Franchthi Cave', in S.C. Humphreys and King, H. (eds) *Mortality and Immortality: The Anthropology and Archaeology of Death*, pp. 79–101, London: Academic.

Jacobsen, T. and Farrand, W.R. (1988) *Franchthi Cave and Paralia: Maps, Plans and Sections*, Bloomington, Ind.: Indiana University Press.

Jamet, M. (1982) 'Étude netectonique de Corfou et étude paléomagnetique de sédiments néogènes des ilex de Corfou, Cephalonie et Zanthe', unpublished dissertation, Université de Paris-Sud.

Jochim, M. (1987) 'Late Pleistocene refugia in Europe', in O. Soffer (ed.) *The Pleistocene Old World: Regional Perspectives*, pp. 317–31, New York: Plenum.

Jovanović, B. (1966) 'Hajdučka Vodenica – praistorijsko nalažiste', *Arheološki Pregled* 8: 102–3.

—— (1969) 'Chronological frames of the Iron Gate group of the early Neolithic period', *Archaeologia Iugoslavica* 10: 23–38.

—— (1974) 'Praistorija gornjeg Djerdapa', *Starinar* 22: 1–22.

—— (1982) *Rudna Glava: Najstarije Rudarstvo Bakra na Centralnom Balkanu*, Belgrade: Jugoslav Academy of Sciences.

—— (1984a) 'Hajdučka vodenica, praistorijska nekropola', *Starinar* 33–4: 305–12.

—— (1984b) 'Padina, naselje mezolita i starijeg neolita', *Starinar* 33–4: 159–66.

Jovanović, B. and Glišic, J. (1960) 'Station énéolithique dans la localitié de Kormadin', *Starinar* 11: 113–42.

Jurišić, A. (1960) 'Gradine Zapadne Srbijé, *Arheološko Društvo Jugoslavije, Praistoriska Sekcja*, Ohrid 1: 91–8.

Kaczanowski, M., Kozłowski, J.K. and Makkay, J. (1981) 'Flint hoards from Endrőd, site 39, Hungary (Körös culture)', *Acta Archaeologica Carpathica* 21: 105–17.

Kaiser, T. (1990) 'Ceramic technology', in R.E. Tringham and Krštić, D. (eds) *Selevac: A Neolithic Village in Yugoslavia*, pp. 255–89, Los Angeles: UCLA.

Kaiser, T. and Voytek, B. (1983) 'Sedentism and economic change in the Balkan Neolithic', *Journal of Anthropological Archaeology* 2: 323–53.

Kalicz, N. (1957) 'Tiszazug őskori települései', *Régészeti Füzetek* 8: 1–97.

—— (1970) *Clay Gods: The Neolithic Period and Copper Age in Hungary*, Budapest: Corvina Press.

—— (1976) 'Eine neues kupferzeitliches Wagenmodell aus der Umgebung von Budapest', in H. Mitscha-Marheim, Friesinger, H, and Kerchler, H. (eds) *Festschrift für Richard Pittioni zum siebzigen Geburtstag*, pp. 186–202, Vienna: Deuticke

—— (1983) 'Die Körös-Starčevo-Kulturen und ihre Bezeihungen zur Linearbandkeramik', *Nachrichten aus Niedersachsens Urgeschichte* 52: 91–130.

Kalicz, N. and Makkay, J. (1977) *Die Linienbandkeramik in der Grossen Ungarischen Tiefebene*, Budapest: Akadémiai Kiadó.

Kalicz, N. and Raczky, P. (1980–1) 'Siedlung der Körös-Kultur in Szolnok-Szanda', *Mitteilungen des Archäologischen Instituts der Ungarischen Akademie der Wissenschaften* 10–11: 13–24.

—— (1984) 'Preliminary report on the 1977–1982 excavations at the Neolithic and Bronze Age tell settlement of Berettyóújfalu-Herpály, part I', *Acta Archaeologica Academiae Scientiarum Hungaricae* 36: 85–136.

—— (1987) 'Berettyóújfalu-Herpály: a settlement of the Herpály culture', in P. Raczky (ed.) *The Late Neolithic of the Tisza Region*, pp. 105–25, Budapest: Akaémiai Kiadó.

Katincharov, R. (1980) 'Les rites funéraires pendant l'âge du bronze en Bulgarie', *Thracia* 5: 167–72.

Katincharov, R. and Matsanova, V. (1993) 'Razkopki na selishnata mogila pri s. Yunatsite, Pazardzhisko', in V. Nikolov (ed.) *Praistoricheski Nakhodki i Izsledvaniya. Sbornik v Pamet na Prof. Georgi I. Georgiev*, pp. 155–73, Sofia: Bulgarskata Akademiya na Vaukite.

—— (1995) 'The tell near the village of Yunatsite, Pazardjik district', *Reports of Prehistoric Research Projects* 1, 1: 11–14.

Katincharov, R., Merpert, N., Titov, V., Matsanova, V. and Avilova, L. (1995) *Selishtna Mogila pri Selo Yunatsite (Pazardzhishko)*, vol. 1, Sofia: Agato.

Keighley, J.M. (1986) 'The pottery of phases I and II', in A.C. Renfrew, Gimbutas, M., and Elster, E. (eds) *Excavations at Sitagroi: A Prehistoric Village in Northeast Greece*, vol. 1, pp. 345–92, Los Angeles: UCLA.

Kertész, R. (1996) 'The Mesolithic in the Great Hungarian Plain', in Tálas, L. (ed.) *At the Fringes of the Three Worlds: Hunter-gatherers and Farmers in the Middle Tisza Valley*, pp. 5–34, Budapest: Akadémiai Kiadó.

Kitov, G., Panayotov, I. and Pavlov, P. (1991) *Mogilni Nekropoli v Loveshkiya kraj. Ranna Bronzova Epokha (Nekropolut Goran-Slatina)*, Sofia: Bulgarskata Akademiya na Naukite.

Kokkinidou, D. and Nikolaidou, M. (1997) 'Body imagery in the Aegean Neolithic: ideological implications of anthropomorphic figurines', in J. Moore and Scott, E. (eds) *Invisible People and Processes: Writing Gender and Childhood into European Archaeology*, pp. 88–112, Leicester: Leicester University Press.

Korek, J. (1951) 'Ein Gräberfeld der Badener Kultur bei Alsónémedi', *Acta Archaeologica Academiae Scientiarum Hungaricae* 1: 35–51.

—— (1987) 'Szegvár-Tüzköves. A settlement of the Tisza culture', in P. Raczky and Tálas, L. (eds) *The Late Neolithic of the Tisza Region*, pp. 47–60, Budapest: Akadémiai Kiadó.

Kosse, K. (1979) *Settlement Ecology of the Körös and Linear Pottery Cultures in Hungary*, Oxford: British Archaeological Reports.

Kotsakis, K. (1981) 'Tria oikimata tou oikismou tou sesklou. Anaskafiki ereuna', *Anthropologika* 2: 87–108.

—— (1982) 'Kerameike tehnologia kai kerameike diaphoropoisesei: problemata tes gramptes kerameikis tes meses Neolithikis Epochis tou Sesklou', unpublished PhD dissertation, University of Thessaloniki.

—— (1995) 'The use of habitational space in Neolithic Sesklo', in J.C. Decourt, Helly, B and Gallis, K. (eds) *La Thessalie, Colloque international d'archéologie: 15 années de recherches (1975–1990), bilans et perspectives*, pp. 125–30. Athens: Tameion Archeologikon Poron.

Kotsos, S. (1992) 'Anaskafi neolithikou oikismou sti biomihaniki periohi Drosias-Edessas', *To Arhaiologiko Ergo sti Makedonia kai Thraki* 6: 195–202.

Koukouli-Chrysanthaki, H. (1993) 'Dikili Tash', *To Ergon tis Arxaiologikis* 1993: 68–75.

Kowalski, K. (1982) 'Animal remains: general remarks', in J.K. Kozłowski (ed.) *Excavation in the Bacho Kiro Cave (Bulgaria): Final Report*, pp. 66–74, Warsaw: Państwowe Wydawnictwo Naukowe.

Kozłowksi, J.K. (1975) 'Badania nad przejšciem od środkowego do górnego pale-olitu na Balkanach', *Przeglad Archeologiczke* 23: 5–48.

—— (1979) 'Le Bachokirien – La plus ancienne industrie de Paléolithique supérieur en Europe', *Prace Archeologiczne* 28: 77–89.

—— (ed.) (1982a) *Excavation in the Bacho Kiro Cave (Bulgaria): Final Report*, Warsaw: Państwowe Wydawnictwo Naukowe.

—— (1982b) 'La néolithisation de la zone Balkano-Danubienne de point de vue des industries lithiques', *Prace Archeologiczne* 33: 131–70.

—— (1984) 'Earliest Upper Palaeolithic habitation structures from Bacho Kiro Cave', in H. Berke, Hahn, J. and Kind, C.-L. (eds) *Jungpaläolithische Siedlungsstrukturen in Europa*, pp. 109–28, Tübingen: Verlag Archaeologica Venatoria.

—— (1988) 'Transition from the Middle to the early Upper Palaeolithic in central Europe and the Balkans', in J.F. Hoffecker and Wolf, C.A. (eds) *The Early Upper Palaeolithic: Evidence from Europe and the Near East*, pp. 193–236, Oxford: British Archaeological Reports.

—— (1989) 'The neolithization of southeastern Europe: an alternative approach', in S. Bökönyi (ed.) *Neolithic of Southeastern Europe and its Near Eastern Connections*, pp. 131–48, Budapest: Instituti Archaeologici Academiae Scientiarum Hungaricae Budapestini.

—— (1992) 'The Balkans in the Middle and Upper Palaeolithic: the gate to Europe or a cul-de-sac?', *Proceedings of the Prehistoric Society* 58: 1–20.

Kozłowski, J.K. and Kozłowski, S.K. (1979) *Upper Palaeolithic and Mesolithic in Europe: Taxonomy and Palaeohistory*, Warsaw: Polskiej Akademii Nauk.

Kozłowski, J.K. and Sirakov, N. (1974) 'Stanowiski środkowego paleolitu w Dewni pod Warna (Bulgaria)', *Sprawozdanie Archaeologizne* 26: 11–29.

Kozłowski, J.K., Dagnan-Ginter, A., Gatsov, I. and Sirakova, S. (1982) 'Upper Palaeolithic assemblages', in J.K. Kozłowski (ed.) *Excavation in the Bacho Kiro Cave (Bulgaria): Final Report*, pp. 119–67, Warsaw: Państwowe Wydawnictwo Naukowe.

Kozłowski, J.K., Laville, H. and Sirakov, N. (1989) 'Une nouvelle séquence géologique et archéologique dans les Balkans: la Grotte Temnata à Karlukovo (Bulgarie du Sud)', *L'Anthropologie* 93, 1: 159–72.

Kozłowski, J.K., Laville, H. and Ginter, B. (1992) *Temnata Cave: Excavations in Karlukovo Karst Area Bulgaria*, vol. 1(1), Kraków: Jagellonian University Press.

Kozłowski, J.K., Laville, H. and Ginter, B. (1994) *Temnata Cave: Excavations in Karlukovo Karst Area, Bulgaria*, vol. 1(2). Kraków: Jagellonian University Press.

Kozłowski, S. (1988) 'The pre-neolithic base of the early Neolithic stone industries in Europe', in J.K. Kozłowski and Kozłowski, S.K. (eds) *Chipped Stone Industries of the Early Farming Cultures in Europe*, pp. 9–18, Warsaw: Archaeologia Interregionalis.

Kraft, J.C. and Rapp, G.J. (1975) 'Late Holocene paleogeography of the coastal plain of the the Gulf of Messenia, Greece, and its relationships to archeological settings and coastal change', *Geological Society of America Bulletin* 86: 1191–1208.

Kraft, J.C., Aschenbrenner, S.E. and Rapp, G.J. (1977) 'Palaeogeographic reconstructions of coastal Aegean archaeological sites', *Science* 195: 941–47.

Kraft, J.C., Kayan, I. and Erol, D. (1992) 'Un site du Néolithique ancien près du village Kovačevo', *Studia Praehistorica* 11–2: 62–7.

Kretzoi, M. and Dobosi, V. (eds) (1990) *Vértesszölös: Man, Site and Culture*, Budapest: Akaémiai Kiadó.

Kroll, H. (1981) 'Thessalische Kulturpflanzen', *Zeitschrift für Archäologie* 15: 97.

—— (1991) 'Südosteuropa', in W. van Zeist, Wasylikowa, K. and Behre, K.-E. (eds) *Progress in Old World Palaeoethnobotany*, pp. 161–77, Rotterdam: Brill.

Krustev, K. (1987) 'Composition of native gold from some alluvial places in south west Bulgaria', *Review of the Bulgarian Geological Society* 48, 2: 87–94.

Kubiak, H. and Nadachowski, A. (1982) 'Artiodactyla', in J.K. Kozłowski (ed.) *Excavation in the Bacho Kiro Cave (Bulgaria): Final Report*, pp. 61–5, Warsaw: Państwowe Wydawnictwo Naukowe.

Kutzián, I. (1944) *The Körös Culture: Dissertationes Pannonicae 23*, Budapest: Universitatis de Petro Pazmany Nominatae Budapestinensis Provenientes.

Kyparissi-Apostolika, N. (1995) 'Prehistoric inhabitation in Theopetra Cave, Thessaly', in J.C. Decourt, B. Helly and K. Gallis (eds) *La Thessalie, Colloque international d'archéologie: 15 années de recherches (1975–1990), bilans et perspectives*, pp. 103–8, Athens: Tameion Archaeologikon Poron.

Lambeck, K. (1995) 'Late Pleistocene and Holocene sea-level change in Greece and southwestern Turkey: a separation of eustatic, isostatic and tectonic contributions', *Geophysical Journal International* 122: 1022–44.

—— (1996) 'Sea-level change and shore-line evolution in Aegean Greece since Upper Palaeolithic time', *Antiquity* 70: 588–611.

Larje, R. (1987) 'Animal bones', in P. Hellström (ed.) *Paradeisos: A Late Neolithic Settlement in Aegean Thrace*, pp. 89–118, Stockholm: Medelhavsmuseet.

Lazarovici, Gh. (1970) 'Cultura Vinča în Banat', *Acta Musei Napocensis* 7: 473–88.

—— (1979) *Neoliticul Banatului*, Cluj-Napoca: Muzeul de Istorie de Transylvaniei.

Laville, H., Delpeche, F., Ferrier, C., Guadelli, J-L., Marambat, L., Pazdur, M. and Popov, V.V. (1994) 'Le cadre chronologique et paléoenvironnemental des occupations gravettiennes et épigravettiennes', in J.K. Kozłowski, Laville, H. and Ginter, B. (eds) *Temnata Cave: Excavations in Karlukovo Karst Area Bulgaria*, vol. 1(2), pp. 315–26, Kraków: Jagellonian University Press.

Lăzurcă, E. (1980) 'Raport asupra noilor cercetări arheologice de la Baia (Hamangia), jud. Tulcea', *Peuce* 10: 13–19.

Leahu, V. (1963) 'Sapaturile arheologice de salvare de la Giulesti Sîrbi', *Cercetări Arheologice î Bucuresti* 1: 123–45.

Legge, A.J. (1990) 'Animals, economy and environment', in R.E. Tringham and Krstić, D. (eds) *Selevac: A Neolithic Village in Yugoslavia*, pp. 215–236, Los Angeles: UCLA.

Leković, V. (1985) 'The Starčevo mortuary practices', *Godišnjak* 23: 157–72.

—— (1988a) 'Šašinci', in D. Srejović (ed.) *Neolithic of Serbia: Archaeological Research 1948–1988*, pp. 94–5, Belgrade: University of Belgrade.

—— (1988b) 'Zlatara-Ruma', in D. Srejović (ed.) *Neolithic of Serbia: Archaeological Research 1948–1988*, pp. 108–9, Belgrade: University of Belgrade.

Leroi-Gourhan, A. (1964) 'Découvertes paléolithiques en Elide', *Bulletin correspondance hellénique* 88: 1–8.

Leshtakov, K. (in press) 'Spasitelni razkopki na obekt Tsiganova mogila 1993', *Arkheologiya*.

Letica, Z. (1988) 'Anthropomorphic and zoomorphic figurines from Divostin', in A. McPherron and Srejović, D. (eds) *Divostin and the Neolithic of Central Serbia*, pp. 173–201, Pittsburgh, Penn.: Department of Anthropology, University of Pittsburgh.

Levine, M. (1990) 'Dereivka and the problem of horse domestication', *Antiquity* 64: 727–40.

Lieberman, D.E. (1993) The rise and fall of seasonal mobility among hunter-gatherers: the case for the southern Levant', *Current Anthropology* 34: 599–631.

Lisitsyna, G.N. and Filopovich, L.A. (1980) 'Paleoethnobotanicheskie nakhokki na Balkanskom polostrove', *Studia Praehistorica* 4: 5–90.

Longacre, W.A. (1995) 'Why did they invent pottery anyway?', in W. Barnett and Hoopes, J. (eds) *The Emergence of Pottery*, pp. 277–80, Washington: Smithsonian Institution.

Lyneis, M.M. (1988) 'Antler and bone artefacts from Divostin', in A. McPherron and Srejović, D. (eds) *Divostin and the Neolithic of Central Serbia*, pp. 301–244, Pittsburgh, Penn.: Department of Anthropology, University of Pittsburgh.

McGeehan-Liritzis, V. and Gale, N.H. (1988) 'Chemical and lead isotope analysis of Greek late Neolithic and early Bronze Age metals', *Archaeometry* 30: 201–230.

McPherron, A. (1988a) 'Introduction', in A. McPherron and Srejović D. (eds), *Divostin and the Neolithic of Central Serbia*, pp. 1–94, Pittsburgh, Penn.: Department of Anthropology, University of Pittsburgh.

—— (1988b) 'Miscellaneous small artifacts', in A. McPherron and Srejović, D. (eds) *Divostin and the Neolithic of Central Serbia*, pp. 315–26, Pittsburgh, Penn.: Department of Anthropology, University of Pittsburgh.

McPherron, A. and Christopher, K.C. (1988) 'The Balkan Neolithic and the Divostin project in perspective', in A. McPherron and Srejović, D. (eds) *Divostin and the Neolithic of Central Serbia*, pp. 463–89, Pittsburgh, Penn.: Department of Anthropology, University of Pittsburgh.

McPherron, A. and Gunn, J. (1988) 'Quantitative analysis of excavated materials at Divostin', in A. McPherron and Srejović, D. (eds) *Divostin and the Neolithic of Central Serbia*, pp. 359–78, Pittsburgh, Penn.: Department of Anthropology, University of Pittsburgh.

McPherron, A. and Srejović, D. (eds) (1988) *Divostin and the Neolithic of Central Serbia*, Pittsburgh, Penn.: Department of Anthropology, University of Pittsburgh.

McPherron, A., Aitken, M.J. and Bucha, V. (1988) 'Absolute dating of Divostin, Grivac-Barice and Banja', in A. McPherron and Srejović, D. (eds) *Divostin and the Neolithic of Central Serbia*, pp. 379–88, Pittsburgh, Penn.: Department of Anthropology, University of Pittsburgh.

McPherron, A., Rasson, J. and Galdikas, B. (1988b) 'Other artifact categories', in A. McPherron and Srejović, D. (eds) *Divostin and the Neolithic of Central Serbia*, pp. 325–36, Pittsburgh, Penn.: Department of Anthropology, University of Pittsburgh.

Madas, D. (1988) 'Ceramic vessels from the Divostin II house floors', in A. McPherron and Srejović, D. (eds) *Divostin and the Neolithic of Central Serbia*, pp. 143–69, Pittsburgh, Penn.: Department of Anthropology, University of Pittsburgh.

Madeyska. T. (1982) 'Lithological and sedimentological analysis of the cave deposits', in J.K. Kozłowski (ed.) *Excavation in the Bacho Kiro Cave (Bulgaria): Final Report*, pp. 13–26, Warsaw: Państwowe Wydawnictwo Naukowe.

Makkay, J. (1982a) *A Magyarországi Neolitikum Kutatásának új Eredményei. Az Időrend és a Népi Azonosítás Kérései*, Budapest: Akadémiai Kiadó.

—— (1982b) 'Some comments on the settlement patterns of the Alföld Linear Pottery', in B. Chropovsky (ed.) *Siedlungen der Kultur mit Linearkeramik in Europa*, pp. 157–66, Nitra.

—— (1984) *Early Stamp Seals in South-east Europe*, Budapest: Akadémiai Kiadó.

318

—— (1992) 'Excavations at the Körös culture settlement of Endrőd-Öregszőlők 119 in 1986–1989', in S. Bökönyi (ed.) *Landscape and Cultural Changes in South-east Hungary, I: Reports on the Gyomaendrőd Project*, pp. 121–93, Budapest: Institute of Archaeology, Hungarian Academy of Sciences.

—— (1993) 'Comparisons of some Chalcolithic and EBA types from Anatolia, the Aegean and the SE Balkans', *Archaia Makedonia* 5: 821–23.

Mallory, J.P. (1989) *In Search of the Indo-Europeans*, London: Thames and Hudson.

Maniatis, Y. and Tite, M.S. (1981) 'Technological examination of Neolithic-Bronze Age pottery from central and southeast Europe and from the Near East', *Journal of Archaeological Science* 8: 59–76.

Maniatis, Y., Perdikatsis, V. and Kotsakis, K. (1988) 'Assessment of in-site variability of pottery from Sesklo, Thessaly', *Archaeometry* 30: 264–74.

Manson, J.L. (1995) 'Starčevo pottery and Neolithic development in the central Balkans', in W. Barnett and Hoopes, J. (eds) *The Emergence of Pottery*, pp. 65–77. Washington: Smithsonian Institution.

Marambet, L. (1992) 'Paléoenvironnements végétaux à Temnata – la séquence gravetienne et épigravetienne', in J.K. Kozłowski, Laville, H. and Ginter, B. (eds), *Temnata Cave: Excavations in Karlukovo Karst Area, Bulgaria*, vol. 1(2), pp. 101–26, Kraków, Jagellonian University Press.

Marangou, C. (1992) *Eidolia: figurines et miniatures du Néolithique récent et du Bronze ancien en Grèce*, Oxford: British Archaeological Reports.

—— (1996) 'Assembling, displaying and dissembling Neolithic and Eneolithic figurines and models', *Journal of European Archaeology* 4: 177–202.

Marcus, J. (1996) 'The importance of context in interpreting figurines', *Cambridge Archaeological Journal* 6, 2: 285–91.

Margos, A. (1961) 'Mezolit v Bulgariya', *Priroda i Znanie* 9: 17–19.

—— (1978) 'Les sites lacustres dans les lacs de Varna et la nécropole de Varna', *Studia Praehistorica* 1–2: 146–8.

Marinescu-Bîlcu, S., Popovici, D., Trohani, G., Andreescu, R., Bălăşescu, A., Bălteanu, A., Bem, C., Gàl, E., Haită, C., Kessler, E., Moise, D., Radu, V., Tomescu, M., Venczel, M., Vlad, F. and Voinea, V. (1997) 'Archaeological researches at Borduşani-Popină (Ialomiţa County), Preliminary report', *Cercetări Arheologice* 10: 35–143.

Marković, C. (1977) 'The stratigraphy and chronology of the Odmut cave', *Archaeologia Iugoslavica* 15: 7–12.

Marković-Marjanović, J. (1988) 'Geomorphology and geology of the Divostin area', in A. McPherron and Srejović, D. (eds) *Divostin and the Neolithic of Central Serbia*, pp. 21–7, Pittsburgh, Penn.: Department of Anthropology, University of Pittsburgh.

Markovits, A. (1928) 'Peri ton mechri simeron ereunon epi tis lithikis periodou tis Ellados', *Praktika tis Ellinikis Anthropologikis Etaireias* 1928: 114–34.

—— (1932–3) 'Die Zaïmis-Höhle (Kaki-Skala, Megaris, Greichenland)', *Speläologisches Jahrbuch* 13–14: 133–46.

Marshack, A. (1982) 'Non-utilitarian fragment of bone from the Middle Palaeolithic layer', in J.K. Kozłowski (ed.) *Excavation in the Bacho Kiro Cave (Bulgaria): Final Report*, pp. 117–8, Warsaw: Państwowe Wydawnictwo Naukowe.

—— (1995) 'Variabilité de catégorie dans l'imagerie symbolique d'Öküzini et de Karain (Turquie)', *L'Anthropologie* 99, 4: 584–92.

Mateescu, C.N. (1959) 'Sapaturi arheologice la Vadastra', *Materiale* 6: 197–214.

—— (1965) 'Contribution à l'étude de la civilisation de Vadastra: phase Vadastra II', in *Atti del VI Congresso Internazionale delle Scienze Preistoriche e Protostroiche II, Rome*, pp. 258–63, Rome: Union Internationale de Sciences Préhistoriques et Protohistoriques.

Matsanova, V. (1992) 'Tellsiedlung Junazite – die Spätkupferzeit', *Studia Praehistorica* 11–12: 148–61.

Mellars, P. (ed.) (1990) *The Emergence of Modern Humans: An Archaeological Perspective*, Edinburgh: Edinburgh University Press.

Meriç, E. and Sakinc, M. (1988) 'Yarimburgaz Mağarasi Mollusk Kavilari Hakkinda', *Arkeoloji ve Sanat* 40–1: 28–32.

Mertens, S.B. (1996) 'The middle Palaeolithic in Romania', *Current Anthropology* 37, 3: 515–21.

Meskell, L. (1995) 'Goddesses, Gimbutas and "New Age" archaeology', *Antiquity* 69: 74–86.

Mikić, Ž. (1981) *Stanje i Problemi Fizîke Antropologije u Jugolavîjî Praistorijski Periodi*, Sarajevo: Centar za Balkanološka Ispitivanja.

Mikov, V. (1948) 'Praistoricheskoto selishte Krivodol, Vrachansko', *Razkopki i Prouchvaniya* 1: 26–62.

—— (1966) 'Tekhnika na keramichnoto proizvodstvo prez praistoricheskata epokha Bulgariya', *Izvestiya na Arkheologicheskiya Institut* 29: 165–210.

Mikov, V. and Dzhambazov, D. (1960) *Devetashka Peshtera*, Sofia: Bulgarskata Akademiya na Naukite.

Milleker, F. (1938) 'Vorgeschichte des Banats', *Starinar* 2: 123–45.

Miloia, I. (1933) 'Săpăturile dela Parţa (Campania 1931)', *Analele Banatului* 4, 2–4: 171–86.

Milojčić, V. (1955) 'Vorbericht über die Ausgrabungen auf der Otzaki-Magula 1954', *Archäologischer Anzeiger* 70: 157–82.

—— (1960) 'Präkeramisches Neolithikum auf der Balkanhalbinsel', *Germania* 38: 320–35.

—— (1973) 'Zur Frage eines präkeramischen Neolithikums in Mitteleuropa', in *Actes du VIII congres international des sciences préhistoriques et protohistoriques*, vol. 2, pp. 248–52, Belgrad: Union Internationale de Sciences Préhistoriques et Protohistoriques.

—— (1976) 'Die Grabung auf der Agia Sofia-Magula', in V. Milojčić, von den Driesch, A., Enderle, K., Milojčić-von Zumbusch, J. and Kilian, K. (eds) *Die deutschen Ausgrabungen auf Magulen um Larisa in Thessalien*, pp. 4–14. Bonn: Beiträge zur Ur- und Frügeschichtliken Archälogic des Mittelmeer-Kulturraumes.

—— (1983) *Die deutschen Ausgrabungen auf der Otzaki-Magoula in Thessalien II: Das mittlere Neolithikum: Die mittelneolithische Siedlung*, Bonn: Beiträge zur Ur- und Frügeschichtliken Archälogic des Mittelmeer-Kulturraumes.

Milojčić, V., Boesneck, J. and Hopf, M. (1962) *Die deutschen Ausgrabungen auf der Argissa-Magula in Thessalien I: das präkeramische Neolithikum sowie die Tier- und Pflanzenreste*, Bonn: Rudolf Habelt.

Milojčić, V., Boessneck, J. and Schneider, H. (1965) *Paläolithikum um Larissa in Thessalien*, Bonn: Rudolf Habelt.

Milojčić, V., von den Driesch, A., Enderle, K., Milojčić-von Zumbusch, J. and Kilian, K. (1976) *Die deutschen Ausgrabunden auf Magulen um Larisa in Thessalien 1966: Agia Sofia-Magula. Karagyös-Magula. Bunar Baschi*, Bonn: Rudolf Habelt.

Milojčić, V., Zumbusch, J. and Milojčić, V. (1971) *Die deutschen Ausgrabungen auf de Otzaki-Magula in Thessalien I: Das frühe Neolithikum*, Bonn: Beiträge zur Ur- und Frügeschichtliken Archälogic des Mittelmeer-Kulturraumes.

Minzoni-Déroche, A., Menu, M. and Walter, P. (1995) 'The working of pigment during the Aurignacian period: evidence from Üçagizli Cave (Turkey)', *Antiquity* 69: 153–5.

Mirchev, M. (1961) 'Tri pogrebeniya ot eneolitnata epokha', *Izvestiya na Varnenskoto Arkheologichesko Druzhestvo* 12: 117–25.

Mithen, S.J. (1991) 'Ecological interpetations of Palaeolithic art', *Proceedings of the Prehistoric Society* 57, 1: 103–14.

—— (1992) 'Individuals, groups and the Palaeolithic record: a repy to Clark', *Proceedings of the Prehistoric Society* 59: 393–8.

—— (1994a) 'From domain specific to generalized interpretation of the Middle/Upper Palaeolithic transition', in C. Renfrew and Zubrow, E.B.W. (eds) *The Ancient Mind: Elements of Cognitive Archaeology*, pp. 29–39, Cambridge: Cambridge University Press.

—— (1994b) 'Technology and society during the Middle Pleistocene', *Cambridge Archaeological Journal* 4: 1–31.

—— (1995) 'Palaeolithic archaeology and the evolution of mind', *Journal of Archaeological Research* 3, 4: 305–32.

—— (1996) *The Prehistory of Mind*, London: Thames and Hudson.

Mogoşanu, F. (1978) 'Mezoliticul de la Ostrovul Corbuluj o noua asezare de tip Schela Cladovei', *Studii şi Cercetări de Istorie Veche şi Arheologie* 29: 335–51.

—— (1983) 'Paléolithique et épipaléolithique', in V. Dumitrescu, Bolomey, A. and Moroşanu, F. (eds) *Esquisse d'une préhistoire de la Roumanie jusqu' à la fin de l'âge du bronze*, pp. 29–55, Bucureşti: Editura Ştiintifica şi Enciclopedica.

Montet-White, A. (1994) 'Alternative interpretations of the late Upper Palaeolithic in Central Europe', *Annual Review of Anthropology* 23: 483–508.

Mook, W. (1982) 'Radiocarbon dating', in J.K. Kozłowski (ed.) *Excavation in the Bacho Kiro Cave (Bulgaria): Final Report*, p. 168, Warsaw: Państwowe Wydawnictwo Naukowe.

Morintz, S. (1963) 'Die jungsteinzeitlichen Funde in Cernica (Bukarest)', *Dacia* 7: 30–41.

Morrison, I.A. (1968) 'Appendix I, Relative sea-level change in the Saliagos area since Neolithic times', in J.D. Evans and Renfrew, C. (eds) *Excavations at Saliagos near Antiparos*, pp. 92–8, London: Thames and Hudson.

Morrison, P. (1993) 'Holocene landscape evolution of the Langadas Basin, Macedonia: an approach to the evolution of the soil resource for prehistoric settlement', unpublished PhD dissertation, University of Birmingham.

Musées Nationaux. (1989) *Le Premier Or de l'humanité en Bulgaria 5e millénaire*, Paris.

Nandor, F. (1953) 'La trouvaille d'une tombe princière hunnique à Szeged', *Collection Archaeologia Hungarica* 32: 123–45.

Nandris, J. (1970) 'The development and relationships of the earlier Greek Neolithic', *MAN* 5: 192–213.

Necrasov, O. (1964) 'Sur les restes des faunes subfossiles datant de la culture de la Starčevo-Cris, et le problème de la domestication', *Analele Stiintifice ale Universitatii din Iasi* 10: 167–81.

—— (1973) 'Studiul resturilor de faună din şezarea neolitică de la Radovanu, jud Ilfov', *Materiale* 10: 39–45.

Necrasov, O. and Cristescu, M. (1961) 'Sur les méditerranoides du néolithique et de l'énéolithique roumain', *Acta FRN Univers Comen* 5: 201–12.

Necrasov, O. and Gheorghiu, G. (1970) 'Studiul resturilor de faună din aşezarea neolitică de al Izvoarele', *Materiale* 9: 91–6.

Necrasov, O. and Haimovici, S. (1959a) 'Etude de la faune de la station néolithique de Tangâru', *Dacia* 3: 561–70.

—— (1959b) 'Fauna din complexele Boian de lângâ satul Bogata', *Materiale şi Cercetări Archeologica* 5: 127–30.

—— (1962) 'Studiul resturilor de fauna neolitica (cultura Hamangia) descoperite in corsul sapaturilor de la Techirghiol', *Materiale şi Cercetări Archeologica* 8: 175–85.

—— (1966) 'Studiul resturilor de fauna neolitică descoperite în staţiuna Gumelniţa', *Studii şi Cercetări de Istorie Veche* 17, 1: 101–8.

Nemeskéri, J. (1944) 'A vaskúti neolithkori (Körös kultura) csontváz embertani ismertetése', in I. Kutzián (ed.) *The Körös Culture Dissertationes Pannonicae* 23: 149–52, Budapest: Universitatis de Petro Pazmany Nominatae Budapestinensis Provenientes.

—— (1951) Anthropologische Untersuchung der Skelettfunde von Alsónémedi', *Acta Archaeologica Academiae Scientiarum Hungaricae* 1: 55–72.

—— (1961) 'Die wichtigsten anthropologischen Fragen der Urgeschichte in Ungarn', *Anthrop. Közl.* 5: 39–47.

Nemeskéri, J and Szathmary, L. (1978) 'Individual data of the Vlasac anthropological series', in D. Srejović and Letica, Z. (eds) *Vlasac*, vol. II, pp. 285–426, Belgrade: Serbian Academy of Sciences and Arts.

Nestor, I. (1928) 'Zur Chronologie der rumänischen Steinkupferzeit', *Praehistorische Zeitschrift* 19: 23–65.

Ngyen Ban Bin (1985) 'Metodika za izsledvane na kusnoplejstotsenski i rannokholotsenski praistoricheski ansambli ot kremuchni artephakti', unpublished PhD dissertation, Sofia University.

Nica, M. (1976) 'La culture Dudesti en Olténie', *Dacia* 20: 123–45.

Nikolov, B. (1976) 'Mogilni pogrebeniya ot rannata bronzova epokha pri Turnava i Knezha, Vrachanski okrug', *Arkheologiya* 17, 3: 38–51.

—— (1982) 'Epokha rannij bronzy v severo-zapadnoj Bolgarii i nekropol u sela Tyrnava', *Thracia Praehistorica, Supplementum Pulpudeva* 3: 192–200.

—— (1986) 'Signes sur des ouvrages en argile de l'époque préhistorique dans la Bulgarie occidentale', *Studia Praehistorica* 8: 166–84.

Nikolov, V. (1988) 'Karanovo VI-Period in Bulgarien: Belege zur Religion, Gesellschaft und Wirtschaft', in Fol, A. and Lichardus, J. (eds) *Macht, Herrschaft und Gold: Das Gräberfeld von Varna und die Anfänge einer neuen europäischen Zivilisation*, pp. 209–40, Saarbrücken: Moderne Galerie des Saarland-Museums.

—— (1989) 'Das frühneolithische Haus von Sofia-Slatina: Eine Untersuchung zur vorgeschichtlichen Bautechnik', *Germania* 67: 1–49.

—— (ed.) (1992a) *Rannoneolitno Selishte ot Slatina (Sofia)*, Sofia: Bulgarskata Akademiya na Naukite.

—— (1992b) 'Die Untersuchungen der frühneolithischen Siedlung Slatina (Sofia) in den Jahren 1985–1987', *Studia Praehistorica* 11–2: 68–73.

—— (1997a) 'Periodisierung und Chronologie', in S. Hiller and Nikolov, V. (eds), *Karanovo: Die Ausgrabungen im Südsektor 1984–1992*, pp. 49–53, Horn: Ferdinand Berger and Söhne.

—— (1997b) 'Die neolithische Keramik', in S. Hiller and Nikolov, V. (eds), *Karanovo: Die Ausgrabungen im Südsektor 1984–1992*, pp. 105–46, Horn: Ferdinand Berger and Söhne.

Nikolov, V. and Maslarov, K. (1987) *Drevni Selishta kraj Eleshnitsa*, Sofia: Bulgarskata Akademiya na Vaukite.

Nikolova, L. (1995) 'Burials in settlements and flat necropolises during the early Bronze Age in Bulgaria', in D.W. Bailey and Panayotov, I. (eds) *Prehistoric Bulgaria*, pp. 271–5, Madison, Wisc.: Prehistory Press.

Ninov, L. (1986) 'Tierknochen aus der prähistorischen Siedlung Kremenik', *Studia Praehistorica* 8: 152–5.

—— (1990) 'Animal bones from boreholes of early neolithic settlement near village Kovachevo, Blagoevgrad district', *Studia Praehistorica* 10: 197–9.

Ninov, L. and Stanev, P. (1991) 'Zhivotnovydna i lovnostopanska dejnost na nase-lenieto ot neolitnata selishtna mogila Samovodene', *Godishnik na Muzeite v Severna Bulgariya* 17: 39–59.

Nobis, G. (1986) 'Zur fauna der früneolitischen Siedlung Ovčarovo-gorata, Bez. Targoviste (NO Bulgaria)', *Bonner Zoolologische Beitrage* 37, 1: 1–22.

Otte, M. (1985) 'Le Gravettian en Europe', *L'Anthropologie* 89, 4: 479–503.

Ovcharov, D. (1976) 'Eneoliten nekropol do s. Lilyak, Turgovishko', *Arkheologiya* 18, 1: 53–6.

Özdoğan, M. (1983) 'Pendik: a neolithic site of Fikirtepe culture in the Marmara region', in R.M. Boehmer and Hauptmann, H. (eds) *Beiträge zur Alterumskunde Kleinasien, Festschrift für Kirt Bittel*, pp. 401–11, Mainz.

—— (1985) 'The late Chalcolithic pottery of Yarimburgaz Cave', in M. Liverani, Palmieri, A. and Peroni, R. (eds) *Studi di 30 Paletnologia in Onoro di Salvatore M. Puglisi*, pp. 117–89, Rome.

—— (1986) 'Yarimburgaz Cave 1986 excavations', *Arkeoloji ve Sanat* 32–3: 4–17.

—— (1989a) 'Neolithic cultures of northwestern Turkey: a general appraisal of the evidence and some considerations', in S. Bökönyi (ed.) *Neolithic of Southeastern Europe and its Near Eastern Connections*, pp. 201–15, Budapest: Instituti Archaeologici Academiae Scientiarum Hungaricae Budapestini.

—— (1989b) '1988 Yili Trakya ve Marmara Bölgesi Araştirmalari', *VII Araştirma Sonuçlari Toplantisi*: 443–57.

—— (1990) '1989 Yili Marmara Bölgesi Araştirmalari ve Toptepe Kazisi', *XI Kazi Sonuçlari Toplantisi*, 146–54.

—— (1991) 'Yili Marmara Bölgesi Araştirmalari ve Toptepe Kazisi', *XI Kazi Sonuçlari Toplantisi*, 146–54.

—— (1993) 'Vinča and Anatolia: a new look at a very old problem (or redefining Vinča culture from the perspective of Near Eastern tradition)', *Anatolica* 19: 173–93.

—— (1995) 'Neolithic in Turkey: the status of research', *Readings in Prehistory Presented to Halet Çambel*, pp. 41–59, Istanbul: Graphis.

—— (1996) 'Neolithization of Europe: a view from Anatolia. Part I: the problem and the evidence of east Anatolia', *Porcilo* 20: 25–61.

Özdoğan, M. and Dede, N.O. (1991) '1989 Yili Toptepe Kurtarma Kazisi', *Arkeoloji ve Sanat* 6: 12–13.

Özdoğan, M. and Gatsov, I. (1998) 'The aceramic neolithic period in western Turkey and in the Aegean', *Anatolica* 24: 209–32.

Özdoğan, M. and Koyunlu, A. (1986) 'Yarimburgaz Mağarasi 1986 Yili Çalişmalari', *Arkeoloji ve Sanat* 32–3: 4–17.

Özdoğan, N., Miyake, Y. and Dede N.O. (1991) 'An interim report on excavations at Yarimburgaz and Toptepe in eastern Thrace', *Anatolica* 17: 59–121.

Panayotov, I. (1980) 'Metal types and the early Bronze age in Bulgaria', *Pulpudeva* 3: 333–5.

—— (1989) *Yamnata Kultura v Bulgarskite Zemi*, Sofia: Bulgarskata Akademiya na Naukite.

Panayotov, I. and Dergachov, V. (1984) 'Die Ockergrabkultur in Bulgarien (Darstellung des Problems)', *Studia Praehistorica* 7: 99–111.

Panayotov, I, Leshtakov, K., Alexandrov, S., Zmejkova, I., Popova, Ts. and Stephanova, T. (1991) 'Selishte mogila Gulubovo – Kusnokhalkolitna, ranna i sredna Bronzova epokha', in Panayotov, I., Leshtakov, K., Georgieva, R., Alexandrov, S. and Borisov, B. (eds) *Maritsa-Istok. Arkheologicheski Prouchvaniya*, vol. 1, pp. 139–204, Sofia: Jusautor.

Panayotov, I., Gatsov, I. and Popova, Ts. (1992) '"Pompenata stantsiya" bliz s. Maluk Preslavets – ranneneoliticheskoe poselenie s intramuralnymi pogrebiniyami', *Studia Praehistorica* 11–2: 51–61.

Panin, N. (1972) 'Quaternary history of the Danube delta', *Cercetări Marine*: 4: 5–15.

—— (1983) 'Black Sea coast line changes in the last 10,000 years. An attempt at identifying the Danube mouths as described by the ancients', *Dacia* 27, 1–2: 175–84.

Papanthimou, A. and Papasteriou, A. (1993) 'O praistorikos oikismos sto Manadalo: Nea stoixeia stin praistoria tin Makedonias', *Arxaia Makedonia* 5: 1, 207–16.

Papaxatzis, N. (1983) 'I magiki domi tis thriskeias sta neolithika khronia', *Archaiologiki Ephemeris* 1983: 35–43.

Pappa, M. (1993) 'Neolithikas oikismos Makriyialou', *To Arxaiologiko sti Makedonia Kai Thraki* 7: 57–78.

—— (1994) 'Neolithikos oikismos Makriyialou', *To Arxaiologiko Ergo sti Makedonia Kai Thraki* 8: 123–45.

Parker Pearson, M. (1982) 'Mortuary practices, society and ideology: an ethnoarchaeological study', in I. Hodder (ed.) *Symbolic and Structural Archaeology*, pp. 99–113, Cambridge: Cambridge University Press.

Passek, T.S. (1949) *Periodizatsia Tripolskich Poselnii*, Moscow-Leningrad: Akademia Nauk-SSSR.

Păunescu, A. (1964) 'A propos du néolithique ancien de Drăghiceanu et de quelques survivances tardenoisiennes', *Dacia* 8: 297–305.

—— (1978) 'Cercetarile arheologice de la Cuina Turcului-Dubova (Jud. Mehedinti)', *Tibiscus Istorie, Volum Închinat Celei de-a 60 Aniversari a Unirii*, pp. 11–56.

—— (1981) 'Mezoliticul de la Erbiceni şi Ripiceni-Izvor, expresie a tardenoasianului nord-vest pontic', *Studii şi Cercetări de Istorie Veche şi Arheologie* 32, 4: 479–509.

—— (1984) Cronologia Paleoliticului și Mezoliticului din România în context Paleoliticului Central Est și Sud-European, *Studii și Cercetări de Istorie Veche și Arheologie* 35, 3: 235–65.

—— (1989) 'Le Paléolithique et le mésolithique de Roumanie (Un bref aperçu)', *L'Anthropologie* 93, 1: 128–34.

—— (1990) 'Scurtă privire asupra paleoliticului și mezoliticului din Dobrogea', *Studii și Cercetări de Istorie Veche și Arheologie* 41, 3–4: 219–24.

—— (1993) *Ripiceni-Izvor. Paleolitic și Mezolitic*, București: Academiei Române.

Pavúk, J. and Bakamska, A. (1989) 'Beitrag der Ausgrabung in Galabnik zur Erforschung des Neolithikums in Südosteuropa', in S. Bökönyi (ed.) *Neolithic of Southeastern Europe and Its Near Eastern Connections*, pp. 223–31, Budapest: Hungarian Academy of Sciences.

Pavúk, J. and Cochadziev, M. (1984) 'Neolithische Tellsiedlung bei Galabnik in Westbulgarien', *Slovenská Archeológia* 32, 1: 195–228.

Pawlikowski, M. (1992) 'The origin of the lithic raw materials', in J.K. Kozłowski, Laville, H. and Ginter, B. *Temnata Cave: Excavations in Karlukovo Karst Area Bulgaria*, vol. 1(1), pp. 241–88, Kraków: Jagellonian University Press.

Payne, S. (1975) 'Faunal change at Franchthi Cave from 20,000 to 3000 BC', in A.T. Clason (ed.) *Archaeozoological Studies*, pp. 120–31, Oxford: Elsevier.

Pearson, M. (1998) 'Performance as valuation: early Bronze Age burial as theatrical complexity', in D.W. Bailey (ed.) *The Archaeology of Value*, pp. 42–54, Oxford: British Archaeological Reports.

Pejkov, A. (1978) 'Sondazhni razkopki na neolitno selishte v Kurdzhali prez 1972 godina', *Akhrid* 1: 16–7.

—— (1986) 'Zwei interessante Kultgegenstände aus der neolithischen Siedlung in Kardžali', *Studia Praehistorica* 8: 208–11.

Perlès, C. (1987) *Les Industries lithiques raillées de Franchthi (Argolide, Grèce)*, I, *Présentation générale et industries paléolithiques*, Bloomington, Ind.: Indiana University Press.

—— (1988) 'New ways with an old problem: chipped stone assemblages as an index of cultural discontinuity in early Greek prehistory', in E.B. French and Wardle, K.A. (eds) *Problems in Greek Prehistory*, pp. 484–86, Bristol: Bristol Classical Press.

—— (1989) 'La néolithisation de la Grèce', in O. Aurenche and Cauvin, J. (eds) *Néolithisations*, pp. 115–6, Oxford: British Archaeological Reports.

—— (1990) *Les Industries lithiques raillées de Franchthi (Argolide, Grèce)*, II, *Les Industries du mésolithique et du néolithique initial*, Bloomington, Ind.: University of Indiana Press.

—— (1992) 'Systems of exchange and organization of production in Neolithic Greece', *Journal of Mediterranean Archaeology* 5, 2: 115–64.

—— (1994) 'Les débuts du Néolithique en Grèce', *La Recherche* 25: 123–45.

Pernicheva, L. (1978) 'Site et habitations du Chalcolithique en Bulgarie', *Studia Praehistorica* 1–2: 162–9.

—— (1990) 'Le site de Kovatchevo, Néolithique ancien, dans le département de Blagoevgrad', *Studia Praehistorica* 10: 142–96.

—— (1993) 'Ukrepitelnata sistema na rannoneolitnoto selishte Strumsko', in V. Nikolov (ed.) *Praistoricheski Nakhodki i Izsledvaniya. Sbornik v Pamet na Prof. Georgi Il. Georgiev*, pp. 97–102, Sofia: Bulgarskata Akademiya na Naukite.

—— (1995) 'Prehistoric cultures in the Middle Struma Valley: Neolithic and Eneolithic', in D.W. Bailey and Panayotov, I. (eds) *Prehistoric Bulgaria*, pp. 99–140, Madison, Wisc.: Prehistory Press.

Petrescu-Dimboviţa, M. (1954) 'Şantierul arheologic Truşeşti', *Studii şi Cercetări de Istorie Veche* 5, 1–2: 7–28.

Petrobok, J. and Skutil, J. (1950) 'Otevřené Sidliště Aurignacké na Pobitych Kamenech u Varny v Bulharsku', *Sbornik Narodniho Musea v Praze* 4, A1.

Petrović, J. (1984) *Gomolava – Arheološko Nalazište*, Novi Sad: Vojvodanski Muzej u Novom Sadu.

—— (1987) 'Zemunica u naselju starčevačke kulture na Golokutu', *Rad Vojvodanskih Muzeja* 30: 13–28.

—— (1990a) 'Istraživanja lokaliteta Golokut u 1988 godini', *Glasnik Srpskog Arheološkog Društva* 6: 55–8.

—— (1990b) 'Researches at Gomolava', in M. Höneisen (ed.) *Die ersten Bauern*, vol. 2, pp. 99–109, Zurich: Schweizerisches Landesmuseum.

Pilali-Papasteriou, A. and Papaefthimiou-Papanthimou, A. (1989) 'Nees anaskaphikes ereuves sto Mandalo dutikis Makedonias, 1985–1986', *Egnatia* 1: 15–28.

Pine, F. (1996) 'Naming the house and naming the land: kinship and social groups in highland Poland', *Journal of the Royal Anthropological Institute* 2: 443–59.

Pollock, D. (1995) 'Masks and the semiotics of identity', *Journal of the Royal Anthropological Institute* 1: 581–597.

Pope, K.O., Runnels, C.N. and Teh-Lung, K. (1984) 'Dating Middle Palaeolithic red beds in southern Greece', *Nature* 312: 264–6.

Poplin, F. (1991) 'Réflexions sur l'astragale d'or de Varna', in J.-P. Mohen (ed.) *Découverte du Métal*, pp. 31–42, Paris: Picard.

Popov, R. (1912) 'Beiträge zur Vorgeschichte Bulgariens', *Praehistorische Zeitschrift* 4: 88–113.

—— (1931) *Peshterata Temnata Dupka. Novo nakhodishte ot paleolita v Bulgariya.* Sofia: Bulgarskata Akademiya na Vaukite.

Popov, V. (1993) 'Neolitni selishte pri s. Koprivets', *Godishnik na Muzeite na Severna Bulgariya* 19: 23–31.

—— (1994) 'Periodizatsiya i khronologiya na neolitne i khalkolitni kulturi ot porechieto na r. Russenski Lom', *Godishnik na Department Arkheologiya NBU* 1: 294–302.

Popov, V.V. (1986) 'Early Pleistocene rodents from Temnata Dupka cave, N. Bulgaria', *Acta Zoologica Bulgarica* 30: 1–12.

—— (1994) 'Quaternary small mammals from the deposits in Temnata-Prohodna Cave system', in J.K. Kozłowski, Laville, H. and Ginter, B. *Temnata Cave: Excavations in Karlukovo Karst Area Bulgaria*, vol. 1(2), pp. 11–53, Kraków: Jagellonian University Press.

Popova, Ts. (1995) 'Plant remains from Bulgarian prehistory (7000–2000 BC)', in D.W. Bailey and Panayotov, I. (eds) *Prehistoric Bulgaria*, pp. 193–208, Madison, Wisc.: Prehistory Press.

Popp, N. (1969) 'The Quaternary deposits in the Danube valley in Romania and the paleo-Danube river bed', *Dacia* 12: 67–72.

Poulianos, A. (1971) 'Petralona: a middle Pleistocene cave in Greece', *Archaeology* 24: 6–11.

—— (1977) 'Stratigraphy and age of the Petralonian Archanthropus', *Anthropos* 4: 41–6.

Prinz, B. (1987) *Mesolithic Adaptations on the Lower Danube: Vlasac and the Iron Gates Gorge*, Oxford: British Archaeological Reports.

—— (1988) 'The ground stone industry from Divostin', in A. McPherron and Srejović, D. (eds) *Divostin and the Neolithic of Central Serbia*, pp. 255–300, Pittsburgh, Penn.: Department of Anthropology, University of Pittsburgh.

Pyke, G. and Yiouni, P. (1996) *Nea Nikomedeia, the Excavation of an Early Neolithic Village in Northern Greece, 1961–1964*, vol. I, *The Excavation and the Ceramic Assemblage*, Athens: British School at Athens.

Raczky, P. (1982) 'Újkőkor – Neolithic period', in P. Raczky (ed.) *Szolnok Megye a Népek Országútján*, pp. 8–23, 92–9, Szolnok: County Museum.

—— (1982–3) 'Origins of the custom of burying the dead inside houses in South-East Europe', *Szolnok Megyei Múzeumi Évkönyve* 1982–3: 5–10.

—— (1985) 'The cultural and chronological relations of the Tisza region during the middle and the late Neolithic as reflected in the excavations at Öcsöd-Kováshalom', *A Béri Balogh Ádám Múzeum Évkönyve* 13: 103–25.

—— (1987) 'Öcsöd-Kováshalom: a settlement of the Tisza culture', in P. Raczky and Tálas, L. (eds) *The Late Neolithic of the Tisza Region*, pp. 61–83, Szolnok: County Museum.

Raczky, P., Raczky, M. and Seleanu, G. (1985) 'Öcsöd-Kováshalom: the intensive topographical and archaeological investigation of the late neolithic site', *Mitteilungen des Archäologischen Instituts der Ungarischen Akademie der Wissenschaften* 14: 251–78.

Raczky, P., Anders, A., Nagy, E., Kurucz, K., Hajdú, Z. and Meier-Arendt, W. (1997) 'Polgár-Csőszhalom-dűlő', in P. Raczky, Kovács, T. and Anders, A. (eds) *Paths into the Past: Rescue Excavations on the M3 Motorway*, pp. 34–43, Budapest: Magyar Nemzeti Múseum.

Radovanović, I. (1981) *Ranoholocenska Kremena Industrija sa Lokaliteta Padina u Djerdapu*, Belgrade, Arheološki Institut.

—— (1994) 'A review of formal disposal areas in the Mesolithic of Europe', *Starinar* 43–4: 92–103.

—— (1996a) *The Iron Gates Mesolithic*, Ann Arbor, Mich.: International Monographs in Prehistory.

—— (1996b) 'Mesolithic/Neolithic contacts: a case of the Iron Gates region', *Poročilo o Raziskovanju Paleolitika, Neolitika in Eneolitika v Sloveniji* 23: 39–48.

Radulescu, C. and Samson, P. (1991) 'Traces d'activité humaine à la limite Pliocène/Pléistocene dans le bassin dacique (Roumanie)', in E. Bonifay and Vandermeersch, B. (eds) *Les Premiers Européens*, pp. 203–7, Paris: CTHS.

Raduncheva, A. (1976) *Vinitsa. Eneolitno Selishte i Nekropol. (Razkopki i Prouchvaniya 6)*, Sofia: Bulgarskata Akademiya na Naukite.

Rasson, J. (1988) 'Loom weights', in A. McPherron and Srejović, D. (eds) *Divostin and the Neolithic of Central Serbia*, pp. 337–8, Pittsburgh, Penn.: Department of Anthropology, University of Pittsburgh.

Renfrew, C. (1969) 'The autonomy of the south-east European Copper Age', *Proceedings of the Prehistoric Society* 35: 12–47.

—— (1986a) 'Sitagroi in European Prehistory', in A.C. Renfrew, Gimbutas, M., and Elster, E. (eds) *Excavations at Sitagroi: A Prehistoric Village in Northeast Greece*, vol. 1, pp. 477–85, Los Angeles: UCLA.

—— (1986b) 'The excavated areas', in A.C. Renfrew, Gimbutas, M. and Elster, E. (eds) *Excavations at Sitagroi: A Prehistoric Village in Northeast Greece*, vol. 1, pp. 175–222, Los Angeles: UCLA.

—— (1986c) 'Varna and the emergence of wealth in prehistoric Europe', in A. Appadurai (ed.) *The Social Life of Things*, pp. 141–68, Cambridge: Cambridge University Press.

—— (1994) 'The identity of Europe in prehistoric archaeology', *Journal of European Archaeology* 2, 2: 153–74

Renfrew, C., Gimbutas, M. and Elster, E. (eds) (1986) *Excavations at Sitagroi: A Prehistoric Village in Northeast Greece*, vol. 1, Los Angeles: UCLA.

Renfrew, J. (1973) 'Trade and craft specialisation', in D. Theocharis (ed.) *Neolithic Greece*, pp. 179–91, Athens: National Bank of Greece.

Rhomiopoulou, K. and Ridley, C. (1973) 'Prehistoric settlement of Servia (W. Macedonia): excavations 1972', *Athens Annals of Archaeology* 6: 419–24.

Ribarov, G. (1991) 'The osteological material from the sunken settlement at Urdoviza', *Thracia Pontica* 4: 113–18.

Ridley, C. and Wardle, K.A. (1979) 'Rescue excavations at Servia 1971–1973: a preliminary report', *Annual of the British School at Athens* 74: 185–230.

Rodden, R. (1962) 'Excavations at the early Neolithic site at Nea Nikomedeia, Greek Macedonia (1961 season)', *Proceedings of the Prehistoric Society* 28: 267–88.

—— (1964) 'Recent discoveries from prehistoric Macedonia', *Balkan Studies* 5: 109–24.

—— (1965) 'An early Neolithic village in Greece', *Scientific American* 212, 4: 82–92.

Roodenberg, J. (ed.) (1993a) *Anatolia and the Balkans* (Anatolica 19).

—— (1993b) 'Ilipinar X to VI: links and chronology', *Anatolica* 19: 251–61.

—— (1995) *The Ilipinar Excavations I: Five Seasons of Fieldwork in Northwestern Anatolia, 1987–1991*, Istanbul: Dutch Archaeological Institute.

Roodenberg, J., Thissen, L. and Buitenhuis, H. (1990) 'Preliminary report on the archaeological investigations at Ilipinar in NW Anatolia', *Anatolica* 16: 61–144.

Rosetti, D.V. (1934) *Sapaturile de la Vidra. Raport Preliminar*, Bucureşti: Muzeului Municipiului Bucureşti.

—— (1939) 'Steinhkupferzeitliche Plastik aus einem Wohnhügel bei Bukarest', *Jahrbuch für Prähistorische und Ethnographosche Kunst* 12: 123–45.

Runnels, C. (1995) 'Review of Aegean prehistory IV: the stone age of Greece from the Palaeolithic to the advent of the Neolithic', *American Journal of Archaeology* 99: 699–728.

Runnels, C. and van Andel, T. (1993) 'A handaxe from Kokkinopilos, Epirus, and its implications for the Paleolithic of Greece', *Journal of Field Archaeology* 20: 191–203.

Russell, N. (1998) 'Cattle as wealth in Neolithic Europe: where's the beef?', in D.W. Bailey (ed.) *The Archaeology of Value*, pp. 42–54, Oxford: British Archaeological Reports.

Ryan, W.B.F., Pitman, W.C., Major, C.O., Shimkus, K., Moscalenko, V., Jones, G.A., Dimitrov, P., Gorür, N., Sakinç, M. and Seyir, H.Y. (1997a) 'An abrupt drowning of the Black Sea shelf at 7.5 kyr BP', *Fluvial-Marine Interactions* (no editor), pp. 115–25, Bucureşti: National Institute of Marine Geology and Geo-ecology.

Ryan, W.B.F., Pitman, W.C., Major, C.O., Shimkus, K., Moskalenko, V., Jones, G.A., Dimitrov, P., Gorür, N., Sakinç, M. and Seyir, H.Y. (1997b) 'An abrupt drowning of the Black Sea shelf', *Marine Geology* 7: 25–44.

Samson, R. (ed.) (1990) *The Social Archaeology of Houses*, Edinburgh, Edinburgh University Press.

Schachermeyr, F. (1976) *Die agaisshe Frühzeit, 1, Die vormykenischen Perioden*, Vienna: Austrian Academy of Sciences.

Schneider, G., Knoll, H., Gallis, C.J. and Demoule, J.P. (1991) 'Production and distribution of coarse and fine ware pottery in Neolithic Thessaly, Greece', in E. Pernicka and Wagner, G.A. (eds) *Archaeometry 90*, pp. 513–22, Basel: Birkhäuser.

Schwidetzky, I. (1957) 'Die Vinča-Schädel: Vorläufige Mitteilung', *Berichte 5 Tag Deutsch Geschichte Anthropologie Frieburg*, pp. 117–9.

—— (1971–2) 'Menschliche Skelettreste von Vinča', *Glasnik Antropoškog Društva Jugoslavije* 8–9: 101–12.

Séfériadès, M. (1992) 'L'outillage: le métal', in R. Treuil (ed.) *Dikili Tash, village préhistorique de Macédonie orientale: fouilles de Jean Deshayes (1961–1975), vol. I, (Supplément du Bulletin correspondance hellénique 26)*, pp. 113–19, Athens: Ecole Française d'Athènes.

Sekereš, L. (1967) 'Ludaš, Budžak', *Arheološki Pregled* 9: 9–12.

Selmeczi, L. (1969) 'Das Wohnhaus der Körös-gruppe von Tiszajenő: Neuere Haustypen des Frühneolithikums', *A Móra Ferenc Múzeum Évkönyve* 1969, 2: 17–22.

Shackleton, J. and Elderfield, H. (1990) 'Strontium isotope dating of the source of Neolithic European *Spondylus* shell artefacts', *Antiquity* 64: 312–5.

Shackleton, N. and Renfrew, C. (1970) 'Neolithic trade routes realigned by oxygen isotope analyses', *Nature* 228: 1062–5.

Sherratt, A. (1981) 'Plough and pastoralism: aspects of the secondary products revolution', in I. Hodder, Isaac, G. and Hammond, N. (eds) *Pattern of the Past*, pp. 261–305, Cambridge: Cambridge University Press.

—— (1983a) 'The development of Neolithic and Copper Age settlement in the Great Hungrian plain. Part I: The regional setting', *Oxford Journal of Archaeology* 1, 1: 287–316.

—— (1983b) 'Early agrarian settlement in the Körös region of the Great Hungarian Plain', *Acta Archaeologica Hungarica Academiae Scientiarum Hungaricae* 34: 155–69.

—— (1983c) 'The secondary exploitation of animals in the Old World', *World Archaeology* 15: 90–104.

—— (1984) 'The development of Neolithic and Copper Age settlement in the Great Hungrian plain. Part II: Site survey and settlement dynamics', *Oxford Journal of Archaeology* 2, 1: 13–41.

—— (1986a) 'The pottery of phases IV and V: the early Bronze Age', in C. Renfrew, Gimbutas, M. and Elster, E. (eds) *Excavations at Sitagroi: A Prehistoric Village in Northeast Greece*, vol. 1, pp. 429–76, Los Angeles: UCLA.

—— (1986b) 'Two new finds of wooden wheels from later Neolithic and Early Bronze Age Europe', *Oxford Journal of Archaeology* 5: 243–8.

—— (1987) 'Wool, wheels and ploughmarks: local developments or outside introductions in Neolithic Europe?', *Bulletin of the Institute of Archaeology* 23: 1–15.

—— (1993) 'What would a Bronze Age system look like? Relations between temperate Europe and the Mediterannean in later prehistory', *Journal of European Archaeology* 1, 2: 1–56.

—— (1994) 'The transformation of early agrarian Europe: the later Neolithic and Copper Ages 4500–2500 BC', in B. Cunliffe (ed.) *The Oxford Illustrated Prehistory of Europe*, pp. 167–201, Oxford: Oxford University Press.

—— (1997) *Economy and Society in Prehistoric Europe*, Edinburgh: Edinburgh University Press.

Shnirelman, V. (1992) 'Complex hunter-gatherers: exception of common phenomenon', *Dialectical Anthropology* 17: 183–96.

Siklódy, Cs. (1986) 'The enclosure – a sign of territorial organization in the Hungarian Late Neolithic – the non-urban way of development', in A. Fleming (ed.) *The Neolithic of Europe*, pp. 123–45, Southampton: World Archaeological Congress.

Sinclair, A. (1995) 'The technique as a symbol in Late Glacial Europe', *World Archaeology* 27, 1: 50–62.

—— (1998) 'The value of tasks in the late Upper Palaeolithic', in D.W. Bailey (ed.) *The Archaeology of Value*, pp. 10–16, Oxford: British Archaeological Reports.

Sirakov, N. (1979) 'Analytical study of blanks from the Cave Samuilitsa II (an example of application of attribute correlation method)', *Prace Archeologiczne* 28: 65–76.

—— (1983) *Reconstruction of the Middle Palaeolithic Flint Assemblages from the Cave Samuilitza II (Northern Bulgaria) and their Taxonomic Position seen against the Palaeolithic of SE Europe (Folia Quaternaria 55)*, Kraków: Jagellonian University Press.

—— (1992), 'Introduction', in J.K. Kozłowski, Laville, H. and Ginter, B. (1992) *Temnata Cave: Excavations in Karlukovo Karst Area Bulgaria*, vol. 1(1), pp. 13–30, Kraków: Jagellonian University Press.

Sirakov, N. and Tsonev, T. (1995) 'Chipped-stone assemblage of Hotnitsa-vodopada (Eneolithic/early Bronze Age transition in northern Bulgaria) and the problem of the earliest "steppe invasion" in the Balkans', *Préhistoire Européenne* 7: 241–64.

Sirakov, N., Ivanova, S., Sirakova, S. and Gatsov, I. (1993) 'Tipologiya na kamennite orudiya ot kusniya Paleolit', *Arkheologiya* 35, 3: 1–17.

Sirakov, N., Sirakova, S., Ivanova, S., Gatsov, I. and Tsonev, T. (1994) 'The Epigravettian sequence', in B. Ginter, Kozłowski, J.K. and Laville. H. (eds) *Temnata Cave: Excavations in Karlukovo Karst Area Bulgaria*, vol. 1(2), pp. 169–314, Kraków: Jagellonian University Press.

Sirakova, S. (1991) 'The leaf-points from Muselievo', in J.K. Kozłowski (ed.) *Feuilles de pierre: les industries à pointes foliacées de paléolithique supérieur européen*, pp. 63–78, Liége: Université de Liège.

Sirakova, S. and Ivanova, S. (1988) 'La site paléolithique près du village Muselievo, département de Pleven', *Studia Praehistorica* 9: 5–15.

—— (1995) 'Chronology and cultures of the Bulgarian Palaeolithic', in D.W. Bailey and Panayotov, I. (eds) *Prehistoric Bulgaria*, pp. 9–54, Madison, Wisc.: Prehistory Press.

Skakun, N. (1993) 'Agricultural implements in the Neolithic and Eneolithic cultures of Bulgaria', in *Traces et fonction: les gestes retrouvés* (no editor), pp. 361–8, Liege: Études et Recherche Archeólogiques de l'Université de Liège.

Skibo, J.M., Schiffer, M. and Reid, K.C. (1989) 'Organic-tempered pottery: an experimental study', *American Antiquity* 54: 122–46.

Sladić, M. (1986) 'Kula près Mihajlovac – un site préhistorique', *Djerdapske Sveske* 3: 432–42.

Slobozianu, H. (1959) 'Consideratii asupra asezarilor antice din jurul lacurilor Techirghiol şi Agigea', *Materiale* 5: 737–43.

Soffer, O. (1987) 'Upper Palaeolithic conubia, refugia and the archaeological record from eastern Europe', in O. Soffer (ed.) *The Pleistocene Old World: Regional Perspectives*, pp. 333–48, New York: Plenum.

Sordinas, A. (1969) 'Investigations of the prehistory of Corfu during 1964–1966', *Balkan Studies* 10: 393–424.

—— (1970) *Stone Implements from Northwestern Corfu, Greece*, Memphis, Tenn.: Memphis State University Anthropological Research Center.

Srejović, D. (1969) *Lepenski Vir*, Belgrade: Srpska Knijiževna Zadruga.

—— (1972) *Lepenski Vir*, London: Thames and Hudson.

—— (1977) 'The Odmut cave – a new facet of the Mesolithic culture of the Balkan peninsula', *Archaeologia Iugoslavica* 15: 3–6.

—— (1988) 'The Neolithic of Serbia: a review of research', in D. Srejović (ed.) *The Neolithic of Serbia: Archaeological Research 1948–1988*, pp. 5–19, Belgrade: University of Belgrade.

—— (1989) 'The Mesolithic of Serbia and Montenegro', in C. Bonsall (ed.) *The Mesolithic in Europe*, pp. 481–91, Edinburgh: John Donald.

Srejović, D. and Babović, L. (1983) *Umetnost Lepenskog Vira*, Belgrade: Jugoslavija.

Srejović, D. and Letica, Z. (1978a) *Vlasac*, vol 1, *Arheologija*, Belgrade: Serbian Academy of Sciences and Arts.

—— (1978b) *Vlasac*, vol 2, *Geologija–Biologija–Antropologija*, Belgrade: Serbian Academy of Sciences and Arts.

Stalio, B. (1964) 'Novi metalni nalaz iz Pločnika kod Prokuplja', *Zbornik Narodnog Muzeja* 4: 35–45.

Stanchev, D. (1989) 'Nekropol of bronzovata epokha do selo Batin, Rusensko', *Godishnik na Muzei na Severna Bulgariya* 15: 7–13.

Stanev, P. (1979) 'Razkopki na praistoricheskoto selishte pri s. Samovodene, V. Turnovo', *Arkheologicheski Otkritiya i Razkopki za 1978*, 23–4.

—— (1981) 'Razkopki na neolitnoto selishte do s. Samovodene', *Arkheologicheski Otkritiya i Razkopki za 1980*, 13–4.

—— (1982a) 'Arkheologicheski razkopki na neolitnoto selishte pri s. Samovodene', *Arkheologicheski Otkritiya i Razkopki za 1981*, 9–10.

—— (1982b) 'Stratigraphiya i periodizatsiya na neolitnite obekti i kulturi po Bsejna na r. Yantra', *Godishnik na Muzei na Severna Bulgariya* 8: 1–17.

Stanko, V.N. (1992) 'Paleoekologicheskaya situatsiya v mezolite Severnogo Prichernomor'ya', *Studia Praehistorica* 11–2: 18–27.

Starkell, L. (1977) 'Palaeogeography of Europe', *Philosophical Transactions of the Royal Society of London* B, 290: 351–72.

Stefanova, T. (1996) 'A comparative analysis of pottery from the "monochrome early Neolithic horizon" and "Karanovo I horizon" and the problems of the neolithization of Bulgaria', *Poročilo o Raziskovanju Paleolitika, Neolitika in Eneolitika v Sloveniji* 23: 15–38.

Sterud, E.L. and Sterud, A.K. (1974) 'A quantitative analysis of the material remains', *Wissenschaftliche Mitteilungen des Bosniche-Herzegowinischen Landesmuseums* 4, A: 155–355.

Stevanović, M. (1996) 'The age of clay: the social dynamics of house destruction', unpublished PhD dissertation, University of California at Berkeley.

—— (1997) 'The age of clay: the social dynamics of house destruction', *Journal of Anthropological Archaeology* 16: 334–95.

Stringer, C.B. (1983) 'Some further notes on the morphology and dating of the Petralona hominid', *Journal of Human Evolution* 12: 731–42.

Svoboda, J. (1995) 'L'art Gravettien en Moravie: contexte, dates et styles', *L'Anthropologie* 99, 2–3: 258–72.

Svoboda, J. and Simán, K. (1989) 'The middle-upper Palaeolithic in southeastern central Europe (Czechoslovakia and Hungary)', *Journal of World Prehistory* 3, 3: 283–323.

Szekereš, L. (1986) *Kanizsa Múltja a Régészeti Leletek Fényében*, Kanizsa: Kanizsa Monográfiája.

Talalay, L. (1993) *Deities, Dolls, and Devices: Neolithic Figurines from Franchthi Cave, Greece*, Bloomington, Ind.: Indiana University Press.

Tasić, N. (ed.) (1979) *Praistorija Jugoslovenskih*, Sarajevo: Akademiya Nauke i Umjetnosti Bosne i Hercegovine.

Tchodadjivev, S. and Bakamska, A.; see Chokadziev and Bakamska.

Telegin, D.Y. (1973) *Seredno-Stogivska Kultura Epokhi Midi*, Kiev: Naukova Dumka.

—— (1986) *Dereivka: A Settlement and Cemetery of Copper Age Horse-keepers on the Middle Dniepr*, Oxford: British Archaeological Reports.

Theocharis, D. (1958) 'Ek tis prokeramikis Thessalias', *Thessalika* 1: 70–86.

—— (1967) *I augi tn Thessalikis Proïstorias. Arkhi kai proimi ezelizi tin Neolithikis, Thessalika Meletimata 1*, Volos: Philarchaios Hetaireia.

—— (1968) 'Anaskafai en Sesklo', *Praktika Arhaiologikis Etairis* 1968: 24–40.

—— (ed.) (1973) *Neolithic Greece*, Athens: National Bank of Greece.

Thissen, L. (1990) 'Part II, The pottery of Ilipinar: A preliminary assessment', *Anatolica* 16: 80–111

—— (1993a) 'New insights in Balkan-Anatolian connections in the late Chalcolithic: old evidence from the Turkish Black Sea littoral', *Anatolian Studies* 43: 207–37.

—— (1993b) 'Pottery tradition and innovation at Ilipinar', *Anatolica* 19: 295–305.

Todorova [-Simeonova], H. (1971) 'Kusnoeneolitniyat nekropol kraj gr. Devniya-Varnensko', *Izvestiya na Narodniya Muzej Varna* 7: 3–40.

—— (1973a) 'Die frühneolithische Kultur Tsonevo in Nordostbulgarien', *Actes du VIIIe congrés international de l'Union Internationale de Sciences Préhistoriques et Protohistoriques (Belgrad)*, vol. 2, pp. 226–35, Nice: Union Internationale de Sciences Préhistoriques et Protohistoriques.

—— (1973b) 'Novaya Kultura srednego neolita v severo-vostochnoj Bolgarii', *Sovetskaya Arkheologiya* 1973, 4: 16–31.

—— (1975) 'Nai-ranni danni za upotreba na metalu v Bulgariya', in *Sbornik Dokladi, Prvi Simpozium po Istoriya na Minnoto delo v Jugoistochna Evropa, Varna* (no editor), pp 5–13, Sofia: Bulgarskata Akademiya na Naukite.

—— (1978) *The Eneolithie in Bulgaria*, Oxford: British Archaeological Reports.

—— (1981) *Die kupferzeitlichen Äxte und Beile in Bulgarien. (Prähistorische Bronzefunde 9:14)*, Munich: C.H. Beck.

—— (1982) *Die kupferzeitliche Siedlungen in Nordostbulgarien*, Munich: C.H. Beck.

—— (1986) *Kamenno-mednata Epokha v Bulgariya. Peto Khilyadoletie predi Novata Era*, Sofia: Nauka i Izkustvo.

—— (1989a) 'Das Frühneolithikum Nordostbulgariens im Kontext des ostbalkanischen Neolithikums', in S. Hiller (ed.) *Tell Karanovo und das Balkan Neolithikum*, pp. 9–25, Salzburg: Institut für Klassische Archäologie der Universität Salzburg.

—— (1989b) 'Das Frühneolithikum Nordbulgariens im Kontext des ostbalkanischen Neolithikums', in M. Höneisen (ed.) *Die Ersten Bauern*, vol. 2, pp. 71–6, Zurich: Schweizerisches Landesmuseum.

—— (1991) 'Kulturblöcke und Kulturkomplexe im Neolithikum und in der Kupferzeit auf der Balkanhalbinsel', *Symposium Illyro-Thrace*, pp. 153–62, Belgrade: Serbian Academy of Arts and Sciences.

—— (1995a) 'The Neolithic, Eneolithic and Transitional Period in Bulgarian prehistory', in D.W. Bailey and Panayotov, I. (eds) *Prehistoric Bulgaria*, pp. 79–98, Madison, Wisc.: Prehistory Press.

—— (1995b) 'Bemerkungen zum frühen Handelsverkehr während des Neolithikums und des Chalkolithikums im westlichen Schwarzmeeraum', in B. Hansel (ed.) *Handel, Tausch und Verkehr im Bronze- und Früheisenzeitlichen Südosteuropean*, pp. 123–45, Munich: PAS.

Todorova, H. and Toncheva, G. (1975) 'Die äneolitische Pfahlbausiedlung bei Ezerovo im Varnasee', *Germania* 53: 30–46.

Todorova, H. and Vajsov, I. (1993) *Novo-kamennata Epokha v Bulgariya*, Sofia: Nauka i Izkustvo.

Todorova, H., Ivanov, S., Vasilev, V., Hopf, M., Quitta, H. and Kohl, G. (1975) *Selishtnata Mogila pri Golyamo Delchevo (Razkopki i Prouchvaniya 5)*, Sofia: Bulgarskata Akademiya na Naukite.

Todorova, H., Vasilev, V., Janusevic, Z., Kovacheva, M. and Valev, P. (1983) *Ovcharovo (Razkopki i Prouchvaniya 9)*, Sofia: Bulgarskata Akademiya na Naukite.

Tokai University (1990) *A Preliminary Report on the 6th Excavation at Djadovo, Bulgaria, 1989*, Tokyo.

Toncheva, G. (1981) 'Un habitat lacustre de l'âge du bronze ancien dans les environs de la ville de Varna (Ezerovo II)', *Dacia* 25: 41–62.

Toufexis, G. (1989) 'Plastikes parastaseis zoon tis neolithikis Makedonias kai Thessalias', paper presented at *Ancient Macedonia 5*, October 10–15, 1989.

—— (1995) 'Neolithique animal figurines from Thessaly', in J.C. Decourt, Helly, B. and Gallis, K. (eds) *La Thessalie, Colloque international d'archéologie: 15 années de recherches (1975–1990), bilans et perspectives*, pp. 163–68, Athens: Tameion Archeologikon Poron.

Trâncă, G. (1981) 'Studiul preliminar asupra resturilor de faună din aşezarea eneolitică de la Cuptoare-Sfogea', *Banatica* 6: 51–6.

Treuil, R. (1983) *Le Néolithique et le bronze ancien egéens*, Paris: Ecole Française d'Athènes.

—— (ed.) (1992) Dikili Tash: Village préhistorique de Macédoine Orientale 1 (*Bulletin correspondance hellénique* Supplément 24), Paris: Bulletin correspondance hellénique.

Trigger, B. (1989) *A History of Archaeological Thought*, Cambridge: Cambridge University Press.

Tringham, R.E. (1968). 'A preliminary study of the early Neolithic and latest Mesolithic blade industries in south-east and central Europe', in J.M. Coles and Simpson, D.D.A. (eds) *Studies in Ancient Europe*, pp. 45–70, Leicester: Leicester University Press.

—— (1971) *Hunters, Fishers and Farmers of Eastern Europe 6000–3000 BC*, London: Hutchinson.

—— (1972) 'Territorial demarcation of prehistoric settlements', in P. Ucko, Tringham, R.E. and Dimbleby, G.W. (eds) *Man, Settlement and Urbanism*, pp. 463–76, London: Duckworth.

—— (1973) 'The mesolithic of southeastern Europe', in S. Kozłowski (ed.) *The Mesolithic in Europe*, pp. 551–82, Warsaw: University Press.

—— (1991) 'Households with faces', in J.M. Gero and Conkey, M. (eds) *Engendering Archaeology: Women and Prehistory*, pp. 93–131, Oxford: Blackwell.

—— (1994) 'Engendered places in prehistory', *Gender, Place and Culture* 1: 169–203.

—— (1995) 'Archaeological houses, households, housework and the home', in D. Benjamin and Stea, D. (eds) *The Home: Words, Interpretations, Meanings and Environments*, pp. 79–107. Aldershot: Avebury.

Tringham, R.E. and Krstić, D. (eds) (1990a) *Selevac: A Neolithic Village in Yugoslavia*, Los Angeles: UCLA.

—— (1990b) 'Selevac and the transformation of southeast European prehistory', in R.E. Tringham and Krstić, D. (eds) *Selevac: A Prehistoric Village in Yugoslavia*, pp. 567–616, Los Angeles: UCLA.

Tringham, R.E., Brukner, B. and Voytek, B. (1985) 'The Opovo project: a study of socio-economic change in the Balkan Neolithic', *Journal of Field Archaeology* 12: 425–44.

Tringham, R.E., McPherron, A., Gunn, J. and Odell, G. (1988) 'The flaked stone industry from Divostin and Banja', in A. McPherron and Srejović, D. (eds) *Divostin and the Neolithic of Central Serbia*, pp. 203–54, Pittsburgh, Penn.: Department of Anthropology, University of Pittsburgh.

Tringham, R.E., Brukner, B., Kaiser, T., Borojević, K., Russell, N., Steli, P., Stevanović, M. and Voytek, B. (1992) 'Excavations at Opovo, 1985–7: socio-economic change in the Balkan Neolithic', *Journal of Field Archaeology* 19: 351–86.

Tringham, R.E. and Stevanović , M. (1990a) 'Field research', in R.E. Tringham and Krstić , D. (eds) *Selevac: A Neolithic Village in Yugoslavia*, pp. 57–214, Los Angeles: UCLA.

Trogmayer, O. (1957) 'Ausgrabung auf Tápe-Lebő', *A Móra Ferenc Múzeum Évkönyve* 1957: 19–58.

Tsountas, Ch. (1908) *Ai Proïstorikai Akropoleis Diminiou kai Sesklou*, Athens: Sakellariou.

Tsuneki, A. (1987) 'A reconsideration of *Spondylus* shell rings from Agia Sofia magoula, Greece', *Bulletin of the Ancient Orient Museum* 9: 1–15.

—— (1989) 'The manufacture of *spondylus* shell objects at Neolithic Dimini, Greece', *Orient* 25: 1–21.

Turner, J. and Greig, J.R.A. (1986) 'Vegetational history', in C. Renfrew, Gimbutas, M. and Elster, E. (eds) *Excavations at Sitagroi: A Prehistoric Village in Northeast Greece*, vol. 1, pp. 45–54, Los Angeles: UCLA.

Ucko, P. (1962) 'The interpretation of prehistoric anthropomorphic figurines', *Journal of the Royal Anthropological Institute of Great Britain and Ireland* 92: 38–54.

—— (1968) *Anthropomorphic Figurines of Predynastic Egypt and Neolithic Crete, with Comparative Material from the Prehistoric Near East*, London: Andrew Szmidla.

Vajsov, I. (1984) 'Antropomorphniya plastika iz praistoricheskogo poseleniya Kurilo-Kremenitsa Sophiskogo okruga', *Studia Praehistorica* 10: 103–41.

—— (1987) 'Pogrebeniya s idoli ot praistoricheskiya nekropol kraj s. Durankulak, Tolbukhinski okrug', *Dobrudzha* 4: 77–82.

—— (1990a) 'Anthropomorfe Plastik auf dem prähistorichen Gräberfeld bei Durankulak', *Studia Praehistorica* 11–12: 95–106.

—— (1990b) 'La sculpture anthropomorphe du site néolithique d'Oussoe près du village d'Asparoukhovo, département de Varna', *Studia Praehistorica* 10: 103–141.

—— (1992a) 'Die früheste dolche Bulgariens', *Anatolica* 18: 61–9.

—— (1992b) 'Anthropomorphe Plastik aus dem prähistorischen Gräberfeld bei Durankulak', *Studia Praehistorica* 11–12: 95–113.

Valoch, K. (1989) 'The early upper Paleolithic in the eastern part of central Europe', *Anthropologie (Brno)* 27, 2–3: 89–91.

—— (1995) 'The earliest occupation of Europe: eastern central and southeastern Europe', in W. Roebroeks and van Kolfschoten, T. (eds) *The Earliest Occupation of Europe*, pp. 51–9, Leiden: University of Leiden.

Valović, S. (1985) 'Resultati istraživanja vinčanskog naselja u Ratini', *Istraživanja* 2: 95–8.

van Andel, T.H. (1989) 'Late Quaternary sea-level changes and archaeology', *Antiquity* 63: 733–46.

van Andel, T.H. and Runnells, C.N. (1995) 'The earliest farmers in Europe', *Antiquity* 69: 481–500.

van Andel, T.H. and Shackleton, J.C. (1982) 'Late Paleolithic and Mesolithic coastlines of Greece and the Aegean', *Journal of Field Archaeology* 9: 445–54.

van Andel, T.H., Gallis, K. and Toufexis, G. (1995) 'Early Neolithic farming in a Thessalian river landscape', in J. Lewin, Macklin, M.G. and Woodward, J.C. (eds) *Mediterranean Quaternary River Environments*, pp. 131–43, Rotterdam: Balkema.

van der Leeuw, S. (1977) 'Towards a study of the economics of pottery making', in B.L. van Beck, Brandt, R.W. and Groenman-van Wateringe, W. (eds) *Ex Horreo*, pp. 68–76, Amsterdam: Brill.

van Zeist, W. and Bottema, S. (1971) 'Plant husbandry in early Neolithic Nea Nikomedeia, Greece', *Acta Botanica Neerlandica* 20, 5: 524–38.

Vasić, M. (1931–4) *Žurnal* (unpublished fieldnotes).

—— (1932) *Praistorijska Vinča II–IV*, Belgrade: Isdanye Drshavne Stamparije.

—— (1986) 'Compte-rendu des fouilles du site préhistorique à Velesnica 1981–82', *Djerdapske Sveske* 3: 271–301.

Vasilev, V. (1973) 'Analiz na osteologicheskiya material ot Usoe I (v statiya na X Todorova)', *Sovetskaya Arkheologiya* 4: 28–31.

—— (1982) 'Sravnitelinye Issledovaniya roli zhivotnovodstvaiokhotydlya praistoricheskikh poselenij Bolgarii', *Thracia Praehistorica (Supplementum Pulpudeva 3)*: 301–10.

—— (1985) *Izsledvane na Phaunata ot Selishtna Mogila Ovcharovo. Interdistsiplinarni Isledvaniya 13*, Sofia: Bulgarskata Akademiya na Naukite.

Vitelli, K.D. (1989) 'Were pots first made for foods? Some doubts from Franchthi?', *World Archaeology* 21: 17–29.

—— (1993a) *Franchthi Neolithic Pottery*, vol. 1, *Classification and Ceramic Phases 1 and 2*, Bloomington, Ind.: Indiana University Press.

—— (1993b) 'Power to the potters: comment on Perlès' "Systems of exchange and organization of production in Neolithic Greece"', *Journal of Mediterranean Archaeology* 6: 247–57.

—— (1995) 'Pots, potters, and the shaping of Greek Neolithic society', in W. Barnett and Hoopes, J. (eds) *The Emergence of Pottery*, pp. 55–64. Washington: Smithsonian Institution.

Vlassa, N. (1967) 'Unele probleme ale neoliticuli Transilvaniei', *Acta Musei Napocensis* 4: 403–23.

—— (1969) 'Einige Bemerkungen zu Fragen des Neolithikums in Siebenburgen', *Studijne Zvesti AUSAV* 17: 413–40.

Volschi, W. and Irimia, M. (1968) 'Descoperiri arheologice la Mangalia şi Lamanu, aparţinînd culturii Hamangia', *Pontica* 1: 45–87.

von den Driesch, A. and Enderle, K. (1976) 'Die Tierreste aus der Agia-Sofia Magula', in V. Milojčić, von den Driesch, A., Enderle, K., Milojčić-v.Zumbusch, J. and Kilian, K. (1976) *Die Deutschen Ausgrabunden auf Magulen um Larisa in Thessalien 1966: Agia Sofia-Magula. Karagyös-Magula. Bunar Baschi*, pp. 15–54, Bonn: Rudolf Habelt.

Voytek, B. (1990) 'The use of stone resources', in R. Tringham and Krštić, D. (eds) *Selevac: A Neolithic Village in Yugoslavia*, pp. 437–94, Los Angeles: UCLA.

Voytek, B. and Tringham, R. (1989) 'Rethinking the Mesolithic: the case of southeast Europe', in C. Bonsall (ed.) *The Mesolithic in Europe*, pp. 492–99, Edinburgh: John Donald.

Vulpe, A. (1975) *Die Äxte und Beile in Rumänien*, II, Munich: Beck.

Wace, A.J.B and Thompson, M.S. (1912) *Prehistoric Thessaly*, Cambridge: Cambridge University Press.

Wagner, P. (1966) *The Human Use of the Earth*, Glencoe, Ill.: Free Press.

Wardle, K.A. (ed.) (1996) *Nea Nikomedeia: The Excavations of an Early Neolithic Farming Village in Northern Greece 1961–1964*, London: British School at Athens.

Webster, G. (1990) 'Labor control and emergent stratification in prehistoric Europe', *Current Anthropology* 31: 337–66.

Weisshaar, H.-J. (1989) *Die deutschen Ausgrabungen auf de Pevkakia-Magoula in Thessalien I: Das späte Neolithikum und das Chalkolithikum*, Bonn: Beiträge zur Ur- und Frügeschichtlicken Archälogie des Mittelmeer-Kutturraumes.

Whittle, A. (1996) *Europe in the Neolithic: The Creation of New Worlds*, Cambridge: Cambridge University Press.

—— (1998) 'Fish, faces and fingers: presences and symbolic identities in the Mesolithic-Neolithic transition in the Carpathian basin', *Documenta Praehistorica (Slovenia)* 25: 133–50.

Wijnen, M. (1982) *The Early Neolithic I Settlement at Sesklo: An Early Farming Community in Thessaly, Greece*, Leiden: Analecta Praehistorica Leidensia.

—— (1992) 'Building remains of the early Neolithic period at Sesklo', *Diethes Sinerio gia tin Arhaia Thessalia sti Mnimi tou D.P. Theohari* (no editor), pp. 55–63, Athens: Tameion Archeologikon Poron.

—— (1993) 'Early ceramics: local manufacture versus widespread distribution', *Anatolica* 19: 319–27.

—— (1995) 'Neolithic pottery from Sesklo – technological aspects', in J.C. Decourt, Helly, B. and Gallis, K. (eds) *La Thessalie: Colloque international d'archéologie: 15 années de recherches (1975–1990), bilans et perspectives*, pp. 149–54, Athens: Tameio Arhaeologikon poron kai Apallotrioseon.

Wilkie, N.C. (1993) 'The Grevena Project', *Arhaia Makedonia* 5: 1747–55.

Willis, K. (1994) 'The vegetational history of the Balkans', *Quaternary Science Review* 13: 759–88.

—— (1995) 'The pollen-edientological evidence for the beginning of agriculture in southeastern Europe and Anatolia', *Poročilo o Raziskovanju Paleolitika, Neolitika in Eneolitika v Sloveniji* 12: 9–24.

Willis, K. and Bennett, K.D. (1996) 'The Neolithic transition in the Balkans: replies to Magri and to Edwards et al.', *Holocene* 6: 123.

Willms, C. (1985) 'Neolithischer Spondylusschmuck: hundert Jahre Forschung', *Germania* 63: 331–43.

Winn, S. and Shimabuku, D. (1989a) 'Architecture and sequence of building remains', in M. Gimbutas, Winn, S. and Shimabuku, D. (eds) *Achilleion: A Neolithic Settlement in Thessaly, Greece*, pp. 32–68, Los Angeles: UCLA.

—— (1989b) 'Pottery', in M. Gimbutas, Winn, S. and Shimabuku, D. (eds) *Achilleion: A Neolithic Settlement in Thessaly, Greece*, pp. 75–164, Los Angeles: UCLA.

—— (1989c) 'Bone and ground stone tools', in M. Gimbutas, Winn, S. and Shimabuku, D. (eds) *Achilleion: A Neolithic Settlement in Thessaly, Greece*, pp. 259–72, Los Angeles: UCLA.

Woodward, J.C., Lewin, J. and Macklin, M.G. (1995) 'Glaciation, river behaviour and Palaeolithic settlement in upland northwest Greece', in J. Lewin, Macklin, M.G. and Woodward, J.C. (eds) *Mediterranean Quaternary River Environments*, pp. 115–29, Rotterdam, Balkema.

Xirotiris, N.I. (1982) 'Apotelesmata tis anthropologikis ezetaseos ton kamenon oston apo ti Soufli Magoula kai tin Platia Magoula Zarkou', in K.I. Gallis (ed.) *Kauseis Nekron apo ti Neolthiki Epohi sti Thessalia*, pp. 190–9, Athens: Tameion Archeologikon Poron.

Yakar, J. (1996) 'The neolithic transformation in the Near East and Anatolia's role in the neolithization of southeastern Europe', *Poročilo o Raziskovanju Paleolitika, Neolitika in Eneolitika v Sloveniji* 23: 1–14.

Yalcinkaya, I., Leotard, J.-M., Kartal, M., Otte, M., Bar-Yosef, O., Carmi, I., Gautier, A., Gilot, E., Goldberg, P., Kozłowski, J., Lieberman, D., Lopez-Bayon, I., Pawlikowski, M., Thiebault, St., Ancio, V., Patou, M., Emery-Berbier, A. and Bonjean, D. (1995) 'Les occupations tardiglaciaires de site d'Öküzini (sud-ouest de la Turquie) résultats préliminaires', *L'Anthropologie* 99, 4: 562–83.

Yanushevich, Z. (1983) 'Nakodki kulturnukh rastenij iz pozdneneoliticheskikh sloev s. Ovcharovo', in H. Todorova, Vasilev, V., Janusevic, Z., Kovacheva, M. and Valev, P. *Ovcharovo. (Razkopki i Prouchvania 9)*, pp. 106–18, Sofia: Bulgarskata Akademiya na Naukite.

Yiouni, P. (1996) 'The early Neolithic pottery: functional analysis', in G. Pyke and Yiouni, P. (eds) *Nea Nikomedeia, the Excavation of an Early Neolithic Village in Northern Greece, 1961–1964*, I, *The Excavation and the Ceramic Assemblage*, pp. 181–93, Athens, British School (*Annual of the British School at Athens Supplement 25*).

Zanger, E. (1991) 'Prehistoric coastal environments in Greece: the vanished landscapes of Dimini Bay and Lake Lerna', *Journal of Field Archaeology* 18: 1–16.

Živanović, S. (1977) 'Vinča skeletons studied at the Gomolava site, Yugoslavia', *Current Anthropology* 18, 3: 533–4.

—— (1986) 'Restes des ossements humains à Velesnica', *Djerdapske Sveske* 3: 286–8.

Zoffman, Z. (1983) 'Prehistorical skeletal remains from Lepenski Vir (Iron Gate, Yugoslavia)', *Homo* 34: 129–48.

—— (1987a) 'Antropološska obrada starčevačkog skeleta sa lokaliteta Golokut', *Rad Vojvodanskih Muzeja* 30: 29–31.

—— (1987b) 'Das anthropologische Material das spätneolitischen Gräberfelds von Hrtkovci – Gomolava', *Rad Vojvodanskih Muzeja* 30: 43–69.

—— (1988) 'Human skeletal remains from Divostin, in A. McPherron and Srejović, D. (eds) *Divostin and the Neolithic of Central Serbia*, pp. 447–56, Pittsburgh, Penn.: Department of Anthropology, University of Pittsburgh.

Zvelebil, M. and Dolukhanov, P. (1991) 'Transition to farming in eastern and northern Europe', *Journal of World Prehistory* 5: 233–78.

INDEX

INDEX

Rumex 147
Ruse 220, 231, Fig. 4.1
Russell, N. 184

Sabac-Jela 184
Sadievo 223
Sadovec Fig. 7.1
Salcuţa 240, Fig. 7.1
Salcuţa culture: animals of 182;
  pottery of 226; tells of 160
Samovodyane 60, 154, Figs 2.1, 4.1;
  furniture models at 107
Samuilitsa 28, 288–9 n. 2, Fig. 1.1
Sandalja 288 n. 2,
Sapareva Banya Fig. 2.1; figurines at
  98; sealing-stamps at 109
Sava 188, 220, Fig. 4.1; lidded vessel
  from Fig. 5.9
sceptre 197, 204, 219
Schela Cladovei Fig. 2.1, Table 2.1;
  burial at 117, 119; pottery at 89
schist 206
sealing-stamps 109–10, 112, 234, 282
secondary products 106, 183, 177, 257,
  258–9, 279; see also looms; milk;
  ploughs; sieves; spindle whorls;
  textiles; vehicles
sedentism 9, 263–4
Selanovtsi 246
Selevac 77, 161, 162–5, 179, 183, 187,
  188, 209, 210, 217, 223, 228, 229,
  234, 274, 275, Fig. 4.1
Servia 47, 171, 226, Figs 2.1, 4.1
Sesklo 43, 44–5, 171, 175, 180, 213,
  226, 269, Figs 2.1, 2.2; body
  ornamentation at 108; pottery at 77,
  78, 82–3; sealing-stamps at 109, 110
settlements 39–75, 153–77, 240–5; flat
  43; locations of 43, 46, 49, 50, 52,
  57, 60, 63, 72, 141, 142–3, 157,
  162, 256; see also built environment;
  camps; tells; villages
sheep see ovicaprids
shell 107, 196, 222–3, 272, 279; as
  grave-goods 117, 119, 120, 122, 123,
  277; in Palaeolithic 29; at Franchthi
  34; see also Dentalium; mollusc;
  Spondylus gaederopus
Shemshovo 243
Shiroka Polyana 28, 288–9 n. 2, Fig. 1.1
Sidari 34, 35, Fig. 1.1; flaked stone at
  127

sieves 92, 183, 258
silver 247, 250
Sirakov, N. 255–6
Sitagroi 166, 170, 180, 183, 213, 217,
  222, 225, 242, Figs 4.1, 7.1;
  anthropomorphic figurines from 229,
  232; burnt building at Fig. 7.2;
  pottery from 226, 252–3, Fig. 7.4;
  zoomorph from 184
skills 28–9
Slatina 53, 61, 273, Figs 2.1, 2.4;
  anthropographic pot at 101; plants
  at 145; sealing-stamps at 109
Slatino 166, 180, 181, 191, 211, 217,
  225, 226, 229, 235, 275, Figs 4.1,
  5.7
Smolnitsa Fig. 7.1
social cohesion 74, 94, 237–8, 266,
  268–9, 280
social structure and organization 9,
  149, 203, 238, 266, 269–70, 280,
  293
sociopolitics 150, 238
Sofronievo 220, Fig. 4.1
soils 150, 187–8; cultivation and 142;
  grazing and 134–5, 256
Souphli 44, 171, 274, Fig. 2.1; burial
  at 123; pottery at 78
Sozopol 240, 243, 252, Fig. 7.1
space: arrangement of people within
  272–83; division of 43, 44, 45, 50,
  51, 53–4, 56, 61, 64, 66, 68–70,
  74–5, 83, 159, 161, 169, 170, 171,
  222; extra-mural 43, 44, 50, 51, 56,
  58, 59, 73, 74, 258; intra-mural 43,
  67, 69, 72, 73, 82, 95, 157, 163,
  174, 264–7, 273; organization of 9,
  23–6, 44, 45, 47, 68–9, 162, 163,
  171, 244; perception of 160, 172;
  private 273; segregation of 74, 190,
  222, 244, 267; use of partitions
  within 46, 53–4, 61, 153, 155,
  157–8, 168, 173, 273, 275, Fig. 5.4
spear-heads 254, 255
spelt wheat 139, 178
spindle-whorls 234, 258
Spondylus gaederopus 108, 171, 196,
  197, 204, 206, 207, 222, 236, 279,
  282
Sredny-Stog culture 258
Stalijska Mahala Fig. 7.1
stamps see sealing-stamps